WOMEN'S WAYS OF MAKING IT IN RHETORIC AND COMPOSITION

This volume explores how women in the field of rhetoric and composition have succeeded, despite the challenges inherent in the circumstances of their work. Focusing on those women generally viewed as "successful" in rhetoric and composition, this volume relates their stories of successes (and failures) to serve as models for other women in the profession who aspire to "make it," too: to succeed as women academics in a sea of gender and disciplinary bias and to have a life, as well.

Building on the gains made by several generations of rhetoric and composition scholars, this volume provides strategies for a newer generation of scholars entering the field and, in so doing, broadens the support base for women in the field by connecting them with a greater web of women in the profession. Offering frank discussion of professional and personal struggles as well as providing reference materials addressing these concerns, solid career advice, and inspirational narratives told by women who have "made it" in the field of rhetoric and composition, this work highlights such common concerns as:

- dealing with sexism on the job market and in the tenure and promotion process,
- maintaining a balance between career and family,
- finding ways to earn scholarly and/or administrative respect,
- mentoring junior women,
- becoming productive and finding one's voice in scholarship, and
- struggling to say "no" to unrewarded service work.

The profiles of individual successful women describe each woman's methods for success, examine the price each has paid for that success, and pass along the advice each has to offer other women who are beginning a career in the field or attempting to jumpstart an existing career. With resources and general advice for women in the field of rhetoric and composition to guide them through their careers—as they become, survive, and thrive as professionals in the discipline—this book is must-have reading for every woman making her career in rhetoric and composition.

Michelle Ballif is Associate Professor of English at the University of Georgia.

Diane Davis is Associate Professor of Rhetoric & Writing and English at the University of Texas at Austin.

Roxanne Mountford is Associate Professor of English at the University of Arizona.

WOMEN'S WAYS OF MAKING IT IN RHETORIC AND COMPOSITION

Michelle Ballif,
Diane Davis,
and
Roxanne Mountford

NEW YORK AND LONDON

First published 2008
by Routledge
270 Madison Ave, New York, NY 10016

Simultaneously published in the UK
by Routledge
2 Park Square, Milton Park, Abingdon, Oxon OX14 4RN

Routledge is an imprint of the Taylor & Francis Group, an informa business

Typeset in Times New Roman
by Bookcraft Ltd, Stroud, Gloucestershire, UK
Printed and bound in the United States of America on acid-free paper by
Sheridan Books, Inc., MI

Photos used on the paperback cover were supplied by the women featured in this volume and are used with their permission.

Library of Congress Cataloging in Publication Data
Ballif, Michelle, 1964–
Women's Ways of Making It in Rhetoric and Composition by Michelle Ballif, Diane Davis and Roxanne Mountford.
p. cm.
1. English language Rhetoric Study and teaching. I. Davis, Diane. II. Mountford, Roxanne, 1962– III. Title
PE1404B264 2008
808'.0420711–dc22
2007038757

ISBN10: 0-8058-4444-9 (HB)
ISBN10: 0-8058-4445-7 (PB)
ISBN10: 0-203-92984-5 (EB)

ISBN13: 978-0-8058-4444-3 (HB)
ISBN13: 978-0-8058-4445-0 (PB)
ISBN13: 978-0-203-92984-1 (EB)

CONTENTS

PREFACE

The inspiration for this project came many years ago, when Michelle and Diane were in graduate school together. They both admired a female faculty member who seemed to have "it"—whatever that "it" is: she was always impeccably dressed, impeccably prepared for the seminars she taught, impeccably articulate, impeccably published. In a word, to name "it", she was impeccably *professional*. Her professional way of being so inspired Michelle and Diane that they were obsessively curious to figure out how she did "it." Indeed, one evening, when their feminism seminar group was invited to her home for an end-of-the-semester social, one of their fellow graduate students, who will remain nameless for her protection, excused herself from the group under the guise of needing to visit the ladies' room. Instead of taking a powder, however, Cynthia Haynes took the opportunity to snoop around, and reported to the group, in hushed whispers, a detailed description of said faculty member's closet. It was, Cynthia reported, impeccable. Skirts, slacks, suits, sweaters: all neatly hung and categorized. It looked, Cynthia said, like walking into a Neiman Marcus showroom. They could only aspire to such discipline and order. Finally Diane—without admitting the closet incident—asked this faculty member how she did "it." And she told them something like this: At 9:00 am, she began her writing with one cigarette; she wrote uninterrupted each morning until noon, at which time she rewarded herself with another cigarette. After lunch, she prepared for her classes, taught, or attended meetings, as scheduled. After dinner, and another cigarette, she read material in her field until she retired for the night. Although not smokers, Michelle and Diane were inspired by her discipline, by her system of orderly production, and they began to wonder, how do other women, other women who have "it," have made "it," do "it"?

The project was further inspired by another conversation about the closets of women in our profession. Roxanne and Diane met at the Rhetoric Society of America conference in 1994 a year or two after the first closet incident. Roxanne had her first academic position at the time, and Diane was getting ready to go on the market. At one of the receptions, their conversation turned, naturally, to what to wear to the MLA interviews. Roxanne called her Ohio State classmates Kris Ratcliffe and Cheryl Glenn to join the conversation, and the three of them regaled Diane with the long list of "fashion don'ts" that their adviser, Andrea A. Lunsford, had given them for the job market: no dangly earrings, no short skirts, no bright colors, no low-cut blouses, no high heels (the list was long). Soon all eyes turned to Diane, who was looking down, taking stock of all the "don'ts" she was violating at that very moment, and they all laughed. Cheryl leaned in and, gesturing to Diane's outfit, offered: "You look great—but don't wear *any of this* into an interview." Kris then recalled that while she dutifully wore a pair of pearl stud earrings for the interviews, she *burned* them after accepting her first job offer. Nevertheless, all three credited Lunsford for providing them with a strong feminist legacy of mentoring, and Diane acknowledged that the interview fashion front may be one arena in which it pays to have a female mentor.

This volume, then, was inspired by the desire to spy on the closets—or the personal and professional choices—of the successful women in our field, in order to see how they "made it." But more than wanting to discover that Sharon Crowley's closet did—at one time—contain a miniskirt (which she admits to having worn while "working" it), the authors wanted to produce a book that would reveal the paths and choices made by women in our field, to provide frank discussion of professional and personal struggles, as well as to provide reference materials addressing these concerns, solid career advice, and inspirational narratives told by women who have "made it" in the field of rhetoric and composition. Seeking to build on the gains made by several generations of rhetoric and composition scholars, the authors hope this book provides successful strategies for a newer generation of scholars entering the field and, by so doing, broadens the support base for women in the field by connecting them with a greater web of women in the profession.

The authors are deeply indebted to those who participated in our study and who consented to subject themselves to our voyeuristic eye. Our hope is that their words of wisdom can make your path to making "it" more successful and more enjoyable.

Huge thanks, also, to Ron Balthazor of the University of Georgia, who constructed the online survey and helped administer it, as well as sort through the data. Thanks to Davida Charney for her help with IRB-speak, to the University of Texas at Austin and to the University of Arizona's Women's Studies Advisory Council for providing special research grants to cover the cost of transcription and transportation to a research site, and to John Kinkade of the University of Texas at Austin and Tammie Kennedy of the University of Arizona, the research assistants who did the transcribing. Thanks to Lourdes Canto, who provided grant support, and Rebecca Dahl, who offered sage advice on IRB issues at the University of Arizona. We are very grateful to everyone who generously offered insights and feedback on this project, including dear friends, respected colleagues, and anonymous reviewers. We also thank Linda Bathgate, Senior Editor, Communication Studies, and Kerry Breen for editorial support and for helping us, finally, to get this volume in press.

Thanks also to Larry Nackerud for all the stall mucking, as well as for help in navigating the strange world of human subjects applications and approvals; to Paul Mowery for finding a way to squeeze grownup playdates into the weekly schedule to keep us sane; and to Bill Endres for his gracious support and good humor throughout the process.

The authors would like to dedicate this volume to all the women in our field who inspire us by their successes.

Michelle Ballif
Diane Davis
Roxanne Mountford

INTRODUCTION

> Women in our field have been absolutely heroic in carrying out important research against significant odds that those in other fields, like literary studies, simply do not face; and finding ways to make the university more inclusive of women and underrepresented groups and more accepting of collaboration, which is a mode of scholarship practiced by many in rhetoric and writing.
>
> —anonymous survey respondent

The academic field of rhetoric and composition has long been hailed as a "feminized" field, a characterization of multiple valences: a majority of scholars and practitioners in the field are women, and the work itself has been viewed (and often celebrated) as "women's work."[1] As a result, as the research has revealed, scholars in the field of rhetoric and composition face unique challenges in the world of academe, specifically, according to Theresa Enos, salary, promotion, and workload inequities. As demonstrated by both statistical data and anecdotal evidence, such as that provided by the research of Enos, Louise Wetherbee Phelps, and Janet Emig, rhetoric and composition academics, specifically *women* rhetoric and composition academics, face different challenges and issues (if not in kind, certainly in degree) than do other female academics. This is not to suggest, however, that the work doesn't have its own reward, as many of our survey respondents and profiled women attested. On the contrary, these women extolled the profession and their role in it: to teach with commitment, to pursue research with passion, to mentor students and colleagues, and to build writing programs that made an institutional—if not personal—difference. Nevertheless, these women acknowledged that the work as a woman in academe is not without its particular challenges. Further, they acknowledge that their area of specialty subjected them to additional challenges. Specifically, these additional challenges have to do with pay, administrative expectations, and tenure and promotion.

Concerning Pay Issues Women's salaries are demonstrably lower than men's in the majority (if not all) academic fields: "In 2005–06, across all ranks and all institutions, the average salary for women faculty was 81 percent of the amount earned by men" (West and Curtis 11). Women's salaries in rhetoric and composition are potentially the lowest, as it is a teaching-heavy specialty, and statistics provided by the 1988 National Survey of Postsecondary Faculty argue that "the more time faculty spend on teaching … the lower the pay" (quoted in Gebhardt, "Evolving Approaches" 10). Rhetoric/composition practitioners spend more time on teaching than their English studies counterparts because they are typically teaching (and mentoring) not only students but graduate teaching assistants (who will teach the college writing courses) (Roen, "Administration as Scholarship and Teaching"). Time spent on teaching, mentoring, and writing program administration is time not spent on research and other monetarily rewarded activities. As the 1988 National Survey notes, "the more time spent on research and the greater the scholarly productivity … the greater the pay" (quoted in Gebhardt 10).

Concerning Administrative Expectations Rhetoric/composition is perceived as a "service" to the university at large (and to the community's taxpayers) to teach basic literacy skills to students. Hence the need for writing programs, such as First-year Composition and Writing across the Curriculum programs, which typically are directed by rhetoric/composition scholars—most likely female scholars (as many as 70 percent of rhetoric/composition scholars may be women [Enos, "Mentoring and (Wo)mentoring" 141]). Scholars in other disciplines are rarely asked to administer programs of such a size and magnitude. Further, scholars in other disciplines are rarely *expected* to administer. That is, although women in other disciplines may have administrative responsibilities, such as chairing a department, their administrative service is not a specific function of their area of study. Women in rhetoric and composition, unlike women in other academic fields, then—as a result of their *expected* administrative demands—earn lower pay, have greater demands on their time, and risk being denied tenure and promotion because administrative work does not typically result in scholarly publications or the kind of scholarly work that is rewarded by the academy. Further, although women in all academic fields (simply because they are women) typically shoulder the time-consuming burden of caring for children as well as aging parents, female rhetoric/composition scholars may find that administrative demands further complicate their abilities to handle family responsibilities. Additionally, other administrative appointments, such as chairing a department or serving as an associate dean, typically involve a sizeable pay rate increase, whereas running a writing program typically does not.

Concerning Tenure and Promotion Issues Although women in other academic disciplines suffer sexism in the tenure and promotion process, women in rhetoric and composition are further disadvantaged. This is due to a) administrative duties interfering with scholarly productivity, b) administrative work not "counting" toward tenure and promotion (Leverenz, "Tenure and Promotion"), and c) English studies colleagues not recognizing studies in rhetoric and composition as "real" scholarship (Gebhardt, "Evolving Approaches"; Schilb, "Scholarship in Composition and Literature").

Well, no doubt you're thinking: Tell me something new. This is precisely the goal of this volume. We do not aim to prove that women in academe, generally, or in rhetoric and composition, specifically, have unique challenges; we believe that this claim has been sufficiently argued. We will demonstrate, rather, how—in the words of our survey respondent quoted above—"women in our field have been absolutely heroic … against significant odds." That is: we will demonstrate how women have succeeded in spite of these challenges, hence our title: *Women's Ways of Making It in Rhetoric and Composition*.

Our focus will be on those women who have "made it" in our profession, specifically on a number of those women who were identified as "successful" in rhetoric and composition by our online survey respondents. This volume aims to relate their stories of success (and failures) to serve as models for other women in the profession who aspire to "make it," too: to succeed as women academics in a sea of gender and disciplinary bias and to have a life, as well. Our focus on women in tenure-track and tenured positions is in no way meant to ignore the number of women in non-tenure-track or non-tenured positions or part-time positions across the country, who represent approximately 80 percent of those teaching writing (Schell 6). Eileen E. Schell's work, for instance, reveals that "[a]lthough a significant number of women have earned PhDs and attained tenure-track positions in English Studies and Rhetoric and Composition, many women still function as an army of labor, a 'disposable' and/or 'recyclable' work force composed of part-time and temporary nontenure-track teachers" (8).

According to the American Council on Education's report "An Agenda for Excellence: Creating Flexibility in Tenure-Track Faculty Careers" (2005), "[i]n fall 2001, 56 percent of all undergraduate, graduate, and professional students enrolled in the U.S. degree-granting colleges and universities were women. However, the representation of women in the full-time tenure-track and tenured faculty ranks stands at only 34 percent" ("Quick Facts"). Additionally, women "who do enter tenure-track positions are 20 percent less likely than their male colleagues to achieve tenure … . University of California, Berkeley researchers refer to the phenomenon as the 'leaking pipeline for women PhDs,' in which women enter and complete doctoral programs but disproportionately drop out of the running for tenure-track positions" (8).

We acknowledge that the reasons for this "leaking pipeline" are infinitely complex—and our survey respondents supplied a variety of compelling explanations: first, as one survey respondent noted, the entire path to a tenure-track position is designed for young men (not middle-aged women—or perhaps any women). The idealized career path of entering PhD studies immediately post-baccalaureate (or post-master's) denies the reality of the path taken by many women, by necessity: many women's educational trajectories are limited or conditioned by their relationships to their husbands or partners and their family responsibilities, including raising children and caring for aging parents. Due to such responsibilities, the completion of the PhD may be delayed by years, and may be further impeded, for example, by attempting to write a dissertation while teaching as a full-time writing instructor. Hence, the tale of the "leaking pipeline" must acknowledge that women possibly traverse a different and more difficult path to a tenure-track position.

This volume attempts to address this "leaking pipeline" by providing stories and strategies to help women in the field of rhetoric and composition, who so desire, to obtain tenure-track positions after PhD work, to succeed in the tenure and promotion process, and to balance career with personal endeavors. To this end, we surveyed women in our profession through an anonymous survey to capture the perceptions and experiences of gender- and discipline-specific challenges, which they articulated as including: dealing with sexism in the tenure and promotion process, maintaining a balance between career and family, struggling for scholarly and/or administrative respect, mentoring junior women, finding one's voice in scholarship, and struggling to say "no" to unrewarded service work, to mention just a few. Our aim was not to repeat the careful and convincing work done by others, most notably Theresa Enos in her study *Gender Roles and Faculty Lives in Rhetoric and Composition.* Rather, we wanted to solicit strategies for success in dealing with these current challenges. To do so, we conducted in-depth interviews with nine successful women in the field of rhetoric and composition to gather the ways they have addressed these issues in their personal and professional lives. The profiles of these women—Patricia Bizzell, Sharon Crowley, Cheryl Glenn, Susan C. Jarratt, Shirley Wilson Logan, Andrea A. Lunsford, Jacqueline Jones Royster, Cynthia L. Selfe, and Lynn Worsham, who were among those identified by our online survey respondents as being models of success—will describe each woman's methods for success, examine the price each has paid for that success, and pass along the advice each would offer to other women just beginning a career in the field or attempting to jumpstart an existing career. Additionally, this volume will offer resources and general advice for women in the field of rhetoric and composition to guide them through their careers—as they become, thrive, and survive as professionals in the discipline.

Literature Review

An abundance of research has documented what we, as women, have long experienced: the academy is a sexist institution and environment. Paula J. Caplan's "The Maleness of the Environment" details the subtle and not-so-subtle forms of discrimination faced by women in academe, which can be exacerbated exponentially by being, additionally, a member of another "non-dominant group or being known to be a female member of the women's studies faculty or a feminist" (203), or being known to produce scholarship on gender issues. Likewise,

Lilli S. Hornig's edited *Equal Rites, Unequal Outcomes: Women in American Research Universities*, Nijole V. Benokraitis's "Working in the Ivory Basement: Subtle Sex Discrimination in Higher Education," and the Modern Language Association Committee on the Status of Women in the Profession's report, "Women in the Profession 2000," provide damning evidence that institutions of higher education remain inhospitable to women professionals.[2] Linda K. Kerber argues, in "We Must Make the Academic Workplace More Humane and Equitable," that academic institutions offer little—if any—"coherent benefit policies that make it possible for [women] to be professionals and parents." Indeed, she writes, the academy has

> been especially hapless in reforming policies on pregnancy and related infant and child care … . [Women] say that tenure clocks were set when a male academic profession was blithely unconcerned about biological clocks. Women who are single parents have an especially hard time. Women with roots in the working class, a group that includes a disproportionate number of women of color, are especially hurt by their institution's failure to provide on-site child care and robust health-care coverage (including for partners). (B7)

The American Council on Education's "An Agenda for Excellence: Creating Flexibility in Tenure-Track Faculty Careers" (2005) identifies several structural barriers to female success in the academy:

> The rigid, traditional model of academe particularly affects women and people of color. The barriers that they encounter in their climb up the academic ladder typically stem from the structure of academe (i.e. policies and practices) and/or from the culture of academe (i.e. experiences of isolation, marginalization, tokenism, exclusion, etc.) … . Structural barriers include tenure and promotion policies, which dictate both the kind of work faculty must perform to earn tenure (research vs. teaching vs. service), as well as the way in which they must do the work (independently vs. collaboratively) to be rewarded. Another example of a structural barrier is the probationary period (the pre-tenure years), which poses a problem for women faculty because it often coincides with their prime years for childbearing. ("Quick Facts")

Thus women in academe struggle against sexist institutional practices, encultured sexist behaviors of students and colleagues, all of which are further exacerbated by additional barriers created by institutional and cultural racism, as identified by Nellie Y. McKay's "Minority Faculty in [Mainstream White] Academia," Conchita Y. Battle and Chontrese M. Doswell's edited collection

Building Bridges for Women of Color in Higher Education, Joanne E. Cooper and Dannelle D. Stevens' edited *Tenure in the Sacred Grove: Issues and Strategies for Women and Minority Faculty*, and Mildred Garcia's edited *Succeeding in an Academic Career: A Guide for Faculty of Color*. And, as Toni McNaron's *Poisoned Ivy: Lesbian and Gay Academics Confronting Homophobia* details, as well as Beth Mintz and Esther Rothblum's edited *Lesbians in Academia: Degrees of Freedom*, the academy continues to struggle with institutionalized homophobia.

And, as the research provided by scholars such as Theresa Enos clearly and convincingly reveals, women in academe who study and practice rhetoric and composition find themselves additionally discriminated against for doing "women's work" in a man's world. Enos writes:

> Women's work is characterized by a disproportionate number of women workers (as in the academy's writing programs), it is service oriented (like the teaching of writing in the classrooms of institutions of higher education), it pays less than "men's work" (traditional forms of scholarship), and it is devalued (compared to males, females get fewer promotions and less pay). Thus males as well as females in a feminized field suffer from salary compression and horizontal rather than upward "promotions." ("Gender and Publishing" 558)

The aforementioned Eileen Schell's *Gypsy Academics and Mother-Teachers: Gender, Contingent Labor, and Writing Instruction* and Susan Miller's *Textual Carnivals* also tell the tales of—and statistically document—the "sad women" of rhetoric and composition in the basement of the Ivory Tower (Miller). And so, as this brief literature review demonstrates, we find ourselves where we began: in the face of institutional discrimination against women, as well as against the "feminized" field of rhetoric and composition. How can women professionals in our discipline survive—and thrive—despite these challenges? For answers and advice, we asked the women in our field.

Our Methodology

As mentioned above, we solicited responses to an online survey, aiming to gather basic demographic information in addition to qualitative responses. As we are aware of the complexities of establishing representative samples, we do not claim that these responses are statistically *representative* of all women in our discipline. Rather, our ethnographic method required us to select a represented—not a *representative*—sample. We used the most common form of purposeful sampling: the network (or snowball) method. We began by soliciting feedback from women who currently teach in known PhD programs in rhetoric and composition (using *Rhetoric Review*'s 1999 Survey of Doctoral Programs

[Brown, Jackson, and Enos 2000] as our primary source). We invited participants to identify other women in rhetoric and composition who fit our sampling profile to whom we sent surveys, asking—again—for further "information-rich" potential participants. We depended on survey distribution via the major listservs of our field, WHIRL-L, RHETNET-L, and WPA-L. In the process, we hoped to achieve maximum variation in terms of variables such as: kind of degree-granting institution, public or private institution, lifestyle choice, stage of career (assistant, associate, or full professor), race, region of the country. As our survey response figures indicate, however, we apparently did not gather maximum variation in several key variables, most notably race. Out of 142 respondents, 131 described their racial identity as "Caucasian, non-Hispanic"; 3 identified themselves as "Native American," 4 as "Caucasian, Hispanic," 1 as "Bi/Multi Racial," and 3 as "Other." Not one respondent identified her race as "African American."

The responses do provide us with rich evidence of attitudes, behaviors, attributes, and experiences. Following the standard, well-tested survey methodology as articulated by Don Dillman's *Mail and Internet Surveys: The Tailored Design Method*, we circulated a questionnaire (which was pretested by a number of female academics to maintain face validity), comprising of a series of open-ended and closed-ended inquiries (the survey instrument—along with the corresponding numerical responses to the quantitative questions—can be found in Appendices I and II). The questions aimed to determine what women identified as the main issues challenging women in rhetoric and composition presently, what issues are typically silenced and not addressed, what advice/strategies they had to offer, and what narratives regarding their success they were willing to share with other women in the field.

An additional question—indeed our first question—was to request that our respondents identify, according to their definition of success, a woman who they thought has "made it" in the field of rhetoric and composition. Prior to distributing the survey, we presumed that those selected would be women who share the following characteristics: hold a PhD; are full professors at an academic institution; are tenured; are well published; are cited regularly; have contributed a consummate piece in the field; are frequently keynote speakers at national conferences; are actively mentoring other women in the field; are able to have a "real" life, in addition to their scholarly activities. The survey respondents did name women who met these characteristics, but they also challenged this definition of success by naming women who did not match this set of criteria exactly, thus expanding what it means to have "made it" in our field.

Stories from the Survey: A Snapshot of the Existing Climate

Although the entire volume will report on and draw from the collected set of survey responses, the remainder of this introduction will attempt to summarize the key themes identified through the respondents' stories, beginning with their assessment of the existing climate of the field of rhetoric and composition. The overwhelming number of women who reported instances of sexual discrimination—even sexual harassment—distressed but did not, sadly, surprise us. The women told us of their experiences of having their work co-opted by male colleagues and dissertation directors; of being stalked by male students (and not receiving administrative support or protection); of being "bullied" by misogynist deans and department chairs; of being expected to carry on "innocent" flirtations with higher-ups; and even of being raped by male colleagues.

The women reported that their institutions were not understanding when family crises interfered with their academic responsibilities, as one woman respondent satirically added: "my home institution … is not family friendly unless you are a man in a traditional marriage with a wife at home minding the kids, who can dress them up and bring them to campus for heart-warming Christian holiday events." Another woman reported that she struggled to negotiate her attendance at faculty meetings, which were always scheduled when she was supposed to pick up her children. Although she usually was able to arrange to have someone else pick up her children, on the occasion that she was unsuccessful in this attempt, she told a male colleague that she would have to miss the meeting because her children needed her. To which, he responded: "with a puppy-dog look, 'We need you, too.'"

The survey respondents also told tales of financial discrimination, such as this woman's story: "My husband is also a rhet/comp faculty person in my department … . It has been … difficult seeing my husband get ever-so-slightly better raises than me. The one time I complained, my (male) department chair said, 'You share the same bank account don't you?' I was so stunned that I couldn't even reply." And other survey respondents reported that—in addition to the ubiquitous forms of sexism in the academy—women of color face another set of challenges. One writes:

> Know that men who do the same quality of work will always get more attention, will be rewarded first, and will be resentful if you point out the "coincidences" of the system. Also know that women of color face an even more difficult challenge. White women who do the same work will be rewarded and noticed first—it will be presumed that you, as a woman of color, are "whining" or are just looking out for your own interests.

Others, in response to such sexist environments and experiences, reported that this constant sexist—and often racist—message played havoc, both psychologically and physically, with their sense of self-esteem and sense of self as a professional. One woman reported that, when pregnant, she was harassed by the graduate director at her doctoral institution. She wrote that he "read my pregnant body as a sign of my being an inferior student, someone who was wasting the resources of the department." She was so distraught over the experience that she had trouble nursing her baby; he lost weight as a result, and she suffered recurrent breast infections. Another respondent reported that although there was no overt sexual or physical harassment, the subtle forms of harassment caused a minor health issue to become so severe that she required hospitalization; she further reported that she was diagnosed with acute depression as a result.

The challenge for women in the face of such sexism is, as one respondent put it, "To cultivate a necessary but not toxic skepticism." And for another respondent: "I experienced the normal kinds of sexism and dismissiveness about the kind of work I do. As far as I'm concerned, the best revenge is doing well and working hard." How to persevere and succeed in such an environment—characterized by one respondent as an environment "symptomatic of a crisis of masculinity"—is, indeed, the focus of this volume. In subsequent chapters, we will address various strategies for success, both in principle and in practice. But first, we return to the surveys to identify the major thematic challenges reported by our respondents.

Themes from the Survey

In subsequent chapters, we will address various challenges and provide potential strategies for responding to them. The challenges as identified by our respondents include the following:

Balancing Professional Roles

As expected, one of the recurring problems our respondents identified was the struggle to balance the concurrent roles of teacher, researcher, administrator, and citizen of the university and of the discipline. One woman noted that the demand for research "separated" her from her "primary goal—teaching." She explained: "I still believe teaching is more important than a great deal of what passes for scholarship, but although my university pays lip service to the importance of teaching, it clearly values the name in print more than the person in the classroom." And another woman responds: "After seven years, I still cannot figure out a way to teach composition classes that does not require most of the energy I possess. The time I take to help students learn ensures that my own scholarly work, always last on the list, gets little time at all." Because teaching is such a time-intensive commitment, the biggest challenge, then, for many women was finding the time to conduct their research and to write meaningful articles and books. One woman wrote that her biggest challenge is "to remember that my own research demands time and energy. I have to work very hard to actively structure my life. My research revitalizes me and when I don't do it, my enthusiasm for my job diminishes." Other women identified an additional struggle of attempting to stay current and to publish in two fields—as in the case of those who claim a literary expertise as well as the field of rhetoric and composition: "Probably the most difficult challenge [I have is] bridging the gap between my life as a literary scholar and as a rhetorician." And another reported that her most difficult challenge has been "keeping up with reading the scholarship and doing scholarship in multiple areas."

Also, as expected, a significant recurring problem our respondents identified was the administrative demand and the toll that this service can take on a career, embroiling one in politically inflected turf and financial battles and taking time away from what "really" counts toward tenure and promotion: publications. As discussed above, women in rhetoric and composition face the unique *expectation* to serve in administrative positions; women are often, as one respondent characterized it, "guilted" in administrative work. To be sure, administrative work can be rewarding professionally and personally; however, survey respondents advised, over and over: "Absolutely refuse to be WPA as a new and untenured professor!" Of course, the rationale for this advice is to protect untenured women from risking tenure and promotion possibilities, as writing program administration does not typically result in the kind of work that is rewarded by tenure and promotion committees. This advice is certainly worth thinking about, although others disagree, arguing instead that creating and/or administering large writing programs earned them the respect of upper administration as well as a university-wide reputation, which served them very well during the tenure and review process. However, as we'll discuss in the chapters that follow, more often than not—even if it has been stated to you otherwise—administrative work rarely is a stand-in for or valued as scholarly production.

Working (with) the Rhetoric/Composition and Literary Studies Tension

An additional area of concern, which came as no surprise, was how to negotiate one's position as a rhetoric/composition scholar in an English department, where literary studies reign. As one respondent wrote: "Be ready to be disliked and considered stupid (by lit faculty) for the sort of work you do." Another respondent characterized it this way: "Part of the difficulty was a mostly male literature faculty that did not view composition/rhetoric as a serious discipline, and that viewed the part-timers (mostly women) with disdain—we were referred to in one memorable faculty meeting as 'the housewives.'" And yet another respondent advised: "Do your homework—in the job search, in your research, before committee meetings, etc. Because many faculty members consider rhetoric/composition a field filled with those 'who couldn't make it in a real academic field' (direct quotation from a senior male scholar not at my university), it is imperative that women provide evidence to the contrary. They don't have to do so defensively or apologetically but with an easy, no nonsense self confidence." Despite this tension, as another woman writes, it behooves us all to abandon this "us"/"them" mentality and to learn "how to function in a department where your area of study is not the thing most people care about, where people see one another's successes as threats, and where, for your survival, you need to learn how to build alliances with people outside of your field."

Balancing the Personal with the Professional

An additional predominant, and not-surprising, concern is: how to balance professional and family responsibilities and demands. A significant number of respondents reported that they had partners, children, aging parents, and/or ill siblings under their care; many women reported difficulty in maintaining two-career partnerships, especially when they had to live separately, in different parts of the country, or when they had to ask a husband or partner to relocate to accommodate a career move, or when they had to work in the same department and negotiate the challenges that that arrangement invites.

One respondent wrote that her most difficult challenge was "attending to both professional and personal responsibilities. Being parent, spouse, faculty, and administrator simultaneously was a constant struggle that left me constantly feeling as though I was only fulfilling each role at about 40% of the expectation I'd set for myself (and that I felt others set for me)." And another woman echoed this sentiment by responding that her most difficult challenge was: "Balance. How to have a family and meet career expectations. These expectations come primarily in having chunks of time to allow what I call the 'mind space' needed to think about large projects, such as the book expected of me in order to get tenure," as well as chunks of time to provide "mommy time" for children.

Other women reported that their most difficult challenge was that their professional career required them to be separated, geographically, from their families. One respondent writes: "I don't like being far from my family. I live in Ohio, and my family is in Minnesota. The mobile nature of jobs in higher education demands that we give up what's dear to us—family and stability." And another woman reported: "I feel that I gave up too much of my family and social life to meet the goals of tenure. The years you owe your family cannot be deferred."

Dealing with the Queen Bee

These narratives detail the kinds of all-too-predictable challenges that women face in our profession; however, the survey also revealed a surprising (and shameful) theme: discrimination, harassment, and abuse by other *female* colleagues. One woman reported: "I have actually had the most trouble with women senior to me who think I need to be taught a thing or two or 'put in my place.' I have learned that it's a good idea to seek out their advice first so that they do not feel disrespected." Some of this hazing is subtle, as in this case:

> a senior woman scholar at my university, one known for her feminism and support of women students, didn't speak to me or acknowledge me for the first three years I was there. I said hello in the mailroom or hallway and got nothing back (perhaps she had a hearing problem). The very first time I saw her in the mailroom after the department had voted overwhelmingly to grant me tenure, she gave me the cheeriest and biggest hello. Coincidence? I think not.

Other responses report much more aggressive and openly hostile attacks, such as vocally undermining and scheming ("like high school girls' cattiness) against a candidate's tenure case. One woman reported that a senior woman actually tore up the junior woman's tenure and promotion evaluation materials. Because this so-called "Queen Bee" behavior was so prevalently reported and so damaging to the field of rhetoric and composition, we will address it in greater length in the following chapters. But these related experiences serve as a cautionary tale for the discipline—"feminized" or not, as one respondent suggests: "This experience has reminded me that we need to be careful about too-easy constructions of female-bonding and simplistic views of the caring, collaborative spirit that compositionists tend to attribute to women."

Advice from the Surveys

We wish to reassure the reader, specifically our female reader contemplating a career in the field of rhetoric and composition, that the scenario is not all "doom and gloom," as these narratives may lead one to believe. Our survey questions intended to capture the specific *challenges* that women in the field were struggling with. In hindsight, perhaps we should have asked what specific rewards women in the field enjoyed, in order to present the positive aspects of working in this discipline. We presumed, however, that women in the field would already know intimately the rich rewards of the discipline—as do we, as we experience them whenever we find ourselves passionately absorbed in a research project, or when we hood one of our doctoral students at graduation, or when we aid a struggling student to develop and mature as a writer, or when we work with committed teaching assistants in a composition program. The rewards are many and sustain us semester after semester. However, there are challenges that try us, and we desired to unearth various ways of meeting those challenges. Our survey respondents were very generous with their advice. Although the entire volume will draw from and report on their statements of guidance and counsel, we offer here a number of the key themes of advice:

Begin in Graduate School

Our respondents had a lot to say in response to the question, "If you were to give one piece of advice to a woman about to begin a career in rhetoric and composition, what would it be?" Women advised those just beginning their academic career to make good choices regarding their graduate studies. Although the following two chapters will detail this advice, we offer here—in summary form—some key themes of advice, beginning with the suggestion that women should investigate graduate programs in rhetoric and composition and "apply to programs with well-established 'stars' in the field." Another woman advised: "Be sure to visit all of your graduate school options before you accept any invitation to be admitted to a program, no matter how good that invitation may sound. You will be spending several years of your life with people who will help define your career—it's worthwhile to meet them first." Once enrolled in a graduate program, students were advised to find a dissertation topic early and to select courses and course work that would work toward the dissertation. Another woman advised that students establish a mentor relationship with one who has "good connections," to facilitate publication potential early in one's career.

Find a Mentor/Build a Support System

A strong theme of advice was the exhortation to establish a mentoring relationship with someone smart, savvy, and successful to guide one through career choices and opportunities and to "give focused and field-specific support." This mentor need not be at the same institution; indeed, some women advised finding a mentor who could provide a more global vision of the discipline; others suggested that the mentor have a sense of the local "political landscape" and be able to advise accordingly. In addition to the professional support that a mentor can provide, a number of women advised that one build a personal support system, especially for women with children or who want to have children.

Publish

Our respondents were resounding in their advice that—despite teaching vocations and administrative responsibilities—"Publication is the coinage of power," as aptly stated by one woman. She continues, "if you want the freedom to move, if you want academic respect, you must develop a strong research program and pursue it diligently. In doing so, seek the help of mentors (of both sexes) to help you do so and to protect you from demands on your time that will make this impossible." A healthy and well-published research agenda not only furthers the research mission and knowledge base of the discipline, but it also provides one with protection from many political battles and personal attacks. One woman reported: "I had to deal with a condescending chair and director of graduate studies. I solved the problem by publishing both of them off the chart and embarrassing them." Making time for research and writing is—as we have already noted—one of the most demanding challenges faced by women in rhetoric and composition. However, as one woman advised: "My advice would be: block out a day a week that you will use for your own reading and writing. Don't give up this time for meetings or other university service work. And, likewise, don't give it up for your family either, if you can help it. Remind yourself that you are a professional. Don't give away the time that you need to keep up in the field and feel confident about taking on that label."

Be Collegial

Part of behaving as a professional is being collegial with those with whom you work and associate. It shouldn't take a rocket scientist or Miss Manners to remind us all that we ought to be respectful of others. However, regretfully for all involved, it often takes more: sometimes it requires a negative tenure vote, as one woman reminded us: "Recognize that there's a fourth category in promotion and tenure decisions: collegiality. Recognize that collegiality involves not setting oneself apart as the critic or superior of one's colleagues (a tough task for us self-important, self-lionizing compositionists)." Another woman advised that one develop collegiality by learning "how to build alliances with the people who must work with you." And yet another woman admitted the difficulty of doing so: "I had to learn how to keep my temper and act professionally at all times. It took a long time to learn how to be gracious."

Stay True to Yourself/Be Good to Yourself

Our respondents told us that it was also important that one remain gracious to one's self, as one woman wrote: "My advice is to be generous … especially to yourself. Don't berate or blame yourself when you cannot do everything as well as you would like. Be forgiving." Another woman echoed this sentiment: "My one piece of advice would be to persist—to look forward to your accomplishments and to learn from the mistakes you've made along the way, but don't dwell on them." Other respondents encouraged women to equip themselves with a good sense of humor or play, and warned them to not take themselves too seriously. One advised: "be humble about your work. Do the work and the rewards will come. Don't compare yourself to others." Similarly, our respondents advised women to "never take things personally":

> I think women tend to take much of what we encounter in terms of reaction to ourselves or our work as personal and [directed] at our own perceived deficiencies. The reality, however, is that most of the time such reactions are much more about the [other] person … and his/her problems than they are about us. That took me quite a while to realize, but once I figured that out and could stop feeling defensive or apologetic, I became much more effective.

Of course, when you have a toxic colleague, being good to yourself should include venting with girlfriends, getting a massage, and giving yourself permission to avoid the jerk at all costs. Being gracious to yourself will sometimes involve asking for help when a toxic colleague becomes an active threat to your career.

Our respondents also told us that it was important to keep true to one's sense of self and to one's desires. In the pressure-cooker world of academe, it is easy to get caught up by the current of professional demands. But our respondents advised us: "try to figure out what you value and want, no matter what pressures there are for you to do otherwise," and "stay true to your vision of what you want and who you are." One respondent suggested:

> Give yourself time to reflect and "check" your life once in awhile. Are you going where you WANT to go, or where you think you HAVE to go? … Have fun. Don't forget that YOU and your family are the most important people … in the world! Don't let a provost or president or department chair or tenure review committee or search committee or dissertation committee tell you otherwise. If you aren't having fun, you're doing it wrong! If it doesn't feel good, you're doing it wrong! If you wish you didn't have to do the things you have to do in order to "get there," then you're going to the wrong place! Ask yourself, "Who/What do I think I am?" And then answer honestly.

Have a Life

And, finally, *dance*. One respondent actually advised women to dance more but, thematically, the advice could be grouped with those others who advised women to "have a life" in addition to whatever professional obligations and successes one may embrace. Here is one respondent: "Academia is a profession which is never satisfied: publish more, teach better, serve on more committees … . You can only succeed—and be healthy and happy, I think—by being able to say no, to set limits on your work, and to create other activities you enjoy where you don't have to think about work." As Chapters 6 and 7 will detail, successful women in our discipline have found ways to balance professional and personal goals. Although not an easy balance to maintain, it is a possible one. One woman offers this advice:

> do what you really want to do. Do not do anything you don't really want to do just because you think it would advance your career. For example: if you want to live in a certain part of the country for whatever reason, then just keep job-searching there, find something else to do while you're searching. Or if you want to take a few years off entirely while your kids are small, do it. You'll get back in the game eventually … . It is true, of course, that women have to present better

credentials than men right along the line to get anywhere in academe. No one will forgive you any errors or weaknesses. But you can't let your awareness of that fact make you run scared. Just always put together the best credentials you can, put your best foot forward, and be willing to try unconventional paths if they seem right for you.

Strategies for Success

With this brief introduction of the predominant challenges faced by women currently in the discipline, as well as a quick survey of the thematic advice offered, this volume moves now to more detailed and sustained analyses of the various strategies for those who desire to "make it" in the field of rhetoric and composition. We stress that there is no "one" way to "make it," as the various paths taken by our profiled women indeed attest. There is no "one" answer to the various dilemmas you will face; we will provide the best advice that we have gathered, but we will finally acknowledge that each situation in which you find yourself will require that you respond rhetorically and carefully analyze the situation, your audience, your purpose, and your exigency.

The book is divided into four sections, roughly chronologizing one's professional journey. Depending on the stage of your career, you may want to begin reading at various points of entry, although each chapter does build on previously established strategies and advice.

Section I, "Becoming a Professional," specifically addresses those women who are currently engaged in graduate studies or who are contemplating the profession of rhetoric and composition. Two chapters in this section, "Succeeding as a Graduate Student" and "Succeeding on the Job Market," aim to initiate graduate students into the professional demands of the field, including conference attendance and participation, as well as working with faculty and mentors to compose a successful dissertation and to begin a track record of scholarship and publication. Additionally, these chapters inform graduate students on the intricacies of the job market, advising them how to present themselves as competitive candidates in order to land a tenure-track position.

Section II, "Thriving as a Professional," advises women through the ranks—from untenured, assistant professor to tenured, associate professor to full professor. These chapters ("Succeeding as a Junior Professor," "Succeeding Despite it All: Administration, Politics, and Difficult People," and "Succeeding as a Senior Scholar, Teacher, and Mentor") lay out successful strategies for establishing oneself as a professional, complete with an active research agenda and publication record, in order to make a compelling case for tenure and promotions. Additionally, these chapters offer advice about writing program administration service, specifically how to juggle this demand with competing research and teaching responsibilities. We presume that one will also need advice on how to deal with difficult departmental politics, with difficult students, and with difficult colleagues, specifically of the Queen Bee type, and these chapters address this as well. Finally, we provide advice and strategies for continuing on in rank and seeking another successful promotion. With one's status as a senior scholar in the field comes additional demands and responsibilities, including mentoring junior colleagues and participating in the development of the greater field of rhetoric and composition. We provide advice on how to succeed in this new role.

Section III, "And Having a Life, Too," addresses the concern that a number of our survey respondents noted: how can one find balance between professional and personal responsibilities and goals? How can one maintain mental and physical well-being in the midst of strenuous and conflicting time demands? Along with Section IV, "Being a Professional: Profiles of Success," which provides detailed profiles of the lives and successes of nine women, these chapters aim to offer "real-life" strategies for succeeding professionally and having a life, too.

In sum, this volume provides a rich compilation of various women's ways of making it in rhetoric and composition.

Section I

BECOMING A PROFESSIONAL

1

SUCCEEDING AS A GRADUATE STUDENT

> [I would advise women to] spend more time in graduate school writing a book-quality dissertation, going to conferences and publishing papers.
>
> —anonymous survey respondent

> [My advice would not be] any different than I'd give to a man: work hard, find a good mentor, listen to what people are telling you, and be willing to revise, revise, revise.
>
> —anonymous survey respondent

It's no secret that many associate and full professors in our field today, including some of the successful women we interviewed in this volume, were able to get tenure and promotion with little more than most of you will need to land an MLA interview. Typically, entry-level job candidates in rhetoric and composition will be expected to have published at least one article in a peer-reviewed journal and to have given a handful of presentations at national conferences. They will also be expected to demonstrate excellence in teaching: they'll need a solid teaching record, innovative pedagogical strategies, and a well articulated teaching philosophy. Bottom line: acing your classes and getting your doctorate, even at a top-tier research institution, will probably not be nearly enough to land you a tenure-track position today; you'll also need to build a strong record of scholarly productivity and develop an innovative teaching portfolio. You'll need a good mentor (or two), as well.

Finding a Mentor

There is a significant distinction between a dissertation advisor and a *mentor*, as Penny Gold, co-author of *The Chicago Guide to your Academic Career*, observes. Whereas the former "has an official role that must be fulfilled, which centers on the direction of the dissertation research," the latter "may have little to do with one's dissertation, but is someone ahead of you in academia, usually in your general discipline, if not in your specific field, with whom you come to have a more informal personal relationship."

The mentor is someone you can go to for advice on all sorts of issues in academic life (as troubling as difficulties you may be having with your advisor or as mundane as advice on what to wear for a job interview). Sometimes the advisor plays this role as well, sometimes another faculty member (perhaps even at a different institution), sometimes an advanced graduate student. You can even have more than one mentor, but you'll just have one advisor (Goldsmith, Komlos, and Gold 46).

Ideally, the dissertation advisor will also serve as a mentor, but that's not always the case. Every doctoral student must have a dissertation advisor, as Gold notes, but not all graduate students "find a mentor" (46). Whereas the dissertation advisor's job (save future letters of recommendation) is all but done when the dissertation is defended, one's relation with a mentor transcends any specific academic accomplishment. Indeed, more than a few of our survey respondents reported that the most difficult challenge they've encountered in their academic career thus far is finding a good mentor. One told us: "The biggest challenge I've faced has been a lack of mentoring. I don't think my story is that different from many composition and rhetoric faculty." Another said the most difficult challenge has been "Being the lone person in my field (rhet/comp) at each of my institutions until recently (having no mentor in the field, having to defend my field alone, being solely responsible for curriculum, graduate students, etc.). Please note that this is a rhet/comp issue, not an issue of women scholars." And one respondent, after noting that her most difficult challenge has been "finding good mentors," wrote:

> I came from a small program, had excellent and thoughtful instruction, had opportunities for hands-on training—in writing center, writing consulting, administrative concerns, etc., but I didn't have a network of people established, nor did I know how to take care of my career. I was hired, luckily enough, with someone who not only came from a much bigger program but who was also very savvy about her career. I was also lucky that we decided to work on a book together, an edited collection. The book was published this year, and in that experience I watched how she established contacts in the field. In addition, she showed me how she thought about work—and marketing work. She was forever saying to me, so how will that work translate to your CV? I was lucky to have that influence. And then I've also been lucky to have good and thoughtful people in the field show an interest in my work, and I have mentors I would have never imagined as a result … . When I first started, I was doing work that was different from my dissertation director's interests—and so I really needed different mentors who could give me advice, and I also needed to know where and how to get published.

Mary Morris Heiberger and Julia Miller Vick, co-authors of *The Academic Job Search Handbook*, suggest that "whatever the relationship with your advisor, it is helpful to have as many senior people as possible interested in your success." They encourage you, as a graduate student, to "take advantage of every opportunity to talk to and get to know other faculty members in your department. Ask them for opinions, perspective, and feedback in areas where you genuinely value their expertise." Alongside Gold, they suggest that you also "develop mentors at other institutions," as well as with your peers in the department (35).

Given the ever-increasing pressure to present and publish your work before you defend your dissertation, it would be wise to find at least one mentor well before you decide on a dissertation advisor, or even a dissertation topic. In "Graduate Students as Active Members of the Profession: Some Questions for Mentoring," Janice Lauer suggests that "mentoring is crucial to help individuals map their paths through a department's requirements and make decisions about whether, when, and where to publish" (231). Should you try to get an article or two out before you start dissertating? Should you try to publish a completed chapter from your dissertation while you finish writing the rest of it? As Lauer notes,

> on the job market, those with completed dissertations *and* publications have the best advantage, all other things being equal; but students with a publication or two but *without* a finished dissertation are less competitive and may, if hired, jeopardize their progress toward tenure when they struggle to finish their dissertation while working in a full-time job. (233)

"On the other hand," Lauer continues,

> students starting a new position with a completed dissertation and no publications sometimes are daunted when trying to place an article or a book prospectus without any guidance and find it difficult to generate the number of publications required for promotion and tenure at certain institutions. (233)

For all of these reasons, and more, we encourage you to find a mentor (or two), preferably very early in your graduate career.

The Conference Scene

Academic conferences can be expensive and hassle-filled; they frequently run interference with scheduled vacations, as well, falling during the week of spring break (CCCC), the week before or after Thanksgiving (NCTE, NCA, ASHR), two days after Christmas (MLA), the first few weeks of summer vacation (RSA, C&W), and/or smack dab in the middle of summer break (ISHR). Nonetheless, as Ms. Mentor (Emily Toth) suggests, "conferences are your professional orientation, and you must attend them." To graduate students and assistant professors who counter that they can't afford to go to conferences, she replies—and we concur—that "you can't afford not to," as they are where you "make your professional name" (*Ms. Mentor's Impeccable Advice* 45).

Attending Conferences

Even if you are not giving a talk, there are many reasons to attend the field's national conferences. John Komlos, Gold's co-author, suggests that it is, among other things, "a way to publicize your impending entry into the life of the organization. This is part of the process of your professionalization." At conferences, Komlos continues,

> You will meet scholars who were mere names to you until then. You will exchange information with graduate students from other universities and, though them, learn more about what others are doing in the field. You will sharpen your understanding of the convictions held by others on important unresolved questions in the discipline and develop ideas on the likely directions new research will take. In which direction should your research go when your dissertation is complete and you are no longer so closely attached to your mentor? Participation at a conference will also offer you an early look at how your work will be received by others. (Goldsmith, Komlos, and Gold 73)

In the panel sessions, you'll both be introduced to some of the conversations going on in the field and get some sense of how those conversations are conducted; you'll witness, for instance, the (productive and not so productive) ways in which scholars in rhetoric and writing studies engage in intellectual disagreements. As Komlos puts it, "you will see firsthand how others perform in stressful situations and what the unwritten etiquette of intellectual jousting at such meetings is" (73).

Perhaps even more importantly, attending the field's national conferences will give you the opportunity to meet scholars from around the country with whom you share interests. We cannot say enough about the importance of networking in academia, and scholarly conferences are a great place to do it: the folks attending these meetings are, after all, precisely those who will be in the position one day to open doors for you—to get you speaking gigs, to write you letters of recommendation, and even perhaps to hire you. Of course, it will take some effort on your part: once you get yourself there, you'll need to find ways to make connections and to leave an impression. To achieve the greatest return on your conference investment, in other words, you'll need to learn to schmooze.

Making sure your name tag is visible, attend presentations given by scholars you're interested in and make it a point to talk to them about their work.

Responding during the Q&A part of the panel is one possibility, assuming you can offer something productive to the general conversation (and otherwise, don't raise your hand). In any case, take the opportunity to introduce yourself to the speaker directly after the panel, demonstrate your interest in his or her work, and—perhaps, if it's appropriate—make a connection or two to your own. One survey respondent narrates that "while a graduate student completing work on my dissertation, I simply approached 'Professor A' at a conference at which we were both delivering papers and struck up a conversation about our related interests. That was 15 years ago, and 'Professor A' remains one of my most trusted and dearest colleagues."

Make it a point to introduce yourself to other graduate students doing work you're interested in, as well; exchange email addresses, agree to read each other's work, and consider proposing a panel or roundtable together for the next year's conference. Making connections with other graduate students can be one of the most intellectually and emotionally rewarding parts of the conference scene; it can also turn out to be economically and professionally rewarding, since connecting with a single other graduate student also gives you a certain access to his or her extended network of colleagues and mentors. Indeed, one survey respondent advised: "Build national networks of colleagues in the field who become your friends for life. Start with your graduate school cohort and build out from there."

Presenting Your Work

There are good reasons to start presenting your own work at academic conferences very early in your graduate student career. First of all, the professional conference offers a great forum to test out your ideas, to join the professional "conversation," and to help shape the field's areas of interest. It also gets you a line on your vitae, of course, and your name on the program. But presenting at conferences can also help you become more productive: committing to write an eight-ish page conference paper is a good way to get yourself moving on a larger (and so perhaps more daunting) writing project; indeed, many book chapters and journal articles begin as 20-minute conference presentations. Obviously, as former *JAC* editor Gary A. Olson reminds us, "there is a vast difference between a brief conference paper and an extended, fleshed-out, journal article." The former is typically "short, informal and somewhat general, while the latter is longer, more formal, and meticulously detailed." However, that "vast difference" is precisely the reason he also suggests that "it is wise to begin a project first as a presentation and then later to transform it into a substantive, formal article" ("Publishing" 22). Or a chapter. Writing the paper can give you the focus, the confidence, and the momentum you need to follow through with the larger project.

This is true in part because when you present a piece at a professional conference, you receive an immediate response from your audience. In addition to any verbal feedback you may get during the Q&A and/or after the panel, you'll also get instant non-verbal feedback, which can be at least as important as you begin the process of transforming your presentation into a potential publication. As former *CCC* editor Richard Gebhardt notes, "your audience's body language and expressions will let you gauge the clarity and persuasiveness of your paper" ("Scholarship" 41). Indeed, according to Gebhardt, those journal articles that are developed from conference papers tend to have "greater clarity, impact, and flair than essays written with only an audience of readers in mind" (41).

Of course, it is also possible to go the other way: you could take a selection from a larger writing project and turn it into a conference paper. You might present a section from a completed chapter of your dissertation, for example, or from a seminar paper you're particularly happy with. In this case, however, you'll need to make sure that the presentation itself can stand on its own, without the supportive context from which you snip it. "It must be self-contained," says Komlos, "that is, you should coherently explore a specific question and provide some results with a plausible conclusion, even if still somewhat tentative." Though the "results need not be earth-shattering," he suggests, "there should be some effort to clearly pose a question, develop an idea or a thesis, or resolve a controversy, while holding the audience's attention" (Goldsmith, Komlos, and Gold 69).

When you present a paper at a conference, it's imperative that you stay within the designated time limits. Unless you are instructed otherwise, you can assume that on three-person panels, each speaker gets 20 minutes, and on four-person panels, each speaker gets 15 minutes; the rest of the time (about 25–30 minutes) is designated for the Q&A discussion. It's not unusual *enough* for a couple of speakers, especially on a four-person panel, to go on for so long that there is no time left for the final panelist to speak at all, let alone for any Q&A discussion. Strictly speaking, it is the panel chair's job to hold speakers to their time limit, but it is first of all the speaker's responsibility to have prepared a presentation capable of being delivered within that limit. Going more than a minute or two overtime is more than rude; it's unprofessional and could earn you precisely the wrong sort of reputation.

To help ensure that your presentation will make the right sort of impression, you'll need to practice and time yourself. Read it aloud to yourself and to anyone else who will listen—preferably another graduate student, but in a pinch, a partner, kid, or parent will do. The important thing is to hear yourself reading it, to get a rhythm, to get comfortable pronouncing the words and sentences, and to make sure you can give this paper in a dynamic manner within the time you've been allotted. It takes most people about two minutes to read aloud one page of double-spaced, 12-point type, but that general rule will vary quite a bit depending on the font face (Times New Roman is smaller than Arial, which is smaller than Courier, for example), the accessibility of the content, and the speaker's own sense of pacing and pausing.

There is some contention about whether conference presentations should be typed out and read or presented more extemporaneously from notes or an outline. Occasionally, you may hear someone insist that all presentations *ought* to be talks rather than papers, as if the former is always preferable; however, that is not the case. The decision about whether to talk or read has everything to do with what you want your presentation to accomplish. Often this distinction in aim marks a disciplinary divide: in the field of rhetoric and composition, which is on the Englishy side of rhetorical studies, presentations are typically read, while on the more Speech Commy side they are usually given extemporaneously. However, even *within* rhetoric and composition itself, those whose work takes an empirical focus often deliver talks at conferences, perhaps with the help of slides or charts designed to spotlight very specific statistics or other information. Those whose work takes a more literary or theoretical focus, on the other hand, tend to deliver *papers*. In general, presenters who aim mainly to communicate the results of their own or another's empirical research may be wise to give talks; presenters who aim to inspire more theoretical, philosophical, poetic, or pedagogical reflection and/or to spotlight certain performative effects of language, probably would be better off reading papers. In either case, however, an effective presentation will require practice, practice, practice.

Finding CFPs

The field's most well-known and broadly attended national conferences include the following:

- College Composition and Communication Convention (CCCC or 4Cs)
- Rhetoric Society of America conference (RSA)
- International Society for the History of Rhetoric conference (ISHR)
- American Society for the History of Rhetoric conference (ASHR)
- Computers and Writing conference (C&W)
- conference of the National Council of the Teachers of English (NCTE)
- convention of the Modern Language Association (MLA)
- conference of the National Communication Association (NCA).

The quickest way to find each organization's current Call For Papers (CFP) for its upcoming conference is to go online and check that organization's website. NCTE and the MLA also post the CFPs for the regional conferences that they sponsor. One obvious benefit of responding to a CFP for a regional or graduate student conference is that the proposal acceptance rate is much higher than it is for a national conference: you are very likely to get on the program if you take the time to send off a decent proposal. Generally, regional and graduate student conferences are also much smaller and less pressurized, so it can be less frazzling to present at them and easier to make connections with other attendees.

Major journals in the field regularly publish CFPs for national, regional, and graduate student conferences, too, so when you're looking for a conference, it can be beneficial to flip through those most closely related to your specific interests, such as the following:

- *College Composition and Communication*
- *Philosophy and Rhetoric*
- *Rhetoric Society Quarterly*
- *Journal of Advanced Composition*
- *College English*
- *Computers and Writing*
- *Rhetorica*
- *Rhetoric Review*
- *Pre/Text*
- *Written Communication*
- *Technical Communication Quarterly*
- the *Quarterly Journal of Speech*.

If you don't personally subscribe to any of these journals, your library surely does. Various rhetoric and writing listservs and blogs will also post conference CFPs: for example,

- HRhetor (www.h-net.org/~rhetor)
- WPA (www.ilstu.edu/~ddhesse/wpa/listserv)

are both very good about posting appropriate CFPs, as are

- the Blogora (http://rsa.cwrl.utexas.edu)
- The Rhetorica Network (http://rhetorica.net)
- Kairos News (http://kairosnews.org)

and a handful of personal weblogs hosted by individual rhetoricians.

Responding to CFPs

Before you send off a proposal, be sure to read the CFP very carefully. Pay close attention to the deadline for proposal submissions, the word limit for proposals, the presentation options available, and, perhaps, to the theme of the conference itself. National conferences typically ask you to declare whether you are submitting a paper, a panel, or a roundtable proposal, and it is important to follow the directions for the presentation option you are proposing. If you submit a proposal for a single paper and it is accepted, the conference planners will match your paper up with two or three others to form an ad hoc panel for which they will also assign a title. If you submit a panel proposal, you'll put the panel of speakers together yourself: panel sessions include three to four speakers, each of whom talks for 15 to 20 minutes, respectively. If you propose a roundtable, you'll also put it together yourself: roundtable sessions typically include more than four speakers, each of whom will talk for 5–10 minutes. You may be more likely to get a panel or roundtable proposal accepted than an individual paper proposal, mainly because they are less work for the conference planners. Successful panel and roundtable proposals offer a clearly stated theme/issue/topic that is current, relevant to the field's interests, and often related to the overall conference theme. In addition, successful panel proposals demonstrate a clear connection among the individual paper topics and describe how each of the papers will address the panel theme itself.

Tip: some conference planners don't like multi-speaker proposals in which all participants are from the same institution, so consider hooking up with graduate students or faculty members at other universities.

If you are proposing a panel or paper that is easily recognizable in the field of rhetoric and composition—if the focus is on the history of rhetoric, or one of the specific arts of rhetoric (*ars praedicandi*), or first-year writing, and so on—you may not need to situate your proposal within the general theme of the conference. Roxanne Mountford, for example, rarely attends to the conference theme in her own highly successful proposals, and when she teaches her students how to write one, she tells them three things are necessary:

- Connect your papers with a larger conversation in the field,
- show the importance of your work to the larger conversation, and
- explain what will be in the paper ("In this paper, I will XYZ").

Here, for example, is Mountford's paper proposal for the CCCC in 2003:

> One of the traditional areas of commentary in the history of rhetoric is the art of delivery, the only canon of rhetoric that addresses the body. Prevented from participating in public oratory because of the presumed inferiority of their bodies, women turned to the written word throughout history as a means of resistance. However, feminist theorizing about the body, including the work of Susan Bordo, Judith Butler, and bell hooks, as well as many acts of public resistance by ordinary women, allow us the opportunity to refigure the canon of delivery around the female body. In this presentation I will draw on the work of Sonja Foss, Lisa Ede, Cheryl Glenn, and Andrea Lunsford, and others as well as my own research to outline the contours of what Edward Hall calls "the silent language"—the speech of the body, or delivery—from a feminist perspective.

And here is the panel proposal the three of us submitted for 4Cs 2007, the theme for which was "Representing Identities":

> Rhetoric and composition has long been considered a "feminized"

> field, both because a majority of its scholars and practitioners are women and because the work itself has been depicted as "women's work." As Theresa Enos, Louise Wetherbee Phelps, Janet Emig, and others have aptly demonstrated, one result of our field's status is that women in rhetoric and composition are doubly burdened in a way that other female academics are not. A few years ago, we conducted a national survey of women in the field to determine the specific obstacles they face and their strategies for negotiating them; we then profiled eight successful women scholars whose "ways of making it" were of interest to our survey respondents. That research is the basis for our recent book project, *Women's Ways of Making It in Rhetoric and Composition*, in which we offer women in the field strategies for negotiating the hard realities they face throughout their professional career, from graduate school to promotion to full professor. In the proposed panel, we will offer some of the most significant discoveries from our research. Additionally, because the overwhelming majority of our survey respondents identified themselves as Caucasian, creating an imbalance that we sought to correct through our interviews and study of the literature, we will be joined on the panel by one of the "successful women" we interviewed for the book; this panelist's professional experience includes broad themes common to all women in this field as well as the unique issues familiar to women of color.

These proposals so obviously address concerns in the field that there is no real need to demonstrate a connection to the conference theme.

However, if what you want to propose may not be readily recognizable to program reviewers as significant to the field of rhetoric and composition, if the "larger conversation" to which your work connects is not in rhet/comp but critical theory or philosophy, for example, most people agree that it would help to situate your proposal within the general theme of the conference if it has one (a few do not). At times this will require some creativity, some savvy spinning, and an attempt to incorporate into your proposal some of the vocabulary from the CFP itself. There is no need to pretend that you wholeheartedly embrace the theme of the conference if you don't, of course. Here, for example, is Diane Davis's panel proposal to 4Cs in 2004, which incorporates yet challenges the language of the CFP and the theme of the conference:

> The CFP for this year's 4Cs asks how composition matters today, and it asks us to "consider the quality of our national civic discourse," which is clearly abysmal. Yet, the constant call to turn rhetoric and writing classrooms into courses on public advocacy and civic discourse is not unproblematic; indeed, such a call promotes a very narrow conception of writing, underestimates the diverse and extensive ways in which writing matters in a democratic society, and miscalculates the roles

such notions of writing play in the shaping of student-citizens. Furthermore, the advocative turn risks engendering a trope that is incapable of deploying the apotropaic force of "peace," that is, its "active" ability to turn violence aside. Our panel will examine not only the ways in which "writing" exceeds the intentional signification demanded in civic discourse but also the indissociable connections between the excesses of writing and any notion of peace.

And here is Davis's 2006 proposal:

> The CFP for this year's 4Cs issues an ethical imperative in rhetoric and writing studies to forge new and potentially transdisciplinary alliances in order to meet America's literacy needs. This plea "to embrace diversity and to build coalitions, culture and community" essentially amounts to a call for identification, which Kenneth Burke describes as a relation of con-substantiation, a "middle ground" between individuation and sociality, divisiveness and fusion. Therefore, our panel will examine both the necessarily complex itinerary involved in the processes of identification as such and identification's occasionally perilous intersections with the "art" of persuasion. Our explorations will proceed via three very different "terministic screens": new scientific research on mind reading, the reflexive feedback loops operative in a standard poker match, and the philosophical and psychoanalytic distinctions between narcissism and sociality.

Each of these examples uses the language of the CFP in order to issue certain challenges to the conference theme. If the panel proposal establishes a connection to the CFP, the accompanying individual paper proposals need not do so. Here, for example, is Davis's 2004 paper proposal:

> Speaker 3: "Writing (as) Peace"
>
> In contradistinction to Hobbes and Kant, Levinas proposes that an originary peace precedes the war of all against all. In this paper, I'll suggest that "writing" (as opposed to the signification of a meaning) testifies to this always prior and radically hospitable relationality: writing is, first of all, the communication of communicability as such, the exposition of an irreparable exposedness to radical alterity. Whereas the signification of a meaning/message proffers the figure of identity, of *ipseity*, writing simultaneously evokes the figure of the "toward," or the "being-toward" that signals the extreme non-selfsufficiency of the "subject/citizen" and the originarily peaceful relationality that is the condition of possibility for both an empirical peace and for war.

It's also important that you meet the deadline. National conferences are often huge, so no matter how brilliant your proposal may be, if it comes in late it will likely not be considered. Smaller regional or graduate student conferences may be slightly more forgiving; nonetheless, getting your submission in late makes you look sloppy and unorganized, and that's not the impression you want to create. Almost every CFP will include a word limit for proposals—stick very close to that limit. If your proposal obviously exceeds the word limit, the overworked conference planners may toss it without reading it carefully. Unless explicitly instructed to do so, *never* send the entire paper. Conference planners are often responsible for reading and evaluating huge stacks of proposals, so the last thing you want to do is force them to wade through paragraphs of "background material" before stating your presentation's specific contribution. In general, whether the limit is set at 200 or 1,000 words, you'll want to state the purpose of your presentation very early and very directly in the proposal.

Affording It

Generally, graduate students must fund their own conferencing adventures. But occasionally your department or college will kick through with a small portion of the cost if you are actually presenting a paper. It's worth checking with your faculty mentor or department chair, in any case. There are also several ways to lower the cost of attending a conference. First of all, instead of buying an expensive airline ticket, consider driving to the conference with a group of other graduate students. Instead of staying in the conference hotel, check out other nearby hotels that are less swanky and expensive. Some hotels will provide rollaway beds and allow up to six people in one double room, so consider sharing a room with three or more other graduate students to keep hotel costs down. You won't get much sleep, but you'll probably have a lot of fun.

What to Wear

Be clear about this: when you attend a professional conference as a graduate student, you are already on a kind of job interview (or pre-interview), and you should dress accordingly. In his foreword to Dawn M. Formo and Cheryl Reed's *Job Search in Academe*, Ross Winterowd affirms the significance of the fashion question, relating, as a "representative anecdote," some advice he once gave a dissertating student:

> After he had completed his qualifying examinations and was well underway on his dissertation, one of the brightest students I have ever known came into my office with this question: "What should I do to prepare for the job market?" My advice was this: Cut your hair, and get rid of your beaded headband. Get out of your thongs, holey blue jeans, and T-Shirt with its Rolling Stones emblem. Buy a pair of shoes, a pair

> of gray trousers, a white shirt, and a necktie. And wear them. He did. And he got a job. (xvi)

The point, Winterowd said, was not that this independent soul had sold out to the establishment but that "he did not, through his dress and manner, challenge interviewers to a fight. That is, by 'talking their language' in the way he dressed, he invited them to discuss ideas and values with him" (xvi).

What most interests us here is not whether Winterowd's advice encourages a certain selling out but rather that it is, in any case, thoroughly gendered: what might an equally qualified *female* candidate wear so as to not, through her dress and manner, "challenge interviewers to a fight"? That, we submit, is an infinitely more complicated question. How might she dress in a way that "talks their language" and invites them to "discuss ideas and values" with her? Probably not in gray trousers and a white shirt, nor in the equivalent of a tailored "power suit," both of which could make her appear too ball busting, too scary, too "manly." But not in anything too soft or "feminine," either, as that could make her appear too weak, too unprofessional, too "girly." And we won't even get into the problematics of shoe selection. It's almost a non-issue for a male in grey trousers; he'll be safe in anything short of, say, bright orange high tops (or flipflops). But a woman is faced with all sorts of other issues beyond finding shoes that match her outfit: if the heel is too low and/or if the leather is too soft and comfortable, it could give her a frumpy, earth-muffin, or earth-mother look; if the heel is too high, if the leather is too hard, if the toe is too pointy, and/or if there is too much strappy action going on, she could look too sexy and threatening (plus, her feet will hurt).

So what's a woman to wear?

In 1995, Julie Adair King advised readers of her book *The Smart Woman's Guide to Interviewing and Salary Negotiation* that women interviewing for any position should

> aim for a look that's stylish but conservative. Wear a fashionable business suit in a low-key color, a minimum of jewelry, simple accessories and low-heeled pumps. No low-cut or sheer blouses. No spike heels or sandals. No little-girlish jumpers and no nightclub-hopping mini-skirts or stretch pants. Always dress as if you're interviewing for the CEO's job, no matter what position you're seeking. (84)

Even if you work in one of the "creative fields," King warned, "don't make the mistake of wearing your most avant-garde garb in an effort to show your creative genius. Let your portfolio do the talking in that regard," she advised. "Your appearance should tell the interviewer that you also have a head for business." Of course, choosing the appropriate "business suit" is only one step toward that end, according to King, who added that "sloppy manicures, missing buttons, scuffed shoes, stained lapels or snagged stockings are interpreted as signs that the candidate isn't detail-oriented" (84). And that is (still) not all: "For women, makeup is often a downfall," King continues. "Keep yours subtle: no clown cheeks, iridescent eye shadow, inch-long lashes or glossy purple lipstick. Opt for short nails with clear or pale polish; loud colors, especially bright reds and pinks, denote a yen for parties rather than business" (84–5).

All of this fashion advice for the "businesswoman" may seem a little over the top—not to mention offensive—to women in academia, but wardrobe choices can be a deal-breaker in any sort of job interview. Indeed, when Ms. Mentor weighed in with fashion advice tailored specifically for female academics, she insisted that "the best clothes for a professional woman to wear to a big-time academic conference are dresses or skirts that no one will notice or remember: not too tight, not too short, not too colorful." One reader who called herself "Chic in Canada" quibbled, arguing that while this advice might work for very young female conference attendees who need to look older and wiser, it would be "inappropriate, and perhaps risky, for the female candidate who is 'mature.'" Indeed, Chic writes, a mature woman should avoid looking "frumpy" at all costs; she should instead go for an "earthy, ethnic, or elegant" look. After holding "an international fashion summit," Chic in Canada and Ms. Mentor strike a compromise; both women agree

> that understated elegance can be valuable; that miniskirts are always incorrect, because they look childish; that pants can be risky for conservative schools; and that dressing as a Wall Street banker (gray flannel, little tie) will seem too powerful, and therefore out of place, in academia. Ms. Mentor retains some skepticism about "earthy" and "ethnic," especially if "ethnic" means turbans and swirling fringe, but she and "Chic in Canada" agree that colorful scarves are tasteful and welcome accessories. (Toth, *Ms. Mentor's Impeccable Advice* 47–8)

That was 1992. And fashion advice for women in academe has not changed much, content-wise, over the last decade and a half. One trend that has changed is the skirt requirement: many women now opt to conference and interview in a pant suit, and that is a perfectly acceptable choice today. For women who do choose skirts, Kathryn Hume, distinguished professor of English at Penn State University, did offer a thoroughly pragmatic update to it in 2005: "Make sure your clothes look good when you sit as well as when you stand. By that I mean something pretty specific. A short skirt, no matter how stylish when you stand, will ride halfway up your crotch when you sit in a low armchair. That sends the wrong signal to male interviewers, and is likely to irritate female interviewers as well." Hume also suggests that "if your skirt exposes your knees, wear very opaque panty hose, or your knees will flare white if you sit in a low chair and look like a pair of headlights, drawing attention." And contra Ms. Mentor, Hume advises job seekers that wearing "completely bland clothes" that no one will remember may not be the best strategy. If you want to be remembered by an interview committee, she says, "you should wear at least one unusual bright color" (25–6).

This is all pretty standard wardrobe advice for female graduate students who are presenting at conferences or more officially interviewing; it's designed to help you avoid the typical traps associated with gender prejudices on the job market. The three of us were all separately advised, for example, not to wear big earrings, pants, low necklines, short skirts, bright colors, or high heels. We also got some weirder, more paranoid suggestions, and you will too. One now renowned rhetoric scholar told us that when she was in graduate school she was advised to bind her breasts so that they wouldn't be a distraction in the interview process. We responded to this confession with nervous laughter, and yet the extreme nature of the advice exposes the severity of the problem it aims to address.

It's not impossible, of course, for a female graduate student to ignore most of this fashion advice and still land a good job in the field. In fact, in graduate school two of us regularly gave conference presentations wearing dangling earrings, miniskirts, and strappy-pointy shoes; we toned it down for our MLA and on-campus interviews and both managed to get hired at respected institutions. Nonetheless, we submit that the authors of *Dress Smart Women*, Kim Johnson Gross and Jeff Stone, are correct that "people do judge a book by its cover," and it's something of an open secret that we have paid dearly for our previous fashion choices. We now encourage our own students to choose differently (vi).

Typically, what you decide to wear out of the house is a compromise between what you feel most comfortable in and what specific ethos you're trying to pull off—it is, in other words, a rhetorical choice. At an academic conference, generally speaking, you'll want to assume some version of the sharp, happening, and confident but not arrogant scholar. You'll want to avoid coming off too much like the Reflective Hippy, the Wall Street Banker, or the Playboy Bunny; that is, in general you'll want to steer clear of looks that are too casual, too formal, or too sexy. How you, as a singularly fashioned being, move toward a self-presentation that says "academic professional" will depend mostly on where you begin, on what you're currently most comfortable wearing (whether that be jeans and running shoes, a muumuu and Birkenstocks, or a short black dress and pointy-strappy stilettos). Our advice to you: Take all of the above suggestions into account and then strike a comfortable compromise with your own current wardrobe.

Publishing Your Work

Gary Olson, former editor of *JAC*, observed in 1997 that the "institution-mandated pressure to publish" has helped to turn scholarly publication into a fiercely competitive industry, and he proposed that surviving in this "almost cutthroat environment," will require the adoption of "a kind of *entrepreneurial* spirit." Indeed, to potential objections that scholarship is the same "leisurely, gentlemanly activity" that it always was, Olson argued compellingly that scholarship now "*is* a kind of business activity" and that "published works are the currency with which we purchase tenure, promotion, salary increases, and the respect of colleagues" ("Publishing" 19). Olson's disturbingly accurate depiction of the academic publishing scene can hardly be contested today, more than a decade later—except perhaps to note that things have gotten even worse. Most of you will now need the "currency" of publications to purchase the luxury of a *job interview.*

Graduate students in the field today live under what Christina Murphy, former editor of *Composition Studies*, *Studies in Psychoanalytic Theory*, and *English in Texas*, describes as an ever-increasing pressure to "produce scholarship *as* professionals while they [are] studying to *become* professionals" (6). Hiring committees are on the lookout, among other things, for evidence that a job applicant has the intellectual capacity and productive energy to earn tenure at their institution, and a few well-placed, peer-reviewed scholarly publications can serve as such evidence. Publishing in graduate school won't guarantee that you'll get job interviews, but hitting the job market without any publications will more than likely put you at a disadvantage. Getting an article, book review, or response essay published in any of the field's respected journals helps to demonstrate your ability to enter the scholarly "conversation," which is one indication that you may have what it takes to publish rather than perish in a tenure-track position.

In an ideal world, of course, you would not "clutter the mails, the Net, the journals with your naïve maunderings," as Ms. Mentor baldly puts it; you would not "publish a semicolon before it was ripe." The harsh reality, however, is that "a publish-no-thought-before-its-time academic is an unemployed academic." If you want to be competitive on the job market, you'll have to get your work out there, even if it is not quite ready for prime time. "You cannot wait to be brilliant. You need to make yourself known as soon as possible," Ms. Mentor insists (Toth, *Ms. Mentor's Impeccable Advice* 18). As a graduate student,

> You should be delivering conference papers, and writing book reviews; you should be volunteering to edit manuscripts, judge contests, arrange conferences, chauffeur visiting scholars and writers. You should be sending stuff around, whether its published or not; you should list on your vitae all the pieces that are "in circulation." When an article is turned down, you should study the readers' reports, revise, and send it out again within a week. You must be ambitious; you must aim to publish early and often. That is the only way you'll distinguish yourself from the hordes of people who apply for every tenure-track job—sometimes as many as two thousand for every one job in the humanities. (18–19)

Getting Started

Attending the national conferences and studying the major journals will expose you to the conversations going on in the field and give you some sense of where you might begin to contribute. Even if you have to miss a major conference, you'll learn a lot about current discussions by scanning the conference program. If your goal is publication, however, there is no substitute for reading the field's major journals. One of this volume's profilees, Lynn Worsham, told us that when she was in graduate school she spent every Friday afternoon in the library's current periodicals section reading journals and attuning herself to issues currently under consideration and debate in rhetoric and composition as well as in other fields. This sort of self-assigned homework will not only keep you informed about the issues that rhet/comp scholars find worthy of debate right now, but will also offer you an array of potential writing projects, help you to develop an appropriate author-ethos, and guide you in determining an acceptable method of approach.

Book Reviews

According to Murphy, "one of the most important ways novice professionals can break the print barrier is by publishing book reviews" (11). Many of the field's journals run book reviews consistently, and they are often beating the bushes for qualified colleagues to write them. For this reason, it is somewhat easier to land a book review than a journal article; for the same reason, a book review will probably not *count* quite as much to a search committee as a journal article would. Book reviews, nonetheless, can be solid publications and offer graduate students a great way to make the move into print. To land a book review, you'll need to study the genre. Collect journals in the field that regularly publish them and determine both the types of books they review and the length and style of the reviews they publish. Once you decide on a journal or two to query, send a note to the editor offering to review a certain book of interest to that journal's readership. Occasionally, journals commission submissions and aren't set up to accept uninvited book reviews; however, even then it doesn't hurt to send a query that states your interest. It may well result in an invitation later.

The process is simple and often successful, but it does take some care. Be certain that the forum you select actually runs the sort of book review you're proposing, for example. Obviously, a book review *essay* that discusses a new book's potential contribution to the field in terms of the broader conversation it enters will be of much more use to you as a publication than will a simple thumbs up or down paragraph. Be certain, also, that you offer to review a book that will be of some interest and value for you. Because there is never enough time in graduate school, it's important to economize whenever possible. So consider reviewing a book that is central to a conference presentation or a seminar paper you're currently working on. As Worsham advised, "if you're doing a seminar paper on, say, body politics, then it would be smart to find a recently published book in this area and try to get a book review commissioned. Reading the book supports your preparation for writing the paper, and your publication of the review helps to build your professional credentials" (309, this volume).

The standard book review involves a summary of the book's contents and an evaluation of its merit. However, "the best reviews," says Robin W. Erwin, "teach the reader something about the field in addition to announcing and describing a book." She continues:

> A good review places the targeted book in the context of its field, shows its importance, place, historical or social function, what it offers and does not offer, and any connection to trends in the field. It may identify the academic or philosophical lineage of the author, the identity of the school of thought represented by the book, the place of the book's ideology in the philosophical continuum of the field, or some other quality of the book placed against the texture of the field. When presented in this fashion, the reader learns not only about the book under review, but also about the field. (85)

One note of caution: It may be tempting to *slam* the book you're reviewing, perhaps because it doesn't take your own pet theories or authors into account, it assumes an ideological angle you don't buy, or it fails in some sense to say what you would have said about the topic. *Don't do it.* Any time you write a book review, but especially at this particularly vulnerable time in your budding career, you will want to demonstrate a certain level of collegiality and respect for the work of your future peers and colleagues. If you can't muster that respect, don't write the review; choose another book. It's that simple. We aren't suggesting that you avoid negative critique, not at all. But there is a crucial distinction between a thoughtful critique and a slam: we urge you to refrain from simply dismissing a work, copping a superior attitude, or playing the role of the *sujet supposé savoir* when you offer your evaluative commentary. There are several ethical, professional, and pragmatic reasons for this, not the least of which is that your publications, book reviews included, will be one avenue through which future hiring committees will assess your capacity for collegiality. Indeed, this field is small enough that the author of the book you're reviewing today may well be chairing the search committee for the job you want tomorrow.

Journal Articles

Writing book reviews is a good way to break into print, and a well-placed review essay can help to demonstrate your scholarly potential. Still, it's no secret that one peer-reviewed article in any of the field's national journals typically carries more weight with a search committee than a handful of book reviews. First of all, an article is the fruit of your own research agenda, and getting it accepted for publication in a top-tier journal in the field gives both that agenda and your scholarly potential a significant stamp of approval.

It's not unusual for graduate students to fear that they have nothing to say, nothing to add to existing conversations in the field—no thoughts worth articulating, much less publishing. It can be somewhat intimidating, after all, to try to enter into a scholarly conversation with the very scholars from whom you're learning so much. However, Olson observes that "comparing your own work with that of the most seasoned luminaries in the field is perhaps the most serious mistake any beginning scholar can make, in that it can help prevent you from seeing yourself as a scholar" ("Publishing" 20). Your job is not to win a competition by brilliantly uttering the last word on a topic and putting it forever to rest; your job is to *engage* in and in some way to further the ongoing discussion. That's all. Scholarly work always has a rhetorical context, and you'll want to analyze that context carefully before you speak, as you would if you were joining an already intense conversation at a departmental party. "It's imperative that you read what is currently being said about the subject," Olson suggests, "discover what the positions are and who is taking what position, and, in general, acquire a sense of the larger conversation" (21).

Olson observes that many academics approach scholarship backwards: they know they have to publish *something*, so they look around for a subject and something specific to say about it. "They go back and read what others have written about the subject, searching for some 'original' point. Then they try to write an essay from their research" (21). This method of approach is not only "artificial," Olson warns, but it also demonstrates a fundamental misunderstanding about what "true scholarship entails":

> An active scholar in any field rarely needs to worry about "finding a subject" because that scholar is actively engaged in reading the key journals, studying the new books, attending the major conferences. This person knows intimately what the major scholarly conversations are, who is arguing what points, and where each conversation is leading. Given this scenario, it is difficult to imagine someone *not* having something to say about at least some of the important issues in the field. (21)

Editors very often have to reject manuscripts because "the author quite clearly is unaware of recent developments in the field," Olson continues. "Undoubtedly, such authors are not staying abreast with the published work of their colleagues and, instead, are writing in a vacuum, artificially and mechanically 'searching' for subjects to write about" (21).

As a graduate student, you should already be attending the major conferences and reading the field's journals; that's a given. However, it's important to recognize that graduate school itself offers you a rich intellectual environment, and you should milk it for all it's worth: Talk to your peers about what you're reading, what you're writing, and what you're teaching. Talk to them about potential gaps in the scholarly knowledge on a particular subject that interests you; talk to them about the success or failure of a particular pedagogical approach in your classroom, too, because the classroom can be a great source of inspiration for publications in our field. Form a writing group with the express purpose of helping each other turn your latest conference or seminar papers into published articles. If you're writing your dissertation, share your drafts with your peers and get their advice (along with your dissertation advisor's) about turning a finished chapter into a publication or two.

Whatever it was in its previous life, however, a journal article must be self-contained, address the needs of the new audience, and demonstrate the formality of standard written English. A conference paper tends to be more talky" than an article, for example, and less rigorously researched, documented, and elaborated. When you write a dissertation, you're addressing "the three or four people on your committee" with the express purpose of proving to them "that you can do research and that you have read all of the relevant scholarship in your area," as Komlos observes. Obviously, a journal article should be written for a much broader audience and should be written not so much to prove that you know your stuff as to join the intellectual conversation. And whereas a dissertation chapter may deal with several interlocking themes and arguments, a journal article should develop a "single theme" by "addressing itself to examining an unsolved problem or controversy, to presenting a new way of looking at an old problem, or to opening new avenues to explore. It might, in addition, propose a new conceptualization, synthesize a fragmented literature, or analyze new data" (Goldsmith, Komlos, and Gold 188–9).

Some widely published academics suggest that novice scholars set themselves up for failure by submitting to the most prestigious publication outlets early on; they advocate instead "a steady progression that begins with local outlets—especially regional journals—and culminates with national journals of high repute. The assumption," Murphy tells us, "is that few novices write at such an accomplished level early in their careers as to compete effectively with established scholars with international reputations and a host of publications to their credit" (12–13). But others disagree, arguing that starting at the top is always worth the chance since the worst that can happen is that your submission will be rejected, in which case you are free to resend it to a lesser-known journal. After all, plenty of graduate students in rhetoric and composition do succeed in landing a national publication; over the past few years, each of us has worked with students who, while dissertating, published in top-tier journals.

Still, there is no denying that one has a better chance of getting one's work published in regional journals than in national ones; the review process for regional journals also tends to go much faster, so you'll know sooner whether your work has been accepted for publication or not. The sheer "volume of submissions that major journals receive annually," Murphy observes, both slows down the journal's decision-making and publication processes and lowers one's chances for getting a submission accepted.

Sometimes the number can be in the thousands, and each of these manuscripts must be sent out to several readers as part of the review process. Depending upon the number of manuscripts each reviewer receives, the reviewer might take up to six months to respond. Similarly, the editor may take several months to complete the review process and make a decision. It's not uncommon for the author to wait a year or more to learn of a manuscript's fate; nor is it uncommon for the author to wait a year or two longer to see the manuscript in print (13).

It's important to understand all of this ahead of time, that when you send a piece off to a national journal it could disappear into what feels like a black hole for more than a year and then resurface in the form of a rejection letter. This timetable is worth considering since scholarly journals do not accept multiple submissions: once you send a piece to one journal, you cannot send it to another one until the first journal accepts or rejects it. That can be a crazy-making situation when you're trying to get a solid publication under your belt before you hit the job market. When shooting for a national publication, the key is to send off your manuscript and then to forget it, to immediately turn your focus toward *another* piece to submit elsewhere. Perhaps the best way to cover your bases is to send at least one manuscript to a national journal and at least one other to a lesser-known or regional journal. You might also consider submitting a second piece to an anthology or collection, which is about the same, prestige-wise, as getting an article into a regional journal—but do beware that anthologies tend to take a long time to publish; the wait-time from submission to publication is often longer than it is in a top-tier national journal.

It's important to recognize that there are no one-size-fits-all manuscripts; before submitting your work, you'll need to study the journal carefully, analyze it rhetorically to determine if you've found a good fit. Who reads this journal? What's its scholarly focus? How long are the articles? What's the documentation style? Are most of the articles based in empirical research, theoretical reflection, or informal argumentation? Do any of them even vaguely engage the theme your text engages? According to Komlos, "if a particular journal has published an article on such a theme, perhaps the editor(s) will be willing to do so again on a similar topic" (Goldsmith, Komlos, and Gold 189). On the other hand, if this journal has recently put out a special issue on precisely the issue your manuscript addresses, this may not be the kairotic moment for your submission, even if this journal seems like a good fit in every other way. Once you decide where to send your manuscript, be sure to read and follow the journal's submission guidelines carefully. Typically these can be found in the first few pages of the printed journal or on the journal's website. If the guidelines set a certain word limit or request a certain font, format, line spacing, or documentation style, adapt your manuscript accordingly. Some journals now accept electronic submissions via email, which is very convenient; however, if the submission guidelines ask you for three hard copies and an electronic copy on a floppy disk, that's what you should send them. Finally—and this is for your scholarly ethos—you'll want to comb through your manuscript for typos, grammar issues, and citation problems; do not expect the journal editors to run down missing source information or check a citation for you. Once you've got it all together, write a cover letter, preferably on your institution's letterhead, introducing yourself and your essay to the journal editor and asking him or her to consider your essay for publication; be sure to include your address, phone number, and email address so that the editor can get in touch with you later. Then *send it off.* Don't get sucked into an endless and compulsive cycle of revising and polishing; this is what Komlos refers to as the "self-defeating process of soul-searching procrastination" (192). As Donald Murray wryly notes, writing that never gets sent out never gets published (147). Send it off.

You will likely get a postcard or email from the editor within a month or two letting you know that s/he has received your submission. At this point, the editor has read (or scanned) the piece to make sure it is the sort of work the journal publishes and, if so, to determine which review editors would be most qualified to evaluate it. When the reviewers' evaluations come in, the editor will send them to you along with a letter advising you that your manuscript has been accepted or rejected, or—very often—requesting that you revise your text according to the reviewers' comments and resubmit. It is extremely rare for an article to be accepted outright in a prestigious journal, where the rejection rate can be as high as 90 percent (Goldsmith, Komlos, and Gold, 190). It is not rare, however, for submissions to be rejected outright, and anonymous reviewers' reports can be extraordinarily harsh: "dismissive, nasty, even brutal," as Gold puts it (196). But everyone who regularly publishes also gets such rejection letters, so don't despair or take it personally *when* you get one, too. Gold confesses that she got a brutal rejection letter on the first piece she ever sent out, and that it

> might have discouraged me from ever trying to publish again but for the fact that I shared my distress with a colleague. She told me that she had received comments in a similar vein on an article, that it was quite common, and that I should just turn around and submit it again elsewhere. I did, and the piece was accepted with no requests for revision. (196)

This is a common story: one journal's outright rejection turns into another's lead article. Do read the reviewers' reports carefully, though, even if they are rude and dismissive, because if there is even one helpful suggestion for revision in there somewhere, they've given you a gift, and you are back in business. Treat any rejection letter as a kind of "revise and resubmit"—except that in this case you'll want to revise and resubmit *elsewhere*.

When you get a bona fide revise and resubmit from a journal editor, Gold advises you to read the referees' comments very carefully and then to set up "three categories: the suggestions for change that you agree with and that you will implement, the ones that you disagree with (and why), and the ones that you agree with in principle, but are unwilling to undertake (and why—because they would take too much additional research, take you too far afield from the central argument, etc.)" (196). It never pays simply to ignore one of the referee's comments or to be snitty about those comments in your response to the editor; first of all, the editor clearly respects these readers—s/he chose them to evaluate your manuscript—and, second, more often than not your resubmitted essay will go back to those very same readers for a second round of comments. So if you're not going to take a particular suggestion, explain why in a thoughtful and respectful way.

Suffering both the painfully poky timeline and the often brutal referee reports may be a bit easier for those who understand how the review process works and what is expected of the referees. Occasionally a press will pay a reader a small sum (usually \$100–\$150) to review a book manuscript, but when readers agree to review a manuscript for a journal, they're almost never paid for their time—it's an incredibly important service to the profession, and yet, like most service work in academia, it is both invisible and uncompensated. Frequently, it is also a surprise: Komlos notes that "often the editor does not even inquire if [reviewers] are willing to serve in that capacity, and suddenly an article lands on their desk for judgment." Of course, a reviewer could simply return the envelope to the editor with an apology, but that's really "not considered good form," as Komlos puts it:

> It is much easier to put it aside. Then a few weeks later it is still on the wrong side of the desk and he realizes that he would lose face if he returned it to the editor at such a late date, and he owes him a favor anyhow, and the topic sounds interesting, so perhaps he should move it to a different pile. In the meantime, the author is anxiously hoping for a quick turnaround. Well, it is easy to see that it is a miracle that the refereeing process works as well as it does, and generally it does work acceptably. (195)

You can assume that your manuscript's referees extracted themselves from their own overwhelming schedules to respond to your work, and no matter how brutal or hasty that response may have come off, at some level they were attempting to fulfill a responsibility—to you, to the profession, and/or to the journal's editor. So don't let their comments get you down; read them carefully and learn everything you can from them, and then revise and resubmit somewhere. "The principle is rather simple," says Komlos: "submit, revise, resubmit, publish" (197).

Dissertating

An astonishingly high percentage of ABDs end up never completing the dissertation. There are no doubt many reasons for this, but perhaps one of the rudest is that not every excellent student is cut out to be a scholar, and inasmuch as the dissertation project marks the transition from the former to the latter, it is, so to speak, the first place where the rubber meets the road in academia. Though the dissertation is by far the longest (usually 200–300 pages) and most significant piece of writing you'll do in graduate school, you're expected to do it outside the formal structure of a seminar course—which means that you are mostly on your own, producing this highly invested document without the benefit of progressive deadlines, reading lists, and enlightening class discussions. ABDs are free for the first time in their graduate career to dawdle without any immediately detectable consequences, and many who are sucked into procrastination's black hole early on never make it out again. Succeeding at this final stage of graduate study requires, among other things, the dedication and self-motivation of a *scholar*: if you find that you do not delight in endless hours of solitary writing and research, it may be that a scholar's life is not for you—no matter how much you've enjoyed life as a student—and you may want to visit the career center to start contemplating extra-academic job opportunities.

Most every other professional position you might get with your rhetoric and composition credentials (technical writing, editing, PR, etc.) pays at least as well as academia. So if you don't enjoy scholarship, you should probably get out of the game now, and without an ounce of shame. "The average person changes careers five to ten times in a lifetime," Ms. Mentor reminds us. "The shame is to continue in something one does not love, just because one has begun it. Smart folks stop" (Toth, *Ms. Mentor's Impeccable Advice* 17). Those of you who do love it and stick with it, however, are in for what most will agree is an extremely challenging and thoroughly rewarding career. To succeed you'll need self-direction, willpower, and a love of scholarship; you'll also need a good committee, a sound topic, a self-imposed writing schedule with progressive deadlines, and an enhanced capacity to say "no."

Selecting the Committee

As Jacqueline Fitzpatrick, Jan Secrist, and Debra J. Wright, co-authors of *Secrets for a Successful Dissertation*, bluntly put it, "the selection of the dissertation committee members is the bumpiest decision that the doctoral student makes" (31). It's also one of the most significant, so it is wise to take the time to research and reflect before you make it. The most important member of your dissertation committee is your director, and you'll want to make this selection first, with the greatest of care, before choosing any other committee member. If you chose your graduate program in order to study with a specific professor, your decision may be fairly simple—but do be certain that your intellectual idol is someone you can actually work with. Sometimes he or she is not, in which case you should ask someone else to direct your dissertation. You will want to choose a distinguished scholar who has published widely in the field, of course, since you will benefit from your director's connections, but beyond that, you'll want to choose someone you respect and can work well with. Joan Bolker, author of *Writing your Dissertation in Fifteen Minutes a Day*, concurs, noting that

> Famous advisors are a mixed blessing. The advantages are obvious. But remember that such academics often spend a lot of time away from their own institutions, giving lectures, serving on committees, and the like, and they may not be easily available to you when you need their help. My first dissertation advisor was quite famous, but I quickly discovered that her students often had a hard time graduating, and that she appeared to compete with them and put obstacles in their paths. I remember the moment at which I realized that if I remained her advisee, I'd never finish. If choosing a politically advantageous, famous advisor makes it unlikely that you'll complete your degree, it's clearly not worth it. (21)

Additionally, one of our survey respondents confided that her most difficult career challenge so far was located right up front: "finishing the PhD with almost no support from my advisors." Don't let that be you. Your director's letter of recommendation will be the most important one in your dossier when you apply for jobs, so before you ask anyone to chair your dissertation committee, ask around about him or her, try to determine what sort of reputation this professor has with dissertating students. Komlos recommends talking to *everyone* before making any decisions:

> You should talk to everyone: to teaching and research assistants and to students who are ahead of you in the program as well as to as many faculty members in the department as possible during their office hours to see how compatible their ideas and interests are with your way of thinking about problems. See if the professor seems to respond to you in a positive way. If he is difficult to reach or to talk to, if he is fidgety in your presence, if he keeps on looking at his watch while you talk to him, if he seems disinterested in the issues you raise, or if he is not concentrating on the discussion, then you probably do not have a good candidate for the position you seek to fill. If, however, he is curious about your intellectual development, if he is helpful in solving some problems you present to him, and if he seems to be interested in working with you—in other words, if he appears to be nurturing—then you might, indeed, just have the right mentor for you. (Goldsmith, Komlos, and Gold 49)

Though Komlos appears to have forgotten that there are female dissertation advisors, the point he and Bolker are separately making is significant: you will want to choose as big a name as possible in the field from among those who are interested, curious, and helpful. Fitzpatrick, Secrist, and Wright offer that a "supportive mentor is a good criterion for membership. A committee chair must be strong enough to protect you and your work when the going gets tough and at the same time must be critical when the work is not up to acceptable standards" (31).

When you decide whom you'd like to work with, make an appointment with this professor and ask—in person and with the utmost humility—if he or she would be willing to work with you. It goes without saying that you should not approach a professor you've never had a class with; at the very least, you should have taken one seminar with this professor and you probably should have earned an A in it. At many institutions, faculty members get no compensation for taking on dissertating students, so you are basically asking this person to donate his or her time to you and your project, to take responsibility for seeing you through this process and for doing a lot of networking on your behalf. It is not appropriate to ask this of someone who has not yet had the opportunity to evaluate your work or your work habits. Still, as we noted above, writing a dissertation is like nothing else you'll do in graduate school, so when you meet with this professor, you'll want to express to him or her not only what you hope to work on but also why you need his or her guidance on this project (rather than someone else's). Be ready with descriptions and explanations, and don't be offended if this person turns out to be unable to say yes.

Once your director has signed on to work with you, it's important to get his or her thoughts about other potential committee members and what aspects of the dissertation each of them will be responsible for (feminist theory, *ars praedicandi*, ancient rhetoric, research methodology, and so on). It's never a good idea to leave your director out of this loop because you will need to select a group of people who can work well together. As Fitzpatrick, Secrist, and Wright put it, "after the committee is formed, you will initiate meetings where four or five personalities must blend" (33). At the very least, they propose, "all good (and we stress good) committee members, will (and should) offer respect and support for the student." Beyond that, "research interests, previous working relationships, classroom teacher-student relationship, knowledge of methodology, writing, and editing skills should all be considered when selecting the committee" (31). One of our survey respondents also suggested that you "study your PhD under both men and women who are well known and established in the field." Though your director is the most important member of your committee, you'll also want to keep in mind that each member will have the power to help or hinder your progress *tremendously.* The nightmare committee member who won't approve a single sentence that has not yet ripened into pure perfection or who won't respond to drafts because s/he has an axe to grind with your director is an all too familiar figure in the dissertating lore of most any PhD-granting institution. Don't get stuck with him or her; do your homework.

After your committee is in place, you and your chair will need to decide together on a protocol of interaction between you and its members. If you've already established a very good working relationship with the members of your committee, you may decide to keep the process of engagement fairly loose, leaving you free to request feedback on ideas or sections of writing from anyone or everyone on your committee as you go along and are ready for it. That flat, democratic setup can work well if the situation is right for it, but it is not always a good strategy. Fitzpatrick, Secrist, and Wright note that "some students prefer working with their chair, only occasionally meeting with other committee members, and sending as few drafts as possible to the other members. Often, chairs prefer the same hierarchy" (33). This hierarchical setup is generally recommended because it leaves one committee member, the director, in charge of guiding the project—you know what they say about too many cooks. In this case, all ideas and chapter drafts are routed through the director, who then works with you on them until they are considered fully cooked and ready for feedback from other committee members. Among other things, this prevents the possibility of getting four very different "suggestions" on where to go next or how to make a weak draft stronger.

Selecting a Topic

Selecting a dissertation topic is an act of professional self-definition, since what you choose to work on (or, very often, what chooses you) will "determine which jobs you can aim for, and what you can teach, and what you will be expected to write about for publication," Ms. Mentor advises.

> If you select Charlotte Perkins Gilman, for instance, you will be "marketable" in Women's Studies; American literature, nineteenth and twentieth centuries; and possibly nonfiction, autobiography, and cultural studies. You may love Renaissance poetry, but you will have to bid it adieu as a subject for scholarly inquiry. (Toth, *Ms. Mentor's Impeccable Advice* 16)

At least for a time. In other words, your dissertation topic will define and delimit your first area of expertise in the field. Through another book or a series of focused articles you may earn expert credentials in another area later in your career, but for the duration of your junior professorhood you're pretty much stuck with the expertise you earned through your dissertation-cum-first-book.

This means, among other things, that you need to be passionately invested in your dissertation topic. As one of our survey respondents put it, "write about what obsesses you." Another said, "Identify research about what you're passionate about," and yet another advised: "Do, study, pursue things/issues that you love or care about." Your topic must also be marketable, however; it needs to be compelling to at least three audiences: search committees, book publishers, and tenure review committees. It may be tempting to try to keep your options as open as possible by selecting a broad and sweeping topic—Ms. Mentor's example: "The Rhetoric of Ignatia Quicksilver as Applied to the Works of Shakespeare, Henry James, D. H. Lawrence, Toni Morrison, and Beavis and Butthead"—but that's a bad idea. It is much better to demonstrate in your dissertation that you have substantial expertise in an area or two than it is to suggest that you are a "jill-of-all-trades" with surface-level knowledge in many areas (Toth, *Ms. Mentor's Impeccable Advice* 16). Your topic should be focused and specific enough to make it possible for you to complete your dissertation project in a respectable amount of time, as well. Though, as Maureen Hourigan, author of "From Dissertation to Scholarly Monograph," points out, the pressure to reduce time-to-degree ought not lead you to select an overly obscure topic that no one else has worked on; such narrow or unrecognizable projects may seem safe as dissertations, but they are not likely to fit the needs of potential employers (80).

Your dissertation topic very likely will turn out to be the product of a collaborative effort: you come up with a general area of interest, and your director helps you narrow and focus it into something doable and marketable. If you're having trouble coming up with initial possibilities, think back through the books you've read and papers you've written for seminar classes and ask yourself which readings or critical approaches turned you on and got your synapses firing? Make a list and start there, with what really does it for you intellectually. Are there any potential dissertation topics there? Or, could any item on your list *feed* a dissertation topic? If you're passionate about Marxist theory, for example, perhaps that could be your critical approach to another topic; or perhaps it could be your topic in the form of, say, an analysis of the intersections among rhetorical theory and socialist theory, or a genealogy of socialist influences in composition instruction from 1900 to the present. You might also consider doing a bit of disciplinary translation work, explicating certain significant but not yet overdone aspects of Marxist theory for those of us in field of rhetoric and composition.

It's a good idea to go to your university's physical or electronic library and look through recently completed dissertations in the field, as well. (You'll be surprised, by the way, at the number of them that are perfectly awful, and that will give you some courage to get going if nothing else.) This will help you get a good sense of the array of topics that have been covered in the last several years in your program—are there any trends? Look at the chapter breakdowns to determine how each dissertation approaches and develops its topic. Look for ideas in what those ahead of you have done. Look at the topics of recent book publications in the field, too. Note chapter length and the requisite items covered in the preface, introduction, and conclusion, as well, to get an idea of what's standard and what's possible. It can be helpful to repeat this exercise later, as often as necessary, whenever you feel blocked.

Writing the Prospectus

Once you've selected your committee and they've approved your general dissertation topic, you'll be asked to write a prospectus, a description of your research project that will serve both as a kind of blueprint for you later and as a way to convince your committee that you've got a significant topic and a workable plan of development before you begin. Though it by necessity maps a tentative plan that will very likely change as you write and research, it is not merely a hoop, and you will cheat yourself if you think of it as one. Don't rush it or blow it off or imagine it as a BS document that you've got to throw together to set the *real* process in motion. The prospectus is the beginning of the real process, and you'd be wise to take the time to do it right and make it work for you. On the other hand, you don't want to get stuck in the prospectus; it is, again, a tentative document that must change as you go, so don't allow it to trap you: you don't need all the answers to write a good prospectus. You mostly need to know the questions and how you'll address them.

It typically takes a few months at the very least to produce a good prospectus, and the finished document is usually somewhere near 20 to 25 pages in length. Check with your committee to determine exactly what they expect you to cover, but the prospectus generally includes each of the following elements:

- a detailed description of the issue you plan to address
- an extensive review of the critical literature, which demonstrates your familiarity with the relevant sources and establishes the contribution your project will make to that body of work (this very often turns into the first chapter of your dissertation)
- your research methodology, including a description of your primary sources and the theory or theories grounding your approach to them
- a research plan detailing how you will conduct the research for your project (Will you have to travel to an archive? Will you need to conduct ethnographic research? Will this project require you to apply for grant money? Are your primary texts written in, say, Greek? If so, do you currently read Greek? If not, what's your plan? And so on. A handful of our survey respondents, by the way, told us that if they could do it all over again they would learn Greek and Latin.)
- a thoughtful, chapter-by-chapter description that illuminates the anticipated trajectory of the text
- a preliminary bibliography including the primary and secondary sources you plan to work with.

Plan to keep in close contact with the members of your committee as you write your prospectus, and ask for their feedback frequently. Once the document is complete, you'll submit it to your director; if the director approves it, she or he will submit it to the rest of your committee for evaluation and feedback. The committee will evaluate your project's significance to the field and its feasibility as a dissertation before they approve it. Since the approved prospectus is a kind of contract between you and your committee—indicating that they agree, in principle, that this is a worthwhile project that they will support—each member will read it carefully, with an eye toward spotting potential issues or problems with your proposed project. They'll be asking themselves, for example: is this a solid dissertation project that will make a discernible contribution to the field? Does this review of the literature indicate a firm grasp of the existing material, and is this indeed the most relevant body of literature through which to approach this project's research questions? It's in your interest to address these sorts of questions as explicitly as possible, to tell your audience (in this case, your committee) flat out why your project is significant, interesting, and worthwhile, and what exactly it is that you expect it to contribute to the existing literature and to the field at large.

Writing a Book Instead

Over the last decade or so, it has become increasingly common for ABDs, with the consent and support of their committees, to write their "dissertations" as scholarly monographs intended for publication. Both the dismal state of the job market and the ever-increasing standards for tenure in academia have prompted this shift, and Hourigan encourages graduate students to select a dissertation committee that will embrace the idea (80). "Students in today's economically pressured universities are themselves pressured to reduce the time-to-degree (currently averaging about eight years in the humanities) to five years," Hourigan writes. And due to this pressure, she notes along with Paul Cantor, Gordon Hunter, and Domna Stanton, graduate students often "produce dissertations of no more than 150 pages of 'undigested and unpolished' research that 'must be seriously revised and expanded' before they can be transformed into scholarly monographs" (80). These days, you cannot afford to sign on with a director who thinks of your dissertation as a mere hurdle you must get over as quickly as possible on the way to your degree; you need a director with a broader vision who's willing to help you catch traction early on the field's ever-increasing tenure requirements.

As one of our survey respondents told us, if she could do it all over again, she would

> spend more time in graduate school writing a book-quality dissertation, going to conferences, and publishing papers. It's very difficult to sustain this kind of productivity in graduate school, but it's even more difficult when you're teaching five courses a year, doing program administration, and working under the threat of being fired if you don't publish enough. I wish I'd had more of a "leg up" when I hired in as assistant professor, but I didn't have good advisors or mentors in graduate school, either.

Though you may assume that you'll have more time to write once you get out of graduate school, most everyone will tell you that it's the other way around: you'll have less time to write once you assume the responsibilities of an assistant professor. "Thus, a director who has published extensively in the field of rhetoric and composition," Hourigan writes, "and whose advisees have a history of quickly turning their dissertations into monographs is exactly whom an astute graduate student should seek out" (80).

Obviously, writing a book from the outset will save the newly minted PhD a lot of time and trouble in her first few years as an assistant professor. And to get a good sense of how to do that, Hourigan recommends that ABDs read articles by Robert Armstrong, Frances Halpenny, and Olive Holmes in volumes three and six of *Scholarly Publishing* (1972 and 1975). These pieces on revising the dissertation for publication expose what a writer must "root out" of a standard dissertation before submitting it to a university press for consideration, including "redundancy, an apologetic opening, excessive quoting, an over-abundance of discursive footnotes, and the like." These essays, taken together, Hourigan suggests, can "provide a blueprint for what not to do in the months of dissertation writing that lie ahead" (81). Hume concurs, adding that

> Dissertations written in the old-fashioned way—as dissertations—will suffer problems that must be corrected before they are shown to a press. If you and your supervisor plan ahead, you can avoid that extra stage of revising by writing a book from the very beginning. Here are the differences for you to keep in mind. Dissertations tend to reflect your process of educating yourself in the topic; books simply offer the conclusions. A dissertation spends a lot of time differentiating you from all your predecessors in the field. After all, one of its functions is to prove that you know the field. Your knowledge should and must be assumed in a book. … Dissertations reflect your insecurities regarding your status in the field, often offering far more support for an argument than is necessary, or defining your position by attacking those of others. A book projects the confident voice of an expert telling other experts new ideas that will be of interest to them. … Tone is one of the most obvious characteristics that a publisher will look at. If your manuscript sounds like a dissertation, a press wants nothing to do with it because far too much effort will be required to edit your work into proper professional shape. (86–7)

Before you write one word of your dissertation, be clear with your committee about whether you'll be expected to produce a standard dissertation or if you're free to write a book. Or, as Hourigan and Hume suggest, select only committee members who will give you the latter option. Once you get your committee's approval, make all necessary adjustments to the standard dissertation process.

The purpose of the literature review, for example, is to prove to your committee that you've got a handle on the existing materials relevant to your project. You produce the standard review of the literature for your prospectus, and then, after revisions and updates, it becomes the introduction or the first chapter of your dissertation. It is also, however, the first section you'll need to cut when you turn your dissertation into a book manuscript. And because it comes right up front, it tends to set the tone for the rest of the manuscript. Therefore, Hourigan suggests you produce the "traditional extensive review of the critical literature in the dissertation prospectus" but that you get your committee to allow you to produce a *publishable* introduction or first chapter to the dissertation itself (81).

A warning: If you do get the green light from your committee to write a book manuscript in place of a standard dissertation, you will nonetheless be required to follow your institution's approved format and citation style for dissertations, which tends to be exceptionally rigid. So again, before you write a single word, Komlos recommends that you consult the dissertation office about its requirements. "Redoing the format can be extremely time-consuming; it is much easier to do it correctly the first time. You may be surprised that there is no flexibility in this regard whatsoever. If you know in advance that certain information is needed in the bibliography, you will not have to waste time subsequently looking up the citations again" (Goldsmith, Komlos, and Gold 61).

Forming a Writing Group and Setting Deadlines

As we noted above, writing the dissertation can be an extremely solitary experience because it is outside the seminar structure. Once you've gotten your prospectus approved, you are to a large extent on your own: your graduate student colleagues aren't reading the same material you're reading, and there are no built-in opportunities for discussing with anyone what you're reading or writing about. You should get extensive comments from your advisor on completed chapter drafts, but most dissertating students benefit from a more continuous experience of give-and-take about their progress, their insights, their stammers, and their stalls. One very good way to get this kind of feedback loop going is to form a writing group with graduate students in your program. In the best of all possible worlds, this writing group would consist only of those graduate student colleagues who are also dissertating; however, if that restriction makes for slim pickin's, drop it and include those who are interested in giving and getting feedback on any substantial piece of writing—such as seminar papers, conference papers, and journal articles. Writing groups are generally small (three to five people) and meet regularly to work through ideas, issues, or problems with which group members are currently wrestling, as well as to give and get feedback on drafts.

Some time-conscious ABDs imagine that committing to a writing group would just add one more item to their to-do lists, one more time-sucking activity or procrastination device that would keep them from actually writing their dissertations. And it's true that once you're finished with coursework, you may be called upon by family, friends, advisors, and administrators to take on any number of assignments for which you now, presumably, have plenty of time—so you'll need to learn to protect your writing schedule by saying "no" with a great deal of guilt-free resolve. However, participating in a writing group may in fact be one way to protect your writing time, as the commitment can help to keep you motivated and productively on task. It isn't easy to give yourself deadlines and stick to them as you write your dissertation, but most writers need to set and meet periodic goals to keep them going, to assure their consistent progress. It's more productive to give yourself small writing objectives than huge ones, to work with sections or subsections rather than entire chapters. Baby steps—that's the key. Instead of simply telling yourself "I need to complete chapter 2 this month," sketch out a schedule of smaller, progressive deadlines to get you there: "I'm going to complete section 3.3 of chapter 2 by Sunday." Writing groups can be very helpful in this regard. If you know the group is meeting on Tuesday afternoon, you may be more invested in getting at least an ugly draft of section 3.3 ready and out to them by Sunday for feedback. Such self-imposed, progressive deadlines can be life-savers for any writer, but they are especially helpful for dissertation writers who are not yet accustomed to writing outside a classroom structure. As you become a more experienced writer and scholar, you may or may not give up your work with formal writing groups; however, most successful scholars in this field continue to give and get responses from each other on their writing. The three of us routinely send each other essays and chapters for quick feedback, and we call or email each other for advice when we feel stuck.

Firing Your Director

It happens. Sometimes personalities or schedules or writing styles clash and things just don't work out. Maybe your director is too busy to offer you the kind of guidance you need, maybe your personalities or interests don't gel as well as you thought they would, or maybe your director—let us be blunt—has turned out to be something of an asshole. Indeed, more than one of our survey respondents told us that some of their most difficult experiences in the field thus far happened in graduate school with their directors. One, who did not fire her director but who possibly should have, confided: "I had a very turbulent relationship with my dissertation director. This is probably not new, but a big part of the problem was, I thought, the male/female thing. I 'solved' the problem by giving in and writing [the dissertation] the way he told me to." Another respondent who did not fire her director told us that she finished her dissertation and succeeded despite the fact that he gave her no real guidance:

> My biggest problem was with my dissertation advisor. He was male, but I'm not sure the problem was gender-specific. The difficulty I

> faced was that I really received close to zero guidance and spent a lot of time floundering around before I learned enough on my own to be able to negotiate the final dissertation. I feel very much that it was a non-guided project. Given how well it turned out, I feel very positive about the outcome and my own ability, but along the way I constantly felt undercut. On the one hand, I would receive high praise for my general ability, but the specific text would be either faulted or damned by faint praise. It took me quite a while to understand that this treatment was more about him than about me and to get past it. I found, however, that I pretty much had to figure out my own way of doing this.

A few of our respondents did fire their directors. One, who stuck it out for five long years before giving up, told us:

> My doctoral committee chair was the coldest, meanest woman I've ever met. We began working together because she was such a prominent feminist in the field and she seemed so nice. What I learned over our 5 years of work was that she consistently favored men over women, and that she expected to produce "daughters"—versions of her in different bodies. When I put race at the center of my work, she claimed I was being a bad feminist, and a bad scholar. At times, I would be physically ill (I'd throw up or have anxiety attacks) when I was preparing a paper to turn in, a draft, or getting ready to meet with her during my exams year. When I told her about my anxiety, she laughed. I removed her from my committee after my oral exam and selected a new chair for my dissertation committee, a man.

If you find, for whatever reason, that you have irreconcilable differences with the director you've chosen—if you can't work with her, if he's not giving you the kind of attention and support you feel you need, if her advice about how to proceed on the project consistently conflicts with your own sense of things—you may need to find someone else to direct your dissertation. Fitzpatrick, Secrist, and Wright offer this advice:

> How do you fire a chair? Gently, but with no wiggling around. Write a letter explaining the difficulties, but write with respect and choose your words carefully. Suggest that the member is far too busy to deal with your dissertation. Recognize that the member holds other more important responsibilities. (39)

There is no need, they continue, to "express your secret belief that some professors are so self-absorbed that they haven't time to consider any work other than their own." Professors are generally very busy creatures who, like so many people, sometimes find themselves over-committed. You certainly shouldn't allow yourself to become a casualty of some professor's crammed schedule, but "do be polite," as Fitzpatrick, Secrist, and Wright suggest, especially since "one never knows about the later consequences of firing a member. Politics are both overt and covert at all universities, and there is no point in burning bridges" (39–40). Indeed, our respondent above who did fire her director told us that "she made it clear that my decision was insulting (even though I made it clear that this was for my own mental health and ability to continue). She has consistently shunned me at professional gatherings and disparages my work to her friends and colleagues." So though you may need, for your own "mental health," to get rid of your director, you'll want to do it as politely and delicately as possible.

Demonstrating Excellence in Teaching

The field of rhetoric and composition is invested in pedagogy—extraordinarily so—therefore, whether you hope to land a position at a small liberal arts college or a Research One institution, you should be prepared to demonstrate both interest and excellence in teaching. Though one of our survey respondents advised rhet/comp graduate students to "finish your graduate work as quickly as possible by ignoring the emphasis on teaching and pedagogy," it is our position that, in this particular field, it is not wise to accept a full fellowship that exempts you from teaching for more than a year or maybe two during your graduate education, preferably while you're dissertating. You'll want to gain as much experience as possible in the classroom as the teacher of record (rather than as a TA), and you'll want that experience to be varied—though repetition shrinks prep-time, it's not to your advantage to end up with nine semesters of experience teaching first-year composition and nothing else. If your institution grants you the opportunity to gain other sorts of teaching experiences, take advantage of it; it's important to your professional development and will give you more credibility as a teacher when you enter the job market.

You will no doubt put a lot of time into your teaching while you're in graduate school, and it's imperative that you keep a record of your work. Whenever you teach a class, keep copies of everything: the syllabus, formal and informal assignments, samples of your responses to student papers, and course evaluations. You will need at least some and perhaps all of this material when you go on the job market. Many schools routinely ask job finalists for a teaching portfolio, for example, so it's a good idea to have one ready to go, just in case. The teaching portfolio can be produced on paper or online and typically includes a statement of your teaching philosophy, a sampling of your course syllabi and major assignments, evidence of teaching effectiveness (student evaluations, copies of your comments on student papers, and so on), and perhaps even a video of a class you have taught. If you put your teaching portfolio online, it is acceptable to provide a URL for it on your curriculum vitae. Otherwise, it's generally not a good idea to provide a teaching portfolio until (or unless) it is requested by a search committee.

Most colleges and universities have a Center for Teaching where graduate instructors and faculty members can go to get help creating assignments, designing course syllabi, crafting a teaching philosophy statement, running in-class discussions, gathering student feedback, preparing for peer observation, handling difficult or troubled students, and so on. Many Centers for Teaching will help you put together the entire teaching portfolio, as well, so we suggest that you check into this service if your institution has one. Much of the material included in the teaching portfolio will naturally accrue as you move through your graduate program; you'll just have to hold on to it. The teaching philosophy statement, however, will require some effort, and it is a good idea to start thinking about it early.

Almost every institution will ask job candidates for a teaching philosophy statement, so you will want to prepare it before you go on the market. It's a good idea to look at sample teaching statements online and perhaps in the career center at your institution; it's typically more productive, however, to examine statements written by your fellow graduate students. Because teaching philosophy statements are often required again during the tenure process, your faculty mentors may have one to share with you as well—it never hurts to ask. In general, this document is a concise (a page, maybe two) description of your pedagogical approach, both its philosophical/theoretical backing and its practical applications. Most teaching statements open with a description of the pedagogical objectives derived from the philosophical backing. What do you want your students to get out of your courses beyond the requisite content? Increased capacity for critical thinking, for rhetorical analysis, and/or for internet communications? An ability to collaborate effectively? A heightened level of intellectual curiosity? Whatever your pedagogical objectives, state them explicitly and indicate *why* they are important. Think about this part carefully because it's the heart of your teaching philosophy statement. The rest of the document should describe the concrete classroom methods and assignments you use to accomplish your pedagogical objectives. If you've developed a particularly innovative assignment, describe it in some detail and explain its connection to your overall goals. If you've had the chance to teach different kinds of courses, describe how you achieve your objectives in each. You might also describe an assignment or classroom method that turned out to be unsuccessful; then explain what you learned from it and what you do differently now.

Though it's called a teaching philosophy, you'll nonetheless want to avoid flying off into language that is too abstract or theoretical; keep your references as concrete as possible and focus mostly on actual classroom approaches and experiences rather than hypothetical ones. Also remember that this is *your* teaching philosophy, not some universal form for one, so write in the first person and stick for the most part to the active voice. This document is not a test of your philosophical abilities, in other words; it's meant to demonstrate that you have an actual pedagogical approach, that your method and assignments are meant to accomplish something, something more than randomly filling up classroom hours. As Cindy Moore and Hildy Miller put it in *A Guide to Professional Development For Graduate Students in English*, your teaching philosophy statement "gets at why you do what you do; it gives your varied teaching practices some intellectual coherence" (43). Once you've got a solid draft of your teaching statement, you'll obviously want to run it by your advisor, but we encourage you to workshop it with your peers, as well. Get as much feedback as possible.

What we hope to have demonstrated in this chapter is that succeeding in graduate school will take more than defending the dissertation and managing to stand out in a seminar or two. A successful graduate student is one who uses her time in graduate school to develop as a professional and as a participant in the greater field of rhetoric and composition, one who begins establishing herself as an exemplary scholar, teacher, and colleague. To accomplish this, one survey respondent advised, you must begin by "dig[ging] in wholeheartedly" in graduate school,

> learn[ing] as much as you can with rigor and integrity. Don't be afraid to push when warranted and to explore the richness of the field before committing to any one aspect in particular. In other words, embrace the rhetorical—read situations, experience difference, linger in invention long enough that you know you aren't cutting off promising avenues of inquiry. And, while doing all of this, build community—rhetoric and composition will never work well in a social vacuum.

2

SUCCEEDING ON THE JOB MARKET

> Look very carefully at the politics in the departments to which you apply; make sure your work fits in well and that work in rhetoric is respected … . Find a place that welcomes you, and do good work.
>
> —anonymous survey respondent

You would be wise to start preparing for your job search about the same time you put your dissertation committee together. Begin studying rhetoric and composition job ads in the *Chronicle of Higher Education* and Modern Language Association's *Job Information List* to get a sense of what sorts of positions are out there and how they are defined. You'll also find rhetoric and composition job ads on the same listservs, blogs, and websites that routinely post conference CFPs. H-Rhetor and WPA are particularly good about posting job ads in our field, as is the Rhetoric Society of America website (www.rhetoricsociety.org). Begin studying candidates, too. Departments that are hiring often invite one or two graduate student representatives to be part of the search committee; if your own department happens to be hiring, ask them to consider appointing you as one of the student members. Go to the candidates' job talks and other open presentations to get a sense of how each one approaches the situation, making note of things they do that you'll want to emulate and/or avoid when you're in their position. During hiring season, your department may hold workshops on writing application letters and dissertation descriptions, and on putting together a curriculum vitae and/or teaching portfolio; it may also hold mock interviews for students going on the market for the first time. Attend as many such sessions as you possibly can, as it will give you a good sense of what to expect very early, which should make the entire process less anxiety-producing when the time comes.

And finally: begin studying published advice on the academic job search. There are several very detailed and helpful books on the subject, some of which include sample documents of various application materials, and you should become very familiar with a few of them.[3] To date, none of these books is devoted solely to rhetoric and composition, and we aim here to offer you some field-specific information and advice that will be helpful to you as you go on the job market in rhet/comp; however, our brief contribution is not intended to replace but to accompany the books that offer broad coverage of the academic job search.

Some Background Information

Generally, you'll want to go on the market the same year you finish your dissertation; so if you interview at MLA in December for a position that begins the following September, you should plan to defend your dissertation absolutely no later than early August—but the earlier the better. Be aware that faculty are generally on nine-month contracts and very often leave town or even the country during the summer months. Don't make the mistake of assuming that they will be around for a June, July, or August defense just because that's the timetable you have set for yourself. They may have very different plans, and it is your responsibility to work around them. If you want a summer defense, make certain very early that your entire committee will be able to be there for it. If not, find out what the rules are: how many of them must be physically present for the defense? You may have a five-person committee, but the college may only require that three members be there in person. It could be possible to hook up to another via conference call.

Though you may be tempted for all kinds of reasons to take a full-time teaching position before you finish your dissertation, we don't recommend it, as it is extremely difficult to finish once you assume the demanding role of a full-time lecturer or an assistant professor. Several of our survey respondents told us that the most difficult challenge they had faced in their careers thus far was trying to teach full-time while dissertating (or rather, while *not* finding time to dissertate). "Completing my dissertation while working full-time (teaching 5 classes per semester at a community college) was the most difficult challenge I faced," one respondent told us. Another wrote, bluntly, that the biggest challenge she has faced thus far has been: "completing the PhD while teaching full-time and having a family. TIME!!!" One respondent who, apparently, has been ABD now for seven years, confided that

> The most difficult challenge I have faced is getting time to do the scholarly work that would enable me to finish my doctorate and get a better paying teaching position so that I could live above the poverty level. After seven years, I still cannot figure out a way to teach composition classes that does not require most of the energy I possess. The time I take to help students learn ensures that my own scholarly work, always last on the list, gets little time at all. At present, I feel near complete burn-out, like abandoning my career altogether.

Several of our respondents also told us that if they could begin their careers all over again the one thing they'd do differently would be to "finish my dissertation before taking a full-time job." One wrote "I might decline to begin teaching without a PhD in hand," and another told us: "I would take an extra year in graduate school, not rush into the job market."

You may believe strongly that you'll be able to do your new job well while finishing up your old job (dissertating), and you may be correct, but it will not be easy. And if you begin a tenure-track position while still writing your dissertation, remember that you will be doing that *in place of* making progress toward tenure. As Heiberger and Vick put it,

> In a tight job market, candidates who have completed their degrees are likely to be chosen over those who have not. In addition, once you have accepted a position, you will gain tenure as a result of research done as a junior faculty member. If you begin your research by completing the dissertation, you will already be late by the tenure clock, and in the position of a student with several incompletes, who can never catch up with current work. (21)

If you absolutely must take a job before you finish the dissertation, Heiberger and Vick suggest that you "discuss the situation with faculty members in your department and choose the employment most conducive to finishing the dissertation" (21).

In the field of rhetoric and composition, initial job interviews are typically held at the Modern Language Association conference, which currently takes place 27–30 December each year; beginning in 2010, the conference will take place the first Thursday through Sunday following 2 January each year. Unfortunately, it is usually necessary to register for the conference and book your flight and hotel room before you know if you'll have interviews to attend or when and where they will be held. You should plan to arrive the day before the conference starts and to stay at least two nights, but three nights is safer. This is obviously an expensive gamble, but if you wait until two weeks before the convention to book a flight, assuming there is still one available, it will cost you more. You'll face the same thing with the hotel room: this is a huge conference, and if you wait to secure your room, the main conference hotels, as well as all less expensive hotels in the surrounding areas, will very likely be booked solid. Don't get into this situation; plan early. If a friend is also interviewing, consider sharing a room, as well as cab fare or the airport shuttle. This time, however, it is not wise to bunk with five other graduate student friends in a cheap hotel around the corner; you're going to need to focus during the day and recuperate at night.

Types of Jobs

There are many kinds of academic positions at many sorts of institutions, so you'll want to reflect about what sort of position you really want, as well as what you will be willing to accept. The most prestigious and hardest-to-get academic jobs are at top-tier research institutions, but be prepared: tenure requirements are highest at these institutions, and if you land a job at one of them, you'll be expected to hit the ground running. Research universities are so called because their focus is on research, which means their faculty members are expected to publish constantly in the top journals and with the top presses. Does that sound like an exhilarating challenge or a nightmare to you? Be honest with yourself. Obviously, there are many more jobs available in teaching institutions than in research institutions. In rhetoric and composition, of course, teaching is *always* emphasized and various sorts of administrative duties are standard; so if you land a position in this field at what is commonly referred to as a "Research One" institution, you should be prepared to be everything to everybody: an outstanding teacher, an effective administrator, *and* a publishing machine. One survey respondent told us that she'd advise potential rhet/comp graduate students to decide, *before* they begin a PhD program, "the type of academic position" they'd like after they graduate:

> There are more and more career options in rhet/comp, from teaching-oriented positions to research positions and others in between. Don't be pressured to do the "Level One" research track, if it's not your interest. I went to one of the bigger, more established PhD programs, and we were told, "You should be a scholar, not a full-time teacher." My professional development was geared toward that track, also. That's a lot of pressure in an increasingly tight market. Also, it really runs counter to what I believe should be the rhet/comp ethos. And it's a very male-oriented version of academic success, forcing women with multiple personal commitments to sacrifice greatly.

Still, as we noted above, getting a position at a teaching institution doesn't necessarily exempt you from the requirement to publish. Heiberger and Vick warn, for example, that "four-year colleges of national reputation also require substantial research of their faculty members" (7). And Gold points out that "lack of publishing puts one at risk of 'perishing' in teaching institutions as well, as research and publication are seen to be linked to good teaching" (Goldsmith, Komlos, and Gold 187). The biggest distinction between a research and a teaching institution, especially for those of us in rhetoric and composition, may be that at a research institution faculty members are expected to earn national and international recognition through their publications, whereas faculty at most teaching institutions, Gold suggests, "are expected to make some contribution to their fields through publication, but [they] are not necessarily expected to be leaders in their fields." She continues:

> It is understood that publication has repercussions for one's teaching as well, in addition to being a sign that one is up to date with the field. To

> publish, one has to be willing to work on something until it is polished and convincing and to be willing to take the risk of putting one's ideas out in an arena where they can be criticized. We ask our students to do this all the time, so it's important that we do it also—at the very least, it gives us some additional sympathy for the challenges they face to complete and perfect their work. (186–7)

There are also distinctions to be acknowledged between public and private, secular and religious institutions. A private college may have lots of money for interesting programs, for example, but that luxury may come with certain religious and/or political strings attached; a public college or university, especially if it's not the state's flagship institution, may have serious financial issues that are worth considering (if it has no budget for faculty travel, you'll be paying for your own conference trips, for example, and raises may be both tiny and rare). An institution's geographical location is important to consider, as well. One of our profilees, Patricia Bizzell, told us that she turned down a prestigious job offer from the University of Minnesota because her husband at the time, Bruce Herzberg, didn't want to "live in the frozen north." Another of our profilees, Sharon Crowley, admitted that she left her position at a top-tier research institution (Penn State) for a non-flagship state institution (Arizona State University) because she wanted to go home again to the Arizona desert. It's also important to consider whether you need a large urban area or if you can handle living off the beaten path. Some very good schools—such as RPI, Penn State, Purdue, and Princeton—are located in small college towns with no international airport; often less prestigious schools are situated in a thriving metropolis with good shopping, fine restaurants, and a myriad of cultural attractions. The latter also offer, let's just say it, plenty of young, single people, and this is an important consideration for many new graduates.

On the flipside of that, however, if you're part of a dual-career couple, you'll probably want to zero in on schools located in an area where your partner will also be able to find a job. Bizzell told us that when she graduated she only applied for positions in geographic regions where there were lots of colleges so that Bruce, when he finished the PhD, would be able to find a position nearby. She accepted an offer from the College of the Holy Cross in 1978 mainly for that reason: it's located in Worcester, Massachusetts, home of 170,000 people and a whopping 13 colleges and universities. Several of our survey respondents told us that that their biggest career challenges thus far have been associated with finding desirable positions near their partners and/or families, some of whom were just not movable. One respondent told us her biggest hurdle was "finding a tenure-track position at a research 1 institution in geographical proximity to my family," for instance. Another noted that the only thing she's not happy about in her career thus far is that "I'm far away from my extended family. … I'd like to move, but I can't uproot my husband and family again." And yet another confided:

> I had to find a position within the same geographical region where my husband, also an academic, was employed. I had to accept "any" job and find satisfaction and career opportunities in it. I had to persevere and have faith that I could do satisfying work, and in doing just that I learned the satisfactions of working with open access writers, and I found ways to develop my scholarly and intellectual interests. But it wasn't easy.

Before you send out applications, be as honest as possible with yourself about what you want and need, both in a school and in a location.

WPA Positions

A brief word about accepting a position as a writing program administrator right out of school: be careful. Our survey respondents were near unanimous in advising new graduates to avoid WPA positions of *any* kind—Sharon Crowley added in our interview that you should avoid them "like the plague." First, there is the problem of authority. Running a writing program will require you to make certain philosophically and pedagogically informed decisions that are likely to be unpopular with other folks in the department and perhaps in the administration. Without tenure, this leaves you in an extremely vulnerable position. If you do what you know to be right for the writing program that you're responsible for, you may be risking your career; if you don't, you'll be risking your integrity. Second, there is the problem of finding time to publish. It is typically considered professional suicide for a recent graduate to accept a WPA position at a first- or second-level research institution with heavy publication expectations. Even if such an institution is enlightened enough to offer you course release, summer funds, and plenty of administrative help, your work running the writing program will almost certainly count only as "service," which will mean next to nothing to a tenure and promotion committee. The bottom line is that it will be more difficult for you to publish enough to get tenure than it will be for the other assistant professors in your department who are not in charge of running a large program.

It may be a different story at certain teaching institutions, such as a small liberal arts school or a Community College, where the expectations for publication are much lower and both service work and outstanding teaching count a great deal in tenure and promotion decisions. It may also be different for those whose research interests lie precisely in the WPA arena. If you want to publish work about running or assessing writing programs, training graduate writing instructors, and other professionalization issues, your publishing potential may be fueled by running a program, and you may be the perfect candidate for a "jWPA" (junior-level WPA) position. Indeed, Cynthia L. Selfe told us that's exactly what happened to her: she took the position first and her publishing interests grew out of it. She was able to publish a lot right away precisely because she allowed her work as a WPA to become the center of her research agenda. She encourages students with a strong *interest* in becoming a WPA to do it and then both to publish about it and to use it to make a name for themselves all around campus. The key here, it seems, is true interest. If your passion is not writing administration but Gorgias or Aspasia, it is probably not wise for you to take a WPA position before you get tenure.

Application Materials

Search committees will indicate in the job ad itself what documents they want you to send in with your application letter, along with the deadline for doing so. Assume that there is zero flexibility in this deadline. Indeed, there may be some benefit to getting your application in early: you'll look organized, for one thing, plus the early applications tend to get more attention from search committees, who are often overwhelmed with too many of them as the deadline approaches. Some committees don't want to sift through a lot of material until they are certain you're a worthy candidate, so they start by requesting a letter of application only, a letter and a CV, or perhaps a letter, CV, dissertation abstract, and teaching philosophy statement. If you make the first cut, the committee will contact you and ask you for more materials. Other committees want you to send them everything right up front so they can evaluate all your materials at once: letter, CV, teaching portfolio, statement of teaching philosophy, evidence of effective teaching, sample syllabi, a writing sample, three or four letters of recommendation, and—occasionally—a transcript. If the job ad instructs you to send only a letter and a CV, you should feel free to include a dissertation abstract and teaching philosophy statement as well; it is usually not a good idea, however, to send a teaching portfolio, evidence of effective teaching, writing samples, or letters of recommendation unless you've been asked to do so. You don't want to stand out for bombarding an overworked committee with unasked-for materials that they are not ready to evaluate.

Consider the letter of application a one-way introduction of sorts: you're introducing yourself to the search committee, and they are evaluating your every comma and contraction to determine if they'll ever return the gesture. It is an extremely important document that must be carefully crafted specifically for the intended audience. If you're applying for thirty jobs, you will need thirty distinct versions of this letter. Given that it is usually the search committee's first introduction to you, they will be looking not only for evidence of your qualifications but also for evidence that you'd be a good colleague. The tone of your letter of application can be as important as its content; all too often a well-qualified candidate, in her eagerness to appear brilliant, comes across as arrogant instead. And that is that. Of course, you don't want to lean too far the other way, either. Hume notes that "being too pushy or too sure of your welcome may irritate some readers, but so will your being smarmy or servile" (10). She identifies three spots in the letter of application that are rhetorically tricky, and navigating each one successfully will depend mostly on assuming the appropriate tone:

a) making yourself appear to be the right candidate for the job
b) saying something that shows you have done research on that department
c) saying that you hope to see them at the conference. (9)

Regarding the first, Hume notes that you cannot *tell* the committee that you're the right choice for the job; you need to *show* them by linking your abilities to the specifications they list in their job ad. "You might also try to make plain how your methodology is widely applicable in different sorts of courses and engages students in unexpected ways" (10). In regard to the second tricky spot, your letter should reflect a little knowledge about the department to which you're applying, some understanding about its mission, its geographic location, its course offerings, etc., but without sliding into flattery or false praise. It's not wise to overdo it, and you don't want to lie. But it can be reassuring to a search committee to hear that you grew up in the area (so you know what you're getting into) or that you currently offer a course that would work well with their current course sequence (mention specific course numbers if you can), and so on. Hume suggests that "sometimes a quote from their department mission statement can be put to good use" (10). As for the third tricky spot, you need to indicate that you will be at MLA and that you would welcome the chance to meet with them, but you don't want to sound as if you assume that you'll get an interview. Consider something like this: "I will be attending the MLA convention in New York City, and I would welcome the opportunity to meet with you there."

Job ads will tell you where to send your application materials, and sometimes they'll tell you whom to send them to. If they list a name, "Professor X, Search Committee Chair," your letter of application should begin "Dear Professor X." If there is no name offered, address your letter to the search committee itself: "Dear Search Committee Members." Your letter should open with a direct request to be considered for the position they've advertised: "Please consider my application for the Assistant Professorship in rhetoric and composition, which you advertised in the online edition of the *MLA Job Information List*." Your letter should end with information about how the committee can contact you over the holidays. If you're going to be in Alaska from December 10 to 27, you'll need to give them a way to reach you during that time; give a cell phone number if you have one, and give your email address, as well, if you're sure you will be able to check it.

Both Hume, and Heiberger and Vick offer excellent examples of well-constructed letters of application, CVs, dissertation abstracts, dissertation descriptions, and teaching philosophies. Heiberger and Vick also offer a section on creating a website that includes a kind of online dossier. You should study these sample documents very carefully and use them to help you create effective application materials that nonetheless reflect your own singular interests and expertise. It is imperative that you circulate drafts of your application documents and get feedback on them from your graduate student colleagues and your committee. Once you get your materials ready, different materials for different positions, go back through them one last time. If you used the Save As function in your word processor to create all your letters from one template, only changing a few relevant sentences and such, check again to be certain that you've addressed each letter to the correct contact person. It will not help your case if you accidentally address your University of Florida application letter to the chair of the search committee at the University of Texas. Double check. If you constructed a website with an online dossier, be sure you've listed the URL on your CV; you may also want to refer to it in your letter of application.

It goes without saying, we hope, that you will have combed through each document for typos, punctuation errors, and misspellings. Attend to other aspects of your presentation, as well: the letter should be on your institution's letterhead, formatting should be consistent, and every document you send should have a crisp and professional look. Though you will want to stand out, it is not a good idea to try to do that by using purple paper or gothic font or by binding your documents in a pink folder with a flamingo on the cover. (Even if you were to get the job anyway, because you're that good, you would never live that down with your new colleagues.) Be professional: both in content and presentation. Once you've double checked all your materials carefully, buy some large envelopes (so that you don't have to fold anything), stuff them with the correct documents, and head to the post office.

Setting Up Initial Interviews

Generally, search committees start looking at and evaluating application materials as they come in—a very good reason to get yours in early, before everyone's exhausted. Given that there may be well over a hundred applications for one rhet/comp position, the committee's first order of business is to reduce that number, which is why you don't want to give them any reason to cut you on a technicality, such as a punctuation error or a misspelled name or a late application file: "When a tired committee meets late at night to whittle four hundred applications down to the twenty-five for which they will seek writing samples," Hume writes, "members will eagerly seize on any reason for discarding a candidate" (10). If you make the first cut, the committee will contact you again and ask for more materials, such as writing samples, teaching portfolios, and letters of recommendation; they will then meet again to reduce the number of applicants to a manageable number to interview in person. It's at that point that they will begin calling candidates to invite them to interview, typically at MLA.

Occasionally, you may be asked to interview at 4Cs or another conference, especially if the position opening was approved too late for an MLA interview.

You may also be asked to interview over the phone if the position opens up at an odd time. Or, if you are asked to interview at MLA or another conference that you cannot attend, you may request a phone interview yourself. We recommend that you try to get a face-to-face interview if at all possible, however, even if it means flying to campus at your own expense. Phone interviews are very difficult because the interviewers become disembodied voices; the facial gestures and bodily shifts that typically provide an interviewee crucial information about how her responses are being received, whether she has said enough, or if she has misunderstood the question, are missing.

Sometimes when a search committee chair calls to set up an interview, he or she will offer the names of the other interviewers, as well. If s/he doesn't, ask for them before you hang up. Write those names down. Each time you agree to an interview, start finding out everything you can about the institution, the department, the faculty, and especially the interviewers. Who are these people? What do they teach? What do they publish? What are the institution's goals? Who are the students that attend this school? Most of the time, you can get all the information you need on the internet. Look this place up, study the material you find, print out the best of it, and put it in a folder labeled with that institution's name. In this folder, put all the information you send or receive from the committee, as well. Think about what you might have to offer this program. What might you teach for them? Consider both what you'd do with existing courses and what else you might teach to complement the existing courses. Prepare more generally, as well. If your department isn't hosting mock interview sessions, ask for one. Practice responding to the question "What is your dissertation about?" constantly. Hume suggests that you memorize a ninety-second description of your dissertation and be able to "recite it without hesitation if awakened at three o'clock in the morning" (30). To avoid talking in abstract generalities—a no no—be prepared to "anchor each and every one of your general statements with references to specific texts or evidence or examples" (35). Be prepared for a question about what you'll do after the dissertation, as well; have a solid description of your *next* book project ready to go. Though it may seem impossible to you at the time, there is life after the dissertation, and search committees are eager to confirm that you are not going to turn out to be a one-hit wonder. Indeed, one of our survey respondents suggested that you "think of your dissertation as the beginning of a multi-faceted research project, not the culmination of something." That's good advice. Hume offers a long list of potential interview questions that you may want to use to help you prepare.

When the time comes to pack for the interview, you are faced yet again with the dreaded *What to Wear* question. We will refrain from adding to the advice offered in the previous chapter, except to offer a few packing tips that we lifted from Formo and Reed:

> We found the conference interview to be a two-suit experience. Conferences tend to allow schools to conduct interviews throughout

> the three- to five-day conference. If you have scheduled several interviews over the course of a few days, you should not feel obligated to have a different interview suit for each day. Alternating a suit each day worked well for us. It also made packing a cinch. To keep the suits wrinkle-free and to ensure that you will not be stranded at the conference with only the clothes on your back, we encourage you to pack your interview materials and clothes in two bags: an attaché and a roll-on suitcase, one that fits in the airplane overhead bins.

Contrary to this light-packing advice, some suggest that it's a good idea to make an inventory list before you leave for MLA and take a backup of everything, just in case.

MLA Interviews

When you arrive at your hotel, give yourself the chance to settle in and then spend the evening going over the information in the file folders you've put together for each of the schools with which you'll be interviewing. Go over the application letter you sent each one very carefully because interviewers often begin with a question taken directly from the letter. Go over your writing sample carefully, as well, since it may have been a while since you wrote it and you'll need to be able to respond to questions about it easily and thoughtfully. The night before your interviews begin, you'll also want to get your clothes ready—make sure everything's ironed if it got wrinkled on the trip and that you haven't forgotten anything. Lay out your entire outfit, down to your skivvies and accessories; if anything significant is missing, go shopping. You should also plan to eat a nutritious dinner and hit the sack early that night; it's not a good idea to skip meals or to pull an all-nighter rehearsing your interview responses. By now, you should have practiced enough. It's time to prepare your body for the next day.

Three sorts of interviewing sites are possible at MLA: the interview center, the hotel room, and the hotel suite. The interview center—or "meat market," as it is not-so-affectionately called—refers to a giant ballroom in the hotel that has been divided up into hundreds of interviewing cubes. Schools that can't afford to secure a suite or that wait too long to do so typically end up in this interview center. If one or more of your interviews are scheduled to take place here, go look at it the day before to get yourself accustomed to the space and its limitations. It will be very loud, for one thing, and there will be other interviews taking place all around you; there will likely also be a number of very anxious interviewees with sweaty palms waiting with you. Nervous energy is extremely contagious, so you'll need to be prepared to stay focused and confident. When you arrive for your interview the next day, you'll get your table number from the information desk. Wait for your interview time to roll around and then, even if another interview is still going on at your table, walk up close enough to gesture to the interviewees that you've arrived, and then wait to be invited over. The key in this type of interview is to stay focused and not let the crazy atmosphere interfere with your ability to present yourself professionally and confidently.

Schools that wait too long to get a suite or space in the interview center typically end up holding interviews in a standard hotel room. This means that one or two of your interviewers will be sitting on the bed during your interview, and that can be extremely awkward—the good news is that candidates are usually invited to sit in a chair. If you've got a "bedroom" interview, you'll want to get yourself psychically prepared for it. Since the search committee chair won't know the room number in advance, he or she won't be able to give it to you when the interview is set up; instead, you'll get the name of the hotel and the name of the committee member registered there. When you arrive at the hotel, wait in the lobby until five or six minutes before your designated interview time, and then use the hotel phone to get the front desk to connect you to your party. Someone on the committee will answer and give you the room number. If no one answers the first time, wait a minute and try again. Don't wait until the exact time of your interview to call the room because elevators are notoriously slow in conference hotels—it'll take you a while to get up there. When you arrive, take your seat and try to forget the fact that you're in what is typically considered a very intimate, private space; ignore the fact that some of your interviewers are sitting on the bed and that, given the angle, you can see the top of Professor Q's sock suspenders or Professor Y's knee-high nylons. You are there to interview, and you'll need to stay as focused as possible on that process.

The best conference interviewing site is the hotel suite, which is both more private than the "meat market" and more public and professional than the "bedroom." A suite typically has a separate sitting area with a couch and chairs; the bed may be on the other side of the sitting area or in a separate bedroom. You get the room number for a suite in the same way you get it for a regular hotel room. If you hear voices when you arrive at the door, don't let that stop you from knocking. You may just be hearing the committee members talking among themselves, or the committee may feel free to continue talking to one candidate until another one shows up at the door. Once you're in, the committee will very likely offer you a bottled water, coffee, fruit, or some such refreshment; be very careful what you choose because once you pick it up you will be responsible for it until it's gone—or until you are. Fruit is drippy, cookies are crumbly, pastries are messy, and coffee stains an interview suit. It wouldn't be a catastrophe if you were to dribble your fruit, of course, and it surely wouldn't keep you from getting hired, but it could undermine your confidence and therefore keep you from interviewing as well as you otherwise might. Bottled water is generally the safest bet.

When the chair or some other committee member gives the signal that the interview is coming to a close, the committee may or may not remember to ask if you have any further questions. Either way, you should have one or two prepared ahead of time. If they haven't told you their time-line, be sure to ask about that; you might also ask if they have a few more minutes to tell you which courses they see you teaching and what sort of contribution they hope this hire will make to the department. If you haven't yet had the chance to say something that really wants to be said about your qualifications, ask if there's time for you to make one last point. Make it quickly, though; you don't want to give them the impression that you're hard to get rid of. Shake hands with every member of the committee, thank them for their time, and exit. As soon as you possibly can, sit down and make a few notes about the interview, including any information you learned about the position and their projected time for making a decision.

Campus Interviews

Because MLA interviews take place over the winter holiday, committee members usually won't meet again to make decisions about campus visits until the middle or end of January. In some cases, two months may go by before the committee gets the chance to meet again and decide which candidates to invite to campus, especially if the department is conducting more than one search or if funding for the position becomes uncertain. Typically, however, candidates get campus invitations from the committee in late January or early February. MLA guidelines say that once a school has made you an offer, you have up to two weeks to take it or turn it down. So if your first campus invitation comes in mid-January from your least favorite school, it's a good idea to try to delay the visit at least a week and preferably two. Your first goal, obviously, is to get a job. But you'll also want to avoid getting into the position of having to decide whether to take a job offer from a school you're not wild about before you've even given your first choice a chance to invite you to campus.

Once you accept a campus interview, you'll want to do some more in-depth research on the department and the institution. One survey respondent told us that the most difficult career challenge she had faced thus far was "being at an institution that didn't value the type of research that I was doing"; this problem may be avoidable if you attend to it up front. Another respondent advised, for example, that, as a prospective candidate, you should "find out everything you can about the institution you plan to join—what's their history of raises, how does faculty governance work there, how have they treated others in your area group? In fact, doing institutional history should be part of R/C training." We agree. And this is the time to do it: between the on-campus invitation and the time you arrive there.

When you pack for campus interviews, you'll want to take the weather into account, especially since you are likely to be out in it quite a lot, walking all over campus. Check the weather ahead of time and come prepared for it. If there's snow on the ground, leave the sandals and bring the boots; if it's supposed to rain all week, bring an umbrella. If you live in Arizona and you're interviewing in Wisconsin, don't forget to bring a warm coat, warm shoes, and gloves. The dress code for campus interviews is slightly more relaxed than it is at conferences, partly because candidates are on campus for a few days and will be engaging in several different sorts of activities. The key is to look professional but not stiff. So if the committee is taking you to a crawfish boil for dinner or if they're having a reception for you one night at a faculty member's house, you'll want to wear something appropriate for that venue—if everyone else is wearing jeans, you'll look silly and uncomfortable in your interview suit. On the other hand, you'll want to dress it up again for your presentations, no matter what everyone else is wearing.

Some schools will pay for your plane ticket up front, but most will reimburse you later, so save some room on your credit card. You will usually get an itinerary from the chair of the committee a few days before you leave, but some schools won't have it ready until you arrive. If you get your itinerary early, try to learn all you can about those faculty members scheduled to take you to dinner. (Hume and others suggest that you *request* your itinerary ahead of time.) Campus interviews are typically exhausting—you are "on" non-stop. By now, the search committee has finished its primary obligation: it has discovered you, talked with you, brought you to campus, and introduced you to the faculty, the students, and the administration—all of whom now constitute your interviewers. You'll very likely be scheduled to meet with the dean of the college, someone from the benefits office, writing program administrators, and other program directors. You'll have breakfast, lunch, and dinner with students and faculty, and you will generally be expected to give both a teaching presentation and a scholarly presentation. There will likely be some time devoted to showing you the campus and the city; you may also be scheduled to meet with a local realtor to get housing information.

The teaching presentation may take the form of a formal talk, an informal discussion, or an actual classroom visit. It isn't really possible to prepare until you know, so if the chair (or whoever calls to invite you to campus) isn't specific, you'll need to ask for clarification. If you're required to teach a class, be sure to get as much information as possible about it: What course is it? What will the students have been doing prior to your visit? And what will they do after? Ask for a course syllabus, as well, and find out if this class is held in a computer-assisted classroom. The point of this part of the interview is to demonstrate that you are a committed teacher who is comfortable teaching and knows how to excite and motivate students—so be thoroughly prepared. Bring your handouts or URLs or slides or whatever you need to give an engaged and enthusiastic teaching performance. "Don't make the thoughtless mistake," Formo and Reed warn, "of reading a scholarly paper to a group who wants to assess your ability to engage the attention of undergraduates" (68). On the other hand, if you are asked to give a formal talk about your pedagogical approach, consider offering a longer version of your teaching philosophy statement, full of concrete examples and assignment handouts. If you are asked to meet informally with the faculty to discuss your pedagogy, you can expect a situation that is very similar to the conference interview, except that the focus will be on your teaching rather than your research. You'll want to come prepared to talk and respond to questions about exactly the same material you would have presented in the formal presentation.

The scholarly talk is tricky because it needs to demonstrate both your scholarly brilliance and your ability to talk to non-experts about what you do. Be sure to find out how long your talk should be and how much time you should allow for questions after it. Never go over that time limit—in fact, try to come in a little under it. If you decide to read a section from your dissertation or another piece you've recently completed, be sure you rid it of jargon and deliver it in an engaged, almost conversational manner, interrupting yourself occasionally with explanations and/or asides designed to draw the audience in. Hume suggests that you might "wish at one or two points to say 'If I were teaching this, I would now develop the historical dimension of this idea a bit further' or 'Since I know you need to know how I would handle an idea like this in a class, let me give you the definition of this specialist term as I would in a class and illustrate it'" (73). Unless you are informed otherwise, expect that your talk will be attended by faculty, staff, and graduate students alike, and pitch it accordingly. It is not okay, by the way, to present the same piece of work you sent out as a writing sample; nor is it acceptable to read a journal article that has already been published. Presume that your audience has read what you've sent them and anything you've published so far, and give them something else from your repertoire. But don't give a job talk on something you're just starting to think about or on a dissertation chapter that hasn't yet received thorough feedback from your director.

Many candidates find that dinners are very difficult situations to negotiate during on-campus interviews because the atmosphere is often relaxed, everyone is winding down, ordering drinks, and telling stories about their kids or dogs. It's easy to get sucked into that mood, to let down your guard; however, *you* are still being interviewed. And a very serious question about your research or teaching practices can come out of nowhere: between Professor X's sailing story and Professor Y's confession that he watches soap operas, Professor Z suddenly leans across the table to ask if you sincerely *believe* that a pod-casting assignment belongs in a writing class or why on earth you'd base an argument on the works of Derrida or Ronell or Baudrillard. It's one of those needle-scratching-across-a-record moments: conversation stops, everyone's looking at you, and you're scrambling to get back into your "candidate" ethos. While it's true that you may appear to be a bit stuffy or uptight if you don't share a glass of wine with your hosts, the more they relax the more you'll need to be on your toes. Never drink more than one glass of wine at dinner; nurse it through the entire meal. And if the wait staff constantly refills your glass, you'll need to remain extra-attuned to how much you're drinking. Drink plenty of water, in either case.

Toward the end of your campus visit, you will meet with the chair of the department, who will tell you more about the position and give you the chance to ask some questions. The chair will tell you the salary range for this position and give you information about travel money, research funds, computer allocations, leave possibilities, tenure expectations, and so on. Your questions to the chair in this meeting should reflect a genuine interest in the position and indicate that you are imagining yourself there, but they should not leave the impression that you will be a tough catch or that you'll require them to scramble up a second position to get you. Be sure to ask about the department's time-line: when will the department meet to make a decision? This is also generally a good time to ask some tough but fair questions about gender issues: Have women in the department had a history of succeeding through the tenure and promotion process? Is there a history of salary equity between men and women at this institution and more specifically in the department? If you are joining an English department with few rhetoric and composition scholars, you also might ask about the relationship between scholars in your field and other fields, such as literature. Have there been any tensions? Have rhetoric and composition scholars had a history of succeeding through the tenure and promotion process? You should feel free to ask questions about any of the items the chair brings up, but you will want to reflect upon what your own questions may reveal about you. For example, if you ask about the institution's parental leave policy, the department chair may infer that you're planning to have a family while on the tenure clock. Instead, you might want to ask a general question about the climate on campus for women. One of us put it this way when interviewing for a position: "What is the climate for women like on this campus? For example, do you have a parental leave policy? Do you have a pay equity program? Do you have a good track record of hiring and promoting women and other members of underrepresented groups? Do you offer benefits to partners of employees, regardless of marital status?" Such a series of questions is expected and can get you around the problem of asking only about the one issue that interests you (and could reveal something about you).

It is illegal, for example, for an interviewer to ask you if you're married, have a same-sex partner, need a spousal hire or partner accommodations, and so on, because revealing such personal information is presumed to make a candidate vulnerable to discrimination in the selection process. Keep in mind that the ideal candidate in most cases is set at default (straight white male who is either single or married to a stay-at-home mom); if this weren't the case, there would be no need for federal and state hiring laws. However, we recommend that you use your rhetorical savvy to analyze each situation individually. You could be interviewing at an institution that is not looking for the "default" candidate. If you're interviewing at a rural institution and the interviewers express anxiety about losing the single people they hire, for instance, it might be smart to reveal that you're married or have a life partner—assuming you do. Furthermore, it may actually be a savvy move for a lesbian, bisexual, or transgendered candidate to reveal her sexual orientation if this is a diversity hire and she's white, or if the job is at a liberal, east-coast college or university where being "out" is common and assumed. On the other hand, such a revelation might not be wise if the job is located in a more conservative geographical area or if it's at a private religious college or university. Because this sort of personal information cannot legally be asked of you, we suggest that you offer it when it is useful to you and to withhold it when it is not.

The voting faculty in the department usually won't meet to discuss the candidates until all the campus visits are complete. If there is a great deal of agreement among them about who they want to hire and the dean responds quickly to the request for approval of the hire, the chair may be able to make an offer to that candidate the very same day the faculty votes. If there is some contention about who to hire—or if it takes a while to schedule the meeting itself, or if the dean is in Istanbul for the month—it will take a while longer. If you were the first to visit a campus that is bringing in a total of four candidates for a position, it could be a solid month or more before you hear back from them; if you were the last one to visit, you could conceivably hear back from them the following week. If the faculty votes to make an offer to another candidate, they will not usually inform the other candidates until after their first choice accepts or rejects their offer. If their first choice turns them down, they may elect to move to their second choice; if their second choice also turns them down, they may be willing to make an offer to their third choice. So it's not over until it's over.

Negotiating an Offer

Rumor has it that offers used to be made in our field at MLA, though we have not heard of that happening lately. Rarely, however, an offer will still be extended at the campus visit. When this happens, it is because the faculty decided before you arrived that if you're as good as they think you are, they'll make you an offer. Most often, however, offers are extended over the phone at least a week (and sometimes two months) after you return from your campus interview. Remember that if your initial interview was at MLA, you are legally allowed two weeks to respond to an offer, no matter where it happens. Don't allow yourself to feel pressured or rushed, and never accept the offer without seeing the contract in writing. Ask the chair to email or fax a copy to you so that you can discuss it with your advisor. Once you get the contract (which may be simply a "letter of offer"), read it carefully. If it's fair and comes from your top choice, you may be tempted to accept right away, but don't. Give other schools the chance to make you an offer, as well, and give yourself time to reflect over possible items of negotiation. As Formo and Reed put it, "an unsigned job offer provides you with an important kind of power—not to be abused, but one to be used wisely" (113). We recommend that you actually *do* talk all offers over with your committee; for one thing, they may know more than you do about how things work at any particular university or they may know people there who can give you the scoop about everything.

If you cannot accept an offer without spousal or partner accommodations, the time to disclose that is probably in the phone conversation when the offer is discussed but before the contract or letter of offer is emailed or faxed. It's probably not wise to disclose it earlier, but the department may feel jerked around if you hit them with it for the first time in your counter-offer. This is not an easy conversation, and there is always the possibility that it'll be a deal-breaker, so approach it carefully, and if you intend to take the offer either way, don't pretend that you absolutely can't accept it without such accommodations. Be as honest as possible about this, and respect the fact that this is a very large and, in many cases, unexpected hurdle that the chair may not be able to clear successfully, no matter how much he or she may want to. If the dean won't approve another hire contingent on this one, there is not much a department or chair can do. For more on the complications of spousal and partner hires, see Chapter 7.

Once you get the written contract, look it over carefully and look for potential points for negotiation. "Remember that in the period between the time a department offers you a position and the time you accept it, you are a 'buyer,' in the strongest position to ask for salary or any other special conditions, such as research support, that may be important to you" (164). Some things, of course, are not negotiable. It is standard for tenure-track positions to come with a two- or three-year renewable contract, for example, which means that if, after that time, you are not progressing satisfactorily—or if they simply don't like you—they will be free to dismiss you, no questions asked. "You cannot do anything about this, so put it out of mind," Hume suggests. "Normally, you will be carried through until the tenure review, when final decisions are made," she continues, "unless your teaching is unsatisfactory or unless you are publishing too slowly and are in a research school, in which case, you may be cut off some time before the sixth-year review" (77). But you should know that most other things are potentially negotiable: you can try to negotiate about salary, travel and research funds, computers and other equipment, software, course reductions, and, perhaps, moving expenses. Many of our survey respondents told us that when they accepted their first jobs they didn't realize they could negotiate the terms. For instance, one respondent said that if she could do it all over again she'd "negotiate better!!! I was really stupid when I came to my current appointment. I could have held out for more money and didn't realize it. Moreover, in every situation in which there were issues of load, money, research assistants, and the like, I felt ill-prepared to make a case." We urge you to prepare yourself to make your own case as compellingly as possible and with confidence.

Many deans insist that new PhDs in their college begin with the base salary; however, if you have a lot of teaching experience or have published a lot of articles (or already have a book out), you may be able to negotiate for a few thousand dollars more. Other schools are more flexible, especially if they know another school is bidding for you, too. One of us worked with a student last year who ended up getting 8,000 dollars more than the already good salary she was originally offered. You'll need to do some research to find out what the local pay scale is for assistant professors in the department; the Almanac edition of the *Chronicle of Higher Education* offers a state-by-state breakdown of average faculty salaries, so that may be one place to start. But it may be more helpful to contact the Human Resources Management department or perhaps the campus library—public universities release a detailed budget each year, which includes faculty salaries, and copies are often kept on reserve in the campus library. It's a good idea, while you're at it, to check the pay equity in the department you're considering: do male colleagues consistently earn more than women at the same level? If so, you might consider asking about that, point blank, in your response to the offer. You'll also want to talk to your supervisor to find out what your own department currently offers new assistant professors; with that information, you can do a "cost of living comparison" between the two states. If your research indicates that this salary offer is low, you should counter-offer. Several of our survey respondents said they regretted not negotiating for a higher salary when they accepted their first jobs; one told us that, looking back over her entire career, it's the only thing she'd do differently: "The only thing I think I would do differently is to negotiate strongly for a higher starting salary. I was a bit naïve in that effort and didn't realize how much the initial base pay is negotiable and also the foundation for all future raises."

Travel and research funds are also somewhat negotiable, at least temporarily. Most departments at research institutions pay for a certain number of conference trips, and some of the top schools also offer research accounts for faculty to use to cover various research expenses, including trips to archives and research assistants, though such accounts are very rare in our field. It is often possible, however, to negotiate guaranteed travel and a start-up research fund for the first year or two. A few years ago, one of our students got guaranteed conference money plus a one-time $10,000 research account written into her contract with a tier-one research institution, though that is also rare. Formo and Reed suggest that "a respectable start-up fund for a humanities faculty candidate is $1200" (115). Moving expenses are tricky at some universities, as there is occasionally a university or college-wide rule against going above a certain amount—some won't put any money at all toward moving expenses. But there is often something else they can do for you that will help defray moving costs—more research or travel funds, for example, or a one-time summer research grant. In any case, don't forget to save all your moving receipts so you can write the non-reimbursed expenses off on next year's taxes.

If the offer you're negotiating is from a research institution, you might also consider asking for a temporary course reduction so that you can get a jump start on putting your first book out. If the typical load is a 2/2, you might ask for a 2/1 the first year. Hume suggests that you might also ask for a lopsided load, from a 2/2 to a 3/1 or from a 3/2 to a 4/1, to free up the spring semester and summer for research. Computers, software, and computing accessories are typically purchased from a different pot of money, so there is a good possibility that you'll be able to negotiate about them. Don't order ignorantly, though; do some research to make an intelligent counter-offer complete with rationale explaining why you need the extra goodies. Heiberger and Vick note that some candidates "successfully negotiate to defer starting a position for a semester or a year so that they can complete a dissertation or a research project or give birth and care for a new baby" (165). You never know unless you ask.

Once you have come up with a defensible counter-offer, call the chair and discuss it with him or her. You may be tempted to use email or fax, but it's probably better to pick up the phone. "It is extremely important to conduct your negotiations verbally," say Heiberger and Vick, "usually over the phone, but occasionally in person, rather than by e-mail. Doing so helps preserve the good feeling with potential colleagues which is your working capital once an offer is extended" (164). The chair may be able to agree to some of your terms right away, but for others (such as salary), s/he will very likely need to speak both with the dean and with the department and call you back. Sometimes the chair and/or the dean will not agree to one or more of your terms; if that is the case, try to see if you can negotiate a better deal in another category. For example, one of us negotiated for a better research fund when the chair could not raise the ceiling on the salary. But be careful. If you are perceived to be unreasonable at this stage of the negotiation process, you can lose the offer. When you come to an understanding about the department's response to your counter-offer, ask the chair to send you the new contract—now you need email or fax. Don't accept an offer until you have it in front of you in writing. When you get the revised letter of offer, feel free to think it over, discuss it again with your director, and be certain: once you accept an offer, your job search is over, at least for this season, since you are ethically committed to show up for the position you've accepted and to stay there for a year. After you've made your decision, call the chair again and accept or reject the offer verbally, and then follow it with a letter or email confirming your decision.

If you accept the position, let other departments considering your candidacy know and withdraw from their search. If you decline the position to accept another, "do so very politely," Heiberger and Vick advise:

> Thank the department again for its offer, mention the positive attractions it held for you, and let the committee know where you will be going. Never burn any bridges. You never know when you will meet the chair or a faculty member from that department. You never know when the people you turn down may be able to influence the direction of your career. So always stay on good and polite terms with your colleagues and in other departments, including departments that you have decided to reject. (165)

Your first job search will almost certainly be a grueling experience; there is probably no way around that. But it can also offer you the opportunity, both on paper and in interviews, to define yourself as a scholar and to construct a professional identity for yourself. This may be why one survey respondent, after telling us that the most difficult challenge she had faced in her career so far had been her "initial job search," then went on to describe that search as both "stressful" and "rewarding." Starting your first job is a challenge, as well, and the best advice we can offer as you begin your new career also comes from one of our survey respondents:

> Arm yourself with all the information, theory, and expertise you can acquire, and then don't hesitate to disrupt, interrupt, and engage actively in the conversations of the discipline and institutions in which you reside. Find good women (and men) allies and collaborate, collaborate, collaborate.

Becoming a Professional

ESSENTIAL RESOURCES

Finding a Mentor

Goldsmith, John, John Komlos, and Penny Schine Gold. *The Chicago Guide to Your Academic Career: A Portable Mentor for Scholars from Graduate School through Tenure*

Publishing Your Work

Olson, Gary A. and Todd W. Taylor, eds. *Publishing in Rhetoric and Composition*

Writing the Dissertation

Fitzpatrick, Jacqueline, Jan Secrist, and Debra J. Wright. *Secrets for a Successful Dissertation*

Bolker, Joan. *Writing Your Dissertation in Fifteen Minutes a Day: A Guide to Starting, Revising, and Finishing Your Doctoral Thesis*

The Job Hunt

Hume, Kathryn. *Surviving Your Academic Job Hunt: Advice for Humanities PhDs*

Heiberger, Mary Morris and Julia Miller Vick. *The Academic Job Search Handbook*

Section II

THRIVING AS A PROFESSIONAL

3

SUCCEEDING AS A JUNIOR PROFESSOR

> Keep your boundaries clear. I think as teachers and as administrators, women are often expected to be more nurturing and more available to students and colleagues. But to do so can mean a drain on energies and resources that could go to your own teaching and research. My advice would be: block out a day a week that you will use for your own reading and writing. Don't give up this time for meetings or other university service work. And, likewise, don't give it up for your family, either, if you can help it. Remind yourself that you are a professional. Don't give away the time that you need to keep up in the field and feel confident about taking on that label.
>
> —anonymous survey respondent

Although your academic career will entail various transitions, the "transition from being a graduate student to being an assistant professor is the most difficult" (Goldsmith, Komlos, and Gold 135). Such a claim hardly demeans the difficulties of surviving doctoral studies, including the dreaded dissertation and its defense, nor the soul-emptying exertions of negotiating the job market, including the dreaded MLA hotel-room interviews with strangers and the anguishing on-site campus visits. However, typically these challenges are met with the accompanying support of a major professor and a group of graduate-school friends. Transitioning to an assistant professor position, on the contrary, is typically a solitary journey: not only geographically—as you move, alone, from Texas to Virginia, for example—but also mentally, as you are now wrested from an advising professor, who guided your research and mentored your scholarly work and relations, wrested from your community of fellow graduate students; wrested from end-of-semester deadlines that demanded that seminar papers be completed or exacting graduate-school deadlines that encouraged a dissertation to be defended. You will find yourself bereft, perhaps gladly, of the comfort of your Freshman Composition course, which you taught three or four times a year for three or more years. You will have transitioned to a new world, to a new geographical location with new faces—most nameless, with new demands, new power relations. You are no longer (formally) a student; you are now a colleague. You are now an assistant professor: untenured, to be sure, but you are now a *professional*.

Although you find yourself in a time of a potentially difficult transition, you will discover that this is simultaneously an exciting and rewarding time. Your graduate years of study have been rewarded by a hiring committee, by selecting you out of innumerable applicants to join them and the ranks of colleagues at your new institution. In many ways, the future is fresh before you, and you may find yourself positively giddy at the sight of a horizon of pure possibility. Nevertheless, you will have challenges: mainly, how to balance the demands of research, teaching, and service; and how to prepare yourself for a successful tenure case (and, of course, how to have a life in the meantime), as one survey respondent wrote: "Academia is a profession which is never satisfied: publish more, teach better, serve on more committees. You name it and it's never quite enough. You can only succeed—and be healthy and happy, I think—by being able to say no, to set limits on your work, and to create other activities you enjoy where you don't have to think about work." But before discussing these demands, in turn, and the various political struggles you will now face as an (untenured) assistant professor, we want to remind you—as did the respondents to our online survey—that you should face these challenges with the confidence that you are now a professional: *an appointed university professor.* In what follows, we will discuss how to perform as this newly appointed professional—how to bolster your confidence, how to behave professionally, and how to thrive as a professional.

Professionalize, Professionalize, Professionalize

Nurture and Exert Confidence

Acknowledging the difficulty of this transition from graduate student to assistant professor, many of our survey respondents admitted that the most difficult part of this transition was, as one noted: "a transition into seeing myself as a 'professional'—not just some kid who'd read a lot of books." This difficulty manifested itself as a quick loss of confidence. One respondent reported: "When I started as an assistant professor, I felt a sharp confidence drop. I think this had much to do with the egos/posturing of faculty. While well versed in feminist theory and having been educated in some traditionally masculinist places ..., I was surprised by my own lack of confidence." Another reports that her greatest challenge has been "Rebuilding self-respect after a negative review." And yet another reported that her greatest challenge has been: "overcoming low self-esteem in academia and my fear of failing as a scholar. I was confident as a teacher and very insecure as a researcher. I did not have many positive role models or mentors (male or female), and I was part of a departmental culture that trivialized composition research and the field of composition during the time that I was trying to publish a book and get tenure."

These responses are not unusual, according to Paula J. Caplan, author of *Lifting a Ton of Feathers: A Woman's Guide for Surviving in the Academic World*: "The combination of women's traditionally low self-esteem and the maleness of the academic environment can make it exceedingly difficult for a woman in academia to remember that she is basically intelligent and competent" (76). Caplan argues that a female academician would do well to remind herself that most women around her experience this same lack of confidence, "[c]hances are, then, that if most women's poor opinions of themselves are not justified, your own isn't either" (76). Caplan also advises us women to "[r]ealize that you will rarely or never feel or be completely prepared for whatever task you are about to do … . Academic women are likely, on account of their self-esteem problems and the maleness of the environments, to spend far more time preparing for courses and writing for publication than necessary, because we are always dogged by the certainty that we shall never be able to do a good enough job" (77). Acknowledging such goes a long way to bolster confidence; yet, additionally, Caplan offers a variety of strategies, prime among which is to construct for yourself a "savings bank of support for your self-esteem," whose resources you can tap when the need arises. Caplan suggests that your bank may include positive evaluation comments and thank-you notes from former students; letters of recommendation; reviews of your work in which your contribution was praised.

The academic setting—still sexist in nature—exacerbates the feeling that you're not quite good enough for the job. Janice Neuleib argues that "unwritten, unacknowledged" rules "tell women that they must meet different and more demanding professional standards, sometimes while simultaneously being accused of special privilege under the law" (130). Neuleib advises several ways to counter this predicament, one being: "Understand that nothing matters as much as an impeccable vita," and another being: "Never appeal to your family situation to explain anything you do. It may be the reason for whatever impedes your progress, but you are fighting years of built-up prejudice against women with small children, demanding life partners, pets, or ailing parents. Tell your best friend or your counselor but never the personnel committee" who will evaluate and judge your performance (133–4).

Caplan offers additional suggestions such as learning various, assertive body language and conversational strategies. For example, she writes:

> I have tried quietly but confidently increasing the amount of space I take up when I am in the presence of someone who treats me in demeaning ways. Once, for instance, realizing that I repeatedly pulled my legs and arms close to my torso, leaned forward, and looked up at a man who regularly put me down, I … leaned back against the chair, relaxed my legs, and (in what felt like a daring act) clasped my hands behind my head, elbows pointing outward. I don't think the fellow understood why, but from that time, he treated me with greater respect … . When you are speaking, if you are interrupted, continue talking and

> continue looking at the person to whom you are addressing your concerns … or say something like, "Just a minute, please. I haven't finished my point." (79; 81)

Caplan recommends Nancy Henley's *Body Politics* and Suzette Haden Elgin's *The Gentle Art of Verbal Self-Defense* for further suggestions as to how a woman can adopt verbal and physical behaviors that exude confidence.

One respondent said that her biggest challenge was "being taken seriously." As other respondents noted, to be taken seriously, one needs to behave as a serious professional. (Being serious does not mean, however, that one loses her sense of humor; on the contrary—more on this to come.) She must, writes one respondent, "Do [her] homework—in the job search, in [her] research, before committee meetings, etc. Because many faculty members consider Rhetoric/Composition a field filled with those 'who couldn't make it in a real academic field' (direct quotation from a senior male scholar), it is imperative that women provide evidence to the contrary. They don't have to do so defensively or apologetically but with an easy, no-nonsense self-confidence."

Doing one's homework is an aspect of professionalizing oneself, of seeing oneself as a professional, by engaging with the other professionals in your field and the ideas and publications that define it. Although no longer formally a student, as a professional you have now made a career-long commitment to continue to learn. Such substantive familiarity, if not mastery, builds confidence and will earn you the reputation of being one who should be taken seriously. Here is what our respondents advised: "Go to conferences and get out there—be a part of the conversation in all that you do." "Be smart about what you study—know what the trends are and what seems to be coming around the bend in terms of theory, community need, technology." "Pursue the study of languages, especially Greek and Latin." Learn more classical rhetoric, more history of rhetoric; "do interdisciplinary work—to stretch the field and its sense of its own disciplinarity"; learn qualitative and quantitative methodology. "Read, read, read. Read theory. Read journals. Read outside your field. And never stop reading." Again, although your formal schooling is now behind you, you must continue to do your homework: to develop yourself as a scholar, to present yourself as credible, to contribute to the ongoing conversation that is the field of rhetoric and composition. Doing the work—staying current, presenting at conferences, publishing in peer-reviewed and regarded venues—generously invites your colleagues to take you seriously.

We understand, of course, that a woman in the field of rhetoric and composition has an especially difficult challenge to be taken seriously. Women, as has been well documented, are often dismissed as incapable as academics; and, as has been also well documented, the field of rhetoric and composition is seen as feminine work, and hence dismissed and devalued institutionally. Therefore, not only do you have to work to ensure that you, as a woman, will be taken seriously, but also that your discipline, and the intellectual work that you do, will be taken seriously. How might one ensure a positive reception? Richard Gebhardt advises:

> For instance, how might you mention a recent *CCC* acceptance in a reappointment-review report? For readers inside composition studies, brief mention of the fact—even using cryptic initials rather than the name of the journal—would be significant. But in a personnel report for nonspecialists you should give more detail. For example: In the past year, my article on the "History of Collaborative Narrative" was accepted for future publication in the refereed journal *College Composition and Communication*—the oldest and largest periodical in my field and, with an acceptance rate under 10 percent, one of the most competitive. ("Preparing Yourself" 124–5).

Carrie Leverenz posits a more institutional response by suggesting that the CCCC survey its members to ascertain the "current status of tenure and promotion in rhetoric and composition" in order to judge "how much institutional change is still needed before we can accomplish our goal not just of 'making it' in the university but making a place for what it is we do" (146).

Clearly, educating colleagues on the value of research and scholarship in rhetoric and composition remains a huge challenge, as this survey respondent articulated: "I'm … struggling with the considerable lack of knowledge about and respect for the field of rhetoric and composition among some of my colleagues … . Be prepared for some uninformed views of the field among faculty in other areas of English." Another respondent wrote: "Our scholarly work is a real puzzle to some folks in English. I've been accused of being a social scientist, for example, being told: 'This isn't English.'"

"This isn't English" because the "real" work of English, apparently, is the teaching of literature. In the face of such a strongly held presumption, we are not surprised to hear that one respondent reported that the rhetoric and composition women in her department, were "referred to as 'housewives' in one faculty meeting." The difficulty of being taken seriously in such climates is real, yet there are strategies for meeting this challenge. One such, according to one respondent, is to "Publish like crazy. It's the only way to anchor your ethos as a scholar equal to someone in literature." It is certainly an effective way, as published scholarship is a prime indicator of your success as a professional in academe.

Develop and Practice Professional Behaviors

Being professional means "doing a job competently, even gracefully" (Bennett 42). Being professional means being on time to class, appointments, meetings; being professional means respecting the time and presence of others—don't open your mail during department meetings, for example. Be present to and engaged with your colleagues:

> Primary to my understanding of professional life is collegiality … . I view relationships among colleagues as emanating from respect, including respect for differences, a shared commitment to collective goals, and an awareness of interdependence among individuals … . Most faculty realize that collective welfare depends on the success and commitment of each individual. (Phillips 148)

Of course, most women are socialized to attend to the welfare of a collective body—whether it be a family or a bridge group. So, although we advise that you be responsible to and respectful of your colleagues, we also advise, as did many respondents to our survey, that you do not fall into the "nurturing trap." Here is what a number of women advised: "Resist the nurturing expectations. That is, students/colleagues will often look to you to nurture in a variety of ways that can impede your professional goals or lock you into gender role expectations. If you love providing food, then do. If you don't, don't feel obligated because you are female." And another: "Be careful of the tendency to 'take care' of the 'needs' of our male colleagues and especially those in literature. As women, and especially as women in rhetoric and writing we seem very easily co-opted into doing much of the difficult departmental work."

In many ways, as one survey respondent advised us, female academics must acknowledge that they will "have to unlearn a lot of traditional feminine behaviors. Deference and indirectness will not further her career studies." Gail Evans, author of *Play Like a Man, Win Like a Woman*, engagingly articulates "what men know about success that women need to learn," including cultivating the assertiveness that most women shun. Evans suggests that knowing how men play—and by what rules—helps women compete more successfully. Men, for example, ask for what they want; women hint (65). Norma Carr-Ruffino's *The Promotable Woman* distinguishes, using various scenarios, the differences between being aggressive, nonassertive, passive aggressive, and (the preferred behavior) assertive. She also provides a helpful checklist of questions to ask yourself when you are faced with a situation in which you need to decide whether you are going to respond assertively or not (231–64).

The female academic is, as you can see, asked to re-examine her socially engendered behaviors and to recode such behaviors. A female academic is required to "play like a man," exhibiting assertiveness and confidence; yet, she is also asked to exhibit the typically female behaviors of graciousness and collegiality, without taking on the assumed burden of nurturance. Recoding such behaviors and assuming what might be called stereotypically male behaviors can be a difficult task: when do socially acceptable behaviors of confidence or assertiveness become anti-social behaviors of aggression (whether coded "male" or "female")? One survey respondent acknowledged: "The establishment expects [the female academic] to walk a very thin line between confidence and aggression."

Another survey respondent reported that her biggest challenge, as a woman in academe, was "managing collegiality. Many people come fresh out of grad school with a sense of entitlement and a fierce competitiveness. Trying to establish collaborative, supportive networks with other junior faculty (especially with those in my immediate area of study) has sometimes been a challenge as a result. I've found that other junior people—especially women—tend to treat their junior colleagues with suspicion and manifest weird passive-aggressiveness toward one another." One respondent advised: "Learn how to build alliances with the people who must work with you." Another reported that her biggest challenge was "learning how to keep my temper and act professionally at all times. It took me a long time to learn how to be gracious." To act professional at all times, be confident and assertive, yet gracious and collegial.

The stakes are very high for such professional behavior: "Recognize," one survey respondent advised, "that there's a fourth category in promotion and tenure decisions: collegiality. Recognize that collegiality involves not setting oneself apart as the critic or superior of one's colleagues (a tough task for us self-important, self-lionizing compositionists)." And in "some academic departments, Ms. Mentor is sad to say, social life is not just the main thing in promotion and tenure decisions. It's the only thing. Usually it is called 'collegiality,' a term which may connote (to the unwary) the qualities needed for a community of scholars. Actually, it means charm and fitting in" (Toth, *Ms. Mentor's Impeccable Advice* 69). "In essence," she continues:

> strive to like and be liked. Then, if your teaching and publications are good, your path to tenure should be fairly smooth. For no matter the written policies, a tenure decision is really a Yes or No answer to one question: Do we, the entrenched faculty members, want this person around for another thirty years or more? It's up to you to make sure that they do. But Ms. Mentor adds that it's also up to you not to forget feminist principles. In your soul, while you're smiling and listening, you should distrust hierarchies and slogans, and welcome new ideas, and support other women, and ponder ways to change departmental silliness, fogeyism, or inertia. While you're learning about your new department, and making yourself liked, you can also be waiting for your chance to make a difference. (71)

Being collegial (striving to like and to be liked) means composing yourself with the four qualities of memorable conduct: grace and charisma; confidence; energy; generosity (Sherman 7). …

And, yet, as we know, newly appointed, untenured professors can be called "uncollegial" simply for disagreeing with another (usually tenured) colleague. One survey respondent reported that she worried about her impending tenure vote, as she had disagreed with a senior colleague in a recent faculty meeting, and had heard that the act of disagreeing had been interpreted as uncollegial behavior. The respondent admitted, however, that she perhaps hadn't disagreed in the "most tactful way." Learning to disagree and/or to challenge senior colleagues is no easy lesson. The challenge is doing so without causing the colleague to feel disrespected or dismissed. In many environments, however, the mere act of talking—even if in agreement—can threaten one's reputation of collegial behavior. As Krista Ratcliffe notes, "I remember thinking in my untenured years that I had more freedom of speech as a graduate student than I did as an untenured professor. And I don't think that's simply the rose-colored glasses syndrome. It's not that I didn't speak as an untenured professor; I just felt more pressure when I did" (4).

We acknowledge—as did one survey respondent—that you may be "damned if you do, and damned if you don't" participate in departmental quarrels, debates, and issues. On this point, we then concede that the wise woman will consult her knowing mentors—both local and global—to rhetorically strategize about best behaviors.

Promote Yourself

Perhaps this appears as a mixed message or contradictory advice: some advise the newly appointed professor to lie low, under the radar of departmental fire, and yet some additionally advise this same professor to assertively and actively promote herself. The advice is not so contradictory, at all: You are aiming to make yourself liked—and senior colleagues like junior colleagues who are busy attending to their own business rather than to the departmental business and battles.

You will not only be attending to pursuing and publishing your research agenda, you will need to let your colleagues know that you are actively doing so, and this is the value of self-promotion. According to Taylor and Martin, "The Present-Minded Professor: Controlling One's Career":

> If you have planned your research strategy and gotten out a couple of papers, and you are still waiting to be discovered, don't hold your breath. No one is going to discover you: you have to promote yourself … . It is not inappropriate, rude, pushy, or aggressive to promote yourself … . First, if you have a paper you are particularly proud of, send it to people in the field … . Send it to the people whose work you cited. These are the colleagues who are most likely to be interested in, to profit from, and ultimately to cite your work … . Accompany the paper with a personal note, explaining how the paper might be of interest to the recipient. Understand, however, that three quarters of

> the recipients will chuck your beloved paper in the circular file. A few will read it, they may cite it, and eventually your work will start to be known. Talk about your work. Give brown bag lunches, colloquia, and conference presentations. (24)

Invite scholars to come speak at your university—find the funds to do so, such as an invited-lecturer series. Also invite scholars to be on panelists with you at conferences (24).

The author of *Play Like a Man, Win Like a Woman*, Gail Evans, advises:

> Make sure everyone notices what you do. Stick out your hand and introduce yourself. Let people know that you're smart, that you've met your numbers, that you're on top of your operations. But you can't do this the way a man does. He can get away with boasting. You can't. When guys brag, it reminds them of being on a team. When women brag, men and women hear rudeness and pushiness. You must learn to be your own public relations person in a way that's comfortable for you and works within the culture of your office. So we have to find ways to toot our own horns without making ourselves or our associates uncomfortable. For most of us, the best personal public relations is accomplished in a relationship context. Rather than stand up at a meeting and talk about yourself, find a more personal way to get the word out. (76–8)

An invaluable marketing and self-promoting document is the curriculum vitae, or academic résumé, that displays your academic history, including degrees earned; your teaching experience, including courses taught and/or areas of pedagogical expertise; your scholarly activity, including your publications and conference presentations; any awards, fellowships, or honors you have received; institutional and disciplinary service you have rendered; and your affiliation and memberships to disciplinary organizations (see the "Essential Resources" at the end of Section I for sample CVs and advice for assembling them). Although your institution may prescribe the format and categories of this document, how you present the intellectual work you do to your colleagues—near and far—is something you can control. One survey respondent reported that her mentor was "forever saying to me, 'so how will that work translate to your cv?'" Part of self-promotion is documenting the work that you do and, if done effectively, one respondent noted, you will teach people how to read your work and how to value that work.

Develop Integrity as a Professional

The "embarrassing truth is that our profession is filled with—almost defined by—missed deadlines and broken promises" (Solomon and Solomon, quoted in

Bennett 56). As you strive to like and to be liked—as you strive to be a professional in the world of rhetoric and composition scholars, make yourself memorable by developing the professional quality of follow-through: "If you say you're going to take care of something, do it. You want people to know they can rely on you—just as you want to be able to rely on them" (Goldsmith, Komlos, and Gold 145). If you promise to have a book review completed or a manuscript submitted by a certain date, fulfill your promise. As Solomon and Solomon noted, the "embarrassing truth" is that most academics, including women in rhetoric and composition, do not deliver what they promised, when they promised it, including "the unreliable manuscript reviewer who despite repeated reminders reneges on his or her promise to provide comment, jeopardizing tenure or promotion decisions. Other scholars come to regret depending on colleagues to honor commitments to a collaborative project, as publishers are particularly aware" (Bennett 56).

Or, in conference settings, presenters who have promised to deliver a 15- or 20-minute paper but who then steal time away from their fellow-presenters and respondents, speaking well beyond time limits (Bennett 56). "Rare is the moderator with the courage or ability to hold speakers to time limits. And then there are those who rise from the audience purportedly to engage the speaker only to deliver their own mini-paper in the time devoted to questions from the floor .... Often the academy excuses these behaviors by speaking of professorial inertia or procrastination, thereby bleaching out the moral issues" (Bennett 56).

Behaving with integrity, collegiality, and confidence will help you to thrive as a newly appointed professional in the world of rhetoric and composition. Periodically evaluate your own state of professionalization; additionally, pay careful attention to whatever official reviews you receive. (A sample inventory can be found in Janice Ellig's *What Every Successful Woman Knows* [161].) In these first years, you can develop a solid foundation of professional behavior, working toward finessing the "winning formula"—which, according to Stephanie G. Sherman, is rhetorically calculated as: Memorability = Style × Substance × Timing (2)—in order to develop and to document yourself as a tenurable candidate.

Thriving Through the Tenure Process; Know What is Expected

"It has been said on more than one occasion," one survey respondent reported, "that the department views its relationship to untenured faculty as merely an 'engagement' and not a marriage. This is usually followed with knowing laughter. (I should add that there is a large untenured contingent in the department.)" No doubt about it, the tenure process is painful, seemingly invented to make candidates feel small, inadequate, and lacking, as they struggle to reduce themselves and their worth to a slim dossier of documentation, which will be judged (as suitable "marriage" material) most probably by folks not even in the candidate's field, and who, indeed, may be hostile to her area of research (whether it be theory, composition, or ethnography, for example). One way to handle the anxiety is to arm yourself with as much information as you can about how the process will go and how you will be evaluated and by whom. Each institution will publish its own tenure and promotion requirements, which will also specify the process. Although there will be differences, the typical routine is this: you submit your dossier to a series of judging or evaluative groups. The first group is your department or division, who will decide whether your case is strong enough to move forward—if so, your department head will request external reviewers, from other (usually peer- or aspirant-) institutions, who will comment on your qualifications. When the letters return, and after you have assembled your final dossier (which the letters will become a part of), your case will be evaluated, formally, by your department or division. The second group is your school- or college-wide faculty committee. Your case then moves on to a number of additional evaluative bodies: your Dean; then on to a university faculty committee; still yet on to the Provost; and then the President; and then, finally, on to the Board of Regents (see Whicker et al's chapter "Stepping Through the Tenure Process").

A small, but extremely helpful volume, Marcia Lynn Whicker, Jennie Jacobs Kronenfeld, and Ruth Ann Strickland's *Getting Tenure,* would prove a helpful guide to tenure-track candidates. The volume advises tenure-track candidates to memorize and heed "The Ten Commandments of Tenure," which are identified as the following:

1. Publish, publish, publish!
2. View tenure as a political process.
3. Find out the tenure norms.
4. Document everything.
5. Rely on your record, not on promises of protection.
6. Reinforce research with teaching and service.
7. Do not run your department or university until after tenure.
8. Be a good department citizen.
9. Manage your own professional image.
10. Develop a marketable record. (138)

Our survey respondents, in varying ways, echoed the sentiments—if not the exact wording—of Whicker et al's "commandments." In summary, to survive the tenure process, as well as to succeed and to thrive, you will need to know the specific expectations that your institution, your administration, and your colleagues have of you. Of course, you will have expectations of yourself—including to behave professionally and collegially. You will find that there are official (written) expectations but also, and perhaps more demanding, unofficial expectations, which you will want to discover as quickly as possible. The first thing you are going to want to do is to visit the office of your university's

Provost or Academic Vice President (or equivalent) to secure the official guidelines that your institution has established for tenure and promotion. Typically, these guidelines will be published in a small handbook or as an online document. You may have already accessed these materials during your job search and/or on-campus interview process, but do this again, as soon as you set foot on your campus. The cruel truth is that tenure and promotion policies change, and often there are no grandfather clauses. You may have accepted the job offer under one set of guidelines, and yet you may be evaluated under another. Hence, keep constant vigil for newly adopted policies and procedures and familiarize yourself with them. The second thing you should do is to schedule an appointment with your departmental head or division chair to discuss how the department interprets the university's criteria and/or to see if there are written guidelines (and/or bylaws) specifically applicable to tenure and promotion candidates within your department. Take careful notes, as you may learn how those written criteria may be inflected by unwritten expectations. You will also want to make an appointment after each year's "Annual Review," and/or "Third-Year Review," or after any formal evaluation of you. Typically, these reports will contain some written statement that will address your "Progress Toward Tenure." Take such statements seriously, and discuss with your department head or division chair what the next, best steps toward such progress could be.

Seek a Support Group

The third thing you will want to do, and if you've already read previous chapters you have probably already done so, is to actively seek a network/mentor/support group to help you not only to gather the information (sometimes also known as gossip) about written and unwritten criteria and expectations, but also to support you through the process, which is, unfortunately, an agonizing one. You will need both local, institutional networks, as well as those in the greater field of rhetoric and composition. If you have not already done so, you are advised to seek out a mentor to guide your decisions.

This was advice that our survey respondents overwhelmingly offered: "Networking is important, even vital. If 4Cs is too big and daunting, there are other smaller conferences that will provide collegial support." "Choose strong and supportive mentors." "I would try very hard to be less shy about finding good mentors and a good network of scholarly friendships. I am still stunned at how solitary academic life can be, even now, when there is a fair amount written about collaboration and so on." "[I wish I had asked] for more advice. I wish I hadn't been so independent. I tended to isolate myself from people who could have been very helpful."

Not only did they advise selecting a mentor at your institution ("Get employed at an institution where there is already a woman in the field, preferably in your own department, who can mentor you."), they also advised finding mentors outside your own institution: "the toughest thing for me to handle in my career was learning that the people who were my mentors at my institution didn't necessarily know how to guide me. Not that they were giving me intentionally bad advice, but they just didn't know enough to guide me … . I ended up turning to people in the field for help, which was great, but then I needed to learn how to apply advice from outside the institution to my own environment. That was a challenge." "Network, network, network. You need the revitalization of conferences and friends at other campuses, and you need the support of recommendations for new positions, fellowships, and the P&T process. More importantly, you need the support because the campus is still terribly biased against women—lower salaries, lower % of tenure, lower number hired. In addition, it helps to hook up with another department or college and to make friends outside the realm of your political fights. The most important support I received was from a 10-year women's studies seminar for faculty that I joined and participated in all through the 1980s."

The Trinity of Tenure

Service

Most institutions will judge your tenure worthiness across three categories of accomplishment: service, teaching, and research. Although you are likely budgeted only for teaching and research, most universities have a "service" category for which you are expected to demonstrate some accomplishment. Unless you are associated with "public outreach" efforts, "service" typically translates into service to the academic community: this may include any administrative work that you do, as well as any number of faculty governance positions: faculty senator, university council member, intra- and inter-departmental committees. As a composition and rhetoric specialist, you may be asked and/or required to serve as a writing program administrator. Say "no," our survey respondents overwhelmingly urged, to such kinds of service before tenure: "The 'service' element of a position in composition can overwhelm you. Don't let it." Survey respondents told a number of stories suggesting—even if a candidate were budgeted for writing program service—that at tenure-time, such service did not "count" towards tenurability. Other respondents noted that such service can keep you from doing what you need to be doing: writing and publishing. One survey respondent noted that her "greatest challenge" was "Doing quality research while administrating the Composition Program and teaching." In short, the survey respondents advised: "Beware of administrative responsibilities before tenure." "Don't let them give you too much service or administration too soon. I know countless numbers of women … who, because they're good at this work, have been exploited." (See Chapter 4 for more information on administrative service, including WPA service.) Although you are expected to serve the academic community—and to do it well—remember that (1) you are not being recompensed for this work and (2)—which may amount to the same thing—this service, when push comes to shove, doesn't "count" toward your tenurability. However, your service may serve as the proverbial "icing" on the tenure dossier, demonstrating that you are committed to your institution's welfare (and, hence, you will be favorably viewed as a contributing and positive member of your institution's community) and that you are a collegial faculty member.

For the purposes of this chapter, we will assume that you have avoided administrative appointments thus far, and that your main area of service will be in the names of faculty governance. (If you are in an administrative position or have held such a position, see Chapter 4.) Many universities pride themselves on "faculty governance," which mainly translates into *you* doing advisory work for administrators, which mainly translates into *you* working harder to do work that counts for nothing—and, often, administrators end up doing whatever they want to do anyway. That's the cynical view, of course, and, trust us, there will be many days, when you are writing up committee reports, sitting in on committee meetings, chairing (laboriously loquacious) colleagues, and you will wonder why you can't be at your computer, writing, or in your classroom, teaching, doing the "real" work of the university. But, let's attempt to embrace the value of faculty governance, and, in that spirit, let's see how your committee service can aid your tenure case.

Neil J. Smelser's *Effective Committee Service* offers simple, concrete suggestions—his own 10 "commandments" of effective committee service, including the rules: "Know your assignment," "Know when you are being co-opted," "Follow through on your contributions," and "Rely on humor." Most of these "commandments" have to do with behaving professionally, shouldering your portion of the weight, and refraining from blathering on and on with self-importance:

> it is safe to say that it is much more self-defeating to talk too much than to talk too little in committees. Of course, to say nothing leaves you completely without influence, unless you bend your efforts to influencing other committee members outside meeting times. But giving long-winded speeches or lectures is a sure avenue to creating disgruntlement and making yourself a scapegoat. It generates murmurs during coffee breaks about people who like to hear themselves talk and not-so-subtle suggestions to the chair to "do something about X." In a way this is a curious point to make, because most academics like to talk; but perhaps it is for that very reason that they do not like to hear others talk at length, no matter how intelligent they might sound. (65)

Behaving professionally in committee service will help your colleagues to see you as the kind of colleague that they would like to have around (a.k.a.

tenured and promoted), as well as to have on future committees (no good deed goes unpunished). But another rule is especially important to the untenured professor: "Knowing when you are being co-opted": "In many cases the issue of co-optation does not arise, because the committee itself is not a controversial one or because you do not feel all that strongly about the issues before it. Sometimes, however, you may feel that you are being asked to join a politically meaningful committee because you represent a constituency or a point of view" (62). As Shirley Wilson Logan's profile reveals, many women of color, for example, find themselves being asked to serve on a multitude of committees, so that they might bring a "minority's" perspective to the issue. If this is the case,

> you must decide (a) not to join, if it compromises your point of view, because joining usually means compromising; (b) to join with an eye to representing your point of view but accepting the need to compromise; or (c) to join order to fight for your position but risk marginalization on the committee by doing so. None of these three alternatives is the "right2 one, but you should understand what you are getting yourself in for. (Smelser 62)

Serving on hiring committees and other potentially emotionally (and territorially) inflected committees can be a potential danger zone for the untenured faculty member. In short, committee work—and other forms of faculty governance—has the potential to sidetrack, or worse, undermine your career. But, according to Smelser, "If committee service is transparently not at center stage in your career, how does it fit in?" (98):

> Committee work is found under the categories of service to the university and service to the profession and community. As a rule, these two kinds of activity do not count very heavily in the minds of deans and personnel committees. Even if your performance is stellar in these areas, you are not likely to be rewarded by merit increases or promotions, especially if your research is poor or non-existent and your teaching is mediocre or bad. But if you are completely inactive with respect to service, this will catch up with you and your career, especially if, in the long haul, you earn the unenviable rap that you do not pull your oar. (98–9)

Service work also offers you the opportunity to diversify your network by meeting and working with people in your department who may be outside your field, and who may thus discover that rhet/comp folks aren't so inadequate. It affords you the opportunity to make connections with people who may be voting on your tenure and/or promotion case—either at the departmental level or at the college-wide or university-wide tenure and promotion committees.

Although perhaps unlikely as a junior faculty member, you may also have the opportunity to serve on national association committees, such as the Rhetoric Society of America, or the American Society for the History of Rhetoric. Service to these organizations will not only help you network but will also help build your national reputation as a "player" in rhetoric and composition studies. (In many tenure and promotion guidelines, candidates are asked to demonstrate that they have a national or even international reputation for scholarly excellence.) The people with whom you serve may even end up writing you external letters of reference for your case.

In sum, Smelser writes:

> we can envision three possible career approaches to working on committees. First, you may avoid it altogether. As I have indicated, it is not mandatory for you to participate in committee life, even though failing to do so may have some long-term and indirect negative effects on your career. But if you know yourself to be inept or if you have an unbounded distaste for committee work, you can avoid it by consistently saying no. Sooner or later, moreover, you will not have to say no, because you will cease being asked because you have developed a reputation of being a nonserver … . Second, and at the other extreme, is the committee "junkie," who makes committee service a way of life, compulsively seeking out and serving on every possible committee … . While they often serve the institution well in this capacity, committee "junkies" are frequently the target of ambivalence on the part of their colleagues, because [they may be seen as] shortchanging their other professional obligations of research and teaching. You must be on guard against overserving … . The more effectively you serve, the more often you will be asked to serve again, because administrators and others appreciate your contributions and profit from your free labor. The third career line is intermediate between the two extremes, and, not surprisingly, is the one I recommend. … the role of making responsible and effective committee work a part of your career, but not letting it get out of hand. To safeguard against the latter, it is necessary to maintain two kinds of balance: 1. Balance between committee work and other career considerations … . 2. Balance among different kinds of committee work. (100–1)

Women are advised to be especially vigilant about maintaining and working towards such balances. As women, we may be asked more often than our male counterparts to serve, and to do the lion's share of the work—especially if it entails writing anything: the minutes, the reports, etc. Women, also, as you are probably painfully aware, have difficulty in saying "no" to requests for help or service. Ms. Mentor writes:

> Too many newish professors, especially women, are seduced into thinking that without them, committees will die, their sacred tasks undone. Committees need someone to show up and make the decisions seem important. And few women, even in these liberated days, can resist that siren call: "You are needed" (the academic equivalent of "You are loved") … . Yet Ms. Mentor knows that you do need to be on committees—to be a good department citizen, and to learn how the university works (few corporations are so arcane). The best committees, if you have a choice, have a finite task with a deadline. They meet infrequently, are publicly known and acclaimed, and include professors from other departments, so you'll get to know people. The worst are standing departmental committees that meet every week, generate endless paperwork (minutes, plans, schemes), and will continue to do so, world without end. If they are also about salary recommendations, you can easily make enough enemies in six months to choke your possibilities for tenure forever. (Toth, "Fear")

Teaching

Although the category of teaching is ostensibly a "real" category—unlike the category of service—that is, one that "counts" toward tenure and promotion decisions, at most institutions, the category of research is typically the one category that your colleagues will examine, scrutinize, and value the most. This is not to demean, of course, the value of excellent pedagogical practices; it is, rather, to realistically advise you as to how to focus your pre-tenure energies. Additionally, this is not to advise you to ignore or to be derelict in your role as a teacher. However, stereotypical feminine behaviors, which we have been engendered to embrace, may actually work against our scholarly productivity: we may spend more time working with students to the detriment of our scholarly work (see Chrisler's "Teacher vs. Scholar"). In sum, continually remind yourself, as you journey toward your tenure and promotion judgment, that although you will need to develop an excellent teaching record, you ought not do so at the expense of your scholarship.

Two sources for helping you to develop an excellent teaching record are the relevant chapters in Robert Boice's *Advice for New Faculty Members*, as well as "Developing a Tenurable Teaching Record" from Whicker et al's *Getting Tenure*, which advises that you teach to your strengths; in pre-tenure years, stick to the kinds of courses that work well for you, in format and in content. Although you may be asked to teach courses that are outside your strengths, you will have some input as to what the majority of your teaching assignments are. Whicker et al write: "Here you are well advised before tenure to develop a reasonable number of courses that you teach well and stick to them. Even if you are curious about other subfields and wish to expand into new areas, resist doing so until after you have tenure. Before tenure, your time is better spent teaching and refining courses you do well and developing your tenure in other areas, especially publishing" (92). If you teach a class in a format you enjoy (large lecture or small group), in a field that you have developed some mastery of, you will not only need to spend fewer hours preparing for class (or worrying about class), but also your student evaluations will be/should be stronger, as students tend to reward confident teachers with praise.

The bulk of the portion in your dossier documenting teaching effectiveness will most likely be taken up by student evaluation scores and comments. Additionally, you will most likely have comments from colleagues who have sat in on a class or two taught by you, but, again, the bulk of your documentation will be in the form of student commentary, which means that your tenure case depends in some part on the way that students perceive your teaching effectiveness. This, of course, as Susan A. Basow's research demonstrates, puts you in a double bind: You have just been advised to resist stereotypical feminine behaviors of nurturing and attending to your students, which may put you at risk of not being seen as a scholar by your colleagues. However, as Basow reports, students require that female teachers "demonstrate traditionally feminine traits of warmth, friendliness, helpfulness, and interest in students, in addition to professional competency, in order to get good student ratings" (146). Male professors need only demonstrate professional competency to receive equivalent student ratings (146).

One survey respondent noted that student perceptions and expectations are regionally, if not nationally, inflected, as well as gendered. She writes:

> Where I have been recently hired, students in Western Canada (as opposed to Ohio) were used to a much more authoritative persona than the one I projected, and were used to lecture-memorization classrooms. I wanted a collaborative, inquiry-based classroom and wanted to be myself and be humble. However, they interpreted this persona and teaching method as weakness and a lack of organization. It is as if they took advantage of my vulnerability instead of taking opportunity to make the course more their own by participating alongside me. I got mostly horrible student evaluations at the end of the term, and a few good evaluations. Some other young female professors (more seasoned than I) have advised me to put on my armor and be tough, not to show any weakness at all. I didn't feel comfortable with that, since I aim to teach civic participation in which the authority figure is flexible and open to good persuasion and students have the real hope of effecting change through their in-class rhetoric. The advice of older professors (male and female) berated the students, but encouraged me to keep up with my pedagogical program and just do it with more confidence and not worry about student evaluations. Next term I will try my best to adapt to

> my audience: to explain to students the methods I use and show them how they are the best adapted to achieving the goals I set out to achieve.

In order to win the student-evaluations-number game, you are being asked, therefore, to do some difficult juggling: attend to your students and be nurturing; yet, do so at your own peril with your male colleagues. Such juggling takes constant vigilance.

Hence, it may be wise to supplement student evaluations with additional documentation of your teaching effectiveness. As mentioned above, one alternate form of documentation is to have your colleagues sit in on your classes to observe and to provide a written evaluation of the experience. Sample assignments and syllabi are additional documents that help you make your case, as is evidence of teaching awards received. Another way to document your teaching effectiveness is to make your pedagogical practice a topic of research. Ernest Boyer, in his *Scholarship Reconsidered*, calls this "the scholarship of teaching." As the field of rhetoric and composition is considered primarily a teaching profession, you might find a way to harmonize your teaching practices and your theoretical and scholarly work, by researching and writing about your pedagogical efforts and your students (just be sure to apply for your human subjects' approval!). The attending published articles can document your "scholarship of teaching."

Your teaching responsibilities necessitate that you attend to students, not only in the classroom, but also out of class, such as during office hours:

> To demonstrate that you care about student intellectual development, try to have an open-door policy at least part of the time. This means explaining office hours to the students and inviting them to visit in those periods to talk about the class or any problems they may be having in it. When they see you in your office and actually talk with you outside of class, they see you in more human terms. If you are accessible, concerned, and show students you care about them, they may even grow to like you. There is nothing unethical about being liked. Yet enthusiastic and youthful professors should guard against encouraging crushes and infatuations that some students may develop. Do this by focusing on intellectual topics and avoid discussing your own personal affairs. Meeting with students during regular, predictable office hours establishes a comfort zone. Let students know that you are accessible and approachable and are willing to develop a relationship that will allow you to enhance their intellectual growth and development. But you are their mentor and teacher, not their buddy or date. If they temporarily forget the difference, you should not. Interactions with graduate students may be more intense as you guide major seminar papers, serve on thesis and dissertation committees, and

> advise them on career options. Yet the basic principles of an open-door policy that applied to undergraduate students also applies to graduate students. (Whicker et al 95)

One survey respondent advised that a balance between students and scholarship could be achieved if a candidate were: "to give no more than six months out of the year to her students and her program. The other six, she should put her own writing and research first."

Such a balance is particularly difficult to achieve when working with graduate students. Although there is a certain amount of official and unofficial mentoring expected in regards to your undergraduate students, the expectation—and responsibility—of mentoring graduate students makes a greater demand on your time. Robert A. Gross, in "From 'Old Boys' to Mentors," characterizes this responsibility as such:

> The adviser's responsibility, it seems to me, is to assist students in their particular efforts to acquire professional standing—to call pertinent opportunities to their attention, to read and react to proposals, fellowship applications, conference papers, prospectuses, job letters, and the like, and to foster an awareness of the numerous ways that graduate education can be employed inside and outside the academy, both for a livelihood and in service to the larger community.

This responsibility led Gross to create a statement, which can be accessed online, which details the roles and responsibilities of both parties: graduate student and adviser ("The Adviser-Advisee Relationship"). In his discussion of these responsibilities, he acknowledges that he used to host meals and other such gatherings, but has subsequently stopped doing so, acknowledging that such gatherings could be misconstrued as inappropriate advances. He goes on to say, however, that encounters with students—graduate or otherwise—need not be sterile and impersonal:

> An adviser need not avoid personal conversations with students, but these should serve as opportunities to facilitate academic progress and chart professional paths, not as exercises in amateur psychological counseling. My practice is to ask students what is at stake for them, intellectually and professionally, in a particular project or course of action and to build a conversation from that. ("From" para. 17)

One respondent noted the difficulty of negotiating the boundaries of such personal conversations. She writes:

> I also found it hard to get used to life on a commuter campus where

> students have unstable lives. Little in my training prepared me for learning to respond to students who sit in my office and confide in me about sexual abuse, horrid divorces, employment and health problems, etc. I've had to learn a lot on my own about what's an appropriate, caring, response.

You'll also want to follow up on institution-wide resources for helping students deal with such issues. For example, the University of Georgia's Center for Teaching and Learning provides a directory for handling sensitive student issues; this directory informs the instructor what on-campus resources are available to assist students, such as professional counseling for students with emotional stress or victims of sexual assault, so that the instructor can refer the student to an appropriate resource of qualified aid.

Research

Above all, as you traverse this tenure-track journey, "keep writing and keep your options open .... [W]riting is the key to tenure-track jobs, and publishing is the only way you can move if you need to" (Toth, *Ms. Mentor's Impeccable Advice* 167). Of the three tenure and promotion categories, your research will be the determining and defining category, as our survey respondents noted: "Publication is the coinage of power; if you want the freedom to move, if you want academic respect, you must develop a strong research program and pursue it diligently. In doing so, seek the help of mentors (of both sexes) to help you do so and to protect you from demands on your time that will make this impossible." And when asked what she might do if she were to begin her career all over again, one respondent writes: "I would have spent less time on service and trying to gain my colleagues' respect and more time on my own writing," and yet another: "I would launch my scholarly research agenda more thoroughly—spend more time setting it up and less time on administration in the early years." These are wise words, particularly in academe's current climate of ever-rising research and publication expectations for tenure (Wilson, "A Higher Bar for Earning Tenure").

As a rhetoric and composition scholar, you will face challenges in your pursuit of a research agenda. Many of our respondents indicated that, although they published in rhetoric and composition, they may have been degreed and/or interested in other areas of research, usually of a literary nature. The difficulty of maintaining two research agendas in two different areas can be problematic. This is what our respondents had to say:

> Probably the two most difficult challenges were bridging the gap between my life as a literary scholar and as a rhetorician. When I began my job I had just completed a rhetorical dissertation on Shakespeare, which became eventually my first book. I also had to

> develop graduate courses in Rhetorical Theory. Thus I wrote that first book with undergraduate Shakespeareans and graduate students in rhetoric, but taught no graduate classes in Shakespeare. Keeping up in two fields has been daunting but is finally starting to feel good!

One respondent reported that her first (unsuccessful) tenure case was a function of her department's "inexperience with handling a comp-rhet case: my literary stuff went to one set of reviewers, and my comp-rhet stuff to another, and of course each set said there wasn't enough for tenure here." She went on to say that if she were able to begin her career all over again, she would "probably stop trying to straddle the division between literature and comp-rhetoric. Sadly, because I think I would do less interesting work."

Whether you decide to attempt two research agendas or attempt one, professional scholars acknowledge that: "'Publish or perish' is not a canard for the mature academic professional. He or she must know how to do research and write up the results with sufficient quality as to qualify them for publication. In addition, he or she must be able to integrate research into the teaching process. Not-so-successful professionals may regard publication as an onerous chore and take refuge in claims about the quality of their teaching and the demands it makes on their professional life. But, it is clear that research and teaching are counterparts, and both are essential to professional growth" (Phillips et al, *Survival in the Academy* 132).

When you prepare reports for your annual review, your third-year review, and your tenure and promotion dossier, you will be asked to represent your "Research Agenda"—that is, an account of your research and writing goals and accomplishments. On this topic, our survey respondents provided us with two types of advice, potentially—but not necessarily—contradictory. The first type was advice to write what is "safe," what will give you "respect" from your colleagues—local or elsewhere, and what will "count" toward your tenure and/or promotion cases.

In regards to publishing work that is "safe," Rebecca Moore Howard, a survey respondent who chose to identify herself, offers this advice:

> I'd offer two pieces of advice: First, I'd give the same advice that a wise colleague, Sandra Jamieson, gave me when she saw that my work in authorship was going to make of me a controversial figure: she said that I also needed to take the time to publish in some of my less threatening interests—hence the *Bedford Guide to Teaching Writing in the Disciplines*. Sandra was talking about me establishing myself as a scholar who is developing established discourses as well as forging new ones. It was good advice for keeping myself grounded in the quotidian work of composition, rather than dashing off into ill-founded revisionist theory. My second piece of advice comes from a wise

> partner, who advised me not to publish the most controversial work until after I had tenure. Hence "Sexuality, Textuality" didn't come out until 2000.

In regards to publishing work that would garner "respect," one respondent reported that her greatest professional challenge was "Being at an institution that didn't value the type of research that I was doing." Another respondent reported that if she were to begin her career again, she would "develop scholarly interests that can win your work the respect it deserves in the academy; do not focus strictly on empirical research on college writing because it is associated with service and teaching more often than with scholarship." And another reported that, if she were to begin again, she would begin by "writing an important book that [would] firmly establish my expertise in the field."

In regard to publishing work that would "count" toward tenure and promotion decisions, most agree that one should focus on writing single-authored books. Sadly, as we know, co-authored works, particularly in fields such as ours, don't "count" as documentation of individual contributions to the discipline. Although the benchmark of the single-authored book as the tenurable case is due to change, as Peter Manning argues, "There are always going to be exceptions, but you would be really foolish to count on being one of them" (quoted in Ruark and Montell). One respondent, responding to this reality, wrote: "I have two pieces of advice. First, write a book as soon as possible. Second, prepare to be lonely." Chilling advice to be sure, as is this story:

> During the last year before I go for tenure, I have been told that my scholarship is lacking. Prior to this, I had been told that I was completely on track, and all my review letters suggest this. But now, one faculty member in Rhet/Comp and the chair (a new chair) have decided that I need to have a book, although that is not a requirement of my department. It's completely a power struggle. They don't necessarily want new scholarship; they told me to "slack and hack" my already published articles and turn them into a book. They assured me that I wouldn't have to do any new research to do it. I'm not sure what a "slack and hack" book would add to my field, but the rhet/comp professor (a woman) assured me that it was a "quickie." (This particular professor loves to use masculinized sex terms to describe things.) The Rhet/comp professor said that if she were an outside reviewer, she wouldn't write a letter in support of me getting tenure because all I had were articles (some of which, mind you, are in the #1 journal in my area), even though our department's tenure guidelines say that we have to have 8–12 scholarly articles or a book.

Another, when asked what she would have done differently, if she were to begin her career again, reports:

> On the one hand, I want to say "write a book early in my career" because that is probably why I was denied tenure (even though a book wasn't formally required). On the other hand, I don't think the field needs a book from every just-out-of-grad-school assistant professor. I did a lot of important program building and mentoring in the six years when I wasn't writing a book that might have gotten me tenure. Maybe I would have passed on the job at the research institution that involved the administration of a writing center and computer classrooms. Maybe I should have waited a year and gotten a job at a smaller place where teaching and service count.

There are exceptions, of course, and both Stephen Greenblatt's open letter to the Modern Language Association and the MLA's Taskforce on Evaluating Scholarship for Tenure and Promotion's recommended that "the profession as a whole should … rethink the dominance of the monograph" (3). However, in *today's* university, the single-authored book remains the standard—often even when written guidelines advised otherwise. And our survey respondents urged new tenure-track rhetoricians to focus their research and writing time on the development of book-length work.

But this situation may be changing. Bizzell noted that the state of university presses today may soon dictate major shifts in the tenure requirements at both the college and university level. Though in recent years Holy Cross has required significant publications for tenure, it still does not require a book, and Bizzell told us that that may turn out to be a cutting-edge decision.

> One of the things I like about Holy Cross is that I really believe we tenure teacher-scholars. We value teaching very highly, and we value contributions to the community very highly. The profession is finally catching up with us. I don't know whether you're aware that MLA is getting involved in the "crisis in scholarly publishing." Look in the MLA publication *Profession 2002*, and you will see there a report from the MLA ad hoc committee on the crisis in scholarly publishing. Stephen Greenblatt wrote a letter saying, "Hey, wait a minute! This is crazy. Why are we requiring books for tenure?" Well, they're only questioning it now because they have to, because the presses are tanking, and they can't publish the stuff anymore. So it's sort of for venal reasons, but, fine, I'll take it. So the MLA publication committee, which I'm also a member of, is going to sponsor a special session at MLA 2003 asking: What do we do? If we want to stop this, if we want to turn things around, what do we do? They're going to have a forum and workshops on re-calibrating tenure criteria, and I'm going to make a presentation on how we do it at Holy Cross. They've asked me to do that. Because we were talking about this at the last committee meeting and I was kind of waxing eloquent about well this is what we've

> always done and blah blah blah, and they said, Yeah, great, we want you to come and talk about that. So that's something else I like about Holy Cross. It turns out we're cutting edge.

On the other hand, Sharon Crowley predicts, in *tomorrow's* university, the tenure bar is likely to go so high that tenure itself will become something of a "dead duck," a privilege granted only to a handful of stars and "stars in the making":

> Years ago, when we were working on the first Wyoming committee for CCCC (this would be in '87 or '88 I think), Jim Slevin remarked to me that some day universities would be structured like law firms. Five or six partners to manage things, and hundreds of clerks to do the work. I laughed at the time, thinking he was making a joke. He was right, of course, as he usually is. I see universities retaining around 15–25% of their faculty on tenured lines. The percentage depends on the prestige/status of the university or, for places that don't have that, the intensity of their desire to have it. Higher on either scale raises the percentage of tenured faculty. Affirmative action will be nodded to in hiring tenured faculty as long as doing so enhances public relations.
>
> In this regime all who receive tenure will be stars or stars-in-the-making. Tenure will be in place, not to secure academic freedom, but to protect universities from losing their expensive stars who won't sign on without it. I assume as well that more universities with pretensions to greatness will soon stop tenuring the assistant professors they do hire because they are a risk—nobody knows whether they will become stars or not. Harvard, UVA, others, seldom tenure the assistant profs they hire, and there is nothing to stop other places from pursuing this practice. The ivies and the higher-status public universities can wait for assistant profs to prove their star quality out in the boonies and then hire them away, as they have been doing for years now.

In this "regime," Crowley predicts, the university will be run much like a corporation: everyone who gets a PhD will teach, undergraduates will be taught solely "by untenured faculty on contingent contracts, and perhaps graduate students as well, using the 'life-experience' part-time model that is already in place in some disciplines (you hire Tom Brokaw to teach a grad class in Comm, for example)." In some disciplines, Crowley continues, the tenured stars will teach the occasional grad class, "if only to insure that their universities can attract the most talented graduate students." In other disciplines, stars won't teach at all but will be "wholly funded by subsidiaries of government and corporate agencies who need research." Untenured assistant professors, whose contracts will stipulate large teaching loads, will still be expected to publish, "and those who can will want to publish in order to become stars and therefore tenured. The rest will teach, teach, teach."

These grim predictions envision a very different/dismal response to the current "crisis in scholarly publishing" addressed in MLA's *Profession 2002*. University presses' sinking budgets have already made it extremely difficult for junior faculty members to get their all-important tenure books published. But whereas the MLA committee recommends that universities consider altering their tenure expectations in the face of this problem, Crowley is suggesting that the opposite is likely to happen: both the tenure bar and teaching loads will continue to rise. When we gasped at this possibility, Crowley gave us a reality check:

> As I'm sure you know, there are places now where the composition program is being run by untenured/untenurable faculty, and the cost savings of this expedient will not be lost on the VP for budget affairs. I can think of nothing that stands in the way of this scenario developing over the next ten to twenty years. It virtually assures a quiescent faculty, it's cost-effective, and the few stars are good for public relations. Please tell me I'm daft.

Whether the future of tenure and promotion will transmogrify as Crowley portends (and as Elizabeth Tebeaux predicts), the current tenure system in rhetoric and composition still holds the single-authored book as the gold-standard for successful candidates.

Additionally, successful candidates are expected to supplement the book publication with additional publications, particularly with articles that have been published in peer-reviewed journals. Further, as some institutions have been asked to note, one should publish in journals with reputations of rigorous repute, typically characterized by the rates of circulation and rejection. (See Chapter 1 for advice on publishing journal articles.) Other publication opportunities such as book reviews, text books, and edited collections can supplement a curriculum vitae, but caution must be taken that these projects do not take time away from those publications that do "count" in predictable ways (the single-authored book and well-placed, peer-reviewed journal articles). For example, one respondent noted that if she could have begun her career again, she would have "written fewer textbooks and gotten better contract terms for those I did write." Like textbooks, edited collections can be time-consuming with disproportionate CV cachet. William Germano, in fact, presents "10 Reasons Why You Shouldn't" produce an edited collection. It is time consuming, what might amount to herding a large number of authors, some of whom may end up writing subpar entries, some of whom may end up not writing entries at all; some compose entries beyond the word amount they have been allotted; some do not follow compositional instructions, and you, as an editor, must tactfully negotiate these authors—you may even need to track some authors down and threaten them, tactfully. All this work, and—as has been said many a time—this work does not, ultimately, "count" toward tenure and/or promotion. Having said that, Michelle Ballif acknowledges, she has found the process and product of an edited volume richly rewarding as it broadens her group of acquaintances in the field, and it provides another way to contribute to the general construction of knowledge in the field. Joseph M. Moxley's *Publish, Don't Perish: The Scholar's Guide to Academic Writing and Publishing* provides pragmatic strategies for writing the various kinds of academic projects, as does Gary A. Olson and Todd W. Taylor's *Publishing in Rhetoric and Composition*, and Joseph M. Moxley and Todd Taylor's *Writing and Publishing for Academic Authors.*

The other type of advice we received from our respondents suggested that you simply write about what you "love"—that you pursue those scholarly projects that provide you with passion and that fulfill you as a researcher. As Juanita Rodgers Comfort suggests, one has to "prepare for the ways in which [her] scholarly agenda, and the publishing potential attendant to that agenda, facilitates or constrains access to material rewards of the profession: account for how the 'market value' of the research [she has] chosen to pursue determines job offers, funding for research, tenure/promotion, and invitations to publish, lecture, edit, and review; understand the professional tradeoffs involved in pursuing a 'less marketable' research agenda."

Naomi J. Miller, in her essay "Following Your Scholarly Passions," writes:

> In the search for a balance between personal passions and scholarly trends, if you go with your heart, your niche in the field will emerge. The most fruitful topics for writing and research are rooted in our own passions and convictions. If you ignore your heart and attempt to focus your research instead on hot trends, the pressure of the market can cause you to lose your mind, even your soul. Your voice will lack authenticity, and you may never find your niche. It is important not to disregard the personal origins of our scholarship if we want to tap into the wellsprings of our own creativity.

A proportion of our respondents echoed these words; they advised: "Write about what interests you and don't think that you have to have all the answers before you can contribute meaningful information"; "write about what obsesses you"; "Do the research you want to do; don't just serve the system"; "Do, study, pursue things/issues you love or care about"; "Do what you love and find the most exciting and most full of possibilities for innovative research; do your own research and not someone else's! If you do what you love, you'll love what you do and people will recognize the merit of your work because you'll do it well. Don't let people sidetrack you with their pet projects."

As mentioned above, these two sets of advice may appear contradictory; however, they need not be. In any event, as Whicker et al advise: "When in doubt, write" (85).

Establishing a research agenda requires, of course, that one write and publish, but it also requires that you document and package that research agenda in such a way that it represents you as tenurable. Whicker, et al, advises you to: "Keep good records and copies of all your published and unpublished research .... You will likely be asked to include reprints of your journal articles in your tenure file, and you may be asked to include conference papers as well. Update the publications on your vita regularly, giving proper citations for articles and other research when it appears in print" (85). That is, have ready to hand the actual documents that establish your publication record, and hence that document your research agenda, but also package these publications in such a way that you can present yourself as having a focused, predetermined research agenda. Even if you have three, disparate areas of interest in which you publish, you will want—in your discussions with review committees and in formal reports—to present these publications (and work in progress) as contributing to a greater, focused, over-arching research agenda, so that all of your research will appear to have synergy; it is even helpful to hook your teaching and service contributions insofar as possible to the goals and accomplishments of your research agenda. You will most likely have to translate your work in terms that will be understandable (and perhaps non-threatening) to colleagues, department heads, deans, and tenure and promotion committees.

In short, you will want to: "Demonstrate a coherent ongoing research agenda. When reviewing your tenure file, most colleagues will want to see evidence that you have a coherent ongoing research agenda. If you are a scalpel scholar, the coherence will be more readily obvious than if you are a shotgun scholar. If you have published in a variety of areas, take pains in your personal statement to show the common themes in your research, pointing to articles and papers that fit into each theme or subarea do not appear to be too scattered .... Most important, colleagues and administrators will want evidence that you will continue to publish and conduct research after you receive tenure. Point out ongoing research projects and talk about future research and publishing goals" (Whicker et al 86).

You will also want to demonstrate how your research agenda has been received by fellow scholars in your field in order to establish your reputation as a scholar of rhetoric and composition. In more crass terms, this amounts to searching how many times (and where) your work has been cited and/or used in course syllabi, for example. Other than looking in the index of every new publication, you do have access to various searchable databases and search engines, including Web of Science; NetLibrary; Google Scholar; Academic Search Premiere; even Amazon's "Search Inside the Book" feature will help you mine for citations. These sources, as well as additional tips, can be found at the University of Georgia's Libraries Faculty Liaison's website: http://www.libw.uga.edu/liaison/citationsearch/citesources.html

Many faculty—especially women, who typically have household and childcare responsibilities—wish for teaching releases, grant monies, and other funding opportunities, which allow them the luxury of uninterrupted blocks of time to devote to their research agenda. Such release time however awarded is, indeed, a luxury; yet, as writing productivity expert Robert Boice demonstrates, faculty on release time are no more productive than the so-called "binge" writers, or procrastinators, whom he studies. Indeed, they were less productive than his so-called "regular" writers, those who see writing as part of their regular work day (76). Whicker et al advise that you: "Treat writing as a regular part of your job," which amounts to overcoming the bad habits of the procrastinating student, and acting like a professional, who views "writing and research as a regular part of the job of being a faculty member, setting aside a fixed amount of time in a week to pursue these activities. The bureaucratic model emphasizes regularity of effort rather than the motivation of impending deadlines" (83). One respondent advises similarly, when she writes: "Spend ten hours a week writing for publication. Ignore the papers that need grading, ignore the email that needs answering, unplug the phone, tell your family to go clean their rooms. It's the only way to keep your career going, and the first thing that suffers when you're busy. Don't put yourself last."

This advice echoes with the advice offered by the previously mentioned, writing-productivity expert Boice, who stresses the idea of the "brief, daily session"—based on his extensive research—to increase writing productivity. Although we recommend all of his work as compelling and motivating, his *New Advice for Faculty Members* offers a solid introduction to his work about writing but also applies these principles to teaching and serving, as well. Boice writes: "the great majority of new faculty struggle as scholarly writers; during years 1 and 2, over two-thirds of them produce virtually nothing that 'counts,' despite their earlier plans for substantial new output during that critical period … . For many newcomers, especially those caught up in busyness, this silence continues into years 3 and 4, often well beyond" (103). Boice accounts for this career-ending "silence," with a list of reasons, including:

1. Faculty never learned, as graduate students, to "*write with fluency and constancy.* … Instead, most worked on proposals and dissertations erratically and painfully, often procrastinating their writing far longer than they imagined possible. The mean length of time for dissertation completion in most disciplines … stands now at 4 years, depending on discipline, and is ever growing" (103–4).
2. "*They too often learned to work in isolation*": "Dissertation writers are traditionally left to work alone with little day-to-day direction, and with the expectation they will not bring written materials to committees until the work is essentially finished and perfect" (104).
3. "*Writing, by nature, seems more difficult*" (104), and hence more easily avoided than other work, such as committee work, or reading student papers, or cleaning toilets.
4. "*New faculty who do little of the writing they had planned for years 1 through 3 have so ready and sincere a defense that they can see no alternative explanation*. They are, they almost always say, too busy to write. In the

main, they felt too overloaded by teaching—preparing class materials, grading paper and tests, keeping office hours—to attend to writing in proper fashion. They complain that ongoing demands of teaching and committee work leave few of the large blocks of uninterrupted time they supposedly need for apt writing, or that when they've worked all day at other things, they have no energy or interest left for writing" (105) .

5. "*New faculty often reject simple, efficient ways of writing as counterintuitive, even as insulting*. That is, they prefer to do what they imagine geniuses do as writers: Struggle and suffer" (105).

Boice's simple and counterintuitive advice is: write regularly; write briefly. "What else, besides prewriting, distinguishes the most fluent and successful writers from the rest of us?" he asks. "They work at their craft daily."

> Recent studies of expertise and greatness confirm the importance of constancy. Outstanding writers, scientists, and artists work regularly, day in and day out, at their craft—for years and years of constant practice. They rely on coaches and social networks (even critics and detractors) to direct and hone their patterning of skills. And they learn to limit practice sessions to periods brief enough to minimize fatigue. They know that long, exhausting practice sessions not only persist beyond the point of diminishing returns but that those excesses associate working and performing with mindless rushing and sloppy habits. (137)

In short, write regularly—with constancy; and write briefly—with mindfulness. Translated: no more "binge-writing" and no more marathon (a.k.a. "large blocks of uninterrupted time") writing. See? It's counterintuitive. We all procrastinate ("I can't do *anything* without a deadline"). But, of course, we usually miss the deadline, anyway, sometimes embarrassingly beyond the original due date. And we all think we cannot write unless we have empty days or weeks or months. These two beliefs—or myths—according to writing experts, are the reasons why faculty fail to be as productive as they need to be—even to meet tenure and promotion requirements.

Boice's research bears this out: "In an ambitious attempt to document the effects of BDS [brief, daily sessions], I measured the writing habits and outputs of newly hired professors over six continuous years. I tracked two groups, each with 16 new faculty. The first group began and persisted with clear habits of binge writing. The second group started and continued as regular writers who worked mostly in BDSs" (143). His findings demonstrated that "self-described binge writers evidenced (1) more binges of writing in long, euphoric, fatiguing sessions; (2) fewer hours spent writing on average per week; (3) fewer manuscript pages produced overall; and (4) fewer total manuscripts submitted and accepted in refereed outlets through year 6 on campus" (143). The differences were remarkable … and devastating: "All 16 binge writers failed to write enough to gain retention and tenure; all 16 regular writers were awarded retention and tenure on schedule" (144).

Regular writers—that is, those who practiced brief, daily writing sessions—scheduled a regular time for writing, usually first thing in the morning, and wrote in the same, "comfortable and comforting" location (139). Boice defies any faculty member who says she is "too busy" to find time for a regular, daily writing session: "Every newcomer to the professoriate I've tracked could find at least 5- to 10-minutes a day, no matter how seemingly busy. And everyone I coached found ways, gradually, to add more and more time for writing, usually by utilizing several brief openings during workdays" (140). The clear message: find some time, even just 5 minutes, at first, to write daily.

"When writers work daily on projects—even very briefly—the ideas stay fresh in mind from day to day; so, less warm-up time is needed before writing the next day. … The habit of writing every day helps make the work more welcome, less a struggle. … Because they eventually provide a realistic sense of doing enough and of progressing fast enough, BDSs help reduce pressures to write quickly and perfectly in first drafts" (138). And, you'll be more productive. And, frankly, you'll feel better about yourself as a scholar: "It sounds self-righteous, I know," one faculty member told Boice, "but I feel good now about getting my writing done before I go to campus. It puts me in a bright mood for the day and I've needed that" (140).

Now that you've established your (synergistic) research agenda, disciplined yourself into writing during brief, daily sessions, given conference presentations in order to, as Krista Ratcliffe advises, "build an audience for your work," you have now produced a book manuscript, and you will need to find a venue for its publication. (Although, as Sharon Crowley told us: "not everything that emerges on your computer screen is publishable. When you realize this about something you are working on, make a file and put it away temporarily. Never throw anything away, though. You never know when you might be ready to write about something that was just a glimmer a year, or five years, earlier.")

Your book manuscript will most likely be a revision of your doctoral dissertation; however, as Whicker et al advise, "by all means … do not send the dissertation out unrevised, because everyone will recognize it precisely for what it is: a tortuously written, overly pedantic, unrevised dissertation" (81). (See Maureen M. Hourigan's "From Dissertation to Scholarly Monograph" in Olson's *Publishing in Rhetoric and Composition*.) According to Krista Ratcliffe, "The problems with not knowing how to write books *and* negotiate the publishing process are many: you may write an unpublishable manuscript, you may suffer from writer's block, you may sadly underestimate the time it takes to write the book, you may sadly underestimate the time needed to get your book through the publishing bureaucracy, you may not know what you can and cannot ask for in a book manuscript review (e.g., suggest readers) or in a book contract (e.g., as to retain copyright of your ideas or to have a hardcover *and* paper editions printed)." William Germano's *Getting It Published: A Guide for Scholars and Anyone Else Serious about Serious Books* is written by a former editor at Columbia University Press and Routledge. The book has three goals: "to explain how publishers select manuscripts and publish them; to help the serious writer best present his or her work so that its chances for acceptance will be significantly increased; to show how the process from submission to publication can be made to work, and work well, for both publisher and author" (x). The book succeeds in these goals, and should be of use to you, the hopeful author. It provides helpful strategies, such as how best to revise your work before submission, and it provides insights into the publisher's mind, such as "the fifty-page rule," which means that if a book does not succeed in the first fifty pages, then it will be rejected by the editor. For our purposes, we will focus on sharing the insight he provides about selecting a publisher. He writes: "In deciding which [publishing] house to contact, keep in mind that you're looking for three things: a publisher capable of bringing your book out well and selling it ably (a publisher you will want); a publisher that is likely to want your manuscript—and perhaps even offer you an attractive advance against royalties (a publisher who will want you); a publisher whose imprint will have a positive effect on your academic career (a publisher who will make others want you, too)" (44; see also 43–58). You'll first want to research the publishers to see what they publish, also known as their "lists." For the field of rhetoric and composition, you will note that the publishers that tend to publish works in our field are mainly these: Southern Illinois University Press, SUNY, NCTE, University of Pittsburgh, Hampton Press. Germano relates that his "favorite tool for academic authors is the excellent and under-utilized *AAUP Directory*, an annual publication of the Association of American University Presses. It's a paperback volume, available direct from the offices of the AAUP (71 West 23rd Street, Suite 901, New York, NY 10010)," which lists series, publishing interests, as well as editor contacts. Additionally, you may want to look at the publishers' websites to identify submission guidelines and contacts. If you meet directly with an editor—say at a book exhibit during the 4Cs—Germano advises that you

> keep these tips in mind: *Think of a meeting at a book exhibit as a polite, introductory exchange, not an exhaustive session on your favorite topic.* Every editor knows the moment when the editorial eyes glaze over and a complete stranger launches into a numbing summary of Chapter 8. *If someone known to the editor has recommended the house, say so.* It breaks the ice. It might also help the editor get a quick fix on your work. *Don't plan on handing an editor a packet of manuscript.* Mail it as a follow-up to your chat. *Accept a firm 'it's not for us' as graciously as you can.* An editor may know immediately that your project doesn't fit that press's list. But by all means feel free to ask for suggestions where you might next turn. *If you've had an encouraging conversation at the exhibit, follow up with a note within a week.* Most

> editors have far too much to do after an academic convention. Writing promptly will help keep your name in the editor's mind. *Get an editor's business card.* Even if you're unable to wangle an appointment, you can walk away with contact details and follow up quickly to the right person at the correct address. (51)

Germano admits that: "This book can't choose a press for you. But some generalizations may help you come to the right decision: *The larger the house, the greater its resources.* The greater the resources, the greater the publisher's expectations. This can work for or against your book. *The more important your book is to that house, the more attention it will receive.* The small pond may be perfect for your book. Or it may be too small to do the book justice. *An enthusiastic editor is your champion.* But an editor can't make it all happen by herself. *A highly targeted book has been known practically to sell itself.* But help from the publisher would be deeply appreciated" (56).

Once you decide on which publishing house might have an interest in your manuscript, you will want to send a letter of inquiry—do not call the editor unexpectedly nor email him/her. Be sure to identify the correct contact name—editor—to whom you need to address this letter, and then do so, correctly, by name. The letter serves as a introduction to yourself and to your project: it will, Germano instructs, identify your credentials, and describe the project: its title, its nature, its audience, and its degree of completion. Germano's book is very helpful in that it contains sample letters of proposal—the good, the bad, and the ugly. Germano notes that it is perfectly acceptable to send out multiple inquiry letters to varying presses; however, if you actually submit the manuscript, it is considered unethical to do so without informing all involved (57–8).

If your letter of inquiry is positively received by an editor, he or she will most likely ask you to send the entire manuscript, or a portion thereof, for review in the form of "readers' reports," much like the peer-review process in place for peer-reviewed journals. Germano writes: "Readers' reports can be secured at more than one stage in a manuscript's life. Typically, these junctures are *Submission of a complete manuscript, partial manuscript, or proposal.* If your editor likes your project, whatever its stage, a report is the next step. *Delivery of the completed manuscript.* If you have a contract for a book you haven't completed, expect to have the finished manuscript sent to an outside reviewer. *Delivery of the revised completed manuscript.* And if you have been required to revise your manuscript to accommodate concerns voiced by the first reader's report, expect that the project will again be sent out for review—either to the reader who reviewed it initially, or to yet someone else" (81). The reader is attempting to answer several questions: "Does this manuscript make a significant contribution to the field"? "Does the author demonstrate a mastery of the scholarly literature? What are the particular strengths or weaknesses of the manuscript? What is the project's intended audience?" "What books are the project's competition in the market?" (84).

"How many readers does it take to answer a publisher's concern? According to a long-standing tradition in the university press world, a manuscript must have *two* positive readers' reports" (88). Sometimes a series' editor counts as one review. In light of reports, the editor will decide to reject or to send it on to next step: Then it goes to the "board" which is a group of faculty members, "composed of professors from disciplines in which the press publishes or hopes to publish," who typically meet monthly (83). If the "board" approves the publication of your manuscript, you will be sent a contract. Given the technical nature of this part of the process, we direct you to the chapter in Germano's book that deals explicitly with contracts (97–119).

During this process of manuscript submission (and the same applies to journal-article submissions), you will be subject to the slings and arrows of readers' reports. Unfortunately, some of these comments can be quite mean. Whicker et al advise that you: "Develop a tough ego to be able to handle negative reviews" (83). If not too embarrassed to do so, we often share readers' reports that we have received with our closest friends, so they can shore up our egos, as well as interpret the reports without the emotional inflection or blinders. "A good strategy when an editor returns a verdict is to read an initial decision, quickly read critical reviews, and then set them aside for a week or so while working on other things. This brief hiatus gives you a week or so to accommodate the emotional reality of having to revise the piece on which you have long labored, in some instances, having to make fundamental changes. After a week or two, reread the reviews carefully and seriously to develop a strategy and schedule for making specific changes" (Whicker et al 84). When you return a revised manuscript, in your cover letter, "assist editors and reviewers to see how your revised manuscript has accommodated their concerns … [;] if reviewer-specified changes are not possible, indicate to the editor why" (84).

To thrive as an assistant professor necessitates carefully negotiating a series of real and competing demands on your time, as you strive to succeed as a teacher and a scholar. In addition, as the next chapter will detail, you most likely will have to deal with administrative responsibilities and the challenges of departmental and university life. To succeed, as one survey respondent advised, "remind yourself that you are a professional." And then behave as a professional: a professional teacher, scholar, and colleague.

4

SUCCEEDING DESPITE IT ALL

Administration, Politics, and Difficult People

> [If I could begin my career again,] I would better inform myself of the difficulties of "making it"; I would know better than to assume that one could "make it" on one's focused excellence.
>
> —anonymous survey respondent

We heartily agree with one survey respondent who noted that "there can be enormous professional satisfaction in this field." Many even find great satisfaction in administrative responsibilities, although that work presents additional challenges and demands. Yet, unfortunately, that sense of satisfaction can be tempered by the need to negotiate political quagmires and pits of despair dug by difficult (often *very difficult)* people with whom you must work—and with whom you must remain collegial. This is not to say that all of your colleagues will be difficult. Indeed, you will find, as have we, that your colleagues may become research collaborators and dear friends. However, there will be moments when people, politics, and administrative demands challenge your quest for success. "Making it" often means succeeding despite it all.

Administration Responsibilities and Challenges

As a professional in the world of rhetoric and composition, you will most likely be asked to assume some kind of administrative duty, most likely as a writing program administrator. As we've noted before, an overwhelming number of our survey respondents urged tenure-track women to avoid, insofar as possible, administrative duties until they are not only tenured, but—according to one respondent—in "the late associate professor stage." When asked what she would do differently if she were beginning her career again, this same respondent added: "I would not let the department guilt me into being responsible for their writing program or center." This sentiment was echoed resoundingly by survey respondents. One wrote: "Do NOT take on ANY administrative work of ANY kind other than regular committee service prior to being awarded tenure. In particular, do NOT accept a WPA position of any kind."

Joan C. Chrisler, Linda Herr, and Nelly K. Murstein, in their co-written essay "Women as Faculty Leaders," offer a differing perspective. They write: "If junior faculty wait until after they are tenured to involve themselves in faculty governance, they fail to develop the track record that earns them the opportunity to be perceived as faculty leaders" (190). The authors urge women to involve themselves in faculty governance, otherwise "More and more decisions will be turned over to professional staff and administrators. The faculty will lose its traditional control over the curriculum, subject matter, methods of instruction, faculty status, the requirements for and awarding of degrees, and aspects of student life that relate to the educational process" (190).

Our survey respondents, however, seemed uniform in their advice to avoid administrative—especially writing program administrative—positions until after tenured. Sometimes their advice was conflicted, however. When asked what she would do differently, one respondent told us: "I would have spent less time in administration and focused more fully on my true love: mentoring and teaching. Of course, it is usually as WPA that you get the chance to do the most mentoring of graduate students." But, again, the time-constraints of administration are very real. She writes that that the most difficult part of her career has been, "trying to manage the tension between taking care of other people's goals and projects, especially graduate students' work and needs, as well as administrative responsibilities in WPA and WAC, with my own research." And another wrote that her most difficult challenge was her "administrative work as associate director of composition. It has been much more time consuming and mentally exhausting than I anticipated. I have had a very tough time balancing administrative duties (including what I think should be done by other administrators but isn't going to get done unless I do it!), teaching, and doing some small bit of research . . . . I pitched myself as someone interested in WPA work when I went on the job market and now I'm not so sure . . . . I'd at least go for a position that didn't require me to do them for several years." And yet another:

> I have been WPA for 7 of the 9 years since I was hired here. Balancing the demands of being WPA (the program has 80–85 faculty and 3,800 students a semester) with the need to research and publish has been really difficult. For the first few years, I had major time-management problems, primarily because I had trouble saying "no" at work, which extended my days to the extent that going home in the evening, I had no mental energy left. Having a supportive husband and understanding children has made a great deal of difference—something reinforced by talking to other WPAs who were not so lucky.

That women need to be urged against assuming a writing program administrative position as an untenured faculty member indicates the widespread practice of, according to Theresa Enos, "burdening *untenured* faculty with directing a writing program"—and this "burden," Enos notes, "falls mostly to women."

She speculates that "[m]any times an untenured assistant professor who is a woman is given the job of director of first-year English so that change is kept to a minimum. Many times she is expected, or forced, to act as a care-taker rather than become an innovative administrator because to step out of the drawn lines means risking alienating tenured members of the department who most likely have had some hand in shaping the program" ("Gender and Publishing" 565). One survey respondent's story lends credence to this theory. She reports that her most difficult challenge was

> taking on WPA work [in] my second year of employment with a workforce of lecturers who had taught at the institution for 10–20 years and who enjoyed a sort of defacto tenure. Most were not trained in rhet comp but had developed teaching expertise over the years on their own and by reading textbooks. I was hired to work in computers and composition and most of these lecturers were computer phobic. In addition, my predecessor, who had run the writing program for 12 years, became chair. Hence I was in effect working for/with about 30 tenured people under the pretense of reviving/rethinking the comp program and becoming a "leader" under a chair who had no intention of letting any change in policy or procedure come into effect.

It is no secret that the time and energy required to administer a writing program is time and energy not spent on researching and publishing—often resulting in negative consequences when an untenured WPA is reviewed for tenure and promotion. But what Enos and our survey respondent articulate here is the unspoken challenge faced by writing program administrators: often one is ostensibly hired or appointed as a WPA in order to effect change and innovation; however, the dirty secret is that the powerless (untenured, most likely female) WPA is hired or appointed precisely so that no change could be effected. And damn the earnest woman who tries.

Clearly, the message is: writing program administration takes substantial energy away from other career obligations: teaching and publishing. An additional message: writing program administration subjects one to overt and covert political battles. Yet WPA work has its joys and satisfactions, and it most certainly will increase your professional visibility and your authority on campus. One of the keys to the "queendom," then, is to negotiate or to balance administrative obligations and to learn how to administer effectively.[4]

To this end, one respondent wrote:

> Assuming that she will have, at some point in the near future if not right now, an administrative appointment, I would offer this advice: 1. Cultivate listening skills; 2. Set priorities so that you are not always reacting to forces/pressures around you; you can influence your work environment; 3. Learn to say "no," "Let me think about that and get back to

> you," and "I can't undertake that project right now, but if you want to proceed, I fully support you. Let me know how it goes."; 4. Remember that writing is central to our field—keep your identity as a writer, make time for your writing (whatever form it takes), since every writing administrator and teacher must also be a writer.

And another: "Recognize that some sort of administrative position is inevitable—prepare for it by taking courses (if they're offered) or by shadowing the WPA/Writing Center Director for a time and learning what to expect. Then plan how to handle conflicting demands and set a research agenda accordingly."

Given the historical role that composition programs have played in the curricular requirements of the modern university (see Crowley; Connors; Susan Miller; Berlin), the demand to administer some kind of writing program is a very real one for scholars in the field of rhetoric and composition, as one respondent advises: "Be aware that unless you are primarily interested in composition administration, job opportunities are very limited." Indeed, the institutional conflation of rhetoric and composition studies (as a discipline) with first-year composition administration (as a curricular service) has spawned a diminution of the profession, as well as of the work of the (mostly female) professionals who administer this "service" (see Crowley; Susan Miller). This predicament, as detailed in WPA narratives such as those in Diana George's edited volume *Kitchen Cooks, Plate Twirlers, & Troubadours,* results in "administrative burnout" (survey respondent), as documented by Laura R. Micciche in "More than a Feeling: Disappointment and WPA Work."

Think of Administrative Work as Professional Development and Scholarship

Although we may have little influence on the institutional devaluation of our field, we can take steps to protect our careers—if not our well-being. Jeanne Gunner, in "Professional Advancement of the WPA: Rhetoric and Politics in Tenure and Promotion," argues that the "first and best thing a WPA who is hoping to advance professionally can do is to join the WPA organization, the Council of Writing Program Administrators … . Its journal, *WPA: Writing Program Administration*, is an outlet for WPA scholarship and a source of historical, theoretical, and practical knowledge for all who direct or participate in writing programs" (316–17). The WPA also supports workshops and conferences, as well as a research grant program. Gunner continues, "Professional membership is a way of establishing professional identity. The benefits can't be overestimated: once you make national contact, a wealth of professional opportunities open up. There really is a network out there, and at whatever point you enter it, you gain access to professional projects and sites that provide opportunities for your own professional development. And when you come up for tenure [or promotion], you'll need a community of scholars who can be called on to evaluate your work. The Council of Writing Program Administrators is the primary site for national connection" (322). Joining a national-level community of like-minded administrators will not only provide you with a support group and perhaps a mentor or role model but also with a space for professional development as well as a forum for turning your administrative work into scholarship.

This is important especially for female writing program administrators, as Sally Barr-Ebest's "Gender Differences in Writing Program Administration" details. Although male and female WPAs have many similarities in training and responsibilities, men "publish more, they are paid more, and they are more likely to be tenured" (53). Significantly, Barr-Ebest found that female WPAs spent more time on their administrative duties, presumably time that could have been spent on writing and research agendas, speculating that they did so due to gender-specific norms, including the expectation that women take on nurturing roles and the tendency for women to assume all responsibilities without delegation.

At whatever stage in your career you may find yourself as an administrator—whether as an assistant professor looking towards promotion to associate or as an associate moving toward full professor—you will be wise to fastidiously document your contributions as a WPA and be aware of the realities and politics in tenure and promotion cases, as Gunner details: "Helping colleagues to understand WPA as an academic and scholarly endeavor has been and is a difficult task, and it's likely to continue for some time to be the pivotal issue in WPA tenure cases. Finding time to do research and publish as we direct a writing program is a major challenge, but the level of productivity will not be a factor if the nature of our work is not first valued as scholarly, as in and of itself a foundation for tenure consideration" (315).

Barr-Ebest concurs and advises that a WPA "Educate your dean, department chair, and tenure committee ... . Once your role has been defined, present a completed statement to the department and request that it be made an official part of the guidelines for tenure and promotion. Keep requesting until it's adopted" (68). Gunner continues: "To sound the theme again: WPAs have often been blindsided in the actual review process when they discover, too late, that much of their scholarly administrative work has been discounted. The risks are especially high in traditional literature departments, where not only scholarly administrative work but any work in rhetoric-composition may be seen as second-class, as not true scholarship. And such biases can prevail even in the most collegial environments; as with any unexamined bias, such views can be invisible to those who hold them and then surface at what, for the candidate, is a critically decisive moment" (321). As one survey respondent reported:

> My confidence-shaking event didn't happen to me but to a male colleague. He was denied tenure in his last year after receiving a positive endorsement every previous year. He had published very little, but had been told (as I was) that the administrative work he was doing would be sufficient. Devastated by his experience, and fearing that his betrayal by

> people he trusted did not augur well for my own future, I began to look elsewhere, but at the same time, I talked to my chair (not a Rhet/Comp person). He totally supported the innovations I wanted for the Writing Program and was determined that I succeed. He offered me the opportunity to write a major grant which funded construction/remodeling for computer classrooms, hardware and software purchases, and faculty development. The project—*and the attendant articles*—then resulted in the administrative work I was doing being recognized by the University, and I was tenured and promoted.

The respondent's emphasized clause "*and the attendant articles*" underscores the significant point, as Barr-Ebest advises: "Publish. [Y]ou are unlikely to get tenure, promotion, or merit pay in comprehensive and doctoral level institutions if you don't publish. Writing program administration offers a wealth of opportunities for research. Decide what you're interested in and what methodology suits your temperament and writing style, and start collecting data" (68). A plethora of publications exist that make the case for writing program administration as "intellectual work"—not only prepared statements, as previously referenced, such as "Evaluating the Intellectual Work of Writing Administration" and the MLA's "Making Faculty Work Visible: Reinterpreting Professional Service, Teaching, and Research in the Fields of Language and Literature," but also scholarly treatments of WPA work. Hopefully, the reader will appreciate that these defenses are *publications* and hence serve not only to articulate the contributions of WPAs to the university beyond "service," but that they also serve as contributions to the scholarly conversation that is rewarded by tenure and promotion committees.[5]

"Tenure [and promotion] has historically been associated primarily with research and publication, secondarily with teaching excellence, and almost never with administrative expertise" Gunner reminds us (319). When you do prepare your tenure and/or promotion dossier, keep this in mind (and keep Gunner's article handy). Gunner advises that you document everything: "Administrative work, too, should be documented: procedures you develop for scheduling, handling grade disputes, staff oversight, and hiring issues" (320). Given rhetoric and composition's historical relationship to institutional "service," this bit of advice is particularly savvy:

> Be especially careful in defining which aspects of your work will be placed in the service category, since much of what we know to be intellectual work for a WPA might appear to be service to those unfamiliar with the field. While a WPA's service work is apt to be more extensive and specialized than that of a regular faculty member, you might not want your service profile to look radically different from a typical faculty member's; you do not want to tilt the sense of the whole away from scholarship by creating a service-heavy impression. (320–1)

And Gunner further advises that you educate your tenure and promotion committee as to the work you do. Gunner describes how to do so and provides a sample of an ill-written personal statement and a revised one. Her essay also includes an annotated bibliography.

In this same article, Gunner also provides solid advice on how to negotiate the appointment of a WPA position, as well as the resulting contract. Prior to accepting the position is the "ideal time," she notes, to negotiate the terms for your administrative work that will protect your professional development and advancement (316). Some of her advice: Begin your negotiations with the job description, consulting the Portland Resolution, which "provides a guideline for defining the WPA position and working conditions" (317). She next advises: Define the terms of the contract, of expectations, of benefits and support. "Defining terms is always a good place to start with any project … , [b]ut terms can be renegotiated, so it's not too late to review all [terms] even if you've been in the position for a year or more. The only bad plan is to use your tenure review as the opening point in a dialogue on institutional expectations" (319).

Irene Ward offers additional advice which could be helpful when negotiating the terms of a WPA position: review the job description and duties annually with your department chair (or whoever is your immediate supervisor). She writes: "A large change or a number of smaller changes outside a writing program can innocently swell a WPA's duties and tasks. Keep records of each of these changes and discuss the impact they have on your job with your head or chair at your annual review" ("Developing" 58–9). And, Ward, also urges: "*Negotiate for the training you need: supervisory skills, leadership, and management*" (59). Her bibliography provides a list of companies offering seminars and other professional development opportunities.

Keys to Effective and Credible Leadership

As a leader of a writing program (or even of a search committee), you will need and want to develop effective leadership and administrative skills. For some women, due to the engendering process and life-experiences, assuming a leadership role is a difficult, if not impossible, task, especially given the fact that the writing program administrator position itself is often seen as a subordinate role and even gendered as female, as Susan Miller and others have argued. One result is that your work may very well be devalued, as "women's work"; another is that your administrative work may be subject to gendered expectations—that is, that you should behave "as a woman"—perhaps overtly nurturing or easy to push around. One survey respondent noted: "After I became an administrator, I was surprised at the ways in which my colleagues 'personalized' my decisions. When I made judgments with which some people disagreed, my decision was attributed to personal factors in my life, in ways that I think would not have happened with a male administrator."

If a woman succeeds as a leader, she may be called a "bitch" or a "ball-buster" or worse. If she fails as a leader, she will be called a "woman" or worse. Although not addressing the gender of an administrator, Edward M. White's "Use It or Lose It: Power and the WPA" posits: "Administrators, including WPAs, cannot afford the luxury of powerlessness" (12). He further admonishes administrators to "recognize the fact that all administration deals in power; power games demand aggressive players; assert that you have power (even if you don't) and you can often wield it" (3).

Problematizing this scenario further is the call by some feminist theorists to develop a "feminist" administration style: that is, not only is one asked to "play like a man," but also to "win like/for women." Amy Goodburn and Carrie Shively Leverenz, in their "Feminist Writing Program Administration: Resisting the Bureaucrat Within," examine their own resistance to feminist administrative styles—characterized by "nonhierarchical collaboration, shared leadership, and the recognition of multiple sources of authority" (277). "For example, Louise Wetherbee Phelps suggests that Nel Noddings's 'ethics of care' can provide a starting point for administrators who must decide how to handle the power they inevitably have over others. In this model, the writing program administrator has power, but it is the benevolent power to care for and nurture others" (277–8). Goodburn and Leverenz conclude that their resistance to such efforts is symptomatic of the "bureaucrat within" and can only be challenged by critical self-reflection (288). Hildy Miller offers a critical reflection on such feminist attempts:

> Because of ideological conflict, feminist approaches are likely to be misinterpreted from a masculinist point of view. Leadership can appear weak if receptivity is mistaken for passivity; affective responses such as laughter for lack of seriousness; and the sharing of power for looking to others for direction .... For women administrators [as opposed to women teachers] working in a feminist way, the problems are compounded, since women's authority is still problematic in academic culture ... . If we add to this position a [different] leadership style, it may exacerbate the problems. On the other hand, as studies have shown, when women adopt more masculinist personas, other difficulties may develop. Positive qualities such as assertiveness in men can be seen negatively as domineering behavior in women. The challenge for feminist administrators, particularly if we are women, is to find a "countermodel" of leadership. ("Postmasculinist" 84–5)

Irene Ward notes that most graduate students in composition and rhetoric are not trained in management and leadership (49), and once they find themselves—unprepared—in a leadership position, particularly as writing program administrators, they quickly experience "burnout," which she defines as "emotional exhaustion," "depersonalization of clients," and "feelings of diminished personal accomplishment" (50–1). Ward argues that "Some of the changes to WPA work environment will cost departmental resources, and so will take time and diligence to get into place," but meanwhile, she suggests strategies to keep you productive and sane (58–61). A handful of these have been excerpted here:

"Involve others and build teams." Ward urges WPA administrators to "learn to delegate and develop a style of leadership that empowers others to act effectively" (59). As a primary example, she recommends Lynn Meeks and Christine Hult's "A Co-Mentoring Model of Administration."

"Seek out positive role models." To do so, Ward suggests that one attend the major conventions in our field, most especially the 4Cs, as well as any WPA conferences. Additionally, she recommends that one read the WPA journal and participate in its listserv.

"Develop realistic expectations about what can be accomplished."

"Discover ways to cut down on interruptions that interfere with your other duties, especially the intensely emotional ones." In particular, Ward offers a brilliant strategy for how to deal with student grievances over grades or teaching assistants. She suggests that one make the students fill out a grievance form in writing and leave it in your office, allowing you the luxury of attending to the grievance when you want to do so; this strategy has the added benefit of cutting down on the number of emotional showdowns.

"Balance your life and outside interests with your work." "Try to figure out what is the most productive number of hours you can work per week. How much can you work and still feel focused, calm, and alert?" Find a reasonable answer, and then stick to it (61).

"Stop thinking you are a victim; take control." "Learn to say no, calmly and without anger, when you are asked to do what can't be done with the resources available" (61). She also advises to "Learn the art of the 'trade off.' When given major new responsibilities that can't be realistically integrated with current ones, say to your boss, 'If we do what you ask, we won't be able to continue to do … . Which do you think is most important for us to do, since we can't do both?'" (61).

"Create a list of deal breakers." "Take some time to think about those conditions that would make your job so difficult or disagreeable that you wouldn't want to continue" (61). However, she does offer that piece of advice with the caveat: "However, unless you mean it, it is not a good strategy to threaten to resign" (61).

Regardless of the challenges, effective leaders exhibit and foster the following personality characteristics, according to Joan C. Chrisler, Linda Herr, and Nelly K. Murstein: leaders are "selected by their peers for their duties if they have reputations for being candid, judicious, trustworthy, assertive, fair, loyal, principled, and willing to accept responsibility for their actions. Faculty with integrity inspire confidence in their colleagues as well as in administrators, who may not always agree with them but respect them nonetheless" (196). James M. Kouzes and Barry Z. Posner, authors of *The Jossey-Bass Academic Administrator's Guide to Exemplary Leadership*, write: "As the data clearly show, for people to follow someone *willingly*, the majority of constituents must believe the leader is honest, forward-looking, competent, inspiring" (11). "Credibility," they continue, "is the foundation of leadership" (13), and they offer a "straightforward prescription for establishing credibility. DWYSYWD: Do What You Say You Will Do" (15). In her essay "Women Administrators in Higher Education," Mary K. Madsen identifies two additional characteristics: effective leaders have a sense of humor and a cooperative spirit (210). In addition to personality characteristics, according to Madsen, effective leaders also "must be people of vision who follow world, national, regional, state, and local trends, movements, and forces. They must be voracious readers" (210). Additionally, they "understand the missions of the institutions they serve," and they have a "keen interest in the entire university community" (210). They network assiduously; they "master their math skills," so they can understand and command budgets; they maintain a "high energy level" by taking care of their health (212). In short, Madsen advises, "Successful leaders learn who the movers and shakers are on their campuses … . A woman who seeks to move up must align herself with the doers both to get things accomplished and to be identified as a doer" herself (210).

Kouzes and Posner argue that effective leaders "inspire a shared vision." They write: "Leaders have a desire to make something happen, to change the way things are, to create something that no one else has ever created before. In some ways, leaders live their lives backward. They see pictures in their mind's eye of what the results will look like even before they've started their project … . Their clear image of the future pulls them forward. Yet visions seen only by leaders are insufficient to create an organized movement or a significant change. A person with no constituents is not a leader, and people will not follow until they accept a vision as their own" (5). They also enable and empower others to contribute to the realization of this vision, by allowing a sense of shared ownership (8). To create this sense of shared ownership, Kouzes and Posner argue that

> Identifying who your constituents are and finding out what their common aspirations are is one of the first required steps that leaders take in enlisting others. No matter how grand the dream of an individual visionary, if others don't see in it the possibility of realizing their own hopes and desires, they won't follow. Leaders must show

> others how they, too, will be served by the long-term vision of the future, how their specific needs can be satisfied. (43)

To accomplish this, leaders must use their "outsight," by which Kouzes and Posner mean the faculty to observe and to listen to their constituency in order to stay current with their needs and desires (54).

The Challenge of Difficult People, Difficult Politics, Difficult Departments

In your academic journeys, you will encounter difficult people: whether in the form of nasty, clearly mean-spirited readers' reports or in the form of nasty, clearly mean-spirited colleagues. Presumably, because you have adopted, as advised, a professional attitude and behavior of collegiality, *you* are not one of these difficult people.

Although there are many categories of difficult people, as our survey respondents revealed, here we will address, in varying scenarios, the difficult colleague and the difficult student. Because, as our online survey results revealed, the politics of dealing with difficult female colleagues (a.k.a. "Queen Bees") was an additional and disturbingly thematic challenge, we will address it separately in Chapter 5. A future chapter (Chapter 6) will also address how to deal with the physical and emotional stress that such difficult encounters engender.

The Politics of Dealing with Difficult People

Due to the complex history shared by these two disciplines and to the tension between potentially competing interests and priorities, rhetoric and composition faculty often experience difficulty when dealing with some of their literature colleagues. One respondent offered the following analysis:

> In general, I think the most difficult challenge for women in our field is the ongoing inequity between literature faculty and rhet/comp faculty in English Departments. Many literature faculty overtly show disdain for composition as a course and sometimes as a field. Simultaneously, many literature faculty (especially established full and associate professors) are male. Most faculty in rhet/comp are female and usually occupy relatively new positions in their departments (like assistant professor). In other words, the power is still with the male literature majority, and rhet/comp faculty exist lower in the hierarchy, exacerbating the tendency to devalue work in rhet/comp.

Other women concur that a good deal of their time (and emotional energy) is spent defending writing programs, research in composition, and graduate study in the field "against concerns, fears, and prejudices of literature faculty." One respondent reported "many instances of pettiness and exclusion—negative reappointment votes for junior composition faculty while junior literature faculty got unanimous votes, for example. Most notably, the compositionists were not included in our search for a new director of composition, and the department did not hire the candidate endorsed by the composition faculty."

Although we could all probably tell similar tales of departmental battles involving the rhetoric and composition faculty versus the literature faculty, a number of respondents urged women not to succumb to the "us/them" dichotomy that sustains this narrative. A number of women, likewise, urged others to build bridges to literature faculty, acknowledging that "collegial relations on the job" involve knowing "how to function in a department where your area of study is not the thing most people care about, where people see one another's successes as threats, and where, for your survival, you need to learn how to build alliances with people outside your field." Sharon Crowley advises similarly:

> Befriend as many colleagues as you can, especially those outside of rhetoric and composition. Professional friendships can be immensely rewarding. And they are useful, too. You can learn a great deal about the way your department works from people who have been there for awhile. Junior colleagues can let you know that it's not just you who is being asked to do more than is humanly possible. Literature and creative writing faculty need to know that rhet/comp people are smart and that they have interesting scholarly agendas as well. If faculty in other areas know you, your projects and your professional goals will be that much easier to achieve. Remember that the philosophy prof in the building next door may be serving on the college P&T committee when your case comes up.

Christine Farris, in her 2002 CCCC workshop presentation "30 Things I Can Say I Know for Sure about Dealing with the Dysfunctional Department," warned that we should "resist the understandable temptation to view the department strictly in terms of binaries," and the literature/composition binary would certainly be one of the most compelling dichotomies, but she also names additional binaries: tenured/untenured, scholars/teachers, "cool/uncool." She advises that one should "build connections" by making "several department friends who are not among the usual suspects." Additionally, she advises that one should "not succumb to premature, partial, or paranoid readings (or single interpretations). Consider yourself an ethnographic participant-observer of your own department," and recognize that "alliances and feuds can have ancient and sometimes unusual roots," so "assume nothing." (For more on this, Farris recommends the writing of Carol A. Gallagher.)

One respondent gave this detailed advice for how she dealt with the challenges of literature faculty who appeared to demean or disempower her as a rhetoric and composition scholar:

> My approach for addressing this issue? I sought to do the best, most intellectually stimulating work I could. I was passionate about my work and strived to find ways (intellectually and structurally) to combat the apathy by introducing composition studies into departmental conversations as often as possible. I invited into my classroom just those people I felt were most apathetic about composition studies. (Note: I did this, of course, only after consulting with senior colleagues and strategizing a great deal about the course and class session, etc., to which I'd invite these colleagues.) I shared my work-in-progress broadly among faculty in the department, particularly those known for their careful reading. (Note: Again I consulted often with senior colleagues in composition before forwarding my work to colleagues outside the field.) I worked side-by-side with these colleagues on departmental, college, and university committees—engaging them in debates and issues that took us beyond our disciplinary interests and differences. This allowed them to see me as other than the "person who does composition" (and for me to see them as other than a defined "enemy").

Other women spoke of the difficulty of dealing with colleagues who took every opportunity to reify the hierarchy of "junior" (or untenured) and "senior" (tenured) faculty, resulting in demands for deference and in instances of "infantilization" (Ratcliffe). Krista Ratcliffe advises:

> You may also have a problem finding the right rhetorical stance to take as a newly employed untenured faculty in relation to the tenured faculty. The pitfall to be aware of is that the tenure process can be infantilizing … . I … felt annoyed when a male professor would repeatedly say at a faculty meeting, "What I think Kris is saying is … ." (Luckily I had read Deborah Tannen and recognized the situation for what it was.) The problem of not knowing how to negotiate departmental politics of the warring variety can be devastating … ; the pitfall is the impulse toward melodrama wherein you find yourself preoccupied at all times with the departmental narrative at hand; there's nothing like departmental injustice or craziness to distract you from the business at hand, which is (as Win Horner used to tell me) to publish, publish, publish. Then they can't touch you … or at least not as easily.

Crowley offers this additional advice for how to negotiate departmental politics:

> *Never* burn bridges. If a senior colleague treats you badly, keep this to yourself while you are within the institution's walls. (The only exception

to the "never burn bridges" rule is this: if the offense is very serious—if it amounts to harassment, say— immediately consult with a senior person that you trust and/or the affirmative action officer.) In most cases, though, you should cry/complain/bitch to a spouse, partner, good friend, or colleague elsewhere, instead. If you are mistreated by someone you know on the national scene, keep this to yourself as well. You never know when you might need that person's help. And remember that revenge truly is a dish best served cold.

The Politics of Dealing with Difficult Students

The majority of your students will likely remind you—with their enthusiasm and desire—of the real value of the academic life. However, as you will learn, or as you have already discovered, students may also prove to be some of those difficult people whom you must negotiate. Sometimes students are trouble, of course, simply because they are troubled. And as mentioned in Chapter 3, your campus should have a host of resources, such as professional counseling, to which you could refer troubled students; in no instance should you attempt to counsel such students yourself. Find the institutional support you need to get this student the help that he/she needs. But sometimes students will challenge you because they are taller than you, or because—especially as a graduate teaching assistant—you are only a few years older than they are, or because you advocate feminist principles, or just because you are a woman. One respondent told us: "I observe—again and again and again and again—that women professors are expected to 'give more' to students. My students are INCREDIBLY demanding and are quick to challenge grades, assignments, requirements." Also, because you are a woman, you may experience students, particularly male students, who take issue with your authority in the classroom.

Whatever the cause, according to Robert Boice, "unmanaged and unsettling CI [classroom incivilities] constitute a turning point that can ruin professional careers .... Why? New faculty in their first two or three semesters tend to spend most of their time preparing for teaching (even at research universities), and when they fail at teaching, they lose the self-efficacy they need to meet challenges or research/scholarship and collegiality/professional networking" (*Advice* 98). Boice found that this was especially true of women (98).

As a graduate teaching assistant, prior to your assistant professor appointment, you may have already accumulated strategies for dealing with the problem undergraduate. If not, you may find the strategies offered by the following helpful: Sorcinelli; McKeachie; Richardson; Whicker et al (101–3), and Toth (*Ms. Mentor's Impeccable Advice* 83–104).

Additionally, as a newly appointed assistant professor who now will be asked to teach, mentor, and advise graduate students, many of whom may well be your peers in age, as Krista Ratcliffe notes, "you may initially have a hard time finding the right rhetorical stance to take as an untenured assistant professor in relation to graduate students. Don't get me wrong. Working with graduate students is fun, because their projects are intellectually exciting and because, initially, they may seem more like peers than many of your new colleagues. But the pitfalls to be aware of are (1) giving too much time to their projects and not enough to your own and (2) talking with them about departmental issues that your faculty peers would rather not have circulating on the graduate student grapevine." Working so closely with graduate students has many an additional pitfall to be avoided and/or negotiated, as one respondent writes:

> So far, [the most difficult challenge has been] dealing with the power dynamic in graduate seminars as a young professor; the graduate students at first don't seem to be willing to accept that I have things to offer, and when I spoke to a senior colleague about the problem, I felt like that person took up for the students. There's a way in which one can feel stuck in limbo right out of graduate school.

An additional dynamic that one often must negotiate is that of the powers of attraction between students and instructor, as one respondent admitted: "I have been attracted to male students from time to time and have had to learn to deal with that in silence." Whether the attraction is to male or female students, one is cautioned: study your institution's policy on appropriate and inappropriate relations, lest such dynamics augur the end of your professional career, when you are accused of sexual harassment.

Of course, sexual harassment is illegal, and many of our respondents told tales of the kinds of sexual harassment that they were subjected to and the repercussions such harassment had on their professional performance. In some tales, the harassment was blatantly aggressive (as in the case when one woman was told that all she needed was a "good fuck and a douche bag" to solve her problems) and some less so, as in this case: "I was surprised by the number of tenured, married, male professors in my department who thought I would be interested in providing a little variety in their lives. I became very skilled at playing dumb in response to suggestions and talked a great deal about my family. No one ever pushed the suggestions to the point that I had to confront them directly." And another respondent: "I was a young assistant professor before sexual harassment was legally defined, so it happened all the time. One learned to say 'no' in a humorous way, and to seek out the other female faculty for support. I really enjoyed the sexual harassment information workshop, watching the faces of all the old male faculty as the hip young female lawyer explained the current rules!"

Although earlier strategies of "playing dumb" may have served an earlier generation of women, the law, "the current rules," now provides for more pointed responses. It would behoove you to familiarize yourself with your campus' sexual harassment policy, as well as to consult Bernice Lott and Lisa M. Rocchio's "Standing Up, Talking Back, and Taking Charge: Strategies and Outcomes in Collective Action Against Sexual Harassment," which defines sexual harassment and how to respond to instances of such. Also educative is Maryka Biaggio's "What I've Learned About Addressing Sexual Harassment, Protecting Students, *and* Keeping a Job." The key directive is to document instances of such, as Linda L. Carli explains:

> There are a number of ways of responding to sexist or hostile behavior on the part of students or colleagues. One is to confront them and tell them why their behavior is inappropriate. This is probably most effective with individuals who are exhibiting the behavior unwittingly and who probably would be embarrassed to have it brought to their attention. Individuals who deliberately intend to cause insult are less likely to change in response to a confrontation. For these individuals, and for cases of sexual harassment, records should be kept to document the nature of the harassment or discrimination, its frequency, and your response. Explicitly rejecting the harasser's attentions, such as writing a note to the harasser to explain that you want him to stop his offensive behavior, can make it easier to prove that sexual harassment occurred, should you ever decide to file charges. (291)

Working the Greater Field's Politics

Many respondents encouraged women in our field to "get involved with the work of CCC, on committees or SIGs, and the WPA. You will find great colleagues to support your work, which will be especially important if you end up in a job with few local colleagues in rhetoric and comp." However, we also learned from our survey responses that the field of rhetoric and composition is characterized by a sense of intense competition, of cliquishness, and of big egos, and involvement with the greater, national field of rhetoric and composition subjects the woman in our field to new political challenges and concerns. We were told tales such as these: "So, when it comes to publishing, I ask outside of the colleagues in RC because anything I would be doing is in competition to what they are doing … . To publish and succeed makes others look bad or at least sets egos on fire with jealousy." Another reports that what she has found most challenging is "the ability to become more active in the various professional organizations. There appears to be a tight group of people who are constantly on the boards, publishing, and presenting. I see the same names over and over. I have offered my name and services as a volunteer to several groups (C's, TYTCA, etc.), and I never receive a response. I have paid my financial commitments to these groups, and I have kept up with reading their works. It does bother me a bit."

We were told tales of the political battles waged between those scholars who saw themselves as "compositionists" vs. the "rhetoricians." The "theorists" vs. the "practitioners." And the battle of egos at conferences. One respondent wrote:

> When I was a young assistant professor, I was publicly humiliated by a very prominent scholar (not from the field of rhetoric). After listening to my conference presentation, he began attacking the paper point by point, accused me of an "anti-feminist agenda," and refused to allow me to interrupt his diatribe to respond to his objections. When I finally responded, he dismissed my response out of hand. After the session, a few people in the room told me privately that they had agreed with me. Unfortunately, they were too intimidated to voice an opinion. What did I do? Nothing really at the time. I was appalled, shaken, and furious. Since then, I have been more aware of the power dynamics of conference sessions, and have tried to mentor young scholars.

Other respondents spoke of the politics of publication: of suffering ego-driven readers' reports ("the reviewer described my ms. as 'stupid' and 'illiterate.' … I now know how unnecessarily and gratuitously cruel the reviewer was being, and I recognize that the reviewer was a tiny person, not a great sage, but at the time, I didn't know that. I also know now that the journal editor should never have let that review reach me without tempering it in some way"). They also spoke of suffering the threats of co-opted authorship: "Be generous with your ideas and research, but do not pass them on without your stamp of ownership firmly established."

In order to summarize the advice that our respondents bestowed in how to deal with difficult people and difficult political situations, we offer these concluding remarks from our respondents. The first motto: "Never take things personally and continue to do your work with enthusiasm and ardor," and the second slogan: "cultivate a necessary but not toxic skepticism," work together to summarize the best advice. In the face of the difficulties of challenging people and exasperating situations, develop a skepticism yet don't lose your passion for the work:

> Have a good female mentor, and don't be too trusting. Wish I didn't have to say that. Expect people will be kind and open. When they are not (and are instead backstabbing or manipulative), be ready to protect yourself. And, in the midst of it, try not to lose your idealism and your passion for the work. I know that's a tall order. But, I would say that in order to maintain this, one has to teach regularly (and courses one enjoys). That will be the best reminder for why this work is important and for why the rest is really rather irrelevant in the big scheme.

5

SUCCEEDING AS A SENIOR SCHOLAR, TEACHER, AND MENTOR

> The best way to become a senior scholar is to pursue a scholarly agenda that captures your imagination, that you feel is important and worthwhile, that other trusted colleagues recognize as noteworthy and valuable to the profession, and that makes you want to get up in the morning and write. Once you are a Full Professor—which will come if you have worked steadily on that agenda—your job becomes more than that of being a scholar; instead you have the responsibility of making it possible for others—within your institution, within your field, within your profession—to be the best scholars they can be. That's when the real work and responsibility begins.
>
> —Cynthia L. Selfe

By the time you are tenured and promoted to associate professor, you have in many ways already "made it," defying statistical odds: finishing a PhD, scoring a tenure-track position, successfully surviving the tenure and promotion scrutiny, publishing and teaching—and perhaps even administering programs—along the way: and *as a woman, too.* At this point in your career, you should congratulate yourself and enjoy that new, overwhelming capacity to breathe. Enjoy, too, the more relaxed pace, the unapologetic attitude with which you may now greet your colleagues in the hallway. You may feel the urge, finally, to start an herb garden or to take up a hobby you have forgotten in the demanding, grueling race to tenure.

At this point, you may find that you want to devote more of your time to teaching or administrative assignments, as well. But do not forget that your productivity will continue to be evaluated—each year in annual reviews and perhaps separately in "post-tenure" reviews, which are becoming more and more common. If you want to be promoted to full professor, you'll have to continue to research, to write, to publish, as much as—if not more than—you did before you were tenured and promoted: for now you must clearly establish your *national* or even *international* reputation and contribution to the study of rhetoric and composition. In addition to the continued demand on your research and writing time, you will face new time demands, as you accept new leadership and mentoring responsibilities.

This chapter aims to help you navigate these new challenges. Legend has it that Andrea A. Lunsford passed the coveted "keys to the queendom" of rhetoric and composition studies on to her mentees, much as Merlin guided young Arthur in his quest for the holy grail; and to be honest, before Cheryl Glenn confirmed their fictional status, we had hoped to find those keys and pass them on to you in this chapter. Instead, we discovered what we really already knew: that there are no magic bullets, no simple keys to get you in. Therefore, here we will offer you, in their place, some helpful strategies for navigating this critical stage of your career, along with some solid advice from some of those who have arrived.

New Challenges; New Demands on Your Time

The years you spent preparing for and surviving your tenure and/or promotion ordeal were no doubt extremely demanding, especially in terms of professional productivity and emotional tenacity; however, as an assistant professor, you were very likely protected from other, perhaps less emotionally grueling responsibilities, which nonetheless require a great deal of time and energy. Though you may have told yourself, "now I can finally write the book I wanted to write rather than the 'tenure' book" or "now I can take the professional risks I have always wanted to in my research agenda" or "now I can take on that larger longitudinal study I have long planned"—you could easily find yourself, as a tenured associate professor, with *less* time to do the kind of research you have long dreamed about. You may find yourself directing your institution's writing program, a responsibility you were able to beg out of before you were tenured. You will surely find yourself on more and more departmental and university-wide committees, faculty governance bodies, and even professional association editorial and advisory boards. You will start devoting a month or so of your own summer research time to writing tenure review letters for young scholars in other programs across the country. You will be mentoring junior faculty—on campus and across the nation. And you will be advising more graduate students and directing more dissertations. "One of my students has just become an associate professor," Sharon Crowley reports, "and she was stunned by the number of new tasks that awaited her. For one thing, a new associate can expect to find herself appointed to important college and university committees that require time commitments and a lot of work as well (curriculum committees, for example). Assistant professors are usually spared such assignments." Paula Caplan details a number of these "new tasks":

> In some ways, even more demands may be made on your time and energy than when you were junior faculty. As you become more senior, especially if your teaching is well reviewed and you have published interesting work, more students will want to work with you and have

> you as a supervisor or mentor. Your colleagues in your department will expect you to take on more committee work and administrative duties, since you presumably know the ropes. As a woman, and if you are a member of a non-dominant group other than "women," you will likely be in even greater demand by administrators who are increasingly pressured (or are choosing) to demonstrate that they strive for diversity in committees that deal with such issues as student recruitment, employment and pay equity, and general university administrative work. (*Lifting a Ton of Feathers* 155)

Hence, as a newly tenured or not so newly tenured associate professor, you will have a host of new demands on your time—above and beyond the research and teaching expectations that you have for yourself as well as those held by your institution and department for you to move forward in rank to full professor. Here, we discuss a handful of these professional demands and offer suggestions about how to responsibly and effectively carry them out. But first a note: although these demands may challenge your schedule, they do offer the unique opportunity to invest in the present and future state of our discipline, and that is a rewarding and important endeavor. Such opportunities may also be an investment in your own professional future, as they raise your profile on campus as well as nationally, and even internationally, and this can bolster your case to move forward in rank, so long as it's not done at the expense of your scholarship.

The challenge is to know when to welcome such opportunities and when to decline them. Balancing your professional demands while maintaining a research agenda (and having a life!) is not an easy job, as Shirley Wilson Logan notes:

> All I'm trying to do right now is keep my head down and finish this book! The hardest part, at this point, since I do have some recognition in the field, is to decline all sorts of requests—from reviewing manuscripts and tenure cases to serving on dissertation committees. I suppose the only advice I have in that regard is to choose selectively and mainly "Just say 'no.'"

Serving the Profession

As you succeed in your research agenda and achieve more and more recognition in the field, you will be increasingly asked to serve the profession by reviewing manuscripts submitted for publication and candidates considered for tenure and promotion. Cynthia L. Selfe rightfully extolled the importance of this service, but as Logan advised, you will have to "choose selectively" which reviews to write, and you will need to say "no" to a number of requests. The ability to say "no" came as a revelation to Susan C. Jarratt:

> Once a chair thanked me for writing a letter. I said, "No problem. It must be done." And she said, "Lots of people turn us down." What a revelation! You can say "No!" So I've said "no" to some things. Better to say "no" than to get overloaded and write a weak letter or get behind.

Now that you know that you can say "no," how do you know when to say "no"?

Before long, if it hasn't happened already, you will be contacted by the editor of one of our professional journals or publishing houses, asking you to review a submitted manuscript for publication: this may be a journal article or a book manuscript. Accepting this responsibility should mean that you will review responsibly. To review responsibly requires you to respond constructively and in a timely way. Regrettably for our discipline, this is not always the case. As you may yourself have noticed, it is all too common for a reader to take a year or more to review your submitted manuscript and get it back to the journal editor. Such inexcusable tardiness can make research obsolete and put careers in jeopardy. If you are asked to review a manuscript and you know that you cannot realistically review and respond to the piece in a month's time, then say "no" to the request. Also, say "no" to the request if you cannot compose a constructive response. Even if you are going to recommend to the editor that the manuscript be rejected, there is no cause for nasty and brutish comments to the author. It is astounding—and shameful—that members of the profession responsible for teaching the writing process, revision, and effective responding strategies would themselves respond in ways that are so inharmonious with those practices. Rather than provide feedback, we suggest that you provide what might be called "feed-forward"—that is, provide commentary that gives the author a beginning place for revision. Ballif recalls that the "feed-forward" she got on a submitted essay from one reviewer—whom she suspects was Sharon Crowley—was so helpful that she could not wait to attend to the requested revisions, some of which would require more time, thought, and research. By contrast, Michelle Ballif recalls another very short review—just one single, devastating paragraph—that so disturbed her that she couldn't so much as look at the manuscript for six months or more. Many of you may have similar tales, each one of which is a disgrace to our field. When you review, keep in mind these experiences and respond responsibly: in a timely fashion and constructively. If you cannot do either, then—for the sake of authors everywhere—say "no."

There may be other reasons to say "no" to the request, as well. To protect your research (and personal) time, you may want to place a limit on how many manuscript reviews you will attend to. Patricia Bizzell told us that she reviews for several presses, accepting approximately four or five manuscripts per year: "What I accept depends entirely on my work load at the time of the request; I tend to knock these off almost as soon as they come into the house and I have time to do that." Jarratt aims to review "interesting" article submissions at the rate "of maybe one a month." And, she told us, "I try to make certain that I take one from each journal once a year or half a year, just so they don't drop me from the list" of peer reviewers.

Additionally, you will be asked to serve on tenure and promotion cases, internal as well as external. You may be asked to serve on a tenure and promotion case of a colleague in your department, or—as you gain more and more recognition in the field—you will be increasingly asked to serve as an external reviewer for a candidate by reviewing the candidate's scholarship and recommending—or not—the candidate for promotion.[6] Crowley notes that "Because rhetoric and composition is a relatively small field, there are relatively few senior professors in it. This means that once you become senior in the field, you will get a lot of requests to write support letters for promotion." How do you know when to say "yes" to such requests?

Our profiled women told us that they set a number as a limit that guides them year by year. Jarratt accepts only "one or two letters each summer (though others come up at odd times) because," she explains, "each one takes me almost a week to write." Glenn reviews "usually three to five cases a summer," but she tries to keep the number to three, "telling department heads that I've reached my limit." Lunsford, likewise, aims for no more than three to five cases each year: "For some time, I have set five as the upper limit of tenure/promotion review letters I can write in one summer, and I like to keep that to four if at all possible." And Bizzell told us that she has an informal limit of two to three per year. Selfe did not specify a limit of the number of reviews she might write each year, but she did stress that "I try not to take on more requests than I can responsibly handle."

Bizzell's guideline for accepting such cases is simply: "first come, first served, although I might add another one [beyond two or three] if I happen to know the person's work very well." Likewise, Selfe accepts "the cases of folks whose work is familiar to me—simply so that I have something intelligent and specific to say." Before Jarratt agrees to write a tenure and promotion review letter, she asks herself the following questions:

> Am I interested in the scholarship? Will it help me or teach me something I need to know? And, do I have the time, given other commitments? I now take only one or two letters each summer (though others come up at odd times) because each one takes me almost a week to write. How do you say "no?" I reply fairly quickly (not to leave people hanging) and say that I don't have time to write a very strong letter. Or in some cases, I say that my knowledge of the field of research of the candidate is not strong enough for me to produce a good letter. Chairs are very gracious. They want great letters!

Crowley (who accepts a maximum of five requests such year) provides this advice for how to write a great letter:

> Make sure the requesting university gives you plenty of time to read

> the dossier, especially in the case of a promotion to full professor, because it will probably be immense.
>
> Promotion letters require all the tools in a rhetorician's arsenal. Committees expect long letters, and the letters have to be carefully written so that nothing in the letter can be used against the candidate by someone who is looking for any excuse to deny ….
>
> In our field, you will sometimes be sent a dossier which demonstrates that a candidate for promotion has been saddled with impossible expectations—she was expected to work miracles in the FYC program and publish a book and several articles as well, for example. This happens less frequently than it used to, but it still occurs. In that case, you have to decide whether or not to mention this in your letter, because your criticism of the department can backfire onto the candidate.

Many of our profiled women noted that they were concerned about writing positive letters. If they are unable to write a strong endorsement of a candidate, Glenn, Lunsford, and Bizzell told us that they would decline the request to write the review letter. Here's Bizzell: "I tend to decline 'due to other commitments' if I think I can't write a positive review, which may be irresponsible and chicken-livered of me, but there it is." Likewise Glenn declines weak cases: "When I've received materials for a particularly weak case, I say 'no.' Unfortunately, such a negative response works against the candidate, as department heads keep track of all the no's. But I figure it's better to say 'no' than to write a negative letter when there's no way I can know what that candidate has been put through or endured at that particular institution." Crowley does not

> accept requests to write letters of support for people about whose careers I know nothing because I do not want to discover once I have read the dossier that I cannot write an entirely positive letter. This sounds harsh, I know; but in a small field such as ours relationships are based on professional trust. You cannot afford to betray that trust by writing things that are untrue, even if they are positive.

Lunsford also declines to review a candidate if she cannot honestly write a positive review. "That does not mean," however, Lunsford noted, "that the reviews I write contain no criticism; in order to be credible, such letters need to address weaknesses as well as strengths." Selfe told us that "I try to take on cases that I believe in—and these aren't always those that are conventionally considered the strongest cases."

An additional service is to write other such letters of recommendation, such as for job applications or award nominations. "The longer you are in the profession," Crowley tells us,

> the more students and acquaintances you have. Professional relationships that last over time are rich and rewarding. Some of my students

> are now full professors, and their success and achievement gives me great pleasure. However, relationships such as these do come with one long string attached: requests for letters of recommendation.

Crowley gladly writes such letters, despite the energy and time demanded to do so, because she acknowledges that her mentors and advocates, such as Ed Corbett, Ross Winterowd, and Jim Kinneavy, routinely and "generously supported [her] career from the beginning" by writing such letters for her.

And yet an additional service you may be asked to provide for the greater field of rhetoric and composition studies is to serve on a journal's editorial board or a professional organization's advisory board. Our profiled women agreed that these are, in the words of Glenn, "wonderful opportunities to meet people, work closely with people, and understand how organizations work, succeed, and/or falter." Bizzell noted an additional benefit: national (or international) visibility: "if you are on the way up, it looks nice to have your name there in [an editorial board] list with some eminent people." And Selfe argued that such advisory positions helped her "stay in touch with developments and voices in the field." They also provided her with a "route for helping and advising other scholars in areas that I know something about." Selfe considered this benefit a "professional pleasure as well as a responsibility." Lunsford warned, however, that "these jobs take up enormous amounts of time," so she advised that such service be kept to a minimum until after one is promoted and tenured. Crowley concurs:

> I love serving on editorial boards, because editors get to read all of the cutting-edge work in the field. One of the unsung perks is that if you review a new book for a journal, you get a free copy. And your name on the masthead of a major journal is of course important proof your national standing. But, as with everything else in this profession, you need to decide whether the rewards balance out the costs when you are offered such a position. Make sure the editor tells you how many manuscripts you will be expected to read in a year before you accept.

Mentoring the Next Generation: Students and Junior Faculty

As previous chapters—and our survey respondents—repeatedly advise, one of the keys to success is to find and construct a positive relationship with a mentor, regardless of at what stage of your career you find yourself. However, as a no-longer-junior-faculty member, you will find yourself increasingly tapped to mentor others. No doubt, you will welcome the opportunity to "pay it forward," and to make a positive contribution to a younger generation of scholars. And we encourage you to do so. But you will soon discover that mentoring is a demand on your time, as well.

One important—and time-consuming—mentoring role is directing dissertations, which Crowley notes, "can be fun or it can be *very hard work*" (her emphasis). "A lot of dissertation direction is," according to Crowley, "cheerleading: you need to learn how and when to urge a student forward. And everyone's composing process is different, so you need to learn what works as encouragement for each student, and what doesn't."

Before agreeing to serve as a dissertation director-cum-cheerleader, Crowley advises: "Make sure you know a student's ability and work habits well if you agree to serve as chair of his/her committee; my advice is to say 'no' if you are unsure of a student's ability to complete the dissertation satisfactorily and in a timely manner. This may sound harsh, but there can be heartbreak and angst involved for all concerned when a student is unable to finish." Crowley also says "no" to a student if the proposed dissertation is not of interest or is on a topic with which Crowley is "only vaguely familiar ... because this is not fair to the student and it requires an enormous time commitment from me while I get up to speed." She advises that one can serve as a reader for such a project instead of directing it. "In the best of all possible worlds," Crowley concludes, "you should never chair more than two dissertations at a time. We do not live in that world, of course."

Indeed, Roxanne Mountford typically directs eight to ten doctoral students each year. With this kind of load, many dissertation directors strategize ways to lighten their work. One practical tactic is to suggest or even require that advisees form writing groups. Before Mountford agrees to work with a student, for example, that student must agree to join Mountford and her other advisees in a working writing group, who meet once a month to workshop chapters (or portions thereof) of their dissertations. Every student member reads each other's work and responds in written form, and they then meet either at someone's home, a quiet café, or someplace on campus to discuss possible revisions. Chapters must be workshopped and revised before they are submitted for Mountford's review. The benefits of this writing group are many: it saves the major professor a good deal of responding time, since the student's work has already benefited from substantial review and revision before submission; additionally, it provides a forum for the major professor to discuss general tips on how to organize chapters or how to develop a 200-page argument, for example, as well as to discuss job application letters and CVs. This clearly saves her from having these same conversations eight or ten times. But the biggest benefit, Mountford claims, is that she no longer serves as the sole emotional support system for each student. They call each other between meetings, she notes, to offer encouragement. They are also harder on the drafts than she is much of the time, Mountford claims, which means she spends her time solving problems rather than convincing students they have them.

Theresa Enos warns women to be critically self-reflective of the demand placed on women in rhetoric and composition to mentor: despite the "feminization" of the discipline, women in the field "still do not enjoy the same status of their male counterparts: They make less, they teach more, and theirs is more likely to be the onerous burden of administrative work in writing programs where male faculty occupy most of the real positions with the real titles. All the more reason, then, we should closely examine any mentoring program to see if women are taking on a disproportionate share of the work; women who, I suspect, were not themselves mentored, except perhaps by the patriarchal master-apprentice model" ("Mentoring" 138–9). Despite the warning, Enos acknowledges, "If women faculty members do not take on this additional responsibility for mentoring—female students, primarily—then how can we change some of the deadly discriminatory practices still going on in our graduate programs?" (142). Similarly, Gail Y. Okawa argues that mentoring can become "an activist practice," one that is "critical to the survival and success of graduate students and junior faculty of color in the academic culture, especially fields like English that attempt to perpetuate the discourse of that culture, and especially at predominantly white institutions, which seem, and in some ways are, uninviting and unfriendly to those who have been historically underrepresented or absent" (509).

Collectively, such mentoring can empower a newer generation to work toward more equitable and satisfying working conditions; individually, such mentoring can provide junior faculty and graduate students with a supportive network as well as opportunity to learn about "the nature of power and authority in higher education" (Mountford 49). A mentor can provide what classroom instruction and graduate seminars may not; that is, as Roxanne Mountford argues: graduate students may receive instruction in writing pedagogy but not in administering writing programs, and certainly not in "negotiating power and authority" in academe (50). Effective mentoring provides for graduate students (and junior faculty) a "comprehensive sense of the profession," "a sense of belonging to a larger professional community by offering opportunities for them to gain at least some experience in academic citizenship and to learn about such things as faculty governance, the concept of academic freedom …, and the university as an institution" (MLA Ad Hoc Committee). Of course, effective mentors—in addition to providing a global sense of the profession—also help their mentees with the "nuts and bolts" of putting together a professional career: guiding students through the job market drama, advising junior faculty through the tenure and promotion process.

To do so effectively, Enos suggests creating structural mentoring opportunities, such as weekly meetings between graduate students and "one or more faculty members for purposes of introducing students to the profession" and portfolio keeping, "to involve graduate students and probationary faculty more actively in reciprocally based mentoring relationships" ("Mentoring" 143). She advocates for writing groups, where students can turn seminar papers into publishable papers; indeed, she suggests that we "view required graduate papers as a succession of drafts" and that we implement our "process and peer-group praxis" from our undergraduate writing classes into our graduate courses.

Whereas Enos's advice aims at helping students publish and, therefore, to be active members of the profession, Janice Lauer queries whether we are pushing graduate students into publication too early, before the students have had the opportunity to build a foundation of disciplinary understanding and specialization of knowledge, and hence when they are not yet ready to participate as active members of the profession. Yet she concedes that "students profit from having had some instruction about the processes of publication while they are still in graduate school" ("Graduate Students" 223) in terms of success on the job market and, later, of research productivity necessary to meet promotion and tenure expectations. She bemoans, however, the pervasive "ethics" of publication, which seems to "require bashing others" or setting up "caricatures and stereotypes of the complex positions of others, especially earlier scholars or ideologies" (234). In contrast, she aims to mentor her students according to an "ethics of care," "marked by features that include a willingness to nurture, to act in concrete situations with emotional involvement, to make responsible moral decisions in particular human relations rather than on abstract principles, to step out of one's personal frame of reference into the other's, to be present to the one cared-for rather than to identify with one's possessions (scholarly possessions)—an altruism constructive for the moral agent and the one cared-for" (234). She asks: "Should we not educate students to reshape the field rather than just to survive?" (235).

Janice Neuleib argues that those in leadership roles have the power to reshape and to "change the basic nature" of the system, making it more hospitable for women (see also Gebhardt's "Mentor and Evaluator"). She provides mentoring suggestions to this end, including "Notice when women faculty and graduate students achieve. Women tend to undervalue their own work and to have it either undervalued by the system or valued only when men assign their imprimaturs … . Women must note and affirm other women" (134). "Support senior women faculty members who mentor and champion junior women. Reward this cooperation when appropriate … . Women want men's approval, but they need women's guidance" (134). As Ms. Mentor (Emily Toth) argues, senior faculty who now enjoy the (tenuous) security of tenure and academic freedom should use their power to advocate for women's issues and faculty rights; they should "be organizing for faculty rights; joining and creating unions; making the Faculty Senate really powerful and obnoxious when it needs to be" (*Ms. Mentor's Impeccable Advice* 185–6).

Powerful and Obnoxious: But Not the Queen Bee

Ms. Mentor's point is well taken: what good is "making it," achieving some power in the academe, if you don't then use that power and influence to effect powerful and influential change in the academy? To do so, one may even need to be "obnoxious" or loud-spoken or gruff. But there is a world of difference between such behavior and the infamous "queen bee" behavior exhibited by some women of influence. Women at all ranks resent—and even suffer—from such narcissism and grandstanding and, yes, even bullying: Paula Caplan reports "Many of the women I interviewed, at all levels of academia, made pleas along the lines of, 'Tell your readers not to forget other women once they get to the top'" (*Lifting a Ton of Feathers* 157). Our own survey revealed a surprising (and shameful) theme: that they experienced discrimination, harassment, and abuse by other *female* colleagues.

As detailed in our introductory chapter, one of the surprising and disappointing things we learned from our survey respondents was that some of the most difficult people in our discipline are women, and some of the most difficult political scenarios to negotiate revolved around such difficult women. Although some narratives revealed passive-aggressive or subtle forms of harassment, other responses reported much more aggressive and openly hostile attacks. Here are just two stories:

> One of my composition/rhet colleagues (who has moved on to a new job, thank goodness) actively undermined my position in the department. In some ways, I understand why she did it—she was getting negative reappointment votes and she decided to distance herself from the compositionists. To get on their good side, she talked negatively about us—me in particular. It was just awful, like high school girls' cattiness. And it had real consequences for me. On one occasion, I got hostile emails from a powerful senior colleague based on information she was spreading. I don't even know the extent of the damage done. I can take office politics, but it hurts to have someone I thought of as a friend turn on me.

> A senior faculty member, a woman with a great deal of power on campus, has been harassing me since my arrival at the university. On several occasions she has threatened me and even worked against my tenure, going so far as to tear up my evaluation portfolio. She has also made sure that I do not get to teach grad courses. The Chair and Dean give in to her because frankly they are frightened of the repercussions of her wrath. Despite my recent tenure, she still works to foment trouble for me with upper administration in regards to receiving support for research and travel. My strategy is and will always be to continue getting my work done even if it means that I pay for all research and travel out of my own pocket and mentor grad students outside my University. I have not told anyone outside my school about this situation because I am so embarrassed and believe that it reflects badly on me even though this is a classic case of harassment.

Perhaps we, along with Krista Ratcliffe, are surprised and discouraged by these stories because we "expected sisterhood to be global," but "it ain't," as

Ratcliffe noted in her 2002 CCCC workshop presentation, "What I Didn't Learn in Graduate School":

> In hindsight, I can see that, despite the political nature of my research on feminist theories of rhetoric, I was a naïve graduate student and an even more naïve assistant professor. I expected sisterhood to be global … and I learned that it ain't. That said, however, I owe whatever success I've had in this field not just to my own dogged determination but, quite literally, to the women in our field who have mentored me, inspired me, and befriended me.

We, too, acknowledge our indebtedness to the many women who have paved the way to our collective successes. However, it is also time to acknowledge and address, head on, the fact that some powerful women in the field, maliciously or unconsciously, hamper the success of their female colleagues. We asked our profiled women what advice they would give on this score. Jarratt noted: "There are strong and difficult personalities in academia, and some of them are possessed by women!" However, she also noted that she had no generalizeable advice about how to deal with such "difficult personalities": "This is a question I simply can't answer in the abstract. My thoughts are running to platitudes about patience, tolerance, and generosity, but sometimes it's important to challenge powerful people, and sometimes people misbehave—even women." Lunsford remarked: "My sense is that most of our colleagues—queen bees or not—want to be attended and listened to, and giving the gift of your attention turns out not to be that difficult to do. Some people will be impossible—we all know that—but others, and I think a lot of others, will respond well to being made to feel important and included. (How naïve is that?)." Selfe responded with this analogue:

> My husband Dickie keeps bees, and I never did much like the queens. They are raised exclusively on royal jelly—a bit too rich for my taste—and so they imbibe a sense of privilege as they grow up. But they are also fairly sedentary, mostly confined to the hive where other bees wait on them. That has always seemed mildly distasteful to me. I'd rather be a worker bee; you get to travel, pack pollen, and zoom around in the sun. You get to see the world—from the air, no less—smell cool flowers, come back to the hive when you need a rest, do bee dances. You get to hobnob with other worker bees, who, generally speaking, seem to be swell companions. You get to contribute to the honey production, and people enjoy the fruits of your labor. There's always one queen bee in the hive, but you *don't* have to *like* her, nor do you have to *be like* her. Do your own good work, help others, and feel good about yourself.

We note that all of this advice is offered from the perspective of very successful and *tenured* women, and so from women who are indeed secure enough to ignore the brutalizing behavior of a female colleague—even, perhaps, to be patient and generous with her, to give her the attention she craves. The situation becomes more difficult to negotiate, of course, when the queen's stinger goes after junior colleagues. It may be smart for an untenured faculty member who's being persecuted to lie low, keep working, and publish her way out of there; however, as a now-tenured witness to the problem, you may be ethically obligated to intervene on behalf of your junior colleague. Indeed, Crowley told us that she would not only "intervene" on behalf of her colleague, but also "go beat the shit out of whoever was doing the discriminating or persecuting."

A Time to Reinvent Yourself and Jumpstart Your Research Agenda

Whether your department's established tenure and promotion criteria include a "single-authored," published book or not, your research and publications to date have most likely been based on your PhD dissertation work, which—at this point—may be eight to ten years old. The grueling race to promotion and tenure very likely left you focused on finishing "the book," or publishing articles, typically from your dissertation research. You may find yourself, now, recently promoted and tenured, feeling empty—as though you had "spent" your best idea. Or, alternately, you may have felt as thought you wrote what would be considered your "tenure" book, all the while wishing to publish the book you really wanted to write. You now find yourself in a transitional phase: you are no longer the impassioned, freshly graduated PhD; you are older, hopefully wiser, but certainly more saddled with mundane realities of committee work, writing program administration, faculty governance, mentoring: worthy commitments, without doubt, but all of which can dull the fire and the passion of research that made this long journey so important in the first place. Admittedly, this is beginning to sound like a relationship manual: "the fire has died. How do I reignite the passion?" Or, like a self-help—middle-age-crisis—manual: "who am I when I am no longer who I was?" The issue becomes: how do I jumpstart and reinvent myself not only as an academic and researcher, but also as an aging woman? Tough questions, but you will need to ignite a new research agenda and remain productive: presumably, you want to press on to achieve full professor, but if not, you are advised that the guarantees of tenure do not protect all (Toth, *Ms. Mentor's Impeccable Advice* 188–91), and, as Crowley has repeatedly warned, the very idea of tenure is perhaps nearing its end.

Theresa Enos's research demonstrates that we, as women, in the field of rhetoric and composition—a field dominated by women—are not publishing as much or as often as we might. She writes:

> Overall, males are still publishing more; … Women are doing

> exciting and vigorous scholarship, yet, of all those in four-year and research universities who do not publish, sixty-six percent are women … . According to my survey data, women writing faculty spend more time teaching than men. In the four-year university, women spend sixty-one percent of their time teaching compared to fifty-four percent for men. And in research universities, women spend forty-nine percent of their time teaching compared to forty percent for men. The data show interesting correlations of time spent on research and both age and length of time tenured. Males spend more time on research than females overall (twenty percent to seventeen percent) …. *According to the data, the older the faculty member and the longer tenured, the less research that person does.* ("Gender and Publishing" 561–3, emphasis added)

This evidence (that women publish less than men and that the longer-tenured publish less), coupled with the data that 10 percent of a profession's authors are responsible for 90 percent of the publications (Moxley, "If Not Now" 4), means that post-tenured women need to find a way to reinvigorate their research agendas. Enos calls on Winifred Horner for a possible strategy:

> Getting published means writing a lot, and disciplining our time. For women directing writing programs (and that's a great many of us) it's hard to give equal attention to teaching and research. Winifred Horner has been tireless in her efforts to help women learn from events in her own academic history: we should heed what she learned regarding the heavy administrative burdens placed especially on women when they should be doing research and writing. She scolds and cajoles: If you take on heavy administrative work—especially before tenure—make sure that it is with the agreement that one day a week—or two afternoons a week—you will not be in the office. This is your research time. Stick to it; whatever you do, do not even think you can work anywhere in the building where the composition office is. Do not even try to work at home. Go to the library. Hide, so no one can find you—and they will try. The "problem" will always be there in your office waiting for you the next morning; it can wait till then. ("Gender and Publishing" 570)

Our profiled women offered additional insights about jumpstarting a research agenda. Jarratt writes:

> I think I've faced this scenario, both the challenge of new ideas and the ennui. Perhaps lying fallow for a time isn't bad. Lives have movement: ebbs and flows. Although some scholars seem to be happiest going full bore all the time, others of us may benefit from slacking off for a time.

> There's a time when people are looking to you for the smart comment, the most cutting edge approach: you're very "on" and in the thick of it. But backing off, not having to be the smartest one in the room can be a relief (and a contribution to mental health). Then starting slowly into something new—reading, going to a different conference or a different kind of session, traveling—these might be good ways to start in a new direction. Other things to do might be to write in an exploratory mode, send something to a smaller journal, collaborate with someone new, sit in on a course, think about whether there's anything going on in the world that needs the kind of attention you can bring.

And when Bizzell was asked how she would advise a woman in our field to jumpstart or reinvent herself during her career, she responded:

> I'd like to know the answer to this! I find that I definitely cannot do as much work in a day as I could twenty years ago. I can tell a happy story about finding a new research direction, however. After several years of feeling I was just "tying up loose ends" in research areas where I had already contributed, I have found a new scholarly passion in Judaic studies. I found it by deciding to devote serious study time to something I was deeply interested in, without much thought as to whether it would be productive of work I could publish in my established field. If it resulted in no publications, that was going to be all right with me. I am still at a very preliminary stage in this research—bolstered by my enrolling in a Master's program in Judaic studies during my 2005–06 sabbatical. Even so, I find that I cannot study anything, apparently, without thinking about it rhetorically so this new passion has already resulted in a couple of publications.

Establishing Yourself: Creating a National and International Reputation

One of many institutional promotion-to-full requirements involves demonstrating that you have achieved a national and even international reputation. Of course, to do so, you need a research agenda that guarantees that you will be published in the most reputable journals with the highest number of readership. Crowley tells us: "A national reputation can be got from publishing in every important journal in the field and from publishing good books." To make your case, as Juanita Comfort advised during a workshop presentation at the CCCC, be sure to keep track of the "life cycle of your work." This is no easy job, but what this advice recognizes is that establishing your reputation means establishing the "use value" and impact that your work has had on the greater field of rhetoric and composition. Take time to check regularly reviews of your work, to gather citations of your work, to follow those who have taken your work as foundational to their own research, and, as previous chapters have admonished: document, document, document your findings. It seems self-aggrandizing, and hence uncomfortable to most women—except for the Queen Bees, of course—but it is an important part of building your case for promotion to full professor.[7]

Another way you can establish your national and international reputation is to remain actively involved in our discipline's conferences, as Bizzell advises: "I still think conferences are a good way to promote one's reputation, if we have to think in those terms. Organize panels that showcase your cutting-edge work. Smaller conferences are especially good because you can network there more easily with others with like-minded interests." Selfe also uses conferences as an opportunity to give "rein to [her] natural inclination to enjoy other people and their work":

> Whenever I hear papers I like, or read articles I think particularly smart, I talk to the authors and tell them so—even if it feels awkward and dorky! And the next time I try an edited collection, or I need an article for *Computers and Composition*, I ask them to contribute. Such things generally lead to longer-term relationships that often involve reciprocal exchanges, contributions, and visits.

Such networking—and your growing reputation—may result in your being invited to be featured as a plenary or keynote speaker at the major conferences or to be invited on other campuses as a guest lecturer. These are time-consuming activities, to be sure, taking you away from your classes, research and writing time, and other commitments—such as your life. However, such opportunities can prove to be a key CV-builder, and hence a case for promotion to full. Not all opportunities are created equal, so you will want to use some judgment in selecting which speaking obligations you accept.

But, as in all cases, you will want the presentation to be a part of a larger research agenda. Such presentations can, as Krista Ratcliffe argues, provide an audience for your work. But, clearly, the admonition is to make sure that there are published counterparts of such presentations: not only to further press your reputation and grow your audience but to convince your colleagues back home that you're exceptionally productive. Lunsford advises: "Make every conference presentation one that can easily be turned into a publishable article. Keep an eye out to weaving essays together into a book, and always be thinking about the 'next project.'" Remember: the currency of success in academe is publications, as Bizzell reminds us: "basically, you just have to write good stuff and publish it."

Networking

One hopes that one's publication record will pave the way for such invitations and for a proper recognition of one's influence and reputation in the field. The reality is, of course, that many publications are a function of your relation to those who review such publications for press. And the various invitations may also be a function of your relationship to others in the field, a.k.a.: the "big cheeses." You will also need to establish relationships with the big cheeses, so that they might agree to write you powerful and convincing external review letters for your case to full professor. So, how to appropriately "suck up" to "big cheeses"? Ms. Mentor writes:

> Verily, Ms. Mentor declares, too little is said about post-tenure in the academy. Rare is the sage counsel for those who've more or less Made It—past tenure—and now ask, "How do I scale the heights of full professorhood?" (Or "How do I kick my way through the glass ceiling of perpetual associate professorship?") You need a campaign to make yourself better known among the powerful. Luckily, you do not need buttons or funny hats, and you can use the research skills you already possess to make two bibliographies. The first will list those already among your admirers: readers who have complimented your writings; conference-goers who have praised your papers; on-line pen pals; positive book reviewers. Your second list will be those who might help now. With them, the campaign kicks off. Through e-mail, you may seek out your powerful targets for a chat, although many influential senior professors remain electronic Luddites … . Most Great Ones do eventually appear in the flesh at conferences, however, where they can be accosted and complimented on their work. You are reminded that even when flattery is transparent, the effort is flattering. And so, you should have business cards to exchange at conferences, where you must strive for Visibility. (And if you have to pay your own way to conferences, well, it's a career investment.) You should appear on the general, lofty, wide-ranging panels on "The Profession" or "The Future of…" or "New Directions in … ," rather than narrow readings of a single text … . You should lurk at cash bars and book exhibits and seek opportunities to compliment Big Names on their work—and exchange cards. You can set up conference goals: to distribute twenty cards, for instance. (Toth, *Ms. Mentor's Impeccable Advice* 189–90)

Moving Up or Moving On?

At this transitional phase in your life, one of the choices you may be entertaining is: should I attempt to move up (go to full professor) at this institution, or should I choose to move on at another institution? No doubt, there are many contextual influences: love may have been lost with an administrator or colleague, prohibiting your institutional effectiveness or desire to continue in your role; state legislators may have forestalled proper recompense for your efforts, resulting in a serious case of salary compression; you sense that your research and contributions will be more appreciated at another institution—instances all that may convince you to move on rather than to press for advancement at your own institution. Or, perhaps, you may—in moving on—be presented with opportunities where you may also move up in professorial rank. Or perhaps you may desire to move on to upper-administration work—this is the stage in life where there are choices to be made.

If you desire to move to full professor at your current institution, or elsewhere, review the suggestions in a previous chapter about moving from assistant to associate professor: the foundational recommendations are the same—ascertain a clear understanding of the requirements and keep impeccable records of your accomplishments—which presumes, of course, that you are accomplishing, publishing, establishing yourself as a "player" in the field of rhetoric and composition. Jarratt advised:

> If you can manage it, try to be strategic in your choice of activities—service and administration as well as publication .... If there's a way to use the service and administration realms as material for publication, that can be helpful; moving conference papers to articles, publishing teaching materials. I've found (and I've heard this from others as well) that, without the threat of actually losing your job, and with the many distractions that come after tenure, pushing through to the second book is difficult. Maybe—in selecting the second major project, [I would advise] not going so far afield from the first.

Bizzell advised that it is "especially important at this level to document responses to your work by others—book reviews, citations in the work of others, etc. (and don't assume your committee will do the googling to find out how famous you are)."

However, despite this foundational advice, the move from associate to full professor is more complicated and shrouded with more unspoken protocol and mystery than the move from assistant to associate professor and thus requires savvy, strategy, and support. "Promotion to full is a tricky business," Lunsford told us: "in my experience, departments have varying criteria for this move." Glenn concurred: the move to full "all depends on the institution, the department head, the personnel committee. It all depends—which is not the answer you want, I know. What I know is this: what will get one person promoted to full at one perfectly good institution will not get another person tenure at another perfectly good institution. I have been stunned to find out that some leaders in our field have been held back for a year or two, promoted with hesitation/controversy, or never promoted at all." Bizzell also noted that "at some places, there is an unspoken queue for promotion. Your department may include some 30-year associate professors who have been slogging away at the one book, hoping to get promoted when it is finished. Will anyone consider it bad form if you jump the queue and put yourself up ahead of these worthies? I was concerned about that, so I consulted a couple of the full professors in my department and was told to go ahead."

The best strategy for negotiating this unspoken and unwritten protocol is, according to Lunsford: "to keep in very close touch with the chair and/or dean, so that you know what these shifting criteria may be, to get in writing such expectations as you can, and to look to recent cases of promotion to full to see how they seem to have worked. *Imitatio* can be an especially useful trope at promotion time!"

Employ this trope when assembling your promotion materials. Examine the documents of successful candidates to full professor with an eye to imitating their compelling quality. Assemble your materials, as advised in a previous chapter, rhetorically: to persuade all the various committees of the value of your work, as a sustained (and sustainable) research agenda, and the value of rhetoric and composition studies in general (do not assume that university-wide committees will understand the value and import of such research). Bizzell advises:

> With more material, maybe much more, to consider at this level, your committee will be even more appreciative of an extremely well-organized package that makes it very easy for them to see what's there and what you've accomplished—many executive summaries, electronic indexing guides if you submit electronically or all those pretty tabs and folders from Staples if in paper copy.

Jarratt reminds us of another important strategy if one aims to move to full professor:

> Don't forget to apply for the next promotion! I've noticed with some women (and maybe men, too, I'm not certain), they're so relieved to get tenure that they don't think too much about the next stage. I believe that was my own case; my chair suggested that I go up for promotion. But it's very important. We need more women in the highest ranks.

In Sum: The Keys to the Queendom

We began this chapter acknowledging the mythic nature of the "keys to the queendom," but the sum of all the rich counsel we received from our online survey responses and from our profiled women has led us to believe that there is a solid set of advice that could serve as such: as keys to "making it" in rhetoric and composition. Indeed, Jarratt offered this advice:

> Persistence seems important: developing a base of knowledge and building on it; forging solid connections in your institution but not sacrificing your scholarly life to service commitments; building

> national connections with others in your area by attending conferences, keeping up e-mail connections, and trying to keep current in the scholarship; trying to test ideas through course development; finding a writing plan that works for you. In rhetoric and composition, not being afraid to move outside our field seems important—looking at the intellectual movements in cultural studies, literary studies, feminism, etc. Take advantage of local institutional opportunities for events, collaboration, and individual grants.

And Glenn:

> Publish; collaborate in terms of writing, organizing events/panels; work like hell (say yes); and laugh. Also try to remember that you're always interviewing for a job, especially when you don't know you are. And don't be mean to people, for god's sake, no matter how important you (generic you) think your book is, your panel presentation, your thinking, your collection of essays, your identity, whatever. Life's too short, and memories are too long.

And Crowley:

> Follow your research where it leads you. Try not to take up research assignments that you don't find interesting simply because a friend or colleague asks you to collaborate .... In regard to service: Do what you are told to do by administrators who evaluate you, and make sure that they know you've done it and done it well. Document everything .... Befriend as many colleagues as you can, especially those outside of rhetoric and composition .... [And] *never* burn bridges.

And Lunsford:

> My goodness, I wish I had a set of fool-proof keys to the queendom, but I'm afraid I don't. I'd say that success in our field today is probably more related to personal goals than it was in the past: what I mean by this is it seems possible to me today to set out your own standards for success and to meet them rather than going solely by the goals set by the institution. That might mean having a rich family life AND a rich academic life and find ways to make both those things possible. Just in terms of the profession, I don't think there's anything more important than articulating a question or problem of great personal urgency/importance to you and pursuing it relentlessly. That will always lead to good, strong, sound scholarship.

Selfe had no ready-made keys to hand, but she did tell us the key to her success: "No keys here, I just put my head down and work."

Serving the Future (Women) of Our Discipline

A number of our profiled women felt a profound sense of responsibility to use whatever "keys" they had acquired to make the field of rhetoric and composition a "more representative and inclusive" discipline (Glenn) and to clear a space for new and/or "marginal" work. Jarratt told us:

> I think there's an opportunity within professional organizations, editing journals and newsletters, serving on program committees for conferences, and in reviewing articles to help set a direction for the field. I do think about that; it's important … . To the extent that I can, I'd like to help clear the way for exciting new work, perhaps work on the margins, and try to make sure that there are listening ears—that there's an openness to a new approach.

Likewise, Lunsford told us:

> given my advancing years, … on most days I do recognize that I am entering (or already in) the last phase of my career and indeed of my life. But I am also aware that this phase may, with luck, be a fairly long one and that I may have a good few years left in which to learn and to keep contributing to our field. What I do feel now much more so than earlier in life is the need and desire to provide a platform for the work of others, to make space for others, whenever and wherever I can. Because of my belief in the efficacy of collaboration, I have always had this goal in mind, but it seems more present to me now, and perhaps I feel in a better position to be able to make those spaces open up.

Using such "keys" to open up new spaces, these successful women have translated the aim of "making it" into "making it possible for others" (Selfe).

Thriving as a Professional

ESSENTIAL RESOURCES

Succeeding in Research, Teaching, and Service

Boice, Robert. *Advice for New Faculty Members: Nihil Nimus*

Moxley, Joseph M. and Todd Taylor, eds. *Writing and Publishing for Academic Authors*

Making Your Tenure and Promotion Case

Whicker, Marcia Lynn, Jennie Jacobs Kronenfeld, and Ruth Ann Strickland. *Getting Tenure*

Administering Writing Programs

Brown, Stuart C. and Theresa Enos, eds. *The Writing Program Administrator's Resource*

Ward, Irene, and William J. Carpenter, eds. *The Allyn & Bacon Sourcebook for Writing Program Administrators*

Section III

AND HAVING A LIFE, TOO

6

SEARCHING FOR WELL-BEING

Strategies for Having a Life

> If you don't live a balanced life, your initiatives probably aren't sustainable.
>
> —anonymous survey respondent

> It would be easier to live with a greater clarity of ambition, to follow goals that beckon toward a single upward progression. But perhaps what women have to offer in the world today, in which men and women both must learn to deal with new orders of complexity and rapid change, lies in the very rejection of forced choices: work or home, strength or vulnerability, caring or competition, trust or questioning. Truth may not be so simple.
>
> —Mary Catherine Bateson

Throughout this book, we have focused on strategies for succeeding in your career, gleaned from our survey data, the profile interviews, and the literature. But, as our opening anecdote reveals, it was the color-coded closet of a famous feminist scholar that prompted us to ask the question, "How do successful women organize their lives?" It was not just this woman's productivity as a scholar that intrigued us—it was also her strategies for living. Like many women in higher education, we struggle to find a balance among work, family/love, and leisure/play. And we are not alone. When we asked participants in our national survey to name the most difficult challenge they have faced as women faculty in rhetoric and composition, they overwhelmingly responded that it was how to "have a life" while pursuing a career. These women put their difficulty in remarkably similar terms. One responded, "balancing career, community, and home." Another wrote, "balancing family life and professional life and balancing my own academic work with my administrative work have been the greatest challenges." Still another explained, "balancing both my life as a single parent of a needy child and my intellectual and scholarly pursuits against the demands placed on me as a tenured faculty member." Another wrote, "Managing my time among several important career and personal demands." Of course, the participants in this study voice a problem that is common among women faculty in general. But among women faculty in rhetoric and composition, who often shoulder more administrative duties and additional student mentoring, time constraints are magnified even more. As one respondent put it, "Teaching [writing] is a psychically draining profession. You have to be present for your students and colleagues in so many ways through the workday. Many times I have headed home feeling so emotionally empty that I just wanted to go to bed when I got home and have no further human contact that day."

When we asked our survey participants what they would do differently if they could begin their career over again, we learned that for many, work/life conflicts were a source of deep regret. One wrote, "I would try to have more of the normal things in life. It is no accident that I am single and have no children." Another wrote, "I would probably change careers. My most likely choice would be training and development in the workplace, an area where I could teach, […] and earn a wage that would enable me to adequately support myself and my child." Another commented, "If I could begin all over, I might actually choose a different career—probably law. The reason for this is personal more than anything. I find that academic success requires isolation, and as I get older, this is getting harder. I sometimes wish I had a job that required more personal interaction." Many women faculty reported that finding a balance between the demands of work with other interests and responsibilities was even more difficult than performing the tasks associated with obtaining tenure and promotion. In fact, because of work/life dilemmas, 16 percent of our survey participants reported that they would not choose academic work in rhetoric and composition if they could begin their lives again. Over 10 percent would leave higher education altogether for professional careers, including medicine, law, computer science, and professional writing.

Self-help books for academics are not particularly helpful in responding to this problem. Ms. Mentor [Emily Toth], Kathryn Hume, and others argue that there are too few jobs in the humanities for graduate students with worries about balancing work, family, and leisure to continue on with their career pursuit. For Ms. Mentor, only intrinsic interest in the work is a good enough reason to choose an academic life, in part because the work is too demanding to be sustained for extrinsic rewards (*Ms. Mentor's Impeccable Advice* 14). Ms. Mentor is not alone in her belief. "Don't go into this field unless you can't think of anything better to do with your time," one of our colleagues often says to graduate students. However, this perspective is perplexing to a graduate student or untenured faculty member who does love the work but wants to maintain her equilibrium. While in our experience embracing the difficulties of academic life and doing a thorough self-examination are necessary and helpful, the "love it or leave it" advice suggests that achieving well-being in higher education is relatively impossible unless one's personality, career goals, and academic culture are closely aligned.

Of course, in some ways, the self-help books are right. The problems associated with academic culture are relatively consistent. As one survey participant put it, the academy "encourages the bad behavior of workaholics." Universities rely on a patriarchal model of work and are relatively conservative and inflexible. Medieval universities employed a faculty of clerics who had no (legitimate) families. Later, when university faculty had families, it was assumed that wives and servants would manage all aspects of the private life so that scholars could devote themselves to their work. When women were finally accepted as faculty, the system did not change—rather, they were expected to fit into the system. In a climate that forces all faculty to adjust to a structure that fails to recognize obligations within the private life, women are likely to find it difficult to maintain balance. Indeed, as we previously noted, universities are leaking women and faculty of color; fewer obtain tenure than earn PhDs and many leave before tenure. In real terms, our lives are not supported by the institution's structure. Pregnancy, adoption, child/elder care, marriage/partnership, and health issues are challenging in an academic environment. Equally problematic is the culture, which can be hostile to those perceived to be outsiders (often by virtue of perceived differences of gender, sexual orientation, race, religion, or even region). Such hostility, which comes from both students and colleagues, requires difficult emotional adjustments, or as one survey respondent put it, the ability to handle "the grief [that] just comes with the territory." These issues are largely credited for the disgraceful fact that although women now receive 51 percent of the doctorates in the U.S., the gap between the percentage of tenured women and men in higher education has not changed in 30 years (Trower and Chait).

But the news is not all bad. Higher education affords tenure-track faculty with access to some recognized sources of mental well-being in the workplace, including relatively high levels of control over our work. To the extent that careers in rhetoric and composition provide opportunities for us to do work we are interested in and allow us to control aspects of the job we dislike, they can be extremely rewarding. One can be overworked and yet happy. As Ellen Ostrow puts it, "Balance [in an academic career] comes from your vital engagement in, and personal striving toward, goals that give your life a sense of meaning and purpose."

The women scholars we interviewed for this study are orderly and focused, with lives that emanate discipline. They organize their lives around their work, but in ways that are sustainable and generative. They are women of extraordinary drive who have discovered life strategies that work for them most of the time. It is true that they tend to be, as Cheryl Glenn puts it, "OWOCs": overworking over-committers, who put in long hours every day. But for the women we interviewed, the question was not, "How do I have a life?" but rather, "How do I find the *right balance* of work and outside activities/responsibilities for *me*?" For as we will suggest in this chapter, women faculty in rhetoric and composition have very different relationships with the academy that affect how they define "balance." In addition, over the course of a career, one's sense of balance changes. Drawing on our interview and survey data, in this chapter we respond to the question, "How do I have a life while pursuing a career in rhetoric and composition?" In the next chapter, we address the question, "How do I adjust to academic culture, and to what degree must I do so?" In the process we discuss the emotional side of work, socialization/enculturation in the academia, ways of rejuvenating oneself, and family/partnership issues.

Approaches to "Having a Life": Integration vs. Isolation

Books on academic culture are replete with stories about the socially backward English professor. For example, a maid at a convention hotel during the MLA is reported to have observed the following about the behavior of professors she cleaned up after:

> "I changed their sheets and cleaned their bathrooms, and except for a few slip-slobs, it was a snap," the cleaning woman reported. "They don't throw food around, they don't smoke, they don't drink, they don't even fuck around.
>
> "Who *are* these people?" (Toth, *Ms. Mentor's Impeccable Advice* 57)

Those professors, are, apparently, *us*. In her workshop presentation to a group of women faculty in March 2003, Sharon Crowley said emphatically that a woman who decides to go into this field must be prepared to have no life at all (Crowley worked seven days a week until she was promoted to full professor, when she finally made a point not to work on Saturdays). Of course, women faculty in rhetoric and composition have been known to live it up a little at CCCC or MLA, but more to the point, a common complaint is that our lives are, well, a little dull, and sometimes, isolating and lonely.

The successful women we interviewed work very long hours. Most work at least twelve hours a day, often hours spent in the office away from home. For example, Cynthia L. Selfe arrives at her office each day at around 7:00 am and does not leave until around 7:00 pm. Andrea A. Lunsford and Jacqueline Jones Royster, both administrators at the time of our study, also work long hours in the office. Cheryl Glenn is at her desk at home around 7:00 am each day and stays there until it is time to teach, late in the afternoon. One summer when she was trying to write a textbook, Crowley began working around the clock. "I can only write for about four hours at a time," she told us. When she has had "pretty serious pressure from the publisher to finish a first draft," however, she has written in multiple four-hour sessions in a day. For example, when she was writing the first edition of *Ancient Rhetorics for Contemporary Students*, she had only a single summer available to her. She got up early, wrote for four hours, then took a break to walk or run errands. She came back to write another four hours, and then she slept. After awhile, her cycle of writing and sleeping disconnected her from the outside world. One day her cat nudged her while she was working, and she said, "What do you want?" "I'd realize I hadn't fed her for twelve hours. I'd look up and the clock would say ten, and I would think, 'Oh, it's ten at night.' But I'd look out and the sun was shining—it was ten in the morning. I've had this happen with other writing projects, too. You get sort of transported to another place and you can't really be with anyone. Even your cat is a distraction." Crowley likens such work patterns to addiction and says that she has often surprised herself by working so many hours over a long period of time without coming up for air. But what we learned from Crowley and the others is that they *love* the work they do. The work itself is rejuvenating. It is, in fact, their lives.

As several of the women in our interview study suggested, it is important for women faculty to identify what they want for their careers by first identifying what gives them pleasure. Several scholars described their work as sustaining them. After describing a difficult time in her personal life, Lunsford said, "My work is what has sustained me. My work and my sisters and my women friends have sustained me." When asked what advice she would give a graduate student about to embark on a faculty career, Shirley Wilson Logan responded that a woman needs to locate where her passions are. She used her own work on Ida B. Wells as an example. "I remember that what got me going with [my research] was the Ida Wells stamp that came out," she said. "I was just curious about it; I had never heard of her. It got me looking into her and some of the work she had done." She had been in an adjunct position at the University of Maryland, but when she decided to work on the edited collection *With Pen and Voice*, she decided to apply for a tenure-track position. "I thought, 'Well, I'm going to do this anyway. I might as well get credit.' I would have done it anyway." When asked what advice she would give to a graduate student, she reiterated, "[T]ry to find where your passion is. Because that's going to have to sustain you in times when it's not all roses. But if you have a passion for it, then that's going to keep you going. Because you have to *want* to know or find out whatever it is that you're doing. It can't just be about the profession, or about advancing, or about promotion."

A question frequently asked in faculty development literature is this: "What do you want from academia? How do *you* define a successful career?" In her response to a graduate student who wondered how to find a "marketable" dissertation topic, Ms. Mentor declares, "Academia does not pay well enough for people to sell their souls that way" (Toth, *Ms. Mentor's Impeccable Advice* 14). Instead, she suggests that the graduate student begin immediately to search her soul and discover the answer to the following questions: "What am I really interested in?" and "What do I want to do with my life?" (15). She concludes by arguing, "Ms. Mentor believes that her wise readers should choose pleasure over pain. If living an interesting life inspires them more than the prospect of committing literary criticism, then they should choose life" (17–18). For Ms.

Mentor, if academics do not see academic work in the life they envision, or, rather, life in the academic work, then they should find a different career path.

Our research and review of literature on successful strategies for academic careers suggests that the question, "How can I have a life while being an academic?" is balanced on a faulty dichotomy: work vs. life. Researchers have long observed that, for many people, the most enjoyable moments of life occur on the job (Gardner, Csikszentmihalyi, and Damon 5). Mihaly Csikszentmihalyi studied artists, athletes, and creative professionals (including teachers, surgeons, and musical composers), trying to identify a kind of experience that would cause people to pursue their skill or profession without strong extrinsic rewards (such as status or money). Csikszentmihalyi discovered that when individuals learn complex skills and then are engaged with a highly demanding task equal to those skills, they often experience a level of enjoyment and well-being that he calls "flow" or "optimal experience."

> [W]hen artists, athletes, or creative professionals describe the best times experienced in their favourite activities, they all mention this dynamic between opportunity and ability as crucial. […] [O]ptimal experience or flow as we came to call it using some of the respondents' own terminology, is differentiated from states of boredom, in which there is less to do than one is capable of, and from anxiety, which occurs when things to do are more than one can cope with. (Csikszentmihalyi 17)

While men and women report feeling a sense of "flow" or enjoyment from watching television or driving, the only experiences that offer a long-term sense of well-being occur when one is engaged in a task that is difficult but in which one momentarily loses track of time and self. Paradoxically, this temporary loss of self-reference coupled with a sense of having pushed oneself mentally and/or physically creates a sense of well-being. In other words, as Crowley's story illustrates most dramatically, it is the experience of losing track of time while making progress in one's work or art that offers a person the highest sense of pleasure. And for most people, this sense of pleasure occurs while performing one's job.

Such research goes against commonly held beliefs about work and leisure. The concept of work that informs Western culture begins with the biblical story of creation (Gardner, Csikszentmihalyi, and Damon 15). According to this well-known creation myth, the Garden of Eden provided everything that Adam and Eve needed. It was not until they were driven from Eden that they were consigned to lives of toil. Work, according to Western tradition, is the consequence of human error, not the highest fulfillment of human creativity and ingenuity. Consequently, many Americans believe that their lives would improve if only they didn't have to work (and television feeds this belief with its obsessive focus on the lives of the leisure classes). But studies show that 80 percent of

Americans would not quit their jobs if they were given enough money to live well; and indeed, retirement is often marked by deep psychological distress rather than relief (Gardner, Csikszentmihalyi, and Damon 15).

As early second-wave feminists recognized, work is profoundly good when an individual feels that she is in control over her own labor and has the freedom to make choices about it. Research shows that control over one's work is a key to personal well-being in the workplace (Warr 4). First interested in the debilitating effects of unemployment, Peter Warr studied the way in which institutions shape experience and influence personal well-being. In 1986, Warr established nine "principal environmental influences" on individual experience: opportunity for control, environmental clarity, opportunity for skill use, externally generated goals, variety, opportunity for interpersonal contact, valued social position, availability of money, and physical security. Control can affect an individual's access to all the other environmental factors, as is clearly seen in a study of working women by Maria T. Allison and Margaret Carlisle Duncan. Interested in working women's experience of "flow" or enjoyment, Allison and Duncan studied a group of professionals (faculty and research associates in theater arts, English and biology) and a group of blue-collar workers (factory workers and service providers). They discovered that control was a significant factor of enjoyment for both groups of women in all areas of life (defined in this study as work, interpersonal relationships, and sports and creative activities) (130–5). But women professionals experienced a sense of control and well-being in both their work and personal lives, whereas for blue-collar women workers, lack of control at work led to boredom and frustration. Tenure-track faculty often have remarkable control over their working lives, choosing what hours to work and when and where, and many can enjoy freedom from commuting to their college or university work during summers and between semesters. If they crave interpersonal contact, often they can choose whether to write at home or in their offices or at a coffee shop. To borrow a phrase from Mary Catherine Bateson, academics can "compose their lives" in a myriad of ways because they do enjoy more control over their work than women in many other kinds of organizations.

In short, our research suggests that women faculty may be asking the wrong question about their work/life dilemmas. Rather than ask, "How can I have a life while doing this job?" women faculty who feel a sense of satisfaction in their lives instead ask, "How can I find a balance that sustains me?" We have discovered two strategies that seem to work well for successful women faculty in rhetoric and composition: *integration* of work-life and home-life, and *isolation* of work-life from home-life. Through our interviews, we discovered that both of these strategies have served successful women scholar/teachers very well in achieving a livable balance of working at academic and private pursuits. By *integration* we mean faculty who enjoy socializing with their academic colleagues and therefore fully entwine their personal and professional lives. By *isolation* we refer to faculty who "compartmentalize" their private and professional lives, carefully cultivating both, but keeping them distinct. We begin with the strategy of *integration*, using Cynthia L. Selfe as our exemplar.

Selfe lived and worked in Houghton, Michigan, at the time of our interview with her. Houghton is a small university town, population 7,010, which sits on Portage Lake in Michigan's Upper Peninsula. Married to Dickie Selfe, who at the time was working and teaching at Michigan Tech as well, Cindy Selfe describes her life as a seamless fabric of public and private life. Integration is a key feature of Selfe's working strategy. Selfe's department head and mentor, Art Young, asked her to participate in administrative work as an assistant professor (Michigan Tech did not require her to publish a book for tenure), and Selfe learned from Young to use every opportunity as a platform for publication. She said, "scholarship and the teaching were never separate for me. And the scholarship and the administration were never separate, and scholarship and program direction were never separate," because Young led all junior faculty to find ways to combine scholarship, teaching, and administration. She credits her productivity to Young's philosophy. She explained, "So, even as I'm doing something, I'm thinking, do other colleagues have to do this? How can I write about it? What am I doing that other people might want to know about? Are other people experiencing these challenges?" Indeed, Selfe's experience with integrating scholarship, teaching, and administration gives her a different view of the role of junior faculty in WPA positions. She argues that it is a mistake to withhold such positions from junior faculty. "If that person can integrate the scholarship and the administrative work," she argued, "then I think it's a really totally healthy position." Her advice follows the overall trend of her life, which is to ask every area of her life to address every other. When called upon to do administrative work, Selfe used what she learned in that position to pose research questions that then could be answered through scholarship. For her, scholarship becomes more of a dialogue when it addresses questions of practical academic concern.

In the office by 7:00 am, and not leaving until 7:00 or 8:00 pm, Selfe works long hours at her office, and tries to relax when she is home. But that does not mean that she separates her private and public life. Indeed, for Selfe, such a distinction makes little sense, since her husband and friends are her colleagues. Living in a small college town among faculty with a "great collegial ethic" helped her enact this model of life. Of her colleagues she reported, "[o]ur scholarly life and our academic life and our life outside of school are very integrated. We live a very integrated existence." She explains,

> I work alongside Marilyn Cooper and Diana George and Nancy Grimm and Carol Berkenkotter and Beth Flynn, and those are the same people I have socialized with. So I go from the office talking to Marilyn, to a potluck dinner that Marilyn brings her dog to, to over to Diana's house—we live like two miles away or something. So my work and my life are the same thing. I really do have a life and Dickie is

> a marvelous part of that. Dickie, my husband, is right there, so we carry our work home and carry our home to work.

Every Sunday afternoon in winter, the Selfes invited their colleagues and students to their home in Houghton for a "doggie potluck scrum." Twenty people went out skiing or snowshoeing with their dogs, and all returned to the Selfes' home for the potluck. The Selfes are childless by choice, but their two dogs, Gracie and Bosco, were fully integrated into the life of the department. Selfe credits the size of the town and the collegiality of her department for this integration of work and community. But it is clear that she made the choice to integrate her life and work in very satisfying ways and that was part of the reason her department has a reputation of being so collegial. "My life is so bound up with my work," she said, and in many ways, it is a life in which the whole is larger than the sum of the parts.

Several of the women we interviewed write primarily at home in order to take advantage of the quiet that a home office affords them. A working strategy that sets Selfe apart from the others is her ability to write "in the interstices of [her] day." While at the university, she can write whenever there is a pause in her schedule—between meetings, classes, drop-in visits. She can write even after frequent interruptions. In contrast, one prolific woman scholar, Cheryl Glenn, compartmentalizes her life. She keeps what she calls "bistro hours" at Penn State University, holding office hours and teaching her classes in the late afternoon and evening so that she can write in the morning. One of the reasons she enjoys working at home so much is that she loves the company of her dog, Charley. Glenn therefore takes a different approach to the life/work relationship from Selfe: she practices *isolation* of home life (which, for her, includes writing) from working life (teaching and service). Glenn works very long hours (including the time she writes), but when she quits working late in the evening or when seeing friends or on vacation, she is able to turn off the pressures of work and relax. In fact, she screens phone calls so that her down time is not interrupted by work-related concerns. This is the second successful strategy for life and work used by our interviewees, and it is the more common one.

As studies suggest, women professionals are more likely to feel that their work and home life compete for their time and attention. While the integration (*overlap*) of work and home life can solve this problem, this strategy is not possible for most women with dependent children or elder care responsibilities. Neither is it possible for women whose colleagues do not share the community ethic of Selfe or who find themselves politically or culturally isolated. One way or another, the question of balance is a personal one, and finding that balance is critical. Often the way to gain that balance is to set hard boundaries around work, or to see the cultivation of one's personal life as crucial to one's ability to bring energy to one's work. As Krista Ratcliffe put it in a presentation to other women faculty in rhetoric and composition,

> [B]alancing your career and your life is the most important thing you can do for your own peace of mind. Find something that you love in addition to your work, something that grounds you and reminds you that your value as a person lies beyond your yearly review letters, beyond the sniping of normal departmental politics, beyond acerbic reader comments on your articles and manuscripts, and beyond the impulse to bean count items on your CV. (2)

For some women, of course, the grounding element beyond work is family (partner, children, extended family). But for others it is community, synagogue, church, or volunteer activities. For example, Logan is a deacon at her church, a leadership position that is deeply satisfying to her. (She also has grown children whose schedules she worked around while attending graduate school and teaching as an adjunct faculty member at the University of Maryland.)

Patricia Bizzell is a notable example of a woman who has successfully isolated her home and work life. While a prolific writer with a busy work life, Bizzell always ends work on Friday evenings and does not resume it again until Sunday morning in observance of Shabbat (Sabbath), a day of rest in the Jewish tradition. In our interview with her, Bizzell said, "It's a very valuable thing to have a Sabbath, and I recommend it. From sundown on Friday to sundown on Saturday, we don't answer the phone, we don't turn on the computer, we don't turn on the TV or the radio, we don't drive anywhere. We have a lovely meal Friday night, and we sit at the table for a long time. And then we sit around on Saturday morning, go to synagogue, take a nap Saturday afternoon, we go for a walk." She went on to say that "This was and is precious family time, and rest time, and you have to learn how to do it. It's a real discipline." Bizzell acknowledged that it was difficult for her to stop working for an entire day, but that doing so has been "a lifesaver in many, many ways." She recommends such a day of rest for everyone, and argues that it should not be a day to take children on an outing, but instead a true day of rest. You have to "turn off the world," she emphasized. In addition to reading and taking a walk, in their time together Bizzell and her family listen to classical music (she is a serious aficionado who regularly buys new recordings) and go to concerts and dance performances (modern and classical). Bizzell described her life as rich and full, in part because of this commitment to scheduling a day of rest and in part to their commitment to cultivating interests unrelated to work.

While Bizzell alluded to her workaholic tendencies in our interview with her and wished she did not have to live by her wristwatch, she still finds time for herself. At the end of the day, she is likely to be reading Jewish history or what she calls "junk reading"—detective fiction or other suspense novels just for fun. While she claims to have no "serious hobbies" (she was leading both her department and the Rhetoric Society of America at the time of our interview), Bizzell has a host of activities that she engages in to relax, including walking the dog and cooking (from scratch, when she can). When she does have more time, Bizzell hopes to study advanced Hebrew, garden more seriously, sail, and ride horses. All these activities (both those she has managed to incorporate into her life and those she has not) are, by design, separate from her work (although her study of Jewish history has begun to inform her scholarship).

Whether a life strategy of integration or isolation (or, as for most of us, a combination of the two) works best for a woman faculty member, academic work is seasonal. Faculty with a traditional workload spend more time teaching and offering service to the institution during the nine months of the academic year, while summers are a time of doing research and writing. From year to year, workloads change. This is particularly true for faculty in rhetoric and composition, who are more likely than their colleagues to rotate in and out of administration. For this reason, we encourage women to think of finding balance *seasonally*. Several women we interviewed stressed that their schedule changes day to day, and those with children stressed that the balance between work and family grew easier as their children grew older.

The important point is to remember that well-being is established over time. According to Warr, a healthy person finds a balance among the three broad areas of life experience (love, work, and play), which include family life, employment, and leisure. But this balance must be measured across a lifetime, with alternating periods of strain and relaxation at work, and through different stages of life (Haworth 62). Indeed, without some periods of strain during which we employ high levels of skill to meet a large challenge, such as writing a book or founding a new program, women would not experience significant enjoyment at work. Enjoyment (or "flow") involves "intense involvement; clarity of goals and feedback; deep concentration; transcendence of self; lack of self-consciousness; loss of a sense of time; intrinsically rewarding experience; a balance between skill and challenge" (quoted in Haworth 84–5). Just as this match between skill and challenge are seasonal in jobs, so is finding the balance between teaching, research, service, family, and leisure. Viewed over time, a period of overwork for an important goal such as tenure and promotion is not a problem as long as a faculty member takes significant periods of rest.

Managing Emotions and Time

One of the key ideas in this chapter is enhancing one's well-being by engaging in work, family life, and leisure in ways that are sustaining. However, because the pressures of a tenure-track position in rhetoric and composition are so high—particularly for women—managing one's emotional life can be a difficulty all its own. A strong, guiding principle for the successful women in our study is finding activities that sustain and replenish them when they are under stress. When asked about ways she structures her life to keep herself balanced and productive, Royster said, "I try to keep my priorities straight, and none of them are job-related. There is nothing in any job that I can imagine that would cause me to subvert my commitment to my family or what makes me feel like I'm living a good and ethical life." She has maintained this value throughout a career of important leadership positions, including her current role as Executive Dean of the Ohio State University's Colleges of Arts and Sciences. There are good reasons to maintain this perspective. In his 2005 overview of international studies of factors affecting personal happiness (or overall well-being), Richard Layard reports that family relationships (close relationships in private life) are the single most important determiner of happiness, followed somewhat distantly by financial situation and work (62–6).

What Royster and others have learned is that one must keep professional work in perspective. Time and emotion must be spent on what one values, not only on what the institution values. Within the Benedictine tradition, everything in the life of a community is considered of equal importance; washing dishes is equally important to preaching a homily. Benedictines try to devote the same mindfulness to all tasks, without allowing some to overshadow (and therefore overwhelm) the others. *Nihil nimbus*, "everything in moderation," is the guiding principle of Robert Boice's faculty development work. Drawing on the monastic concept of mindfulness, Boice advocates that faculty always work in moderation, never allowing one task to overwhelm their lives. In this section, we will discuss the management of emotions and time, which is the way to maintain balance and perspective in the midst of demanding academic environments.

While traveling in Italy, one of us encountered an interesting story about an American scholar. She had taken the third-floor apartment of a building in a large Italian city while trying to finish a book. During one two-week period, this scholar worked at a frenzied pace, not stopping to shower or go out to eat or take a stroll in the evenings. Understandably, she was irritable and disheveled. Her Italian neighbors, for whom such habits of work are anathema, were alarmed enough that they met and considered calling an ambulance to take her to the hospital. They thought she was physically or mentally ill. An Italian told us this story to illustrate the difference between American and Italian values: Italians never neglect food, family, friends, or daily exercise.

In an earlier chapter we have discussed Boice's strategies for academic writers. Underneath Boice's advice to set aside a relatively small amount of time for writing but to do it every day is the principle of moderation. The alternative, illustrated in our Italian tale, is what Boice calls *bingeing*, or working intensely and maniacally close to a deadline. He writes,

> Society teaches us to work sporadically and, too often, in great binges and under looming deadlines. … This way of working is not only inefficient and unhealthy; it is also self-perpetuating as well as self-defeating. Because binges, so long as they last, exclude other important tasks that need doing, those too must eventually be binged. And because binges need long periods of uninterrupted time—whole

> mornings, entire days, weekends, vacations, sabbaticals, retirements, perhaps even reincarnations—we suppose that shorter periods … are unsuitable for creative work. Said one binger to me: "The whole morning is shot; I might as well get some errands done at least; I couldn't get any good [work] done now, in what little time remains." (39)

While bingeing, a faculty member allows sustaining activities such as exercise and social interaction to fall away, which wears away her overall sense of well-being. Worse still, work for bingers becomes associated with mania and exhaustion, which anyone would seek to avoid as long as possible. Therefore, many faculty who work in binge sessions are procrastinators prone to anxiety and depression.[8]

As specialists in the teaching of writing, we should know the importance of working in moderation and practice it. But, as Donald Murray reminds us, "most academic writers don't write enough to get up to speed" (quoted in Boice 138), and to write enough, according to Boice and others, one must write daily. Creative writers practice their craft daily; rhetoric and composition faculty preach it, but few actually do it (Hairston 62). The point is that those who work moderately but do so daily are more productive in the long run. They have the time to engage in other activities that bring balance to their lives, and they feel more confident in themselves because they are productive.

The cycle of overwork and avoidance of work is also a problem in teaching. At the beginning of the twentieth century, faculty at Harvard and other institutions often taught composition to classes of 200 students (Connors, "Overwork/Underpay" 112–13); one report on these deplorable working conditions called the reading of themes for so many students "mental drudgery of the most exhausting nature" (Brereton 75). Fred Newton Scott read 3,000 student essays in the year 1895; his counterpart at Harvard, Barrett Wendell, read 170 students themes *every day* in that period (Connors, "Overwork/Underpay" 113). Working conditions considerably improved with the advent of lower class enrollments, but the fact remains that teaching writing is labor intensive. While presumably rhetoric and composition faculty are personally and professionally motivated to read student writing, the reality is that most of us respond to and grade student writing in exhausting binges the day or two before we have promised to give back papers. The principle of *nihil nimbus* applies here as well. We rarely read as generously as we get to the bottom of the pile after an all-night grading session.

An English professor we know in a small college (where the teaching load is 4/4) required all his students to write a précis for every class. When asked how he graded so many papers every week, he responded that he always graded at least five papers a day. By grading "in the interstices" of his day, to use Selfe's term, he was able to handle a relatively large load of grading, help his English majors learn to read critically, and still work at a moderate level of intensity each day. Boice argues that all teaching tasks can be broken down into manageable chunks that can be accomplished each day (39–46). Such tasks can become daily assignments kept on calendars as small deadlines. Lunsford is a veteran list-keeper who writes every task on her daily planner and crosses off each as she finishes the task. The point is to develop a system that allows one to work moderately but daily to avoid the cycle of bingeing and fasting that is so exhausting and emotionally draining to most people. We would do well to think more like Italians: food, family, friends, and exercise are the core of life. Structuring work around this core is an important key to well-being.

But what happens when one works in a hostile environment? How can you manage your emotional life when you are being sabotaged? Recall the story of the assistant professor in Chapter 5 who was being harassed by a full professor who was so powerful that her chair and dean would not stand up to her. Women in our survey reported that colleagues dismissed their work because they were in rhetoric and composition, worked to prevent their own tenure or the tenure of someone they knew, sexually harassed them, paid them less than male colleagues, subjected them to vicious memos and emails attacking their intellectual integrity, and emotionally abused them in public. One respondent was raped by a colleague who drove her home after a university event (so that she could get home safely). The question is, how does one survive in hostile (even dangerous) environments? Here are some suggestions, drawn from our research.

1. Seek outside help immediately. Several survey respondents who dealt with hostile behavior, including threats from administrators, reached out to other faculty in their own department or outside their department and thereby were able to stop the hostile behavior. One woman who received hostile email messages from a colleague copied the dean whenever she replied to her attacker so that a senior administrator would be aware of her problems. Others suggested getting professional help as soon as possible (many women reported debilitating stress-related illnesses from their experiences with hostile colleagues). For example, one respondent wrote, "I have had the experience of a senior faculty member exerting enormous, sustained, patterned psychological pressure on me to run the writing program her way. At first I responded by trying to carry on a dialogue; gradually I realized that her purpose was not conversation but coercion. I responded by withdrawing from contact with her, doing things my way while trying to account for her perspectives and benefit from her expertise, taking Prozac, and getting psychotherapy."

2. Focus on what you can control: your scholarship. For some women faculty, the best way to respond to a hostile work environment is to leave the institution; focusing on your scholarship ensures that you are in a strong position to do so. The women scholars we interviewed said consistently that when they encountered problems at home or at work, focusing on their scholarship gave them a sense of control. Logan said, "I often use work as my way of absorbing personal issues. I just kind of bury myself in my work … . Work has enabled me to sustain other activities I have been tempted to abandon."

3. Reach out to friends and family. In our interview with her, Lunsford said, "I think that [work] can sustain us through enormous turmoil. [But] it also helps to have lots of girlfriends. Can't have too many girlfriends. Or, too many sisters, in my experience." Royster said that she draws support from her husband and children, her mother, and a group of long-time friends. "Now when I really need love and warmth," Royster stated, "I go home to my mom."

When we asked our survey respondents what they would do differently if they could begin their career again, several responded that they'd find a better balance between their career and "more of the normal things in life." For some, the problem was that their lives were all about work. One wrote, "[I'd] spend more time outside the academy." Another replied, "I do wish I'd had a better perspective when starting graduate school—that you have to have balance in your life. Our work is great; it's real, it's important. But you have to have balance." But others who did put off career in order to pursue a rich private life said they would have thrown themselves into their scholarly careers earlier rather than waiting. "Women my age often arrived at their academic positions later than those now coming through the system," one respondent wrote. "Many of us stopped along the way to have children, take other jobs, and defer our ambitions until a later time. I'd go straight through from college to graduate school to PhD to assistant professor, etc., if given another opportunity." Those who pursued careers while taking care of dependent children or elderly parents reported feeling exhausted, but also this: "All these constraints have shaped my perspectives in such substantial ways that I can't imagine myself without their influences. So, I don't know. The past has shaped me, and struggling with difficult circumstances has kept me working to change the future."

The answer to finding a successful way to manage one's life lies in seeking balance and remembering that seasons of strenuous work must be followed by substantial rest. However the balance is achieved, it is important to remember that we have no choice about seeking it. As Royster puts it, "Unfortunately for us, not only are we [women in rhetoric and composition] talented people, we are trained very usefully to do lots and lots of things. My advice … is to be careful what you say yes to. Stop acting like an amoeba that can absorb everything … . My self reflection [is to] … think twice about whether I *should* do something just because I know I *can* do it well." Indeed, the point is to reflect on your priorities and to have the courage to create the life you want.

7

CREATING A LIFE WITHIN/ BEYOND WORK

Family and Academic Culture

> Once I said to a male colleague that my children need me, and he responded with a puppy-dog look, "We need you, too."
>
> —anonymous survey respondent

> The mobile nature of jobs in higher education demands that we give up what's dear to us—family and stability.
>
> —anonymous survey respondent

Perhaps the most common question asked by women who pursue an academic career is: Should I have children, and if so, when? One of our colleagues decided to have a child while writing her dissertation, in a year in which she was supported by a fellowship. She was fortunate and had her baby right on time, during a moment in her career when she could focus only on writing and taking care of her new infant—her grandmother also moved in to help her. She and her husband decided to wait until she was tenured and promoted to try for a second child, but their lives were so busy that eventually they gave up. They had no time to take care of another infant. The window of opportunity for securing tenure and having children occurs simultaneously for most women who attend graduate school in their 20s and 30s. Because higher education is still dominated by men whose wives either don't work or compromise their careers for the family, women faculty feel the pressure to postpone childbearing or to forgo having a family altogether.

Because academic culture is competitive, homogeneous, and conservative, women faculty who do have children face subtle and overt discrimination. Women faculty and graduate students with family obligations are often considered by many to be less serious about their scholarship than others, regardless of their productivity. A senior male colleague of ours once introduced a junior colleague to the new class of graduate students as the mother of a toddler—he made no comments about her research interests or the graduate-level courses she was teaching. In fact, women encounter more resistance and overt sexism in their academic environment when they try to combine family and career than at any other time in their careers—a resistance not commonly applied to male faculty, even when they are active fathers. Why? "Gender is unbending not only because of its infinite availability as a metaphor, but also because of the way it intertwines gender roles with attractive ideals," Joan William argues. "Our hopes and aspirations, our rebellions and proprieties—all are linked with gendered roles and norms. From the norm of parental care to the structure of the erotic, gender exerts built-in headwinds pushing men and women back into line with conventional gender performances" (246–7). Such norms come into focus when gender norms and academic culture are combined. In this chapter we focus on what to do when your academic life and your personal life come into conflict. We focus first on how to juggle the demands of raising children with a full-time academic position. Next we focus on how to survive in a dual-career marriage or partnership. We end by exploring a few of the many problems that arise from women's cultural differences in academic settings.

Combining Family and Career

As we turn to the difficult subject of balancing work and family obligations, including, especially, care of children and aging parents, we confront an irony: many of the women scholars in our study do not have children. And neither do we. Yet a majority of women balance academic work with the care of dependents at home. Their problems are compounded by academic culture. As one respondent put it,

> I have found my colleagues around the country in rhetoric and composition to be completely understanding and supportive when, for example, I might have to miss a conference at which I was invited to speak because of a family crisis (fortunately, it has not happened very often that I have actually had to renege on an invitation that I accepted). The same cannot be said for my colleagues at my home institution, which is not family friendly unless you are a man in a traditional marriage with a wife at home minding the kids, who can dress them up and bring them to campus for heart-warming Christian holiday events, etc.

Respondents with children frequently reported encountering this double standard. For example, one respondent wrote, "The biggest thing that shook my confidence in myself was that when I was in my 30s and 40s, male professors (senior colleagues, supervisors, etc.) assumed I was not a 'serious' scholar or not 'serious' about my career because I had family responsibilities. Those male profs would praise my husband for achievements 'while being an involved parent,' but never even commented on my labors for my family."

In some cases, respondents reported being harassed by senior colleagues during their pregnancies. For example, one respondent was targeted by the graduate director of her PhD program after taking incompletes in a few of her courses due to pregnancy-related health problems. Although men and women students took incompletes routinely in her program (even when no health issues were involved), the director began harassing her.

> I would be called in for meetings. He would give me arbitrary deadlines for incompletes to be finished, implying that if I did not finish the work, my assistantship would be jeopardized. He made me feel ashamed of myself for having taken incompletes in the first place, and ashamed of being pregnant. He read my pregnant body as a sign of my being an inferior student, someone who was wasting the resources of the department. Three weeks after my baby was born, he called me in for a meeting. He expressed great surprise that I intended to teach in the upcoming fall term, saying that he "naturally" assumed that I would take maternity leave, which the university "in its wisdom" would provide—those are his exact words. He tried to force me to take a leave of absence—with no pay and no health insurance benefits—explaining that the choice was not mine to make, but his.

Eventually she called a friend who worked for a more sympathetic professor, and through networking, she was able to stop the graduate director's efforts to push her out of the program. "However, as a direct result of the harassment," she wrote, "I had trouble nursing my baby, who was losing weight, and I had recurrent breast infections. For over two years, I suffered from depression."

The most persistent problem women faculty with children or other family obligations encounter is an academic culture that requires an undivided devotion to work. In this section we focus on strategies for balancing what Mary Blair-Loy calls the competing schemas of *work devotion* and *family devotion*. Blair-Loy argues that "[c]onflict between work and family is a wrenching contradiction between powerful cultural understandings of who we are as competent and moral adults. These cultural understandings shape our most personal understandings of what we owe our careers, our families, and ourselves" (5). Far from a private "juggling" act, work and family obligations are culturally inscribed and define for us "what makes a meaningful and worthwhile life" (4–5). Blair-Loy followed the lives of 76 women executives, two-thirds of whom she identified as "career-committed," one-third of whom she defined as "family-committed." She found that while "the firm and family … are 'greedy institutions' with 'omnivorous' demands for 'exclusive and undivided loyalty,'" the women in her study recognized that they maintained both worlds and therefore could, to some extent, control and redefine the expectations of those around them (10). The key issue for Blair-Loy is challenging the scripts that "hail" women into impossible positions.

One of the scripts in higher education is the persistent belief in the myth of the "ideal worker."

> An ideal worker is someone who enters a profession immediately upon receiving the relevant credential, works his or her way up the career ladder by putting in long hours without interruptions beyond short vacations, and continues in this fashion until retirement age. The ideal worker can contribute financially to the family, but cannot make substantial time commitments to children or other family members without endangering his or her career. Pay and promotion systems, rules around working time, and the beliefs of those from previous generations who have succeeded as ideal workers and currently manage our organizations, are all built upon the presumption that only ideal workers should be hired, retained, and rewarded. (Drago et al 3–4)

Researchers who studied faculty at Pennsylvania State University theorized that the "ideal worker" syndrome would have two results: first, discrimination against faculty involved in dependent care (either of children or parents), and second, "discrimination avoidance," in which faculty "minimize any apparent or actual intrusions of family life on academic commitments," even when their institutions provide support policies for workers with families (4). The study found that faculty at Penn State (particularly at the main campus) were avoiding taking advantage of family leave and other progressive work/family policies, including a one-year "stay" of the tenure clock for parents of new children (biological or adopted). In the period 1992–1999, 500 faculty members became new parents, but only *seven* of this total took a parental leave (and all who did so were women) (6). Statistics and a focus group study suggested that the *climate* at Penn State was somehow reinforcing the "ideal worker" paradigm, which was built around perceived (if not actual) sacrifices that faculty were expected to make during their pre-tenure years.

As a result of such scripts, women faculty avoid bearing children during the crucial pre-tenure phase of their careers. Of the women we interviewed, only one—Jacqueline Jones Royster—had a child while on the tenure-clock. Royster's case is unusual, however, because she had been promoted to associate and had more than enough publications to be tenured at her first institution (Spelman College). The majority of the women we interviewed had their children before they entered graduate school or chose not to have children. An increasing number of women who attend graduate school during their 20s and early 30s are having children while in graduate school. One survey respondent who was pregnant with her second child while writing her dissertation said,

> A number of my colleagues in composition studies have taken a similar approach—having their babies when close to finishing their dissertations, and they've gotten jobs soon afterwards. Though it's tough to juggle a baby, dissertating, teaching, and trying to present at conferences, etc., I think it's definitely doable, and I know the due date of my

> baby gave me incentive like nothing else to work steadily for 20+hrs a week over the last 6–9 mos. Not everyone is supportive of students as mothers, but from the grad students I've talked to in both lit and composition here at [my institution], women who have children during their grad careers are less conflicted than women who want children now that they're about to go on the market. My colleagues in this position are really wondering when they're going to have the opportunity for kids now that they have the pressure to teach and publish. I think we're all waiting for the system to change—or be more flexible—to allow women greater ability to be both mothers and scholars.

The flexibility of the end-stage of graduate school, when students are either studying for comprehensive exams or writing a dissertation and teaching, is a real advantage over the pressures of pre-tenure appointments. Even if birth delays the attainment of a degree, as one respondent put it, "no one cares if it takes you five or seven years to finish, but they *do* care if you take a hiatus after graduating instead of going on the market." But time is the one problem that all tenure-track faculty fight against: the tenure clock, even when it is stopped for a year, is a relentless and inflexible feature of the current academic system.

Women who choose to have children in graduate school increasingly find women mentors who are willing to help them. For example, in their essay "Mentor, May I Mother?," Catherine Gabor, Carrie Shively Leverenz, and Stacia Dunn Neeley discuss their positive experiences with childbirth during graduate school or pre-tenure years due to the intervention of powerful women mentors. When Leverenz was in graduate school at Ohio State, Andrea A. Lunsford hired her as her personal research assistant when she learned that Leverenz was pregnant. Leverenz put in extra hours before the pregnancy and Lunsford's other research assistant put in more after, a job-sharing arrangement that allowed Leverenz to keep her assistantship. Lunsford and the other rhetoric and composition faculty encouraged graduate students to bring their children to all events and welcomed them as part of the family. The essay shows the importance of sustained attention to mentoring as a way to change the climate for women. As Gabor, Leverenz, and Neeley argue, "The long-standing individualism and competitiveness that characterize academic culture make it difficult for academic institutions to see that the challenges women with children face in meeting standards set by and for men without similar family responsibilities is the result of oppressive cultural norms rather than individual failure" (10).

When women do have children of their own or adopt, they often do so only after having completed the academic project they'll need to earn tenure or until after tenure is achieved. Patricia Bizzell adopted her children after she had tenure. As she put it, "[I said to myself,] I'm really busy, I'm trying to get started here, I don't want to have to think about too many things at once, so let's get tenure first. So I got tenure, then [I thought,] OK, now let's have kids." Bizzell had always wanted children, but she discovered that she and ex-husband Bruce Herzberg could not conceive. Bizzell had a sabbatical leave coming up, so they decided to adopt, timing the adoption so that she could care for their new children while on leave. Holy Cross did not have a parental leave plan in the early 1980s when Bizzell was planning her adoption, so she got together with other faculty and crafted a policy, which Holy Cross, a Jesuit institution, accepted. "I'm the first person," she said, "(I'm very proud of this) to take a maternity leave from Holy Cross." The plan allowed her to take a sabbatical leave and maternity leave back to back during the year her girls first arrived from Korea.

Women who plan to have children during their pre-tenure years should research an institution's policies *and* the practices of the unit they hope to join while interviewing for a position. The Penn State study reports wide disparities in the way that institution's progressive work/family policies were implemented. Therefore, even if policies on parental leave, for example, are available online through a human resources office, a job candidate should look for ways to assess the climate for parental leave in the department. It is often wise for job candidates to arrange to meet with the other junior faculty in the department alone to ask more sensitive questions. Or it is sometimes possible to ask an aggregate question of the department head, such as, "How many faculty who have applied for tenure and promotion have received it in the last 10 years? Of that number, how many were provided with pre-tenure and/or some kind of family leave?" Or a job candidate can ask more generally, "What is the climate for women in this university? What steps has the university taken to attract and retain women faculty?" Normally, offering (and not penalizing women for taking) parental leave is part of an institution's overall strategy for retaining the women they have worked so hard to attract. However, we strongly discourage women from broadcasting their plans to have children while on the tenure clock to prospective employers.

Why? Having children is still considered a disadvantage for women academics. According to Mary Ann Mason and Marc Goulden,

> There is a consistent and large gap in achieving tenure between women who have early babies and men who have early babies, and this gap is surprisingly uniform across the disciplines and across types of institutions. While there are some differences among the sciences, the social sciences, and the humanities, and there are some differences between large research universities and small liberal arts colleges, the "baby gap" is robust and consistent. By our definition, an "early baby" is one who joins the household prior to five years after his or her parent completes the PhD. ("Do Babies Matter")

Mason and Goulden reviewed longitudinal data of 160,000 faculty in the sciences, social sciences, and humanities. Of the data collected between 1973 and 1999, they discovered that having "early babies" is helpful to men on the tenure-track, but it is a strong disadvantage for women. As a result, women on the tenure-track avoid having children. Mason and Goulden measured the number of faculty with children in the household 12 to 14 years following the PhD. They found that a full 62 percent of tenured women in the humanities and social sciences were without children, while only 39 percent of tenured men in the same disciplines were without children ("Do Babies Matter?"). Importantly, the baby gap evaporates when women in non-tenure-track positions are included in the study. Women in these positions were more likely to have children.

How do women (and men) faculty get their work done while taking care of small children at home? Clearly, there is no easy answer to this question. Raising children takes time, and the time must come from somewhere. Institutions have an important role to play in helping women meet these demands. For example, many universities offer childcare facilities on-campus for a fee, which allow parents to drop off their young children and visit them during the day, whenever they wish. Innovative universities sometimes combine childcare centers with ongoing research in early childhood development and education, thus allowing research funding to defray the cost of childcare for parents who are willing to enroll their children in a study. Others heavily subsidize childcare for all employees. At the department level, faculty with young children can be given reduced service loads or service loads that require no regular meetings. But women who choose to have a family before tenure (and it is considered to be a choice), must be prepared to swim against the tide, particularly in the top-tier research institutions.

Women (and men) who want to be in institutions that are supportive of family life may wish to look at second-tier universities and private colleges, where emphasis is placed far more on teaching than on research and publication. Much of the literature on work/family problems is based on first-tier research universities, where the overall percentage of women in tenure-track positions is especially low compared with men (for example, Mason and Gould reported in 2002 that University of California, Berkeley, had only 281 women faculty on campus, but 1,002 male faculty members) ("Do Babies Matter?"). In a discussion of these issues on a composition listserv, one woman wrote,

> At our small state university, my impression is that the number of male and female faculty is about even. In our department, women outnumber men in our tenure-line faculty. Faculty children are regularly seen in the hall and at campus events. It's generally accepted that we have lives outside of campus (after all, many of our students do).

The sheer number of faculty actively involved in child-rearing is likely to have a positive effect on department-level support for working parents. It is important to note that men on the tenure-track have long had children and (as we note above) have *more* children overall than women in equivalent positions. It makes a difference, however, when those men ask for parental leave, bring their children to the office, and otherwise visibly participate in childcare.

Here are some other strategies we have learned from women in rhetoric and composition with children:

1. If you want to have children, don't wait too long to get started. Fertility decreases dramatically after age 35 while complications (including especially chromosomal abnormalities resulting in miscarriage and retardation) dramatically increase (Varner 2). Some women who wanted children but waited until they had tenure found they couldn't have them. Age also impacts adoption; the older the couple, the less desirable they appear to adoption agencies (see Britt). One survey respondent who wanted children but waited too long wrote, "I will regret it forever."

2. Get connected with other parents in your institution. Graduate students who are mothers in one of our departments share babysitting duties, which has been beneficial for their children, who have grown up together. A group of faculty can have a greater effect on institutions than any individual faculty member alone, as Bizzell's story clearly shows. Find out about nationwide efforts to change institutional structures that impede women faculty from having children. The Alfred P. Sloane foundation has been supporting research nationwide (including the Penn State study) on this subject. Louise Wetherbee Phelps has been participating in a Sloane-sponsored project through ACE. Based on her work with this organization, she tells us,

> I think many schools are going to be putting in polices that either lengthen tenure clocks or have policies for stopping them based on having children, for both women and men, and also there will be many other policies intended to deal with this issue for women having babies. Even for grad students, in one case I know of. The basis for it will be competing for these women in a situation where a great deal of hiring needs to be done, and a lot of those hired will be women, … or involve couples who are going to take this into consideration.

For example, the University of Michigan is considering putting in place a 10-year tenure clock for all faculty to better accommodate the realities of faculty lives (Wilson, "Off the Clock").

3. If you are planning to have a child (biological or adopted) while on the tenure clock, plan carefully if you are able. Most institutions offer one semester of parental leave to their faculty, so women try to time their pregnancies to take advantage of the longest possible break, for example by having their children at the end of Spring Semester or during summers. Begin looking for quality childcare during pregnancy or while waiting for adoption to go through, since most university childcare centers and many other good sources of childcare have long waiting lists. Talk to your department head about arranging an advantageous teaching schedule when you return.

4. Don't participate in "discrimination avoidance." Take advantage of all institution-wide support offered you, including parental leave. Ask for what you need from your department and put the onus on them to support you. If the answer is "no," then at least you have put your department head on notice of the need for greater support (the second person who asks may get a "yes"). While dean of the College of Humanities, Annette Kolodny became an important ally for campus-wide change after discovering the child of a night-shift custodian sleeping alone in a women's restroom in the Humanities building (285). Administrators can become important advocates for change, but only if they know the needs of their faculty, staff, and students. Point administrators toward some of the literature on how to create family-friendly institutional policies (for example, Coiner; N. Miller, "Of Parents Born"; ACE, "An Agenda for Excellence") or urge women's groups on campus to do so.

Women in our field report having received some of the following non-trivial support from their departments: using the department refrigerator to store breast milk, receiving reduced service loads (on committees that meet rarely or only online), bringing their children to the office on school holidays, and receiving teaching schedules built around childcare issues. It is important to note that academic maven Ms. Mentor warns strongly against women bringing children to the office *ever*, which may be good advice where the myth of the "ideal worker" is strongly at play. She writes, "a woman seen with a baby is believed to be 'un-serious.' Viewing herself as a mom first, she's thought likely to drop her career at any moment. This unfair characterization is almost universal ..." (Toth, *Ms. Mentor's Impeccable Advice* 119). But, we contend, fewer and fewer institutions fall into this category. If you never see children around, we recommend asking the department head and/or senior colleagues, since some institutions do discourage bringing children to campus for safety reasons or because of the bias cited by Ms. Mentor.

5. If you have a supportive partner, find a way to share the load with him or her
There are women in rhetoric and composition whose partner stays home with the child so that they can work. One graduate student we know chose a position in an area with a low cost of living rate specifically so that her husband could stay home with their pre-school children. Dual academic couples can sometimes stagger their sabbatical and/or parental leaves so that a new child has a parent home for more than a year. The worst situation is to be a single academic parent with children; however, even in this case, local family (when available) can provide much-needed help. Some single mothers go to graduate school where they can receive family support; for example, while studying and teaching at the University of Texas, Susan C. Jarratt lived between Austin and San Antonio so

her parents could help her with childcare. Other women try to find academic positions near family.

6. Find ways to involve children in some of your academic tasks. For example, Brenda Jo Brueggemann and her husband James Fredal set aside "family writing time" with their two children when they were younger. Everyone went off to write something and came back together to share what they wrote. This practice allowed Brueggemann and Fredal to work on their academic writing while encouraging their children to see themselves as writers, too. If your department does not have a practice of inviting children to parties, throw one yourself and invite children to go. This practice of "integration" can be helpful to you and to your children, since it provides you with another way to connect with your colleagues. It is also helpful to your children. Children of academics often find it helpful to grow up knowing other faculty kids, since they are unlikely to meet children like themselves in school (two of us—Ballif and Mountford—were a child of a professor and benefited from such socialization).

7. Practice "rotation." Brueggemann and Fredal rotate all aspects of work/ family life. They alternate research leaves in the summer so that each has an opportunity to go abroad. They try not to accept heavy teaching loads in the same academic term. Each workday they rotate a "no meetings after 3:00 pm" moratorium so that one of them is home when their children come home from school. On weekend days, they rotate primary responsibility for childcare, leaving one parent free to work on other tasks. "Sunday late afternoons through evening anymore we *all* are doing 'homework' together now that the kids are older," Brueggemann writes. "And yes, that's a strategy too. Our dining room always has been the central room in our house. Big table there. Central computer (desktop) is also there. Stereo there. (It's the biggest room in our 1928 house.) We also have two laptops on wireless that can also go at the table. We *all* work there together."

Academic Couples

An increasing number of professionals in our field are married to or partnered with each other, or are married or partnered with an academic in another area (professor or administrator). Four examples from our own research include Cheryl Glenn and her husband Jon Olson, Jacqueline Jones Royster and her husband Patrick Royster, Cynthia L. Selfe and her husband Dickie Selfe, and Lynn Worsham and her husband Gary Olson. Most institutions have found that having a spousal hiring policy is an invaluable part of their recruitment and retention efforts. However, for dual-career couples, there are three key problems: first, how to find two positions in the same university (in the same department or even in the same field); second, how to preserve the relationship while sharing the same general working conditions, within the same university or in a neighboring one; and third, how to survive a long-distance relationship when positions in the same geographical area cannot be found.

Anti-nepotism policies, which precluded the hiring of faculty who were part of the same family, were widespread in the twentieth century. The rules affected women of earlier generations far more than men, since women were more likely to be the trailing spouse or to have less seniority, in the case of faculty who married after they were hired. As Lilli S. Hornig points out, given the way in which anti-nepotism rules were applied, it seemed clear that they were designed primarily to preclude academic couples from holding equivalent faculty positions. For example, universities with such rules often hired wives of faculty members to serve as librarians or secretaries (249). In addition, schools sometimes hired brothers to serve as faculty, while refusing to hire well-qualified wives of faculty members. Hornig suggests that

> [T]he real issue in nepotism regulation had little to do with kinship in general but was specifically intended to preclude faculty positions for wives. Coincidentally, the widespread application of antinepotism policies solely to hiring wives suggests strongly that the presence of wives qualified to be faculty was not rare and that administrators and faculty members were indeed often strongly antifemale. (250)

Fortunately, anti-nepotism policies and practices have been quietly dropped as the advantages of hiring academic couples have become clear. From the point of view of administrators, spousal/partner hiring enables the recruitment of desirable faculty, provides stability (in the form of "institutional attachment and loyalty every college and university hopes for among its faculty"), improves morale among employees, and sometimes is a bargain (when couples trade a dual hire for a salary increase) (251). It is important to note that historically black colleges and universities founded by African American organizations regularly employed dual-career couples throughout their histories for exactly these perceived benefits (Perkins). "African Americans stressed that the talents of all its members were needed for the advancement and 'uplift' of the race," Perkins argues; whereas white women were expected to stay home, black women were expected to use their education for the benefit of others, even when married with children (81).

There are clear benefits for women academics whose partners are in academe. In 1989, Helen S. Astin and Jeffrey F. Milem reviewed 51,574 surveys of faculty in 432 institutions. Thirty-five percent of men and 40 percent of women indicated that their spouse/partner was an academic. Astin and Milem compared the productivity of single women, women partnered with nonacademic partners/spouses, and women partnered with academic partners/spouses. They ran a similar comparison of men. Empirical evidence drawn from this study suggests that the most productive women are in partnership/marriage with another academic. However, men with academic spouses/partners are *less* productive than men who are single or married/partnered with nonacademic spouses/partners. Marriage/partnership with an academic seems to confer on both a level of equality that is an historic gain for women, but an historic adjustment of advantage for men. As the authors put it, "men's professional attainments are apparently not achieved at the expense of their partners in academia" (141). Other advantages for women may include "greater access to academic networks, information, and social support" (140), although this could only be true when the woman is the less senior member of the couple. An advantage for all academic couples (including same-sex) is the opportunity to exchange ideas and take advantage of the relative flexibility of academic life (St. John-Parsons 41).

The most ideal situation for an institution (and for the academic couple) occurs when couples apply for open positions and are reviewed through the usual processes. In the absence of anti-nepotism rules, their hire is part of the regular procedures in place, and faculty hiring committees can review their applications alongside other candidates. Knowing they have a need for a number of new hires, some departments wisely advertise for two or more generalists in a single year, which opens the way for academic couples to apply. However, the more common—and more difficult—course is the creation of a spouse or partner hire, which is normally funded on a case-by-case basis by an academic dean or provost. Often, a spouse or partner hire comes from an existing pool of "lines" left over from vacancies that may or may not be "owed" the department that will receive the spousal hire. Or occasionally, a college or university has a pool of funds set aside for recruitment or retention of faculty, and the funds for a spouse or partner hire can be drawn from this account. Wealthier departments and colleges will sometimes pay for the spouse or partner hire in a different unit if it means they can recruit a faculty member they want. So if you are fortunate enough to be partnered with a famous professor of biomechanical engineering, for example, another university might offer to create and fund a new position for you if your partner would go, too.

Much can go wrong with spouse or partner hires. All hiring tends to bring out latent divisions among the faculty, and spouse/partner hiring can be especially fraught with conflict. The first consideration for departments is whether or not they want to hire or retain a particular faculty member enough to hire their spouse/partner (assuming the partner hire will be internal). The second consideration is whether the spouse/partner meets existing criteria for the position being created for him or her. The hire could be contested on the largely subjective grounds of merit. The public meltdown in the University of Georgia's history department after the faculty failed to approve a spousal hire for a senior scholar is a case in point (Fogg 20). However, the danger for the institution should the merit of the partner/spouse be contested is losing the opportunity to hire/retain two people; too many other institutions would be willing to hire both. (The University of Georgia lost its senior history professor and his spouse, who was a tenured professor of US history at UCLA, to the University of British Columbia.) Ultimately, it is worth it to seek a spouse/partner hire, since doing so is increasingly accepted as a matter of course by both administrators and faculty.

Unfortunately, there is no generally accepted way to let an institution know that you will be seeking a position for your spouse or partner as a condition of your hire. And since it is illegal for an institution to ask about your private life, a search committee cannot ask you about it. In our view, your approach should depend on what stage you are in your career. New assistant professors are hired primarily on their promise, not on an extensive track record of success. Their value to a department has not yet been proven, so bringing up the need for a partner hire early in the hiring process (for example, in the letter of application or even MLA interview) is probably not a good idea. Of course, if there are two positions open and your spouse or partner has applied for the other one, it may be beneficial to let the hiring committee know *if* you both receive an invitation for an MLA interview. It could improve your position, since an offer to a couple more likely ensures two acceptances. If your partner needs a position but none has been advertised for which he or she can apply, you should not bring up this problem until an institution is interested in you. Some experts suggest that the best time to break the news to the department head is during the on-campus interview, but before the offer is made (it takes time to put together a partner hire, they argue, and breaking the news at the time of offer is too late). Others argue that it is best to wait until the verbal offer is made; the hiring of a partner then becomes a point of negotiation (for further tips on interviewing and negotiating for your first job, see Chapter 2). If you are a more senior scholar, your private life is more likely to be known (let's face it: we are a close-knit and gossipy field) or the issue of a partner hire more expected, so you probably lose nothing by explaining in your letter of application that you are seeking to improve the employment picture both for you and your partner. Such a move also answers a question frequently asked by hiring committees: would this senior scholar really leave Green Pastures U to come to our school? Obviously, the more accomplished you are in all areas, and the more accomplished your spouse or partner, the better your opportunities. It is important to remember that your institution must see something to gain from the arrangement. Therefore, if your college or university agrees to hire you and your spouse or partner at salaries you'd prefer to see higher, keep in mind that getting two people for a bargain is one of the benefits of partner hires to the institution.

Sometimes an academic couple in the same field makes a conscious decision to diversify what they have to offer another institution. That was the case for Lynn Worsham and Gary Olson. Worsham's department at the University of South Florida was falling apart following an ethics investigation, so as soon as it was possible, she and Olson looked for a university that would provide good positions for them both. They were able to do so because several years earlier Olson had had an opportunity to move into administration, and they decided that it would be good for them both for him to do so. They now work at Illinois State University where Olson is Dean of the College of Arts and Sciences and Worsham is a full professor in the English Department. Worsham said, "We both benefited: he is pursuing a line of work that he is quite good at, and I have joined a wonderful faculty in a department that is genuinely attempting to create innovative programs on the graduate and undergraduate levels." Importantly, Worsham took her journal *JAC* with her, which was a benefit to the thriving graduate program at ISU. But the key to Worsham and Olson's academic job search is that Olson added significant administrative experience to his CV, which made him eligible for a different kind of academic position.

Finding time to be together is easier for academic partners with flexible hours, so Worsham and Olson must work to carve out moments for themselves. Olson works 15 hours a day as well as weekends in his position, and Worsham works long hours on the journal and other responsibilities. They spend time together every evening talking about the day, and they try to attend each other's professional meetings and "to make a little vacation of it." "We take a few extra days and spend them together taking in the sights and enjoying the local restaurants," Worsham told us. "Since we've been in Illinois, we've gone to Florida regularly to see our friends there, and we've gone to Chicago several times."

Because department-level politics often seem to turn on how many votes there are to hire this person or that, or to reform this curriculum versus pursuing the status quo, academic couples within the same department can be perceived as threatening, particularly if the department has no experience with them. Some academic couples make a principled effort not to talk about department politics at home (Brueggemann keeps an imaginary can of "stop it" close by when department politics come up at home). Refraining from talking about work at home prevents the "spillover" effect—"the transfer of mood, affect, and behavior between work and home," which can have a negative effect on both work and home environment (Roehling, Moen, and Batt 101; see also Montgomery). Another advantage of not "talking shop" at home is being able to claim independence on departmental votes (dual-career couples in the same department are frequently asked whether or not they talk about department issues at home). Others participate on different committees, whenever possible, and in general try to operate in a public way as the individuals they are.

Nevertheless, there are some situations that academic couples should always avoid. Most state and private agencies ask that employees refrain from engaging in acts that constitute a conflict of interest.

> Possible conflicts of interest are generally defined to include financial interest, as in salary or other compensation decisions, and other material or personal interests that might be affected by one relative having jurisdiction over another. The concerns are therefore quite broad and certainly include situations such as one partner in a couple having a voice in decisions concerning the other's promotion and compensation, access to departmental and other institutional resources, and so on. (Hornig 250)

Some colleges and universities are quite clear about rules on conflict of interest, whereas others are not. Sometimes academic couples will need to draw the lines themselves. For example, a faculty member should probably not agree to take on the role of writing program administrator if it means supervising a partner or spouse who is teaching in a non-tenure-track position (particularly one that is negotiated year to year). This can be a painful stance to take when your department is desperate for a WPA. Similarly, it would be inappropriate for a faculty member to accept a role that will involve direct contact with her spouse or partner's tenure and promotion decision. Both are a clear conflict of interest, since you (and your partner/spouse) stand to gain monetarily. Everyone gains when the sun shines through departmental procedures and conflicts of interest are avoided both in perception and practice.

For some women faculty, the key problem is that their partner or spouse either cannot move or will not move with them to the academic position they want. Several survey respondents expressed frustration with being stuck in lower-level positions because their husbands would not move with them. In one case, a woman discovered that her department head was not going to support her tenure and promotion. She wrote,

> I decided to withdraw my case and work the rest of my contract while looking for another position elsewhere. I am about to interview for several positions in other states. I have been careful to choose departments that have a closer alliance with the kind of work I am doing. The very positive response to my applications has boosted my self-confidence. Unfortunately, my husband does not want to move from where we are, but I've made the decision, regardless of his final decision, to go where I can find the most fulfilling work.

Many respondents who molded their careers around their husband's (in every case where this complaint was raised, it was always with a husband and not a partner of either sex), regretted having done so. For example, in response to our question, "If you could begin your career all over again, what you do differently?" one respondent wrote, "I'd get a PhD in Rhetoric/Composition rather than literature; and I would leave my marriage earlier than I did. I know that sounds bad, but I let myself get stuck in adjuncting for years because my husband refused to consider moving." Several other respondents reported that they had taken lesser positions because of their husbands' careers, in one case without regret, since the lesser institution was willing to employ both the respondent and her husband (a literature professor with fewer prospects).

Only one respondent to our survey reported being in a long-distance relationship. She reported that if she could begin her career again, she would have gone to law school. The reason was that while she loved her job, she lived 10 hours away from her partner, which she described as "a nightmare." It is in part because "freeway flyer" relationships are so unsustainable that universities are increasingly willing to hire spouses and partners of their faculty. In fact, Hornig reports that even the top-tier universities have adopted programs for hiring partners in order to retain their faculty. In 1993, Stanford University conducted a major study of women faculty who resigned to pursue other academic positions and discovered that one-third did so because of their partner's employment situation (255). However, even when a partner hire is impossible, there are some options for dual-career couples. For example, Bizzell took a job in an area saturated with colleges and universities so that Herzberg would have a better opportunity to find an academic position when he was ready. Some women take a strong academic position early in their careers knowing that they will have a commuter relationship for a short time but in the long run will be able to move to a wider range of institutions where their partner or spouse can join them. Some opt to commute to their institution, renting a room for several days a week and flying or driving home to their families on the weekends (Karen LeFevre commuted to Rensselaer Polytechnic in Troy, New York, from Burlington, Vermont, for her entire career). The Cornell Couples and Careers Survey, reported in *It's About Time: Couples and Careers*, revealed that women who made the longest commutes had the highest earning potential (Hofmeister 72). Therefore, an important consideration for women who choose careers in rhetoric and composition is their overall earning potential relative to their partner's.

A final consideration for women in rhetoric and composition with partners is whether or not to ask the partner to follow them in their careers. Two survey respondents noted that their husbands were willing to trail after them; of the two, one woman decided to stay in a lower-level position rather than ask her husband to move, and the other reported that her husband did follow her. In her case, the resistance came from others who thought her husband wouldn't support her.

> I remember when I was getting my MA at a small Catholic university where all but one professor was male. I asked a male professor who had encouraged me academically if I should pursue my PhD and his first response was to ask me what my husband would do while I was in grad school … . Lucky for me, my husband has followed me to grad school and to two tenure-track jobs. I know too many women who are still held back by husbands who wouldn't follow them to a job or their own fear that taking an academic job would ruin their marriages. I'm interested in knowing how many women who are denied tenure just quit because they won't ask their husbands and family to move. When I was denied tenure, I gave my husband the option of finding a job somewhere else and I'd follow him, but he said no. So this isn't a story of being harassed but a story of being subtly told that I might not be able to have an academic career because my husband wouldn't like it.

When we look at the women scholars we interviewed, we note that only one—Shirley Wilson Logan—was geographically restricted because of her husband's position. Unexpectedly, Lunsford's husband decided not to move with her to Ohio State from Vancouver, British Columbia, which was a very painful moment in her life. The other women we interviewed were either single or moved with their husbands to the same institutions (Royster reports that her move to Ohio State was prompted by her husband seeking a better position). Of the three of us, two have husbands who have moved with us for our careers (though in both cases, we chose the institution and location in part to accommodate our partners). It is possible to find supportive partners, and our research shows the value of family and partners to women faculty members' overall well-being.

What Mentors Failed To Mention about Academic Culture

We have already addressed many of the most difficult aspects of academic life for women in rhetoric and composition. But there are a few more worth addressing. Consider this section to be the "women's room" guide to academic life.

Your greatest enemy in your academic life may not be a man. As we have discussed in earlier chapters, the Queen Bee syndrome seems to be especially acute in our field. Womanist scholars are more vocal about the Queen Bee syndrome (see especially hooks), but white feminists have been unwilling to talk about the problem as openly. Queen Bees cause deep emotional stress in the women around them. For example, when we asked our survey respondents to discuss any situation that had arisen in their careers that was especially difficult to talk about, many respondents reported on the emotional damage done to them by a senior woman in their department. In Chapter 2, we recount the story of one respondent whose doctoral committee chair was a woman especially cruel to her. The chair was a prominent feminist who belittled the respondent when she decided to focus her dissertation on race, causing her to suffer anxiety attacks. Eventually the respondent removed this Queen Bee from her committee. Afterward,

> She made it clear that my decision was insulting (even though I made it clear that this was for my own mental health and ability to continue). She has consistently shunned me at professional gatherings and disparages my work to her friends and colleagues. She has made it difficult for me to take any white women feminists seriously because she caused me so much psychic pain.

Another respondent made a similar statement: "[A] woman professor … went after my mixedblood heritage, wanting me to 'explain my indianess.' I thought to ask her to explain her whiteness, but resolved the situation by creating a project to demonstrate indigenous knowledge. I wonder why women do this to one another, and I believe in … these cases, … women have bought into male-dominated westernized ways of thinking. I would like for us to stop hurting each other, to instead become caring of one another."

But how does one deal with the emotional crisis brought on by such incidents? Our research suggests two uncomfortable truths: Queen Bees may not recognize that they are causing emotional crises in others, and yet, Queen Bees are widespread in our field. About a third of our survey respondents reported that they were emotionally sabotaged or abused by another woman. So our first suggestion is that when you have experienced abuse at the hands of anyone in your career, seek professional help. Second, assume that, in the words of our survey respondent, you have been "westernized" to favor men, those who are culturally and ethnically like you, and those who are in hierarchy above you. Work tirelessly against this conditioning so that you don't become part of the problem. Third, keep in mind that there is no good way to handle a biased and abusive colleague: if you speak up, you're likely to be punished in some way, but if you don't speak up, you're likely to become ill. Be careful to select someone who is trustworthy to tell what is happening to you and do your best to avoid a direct confrontation with the abuser. A Queen Bee is normally a narcissistic individual, excessively self-absorbed in order to protect deep internal feelings of inferiority. She cannot be reasoned with and will do anything to protect her public image. In short, Queen Bees are tragic but dangerous individuals.

Some of the women we interviewed believed that the only real way to deal with emotional crises created by Queen Bees was by avoiding them and not allowing them to change how you behave. Selfe argues,

> If you pay attention to those people, or … if you let their *problems* flavor your life, then you've lost the battle; you've *become* them. My advice is, "Hey, look, you've got to look after yourself. Here's the cool work you can do here. Here are the opportunities. If opportunity knocks, open the door. Do your work. Do what you want to do. Have some fun. And ignore the behavior that is unproductive, because if you let it influence you, you *become* that problem or that kind of person. You can do better than that."

In our experience, having a community of women outside the academy or in other departments who are part of the solution (by mentoring other women or serving on committees designed to help women in their careers) can be helpful in counteracting the toxic effects of Queen Bees. Exercise and meditative practices (including yoga) can also be very beneficial in counteracting stress, which produces hormones harmful to the immune system and can, over time, lead to anxiety disorders and depression. But nothing can take the place of professional counseling and the revenge of living well.

If you are a woman of an under-represented group in the field, you probably already know that the discrimination of the academy is the type that threatens to kill with a thousand cuts. If you are a graduate student or assistant professor, we urge you to join one of the caucuses of the MLA (for a complete list of Allied and Affiliated Organizations, visit the MLA website at www.mla.org), NCTE (which includes the American Indian Causus, Asian/Asian American Caucus, Black Caucus, and Latino Caucus), or CCCC (including the Special Interest Groups and Coalitions, such as the Coalition of Women Scholars in the History of Rhetoric). Women from under-represented groups suffer from isolation as well as discrimination and so urgently need to find a cohort, mentors, and sponsors (powerful supporters in the administration). Many universities have become sensitized to the need to protect women from under-represented groups from excessive requests for their service, particularly to "diversify" committees or mentor students with similar backgrounds. Nevertheless, life for faculty in the majority group comes without the difficulties that you have, and so some of the "grief that goes with the territory" involves speaking up and occasionally educating those around you—or choosing to ignore it. An especially good book on this subject is *Black Women in the Academy: Promises and Perils*, by a group of black women administrators and faculty.

If you are reading this section and are of the majority group (for example, in the racial majority, heterosexual, ethnically Christian, abled), try to remember that your privilege is invisible to you but also that the skills and abilities and privileges of others unlike you are also invisible to you. The pernicious stereotypes in higher education almost always focus on academic ability. Royster's story of her colleagues who assumed that the underperforming English majors at Ohio State were all black students (see her profile) is a case in point (they held a "B" average—the underperforming students were white). But in addition, keep in mind that it can be exhausting to be different from others, and so offer your friendship and be a good colleague.

Higher education is quite elitist. Faculty from a working-class background often struggle with cultural differences that grow out of differing economic status. Women in higher education tend to come from more educated families (Astin and Milem 131), which can make the isolation for working-class women quite difficult. Knowledge of wine, food, music, and travel are part of the cultural currency in academic circles, even in graduate school. Working-class academics are more likely to choose positions closer to their families, to struggle with implicit social norms, and to suffer more from the economic deprivations of graduate school, since they have no help from home (in some cases, working-class graduate students feel compelled to use what little money they have to help struggling family members). There have been several important books on this subject, the most recent of which is Kathleen A. Welsch's *Those Winter Sundays: Female Academics and Their Working-Class Parents*.[9]

We have focused on the problems of accommodating career and family, but an equally difficult problem for women is being single. Worsham suggests that academic culture is a "couples" culture, which means that single women may find themselves somewhat isolated, particularly when their universities are in small towns. Couples naturally tend to socialize with other couples, particularly when they have children, since other parents can be an invaluable resource for information and support. Imagine trying to date in a town the size of Houghton, Michigan. Cindy Selfe tells the story of going through the grocery line in Houghton and being told by the check-out clerk that she didn't need to buy Grape-Nuts cereal because her husband Dickie had bought a box earlier in the day. Sara M. Bradshaw wrote a first-person account for the *Chronicle of Higher Education* about leaving higher education altogether after landing a job as an historian in a small town as a single woman. She simply had no way to meet anyone to date (she argues that higher education has no "office culture," which is important for single women). Single women do well to take positions in urban centers, if they can, where their chances of meeting other single professionals are stronger (this is particularly important for lesbian and bisexual women). Dating services can also be helpful.

Single women's personal lives are the subject of frequent gossip, and the speculation can be intrusive. In our experience, the best way to deal with gossip of this nature is to find out who is spreading the rumor and nip it in the bud as soon as possible. Other problems include finding that one's colleagues assume that you have more time to assume service and administrative obligations because you are single. Some single women complain that they have no way to stop the tenure clock, unless they fall ill, and they do not have the same access to favorable schedules that women with children do (such as Brueggemann's rotating practice of not scheduling meetings after 3:00 pm). On the other hand, our research shows that many women envy the freedoms of single women faculty, including their mobility and availability to take higher-paid administrative positions.

Lesbian, bisexual, and transgendered faculty play an increasingly important role in higher education. However, without a vibrant LGBT community, it is difficult for lesbian, bisexual, and transgendered women to network and find support, even if they have a partner. Travel is especially crucial for LGBT faculty, and we find that some of our LGBT colleagues tend to live in other places during summers and sabbaticals or even to commute to our universities from larger urban centers. While the lack of federal protection and the ongoing hostility toward gay marriage make the choice of location especially important for LGBT faculty, universities are increasingly finding ways to offer benefits and bias protection to their employees. The *Chronicle* recently offered a first-person account of a gay faculty member in the humanities whose partner was offered a position in a move to retain him (Bennett and Lindsey). A question for some is whether or not to come out on the job, particularly where there are few other LGBT faculty. Some lesbians and bisexual women solve this problem by allowing their butch clothing and hairstyle make the announcement for them. One of our colleagues, the head of a women's studies department, wears jeans, T-shirts and red Converse sneakers every day. She argues that because of her dress, she has been challenged less by students than her feminine-appearing colleagues. Of course, women should never feel compelled to make an issue of their sexual orientation one way or the other, since in most cases, colleagues will not care. For other perspectives on this issue, we recommend Susan Talburt's edited collection, *Subject to Identity: Knowledge, Sexuality, and Academic Practices in Higher Education.*

There are many other lifestyle issues that come from being the only person like oneself in a college or university. Regional differences can be very difficult to navigate, particularly given the cultural conservatism of many colleges and universities. Unless you are willing to sign a statement of faith, you are unlikely to find yourself in a school with an evangelical Protestant mission, where lifestyle violations such as drinking alcohol can bring about dismissal. Nevertheless, paying attention to cultural norms and trying not to flout them is always a good idea. Faculty in the east and south tend to dress more formally than their colleagues in the west. Casual swearing is the norm on some campuses, all but forbidden on others (students, in particular, can be sensitive about this issue and will often bring up their faculty members' swearing in their evaluations). Even footwear can evoke comments. While teaching at Rensselaer, Roxanne Mountford wore Birkenstock sandals to a faculty party one summer evening and her colleague Lee Odell (a former Texan) said, mockingly, "in Texas, we shoot people who wear Birkenstocks!" When she heard this story, Diane Davis, who is a native Texan, was appalled—that Mountford would wear such ugly sandals. Therefore, we recommend that you cultivate a sense of humor about regional/ethnic differences, blend in when it is possible to do so, and focus on what really matters—the work. Sometimes the best approach to such issues is to follow Royster, who contends that nothing in academic life will force her to compromise her ethics. So, if you are a vegetarian in a department of meat-eaters, or ride your bike for environmental purposes and therefore must forgo the formalwear, we encourage you not to compromise your ethics, even if it means that you stand out on your campus.

In the epigraph to this chapter, we quote Catherine Bateson, who encourages women to refuse all "forced choices," but instead to craft the life they want. If it were easy to do so, books like ours would be unnecessary. Nevertheless, one of the constant themes in the lives of the women we interviewed, the women we are, and the women we know is that we do what we do in part because we immersed ourselves in books about the stories of others' lives as children. Women who read always have a line of flight available to them, because they know that other ways of being are possible. Women who write offer a line of flight to others. We offer these words of women in rhetoric and composition as possible lines of flight, but we also encourage women to show us other ways of making it in rhetoric and composition.

And Having a Life, Too

ESSENTIAL RESOURCES

Finding Happiness in Work

Mihaly Csikszentmihalyi. *Finding Flow: The Psychology of Engagement with Everyday Life*

Managing Time and Emotions

Robert Boice. *Advice for New Faculty Members: Nihil Nimus*

Managing Family and Career

Constance Coiner and Diana Hume George, eds. *The Family Track: Keeping Your Faculties While You Mentor, Nurture, Teach, and Serve*

Academic Couples

Marianne A. Ferber and Jane W. Loeb, eds. *Academic Couples: Problems and Promises*

Black Women Academics

Lois Benjamin, ed. *Black Women in the Academy: Promises and Perils*

LGBT Academics

Susan Talbert, ed. *Subject to Identity: Knowledge, Sexuality, and Academic Practices in Higher Education*

Working-Class Academics

Alan Shepherd, John McMillan and Gary Tate, eds. *Coming to Class: Pedagogy and the Social Class of Teachers*

Section IV

BEING A PROFESSIONAL

Profiles of Success

8

PATRICIA BIZZELL

Patricia Bizzell is currently professor of English at the College of the Holy Cross. A nationally recognized authority in writing pedagogy and rhetorical theory, Bizzell is perhaps best known for her book *The Rhetorical Tradition: Readings from Classical Times to the Present*, which she co-authored with Bruce Herzberg and which received the National Council of Teachers of English Outstanding Book Award in 1992. She earned her BA in English from Wellesley College and then her PhD in English from Rutgers in 1975. She served as the Assistant Director of Composition at Rutgers in a non-tenure-track position for three years before joining the faculty in the English department at Holy Cross in 1978. She created both the institution's writing across the curriculum program and its peer tutoring workshop before she earned tenure a mere three years later (1981). Bizzell directed those programs from 1981 to 1994, going to full professor in 1988. She served as chair of the English department from 2001 to 2005 and as president of the Rhetoric Society of America from 2004 to 2006. Now a renowned scholar of rhetoric and writing with numerous publications and honors, Bizzell has chosen to remain at Holy Cross, where she has been teaching literature, writing, and rhetoric for more than 28 years.

Background

Bizzell was born in Chicago but grew up in Northbrook, Illinois, which at the time was a "little village surrounded by cow pastures" but which grew into an upscale suburb. She told us that she was a rather sickly child, forced to spend a lot of time in bed alone, so she read constantly and can't remember a time when she couldn't read. She enjoyed making her own books as a kid, drawing or cutting out pictures from magazines and writing stories to go with them. So it was no big surprise when she became an English major in college: "I always knew I would be an English major."

However, neither of Bizzell's parents had a background in education, and she suspects they "weren't totally convinced" that she and her sister needed to go to college. Her mother, who was raised in Kansas, graduated high school and moved to "the big city" (Kansas City) to find work as a secretary. There she met

Bizzell's father, who grew up in a small town in Oklahoma and had attended the University of Oklahoma for a while but didn't graduate. He was the youngest of nine siblings, so he supported himself while attending college by running a gas station. His imaginative gas-selling gimmicks were so effective that his little station sold more gas than any of the company's other stations, so they promptly transferred him to their advertising department—eventually, he was hired away by the Chicago-based Leo Burnett Agency, one of the top ad agencies in the country. So Bizzell's parents moved to Chicago and had their children; her mother was a full-time homemaker throughout Bizzell's childhood, and "in their universe," Bizzell told us, "it was just not a foregone conclusion" that their daughters should go to college—because they were *daughters*. Bizzell's parents "had very traditional ideas about gender roles and so forth."

However, Bizzell was an exceptional student; reading and writing came very easily for her, and she loved school. So her parents' friends frequently suggested that she should go to college, and her parents listened:

> They were social climbers; that's a good way of describing them, but without sounding too negative. They wanted to get out of the country, off the farm, and up the social ladder, and they succeeded very well. They started out with nothing; my mom was literally barefoot and hungry on the farm as a kid. And they ended up living in this very tony suburb in a very nice house with the cars they always wanted to drive and furs and jewels and all the material things they always wanted. But they studied it because they weren't to the manor born. I think they were always very good at picking up cues from the people around them about how to do it. I remember my mother telling me the first time she ever went to a dinner party where she saw more than three pieces of cutlery on the table next to the plate, and she panicked. She didn't know what it was for, but she watched the hostess, and when the hostess picked up one of the utensils then she picked it up. I think what happened was, the men at my dad's country club let him know that if he had a daughter who could get into and graduate from Wellesley, he ought to let her go there. So that's how it happened. My sister didn't go to college. She just wasn't interested, really. She started college in a state school out in Illinois, and after a semester said, This isn't for me. Both my folks didn't care, didn't really insist. In fact, she had a much more lucrative career than I did anyway: she was a fashion model. Of all things.

Bizzell's parents paid for her undergraduate education at Wellesley and were by that time supportive of her decision to go, even if they never quite understood it. And they must have been very proud at a certain level because when she graduated, they gave her a car as a graduation present. They did not fund her graduate education, however; they thought she should get a job or, as Bizzell told us, "what they really thought I should do is get married. I think they were proud of my accomplishments, but they really didn't get it. It wasn't the kind of thing they could understand or appreciate, really. And when I did get married, they didn't understand why I didn't quit working then."

> They thought "OK, fine, if she likes to do this [teach], that's fine, but now she's married, and now the serious business of life starts—you start having babies and stop spritzing around with this job." I continued to work. And then when we had kids, they thought, "Surely she's going to quit working now." Well, no, I'm still working. Frankly, they kind of thought, "Gee, is Bruce not a good provider? What's the problem here? How come she's still working?" I think they never stopped thinking that at some point I would decide we had enough money so that I could quit working. They just really didn't get it.

Bizzell went to Rutgers for her PhD, again English, supporting herself through graduate school with scholarships and teaching. There was never any question that her doctorate would be in English. "At the time I was graduating from college I was thinking, How can I keep this going? This is so much fun." She wasn't thinking so much about a future career as she was about how to "stay in the game of words." She and her friends were into writing poetry, and many of them were going to New York City to try to make it on the literary scene. But Bizzell told us she didn't think she was a good enough poet to do that; she also hoped to do something a little more "socially relevant." She decided she could do that and stay in the word game by becoming a teacher, and she enrolled at Rutgers.

At Rutgers, she got a very traditional literary training, specializing in American Literature and finally writing her dissertation on F. Scott Fitzgerald. Though she had every intention of becoming a literature professor, she also taught composition in Rutgers's huge, multi-course comp program, and she got into it. There wasn't much out there on teaching writing in the early 1970s, but Bizzell started researching and reading whatever she could in that arena, and she decided she'd like to work in composition as well as in literature. It turns out that Janet Emig was a professor in the School of Education at Rutgers while Bizzell was a grad student in English, but she had never heard of Emig's work. "I could have walked across the quad and taken a course with her, [but] I didn't know anything about her. Until rather late, I didn't really realize that there was … already beginning to be a body of scholarship in this field." When Bizzell got her PhD in 1975, Rutgers hired her as its Assistant Director of Composition—a full-time but non-tenure-track assistant professor position, which both David Bartholomae and Linda Flower had held previously. Bizzell was the Assistant Director for three years before she accepted the position with Holy Cross, and during that time, in the spring of 1978, she taught Rutgers's very first graduate course in rhetoric and composition.

Strategies for Success

Relationships

Bizzell told us explicitly that she has always put her relationships first, before her career, and she advises others to do the same. She met Bruce Herzberg while they were both in graduate school, and they married in 1977. She told us that she had never really thought about whether she would marry—she wasn't opposed to it but it also wasn't something she necessarily desired. Bruce, however, did want to get married: "He talked me into it, basically. And I said, Well, OK, I'm willing to give this a try. I love the guy; let's see what happens." Because Bizzell's Assistant Director position wasn't tenure-track, she had been looking for a permanent position all along, and she and Herzberg decided that if she found one, he would go with her while he finished his dissertation. But because he would be moving with her, she applied only for positions in parts of the country where there were a lot of colleges and therefore many opportunities for him to find a position in the same area. They did not want to teach in the same department, Bizzell told us, but they didn't want to have a commuter marriage, either. The fact that the College of the Holy Cross is located "smack dab in the middle of one of the highest concentrations of colleges and universities in the country" was a huge plus for it and one of the main reasons she took the job in 1978:

> Bruce was really, I think, very courageous about this. He moved with me; I had the tenure-line job at Holy Cross. He didn't have a job. He worked part-time at Clark University for a while, which is in Worcester. He then went into the computer business with the husbands of two of my college roommates who were living in Massachusetts. I renewed connections with them, and these gentlemen had a software consulting firm where they wrote software documentation, they rewrote programs, they did custom software for companies and so forth, so really kind of communication specialists but with a computer orientation. He went to work for them. He had been an undergraduate physics major, so this was no problem for him. And he worked for them for several years. He did a lot of their training; he was kind of their teacher on staff. But he also did programming and documentation and all that kind of stuff. And then eventually he got a tenure-line job, I don't know, when did he start working at Bentley? Probably, it was like maybe three or four years after we moved up there he got the job at Bentley College, where he's been ever since, and he's been very happy.

Bizzell told us that Herzberg has remained at Bentley in part because she has been so happy at Holy Cross and wanted to stay there. And yet, she told us, "he never in any way made me feel that he was making a big sacrifice to do this or that he was threatened by the fact that I was ahead of him professionally, in terms of getting into a tenure-line sooner and so forth, moving along the professional path ahead of him." What's important for our readers, as Bizzell reminded us, is that she and Herzberg made professional decisions based on what they thought would be best for their relationship. They put the relationship first:

> We put that first, and I think it has worked out for us. We've had a lot of success. So if folks are reading this book and want to know words of wisdom from Pat Bizzell, one I would give them is put your relationships first and don't worry about what the professional fallout will be. You'll work it out. You'll get a job. You might have to pass up an opportunity that you regret, but I think relationships are more important. And you have to think about yourself as a whole person. I would add to that: go and live in a part of the country where you want to live. I like New England. I had been up there in college, my husband went to Amherst as an undergrad, so we knew New England, we liked it, we were happy to move there.

College vs. University

Bizzell told us that she might enjoy teaching in a graduate program and that she may "experiment with that at some point, go somewhere a year as a visitor once my kids are out of the house, if that ever happens. They keep bouncing back on us." For now, however, she remains very happy to be teaching a wide variety of courses to undergraduate students. Holy Cross is a beautiful New England college with about 2,800 students, all undergraduates, and Bizzell told us that academically it "is fully the equal of Amherst and Wellesley. It may not have quite the reputation, but having some knowledge of those schools as well, I would say it's really quite a fine school." Bizzell has obviously had many opportunities to move elsewhere, to take a position at a university with a graduate program in rhetoric. Given her well-known ability to create and direct successful writing programs, for example, she could easily have gotten a position as a writing program administrator at a research institution. But Bizzell told us she truly enjoys the freedom she has at Holy Cross to teach a wide variety of classes and that she hasn't wanted to give that up: "There was a time, maybe ten years in, when I could have moved to be a WPA someplace. But I didn't want to be a WPA. I love the WPA organization, and I've been involved in it over the years; WPAs do excellent work, crucial work in the academy. But I didn't want to be one. I liked what I was doing better. Because I could do this writing administration stuff and meanwhile teach a seminar on Harriet Beecher Stowe if I wanted to."

Bizzell told us that she had one particularly interesting opportunity to go to the University of Minnesota, but she passed that up, too, because Herzberg "didn't want to live in the frozen north." It's beautiful country, she told us, but Herzberg hates the "northern exposure routine," so that was out. They were much more interested in living *together* in a part of the country that they both enjoy than in landing a position at a prestigious university:

> I think folks should consider a variety of factors, not just what your graduate professors tell you to consider, which is to get the most prestigious job at the most prestigious institution you can, and don't take a job at Podunk U because nobody will respect you. I'm at a college, I'm not at a university; Bruce is at a college. And over the years of course we've had many opportunities to move. I like being at a college. I like being where we are. The longer we stay there the more I like it because I have relationships now, I have friendships with people that have developed over twenty years that I don't want to give up. Our kids have grown up there. Worcester is a really nice town, not too big, it's well located. It's a good place to raise kids. So I like it there. I like being at a college, too. I do a lot of teaching. All I do is undergraduate teaching. And I love it.

The teaching load at the College of The Holy Cross is currently 3/2, but for a long time it was 3/3, and Bizzell says she teaches freshman comp every year by choice. Of course, she also has the opportunity to teach almost anything else she wants at the undergraduate level, and that aspect of being at a college appeals to her. She routinely teaches American lit and an introduction to women's studies course in addition to courses in rhetoric and writing; indeed, she taught the first course in women's literature in the department, and she was for a long time one of only two faculty teaching literatures of color. Most recently, in conjunction with Holy Cross's appointment of Danzy Senna to an endowed chair, she taught a course on "passing" in both Chinese-American and African-American literature. For Bizzell, one of the most appealing things about being at Holy Cross is this kind of flexibility about what she teaches.

Bizzell also told us that the students at Holy Cross are very smart—indeed, the one regret she has about teaching at this institution is that the students there are *too* smart, too prepared and pampered, so that she ends up for the most part "educating the upper crust." Though she was relieved to move from Rutgers's huge required composition program to a small college that didn't instate a writing requirement, and though writing's elective status at Holy Cross is what allows her the freedom to teach pretty much whatever she wants to, she does miss working with those first-generation college students who actually *need* help with their writing:

> The one regret that I have about Holy Cross, and this is an unresolved problem, is that the kids at Holy Cross for the most part are really elite kids. When I was at Rutgers I ran what they then called the remedial

> comp program, and I felt like there I was having a more direct socially beneficial effect. Because I could really help kids who were new, first-generation college students who were really struggling, and they're still my favorite students. Now we have some students like that at Holy Cross, and we tend to find each other. In fact, that's one reason I'm having so much fun in my comp class this semester. The deans all know that I want these students in my comp class. And at a place like Holy Cross they can just hand schedule them into my comp class, especially the spring comp class. I often don't teach it in the fall; it depends on what else I'm teaching. My favorite comp class is spring comp because those are the kids who all flopped in the fall.

Still, the upside to educating mostly elite undergraduate students at Holy Cross, she says, is that they could "have their consciousness raised" and then "go out and be in influential positions."

Administration

As we noted, the wide range of teaching opportunities Bizzell enjoys at Holy Cross is an effect, among other things, of the fact that composition is an elective there; there is no required composition program. Until the early 60s, they had a traditional Jesuit curriculum, Bizzell told us, which offered students what it considered progressively more sophisticated studies of discourse, beginning with poetry and ending with theology: in students' freshman year, they would take a year-long course in poetry, and they'd learn grammar by studying poetry; in their sophomore year, they would take a year-long course in rhetoric; in their junior year, it was philosophy; and in their senior year, it was theology. Because Holy Cross had only recently given up that curriculum, they had no intention of returning to it, even in the form of a required writing course. Still, they considered writing and rhetoric very important, and they hired Bizzell, in part, to help them decide what to do with it. Bizzell, a self-proclaimed "closet abolitionist," agreed that required courses are not the best way to deliver writing instruction—she had been a part of the giant comp machine at Rutgers and didn't like it—but she told them that everybody, the whole faculty, should be involved in the teaching of writing, that what they needed was a writing across the curriculum program.

> And that's what I did, I started a writing across the curriculum program, and the other thing I did in order to support the writing across the curriculum program was to start a peer tutoring workshop. No grad students—just undergraduates tutoring undergraduates. So for the first ten or fifteen years I was at Holy Cross I directed writing across the curriculum, and I ran the peer tutoring workshop and trained the tutors.

Right off the bat, Bizzell was a creator and administrator of campus-wide programs. A few of our profilees noted that the demands of administration can challenge one's values, but Bizzell told us that she has tried to make administrative decisions that serve her values:

> I believed it would be better for students if everybody on the faculty took writing as their responsibility. Especially students who were struggling would be better served. Faculty couldn't just say, Oh, well, he can't write, send him over to the English department. And I thought that the peer tutoring in many ways served my values in terms of collaborative work, students helping students. What the tutors learned was wonderful for them, and many of my tutors are now teachers, some are actually in comp and rhet; kids have gone on, actually gone on to graduate school in comp and rhet. And I think being a tutor, or being someone who used the workshop, gave you a good orientation towards doing academic work, less competitive and more collaborative and so forth. Although I have to admit I am a fun-sy girl, I wasn't only looking for fun, I think I was also trying to make the choice to do things that I thought were important.

Bizzell assumed a 2/2 load most of the time she was creating and administering these programs; still, when we gasped at the amount of work she took on instantly at Holy Cross, she admitted that she "probably needed serious therapy. Long ago. [laughter] Workaholic, obsessive personality, type-A, whatever. No, I plead guilty, absolutely." (Cheryl Glenn would say that Bizzell, like every other profilee in this volume, is a member of the OCOWA: Over-Committers, Over-Workers Anonymous.) But Bizzell told us she found it very exciting to start these programs; because there was nothing already in place, she got to set up exactly what she wanted. She worked for the dean, and she was "it," the only comp person on campus—she was their entire writing program. She found this exhilarating, and she loved what she was doing. She also told us that that it was, in part, through her administrative work that she became known around campus very quickly, which made it possible for her to consider going up for tenure early.

Early Tenure

Bizzell and Herzberg were eager to have children, but she felt it was important to get tenure first. In order to speed up the process, she decided to count all three of the years she had taught full-time at Rutgers toward her tenure clock so that she could go up for tenure in her third year at Holy Cross. Bizzell stressed that this was a risky choice, "probably even foolhardy," and one that she would not necessarily recommend to others. But she liked the job and the city, and since Herzberg had not yet landed a tenure-track position, she decided to go for it and find out quickly whether they were going to get to stay in Worcester or if they'd need to move. They got to stay, and her decision to go up early worked out very well for her:

> I knew what they wanted me to do, so by the second year I was there I at least had the programs launched. They weren't doing what I wanted them to do yet, but at least the shape of them had structure, was visible, and, I don't know, I just … don't know why, but I think I had a good sense of how to move into that community and make myself known there. You could nominate yourself to be elected for certain committees, so I immediately got myself onto the curriculum committee, the college curriculum committee, which turned out to be a good move because I could talk about writing there. I have just always kind of been an outspoken person. I always just say what I think, not rudely, I hope. Shortly after I came to Holy Cross, I got elected to the top governance committee there, which was very nice, very flattering, but that also kind of helped me get visibility. And also because I'm doing writing across the curriculum I'm going around to all the departments, I'm meeting people, so I was in a position, perhaps an advantageous position, to come up for tenure relatively early. People in the college knew me.

So along with starting high-profile, college-wide programs, Bizzell also got herself onto high-level and very visible committees, which helped her make a name for herself quickly at her institution. All of this no doubt helped her tenure case when the time came. Nonetheless, it's worth noting that the publication requirements for tenure at Holy Cross at the time were "pretty skimpy," as Bizzell put it. "I got tenure in 1981 or '82. I only had three or four articles published at that time, but that was enough for tenure at Holy Cross then." Currently, in the field of rhetoric and composition, tenure generally involves producing a single-authored book, and if a candidate doesn't have that book in hand or at least in press at the time s/he comes up for tenure, the most selfless and accomplished service record in the world won't save his or her case. However, *with* that book in hand, the kind of service record and name recognition Bizzell accomplished could certainly help to make the case.

Children

Bizzell knew she wanted children, so immediately after earning tenure she and Herzberg tried for a couple of years to get pregnant. When it didn't happen, they adopted biological sisters from Korea. Bizzell told us that there was a time factor involved in this decision: she had a sabbatical coming up, and she wanted to use it in conjunction with maternity leave, which is something she helped to institute at Holy Cross.

> At the time I came to Holy Cross, they had no maternity leave policy at all. Of course they didn't: they hadn't even had women faculty but for a few years. They had Jesuits, for heaven's sake. And the lay faculty they hired in the 60s were all men in traditional marriages who didn't need family leave. So it was a completely different model. So I said, Well, you guys need a maternity policy, and a bunch of us got together and made use of college governance. I'm the first person—I'm very proud of this—to take a maternity leave from Holy Cross. The policy as it then was allowed me to take a semester off at some fraction of my pay; so I thought, Well, what I want to do is combine that semester maternity leave with a year's sabbatical so that I can get basically two years off when I have a baby. And then when it transpired that our kids were going to be adopted, we said, let's get siblings, let's get them at the same time, and I'll have that two-year period off from work to be with them when they're small, so that's what we did. We got these two little girls from Korea, biological sisters; they were two years old and six months old when they came, and I was home with them—not totally full time, I did after a certain point get some part-time daycare so I could continue to do my work.

Bizzell told us that after she adopted her children, she didn't return to work full-time for almost two years, and that she feels very good about that decision.

> I think everyone has to come up with their own solution for how to mesh children and work. If somebody wants to have a baby and go back to work six weeks later full time, that's their business. I wouldn't have wanted to do that. And I would never venture any judgment one way or the other on how another person decides to handle that; that wouldn't have been for me. And as it turns out, I wouldn't have been able to do it because our older daughter had all kinds of issues that needed a lot of special attention. So it was a good thing that we planned it the way that we did.

After her maternity leave, Bizzell went back to work, teaching, directing her programs, and writing her books. But her schedule, she told us, was never the same. "I always tell people that the life that I had before children was reduced to rubble by having children. It was absolutely leveled to the ground. And then a new life was constructed, which included the children. That's how it impacted me. Maybe it wouldn't affect everybody that way. But that's how it affected me."

She described two chief differences between her pre-kids and post-kids life. First, after the children came it became imperative for her to plan her day down to the minute. "This [pointing to her wristwatch] became a manacle … chaining me to the schedule. And I had to do everything. I had to get the kids to daycare, get them to school. I had to go pick them up; I had to follow their schedule." For the first time ever, she had to schedule her writing time, as well. She likes to write in the morning and, like several of our other profilees, had always tried to schedule her classes in the afternoon to give herself long blocks of morning time to write; however, once the kids arrived on the scene, she told us, even her writing had to be scheduled down to the minute.

> I had never worried about that previously. I did it when I felt like it. And I could sort of let an idea gestate and say, OK, I think I'm going to be ready to start working on this next Monday or Tuesday or something. Oh, no, forget about that now. You've got Monday 10 to 12 to work on your writing, and then you won't have another time blocked to do it till Thursday, 3 to 4. So get cracking. Everything had to be done when there was time for it.

The second major post-kids difference she described is related to the first: she began to feel as if she never did anything quite as well as she wanted to do it:

> And that I just had to live with that. That was part of the cost of trying to do all the things I was doing. I never really quite spent enough time with the kids, never really gave them quite enough attention, never really gave my students quite enough attention, never really did all of the writing that I wanted to do. Everything was getting a little shorted. And that was just life. I was just going to have to deal with that. It's psychically draining, and I think our culture sends women many messages that they are inadequate in many ways. We are constantly barraged with that, no matter what choices we make, whether we stay home with our kids full time, whatever we do, we're not good enough. And we get those messages all the time, from multiple sources. I've already suggested my parents were puzzled by the fact that I'm still working, after I had kids. You just have to hold off those messages, that's all. You just have to. I'm doing what I want to do. I wanted to have kids. I want to work. There was never any question in my mind of quitting work to stay home. I would have killed myself long ago if I tried to do that. I love my kids, but I am not a full-time mom. No way could I do that. So I was doing what I wanted to do, and I just had to live with the psychic stress of holding off. You can hold these messages off, but it requires effort. It's like holding a weight off your chest; you can do it, but your muscles are tensed all the time. And I still live with that. Not as much as I did when the kids were small. Now I've got the consequences, so I can say, Gee, would things be better for them—they're both troubled kids, each in her own way—would things be better for them if I had spent more time with them? I don't know. I don't know.

Bizzell noted that today men are often much more involved in childrearing than they were when she was in her 20s and that these are issues that now very often concern men. However, she doesn't feel that they concern men and women equally: "I think they concern women in special ways because the culture addresses women in a special way." Therefore, Bizzell's advice to women in the field is that "if you're going to have kids—with a partner or without a partner—and work, you just, I think, have to realize that you're going to have a little extra psychic tax to pay." Indeed, when we asked Bizzell if there were anything at any level of her professional career that she wishes she could do again differently, she finally, after some time, described as potential regrets certain decisions she had made at this intersection of family and career:

> Thinking about it, looking back, there are things that, maybe things that I regret, maybe opportunities that I regret [not taking]. The whole issue of working full time and having kids has been very, very vexed for me. That's been a real source of stress and pain, and I feel very dissatisfied with the way that I worked that out. But I don't know that I could have done it differently … . I don't know another option.

Negotiating Discrimination

When we asked Bizzell to describe some of the professional struggles she faced and the strategies she used to navigate through them, she told us that she has typically gone with "the honest face ethos":

> Mina Shaughnessy talks about the honest face ethos and how that doesn't cut it in academic writing. And I think she's right on the one hand, but on the other hand, I think my strategy, if there was one, was always just to do what I wanted to do, and to make sure I had all my ducks in a row, and then hope that I would have success. And if I didn't, so be it.

So, for example, when Bizzell joined the English department faculty at Holy Cross and encountered its longstanding tradition of hazing new faculty, she just said "no":

> They had a position that they called—and I'm not kidding you—department thrall. Department thrall was whoever was hired last, and the task of the department thrall was to make the coffee, and … bring the sherry over to the faculty meeting in the library, and any other kind of schlepping stuff that had to be done. A young man had that position when I came to Holy Cross, and he came into my office in great glee the first semester I was there and said, "Oh, I'm so glad I don't have to be department thrall anymore. The job has fallen to you." I said,

> "What's that?" He told me, and I said, "I'm not doing it." … Sorry, no more department thrall. If it's gotta be me, I'm not doing it.

This courageous stance didn't always go over well with everyone. When Bizzell simply said "No" to being the department thrall, both the young man who hoped to pass the job off to her and the young woman who had held the post before him were embarrassed for having done it and a little angry at Bizzell for demonstrating the courage to say "No": "The negative vibes I got were more from them, really, than from the senior faculty because I wasn't sort of playing the game, or I had said the emperor has no clothes or something." Still, Bizzell told us that when she came up for tenure, "there was a virulent faction who tried to get rid of me"; she faced the same small faction of resistance again when she came up for full professor. "So maybe people didn't like me," she told us. "I wasn't mad about it. I hope I wasn't rude. But I just said, 'I'm not doing it. That's not appropriate.'" Bizzell's courage in these situations is perhaps (and among other things) an effect of Bizzell's well-rounded sense of herself, which is not defined solely by her job: "Maybe they didn't like me and they didn't want to tenure me, but that's who I am. I just thought, fine, I'll go elsewhere. I can get another job. I can get a job outside the academy. My husband did. He did it; I can do it. I just wasn't going to be the thrall, and I didn't do it."

Bizzell told us that she owes much of her success to the fact that she focused on doing her job well and making decisions that served her values, without worrying too much about fallout.

> I don't think we live in a perfect world where virtue is always rewarded, but that's what I meant by saying I had my ducks in a row. I felt I was doing my job competently, and I could prove that. Therefore, if I said, you know what, for the next few years, I'm going to have to leave campus every day by 5:15 because if I don't, if I'm late picking up my kids from daycare, they will charge me $5 a minute for every minute I'm late after 5:30, and it takes me about fifteen minutes to get across town, so I'm going to be leaving at 5:15, so if y'all want to have a faculty meeting and you keep talking, you'll see me get up and leave. Don't be offended. I have to go. And some people no doubt thought that was unprofessional. Too bad. Too bad. And I never got mad. I just said, This is what I'm going to do. For me it was better not to get mad. I have a terrible temper, actually, so I try to keep it under control. Plus I think politically in dealing with situations like this, I feel it's more effective not to be mad, not to be defensive, just to say, These are my needs, this is what I'm going to do, and if the institution can't support that, I'll go elsewhere. I can get a job. I've got a PhD. I can get a job somewhere else … . [Y]ou might love this job or you might want to get tenure at this place, but it's not the end of the world if you don't. It's not. You can go elsewhere. As long as you know that, then you decide

> what terms of employment you're willing to accept. That was always my attitude at Holy Cross. If they don't like me, then they'll get rid of me and fine. And there were people who really didn't like me, according to what they wrote on my negative tenure report and my negative promotion report. But they didn't prevail.

We asked Bizzell if she had to deal with a kind of day-to-day hostility from this faction who didn't like or support her, and she told us that she has a very high tolerance for hostility, "particularly certain kinds of male arrogance and hostility. I think I let a lot roll off my back to tell you the truth. I think I'm pretty good at dealing with difficult people because I don't get mad and I do what I want to do anyway. I've found that it's a good strategy to thank people politely for unwanted advice and then follow my own instincts."

Another situation in which Bizzell's calm yet straightforward approach served her well took place in the first year she was at Holy Cross.

> One of these guys who was notorious for flirting with junior faculty tried to flirt with me. He came in my office one day, and I was actually standing looking out the window and didn't hear him come in, and he walked up behind me and put his arms around me and hugged me. From behind. So his arms are across my chest, pinning my arms to my body. I just went like this, just threw him off, basically, and said, "Please don't do that. Don't ever do that again." That was all I had to do with him. That was the end of him. He didn't flirt with me anymore. He was nice to me. I don't know what he thought of me. I didn't go the affirmative action route or report sexual harassment. I don't think we had an affirmative action office in those days. Literally, I don't think we did. I don't think I would have anyway. If he had persisted, sure. But that was enough.

And it continues to serve her well now that she is the department chair:

> I have to say, I'm really not sure what some of the men in my department think of me. I'm the department chair now, and I get vibes from them from time to time that they really don't respect me in that position. Sometimes I feel like they really don't have the same attitude towards me that they would towards one of their own in that position. I'm really not sure what they think of me, but I kind of have a feeling they don't respect me. They'll sometimes feel they don't need to come to the meetings that I call, or I'll send out a memo of some kind and one of them will send me a prissy little correction to something that I've said in the memo, that kind of thing. Helping me out … . Fine. Life is too short to get aggravated about that. I can afford to be generous. I'm

> the chair. I'm sitting pretty. I've had all the professional success anybody could hope to have.

Mentoring

After spending more than two decades creating and running various programs all over campus at Holy Cross, Bizzell is now serving as the chair of the department, and it's worth noting that she seems much less enthusiastic about this particular administrative position:

> Being department chair is great. Actually—what am I saying? I really hate being department chair. I've avoided it all these years. We take it in turns to be chair; we don't hire outside. And I never wanted to be department chair. But I could hide from it because I was running the writing program for many years; then the dean wanted me to run the college honors program, so I did that for a while. I always had some other program that I was running, so I could hide from being department chair. Finally I ran out of places to hide, basically, so I became department chair, and it really has many horrible aspects to it. Which I won't go into, but other horrible aspects besides the one I just mentioned. It's a huge amount of work, an unbelievable amount of work.

However, the one thing she told us she appreciates about chairing the department is that "it does enable me to mentor the junior faculty, particularly the women."

As a graduate student and junior faculty member, Bizzell didn't get much mentoring. She did well, and she went through the program fairly quickly—in and out in five years—but she did it with very little professional and scholarly guidance. She told us that George Kearns, who was not a graduate professor but was the director of the writing program when she was the assistant director, mentored her some in terms of professionalization. He was a full-time administrator running their enormous writing program, and when she was hired as the assistant director, he helped her "learn the ropes." But that was pretty much the extent of it.

> I'll tell you an interesting story. Dave Bartholomae, Don McQuade, and I are all graduates of the Rutgers program. A few years ago Dick Poirier decided—and Dick Poirier of course, is the big, ultra, the god of the graduate program at Rutgers, the high-powered theorist, and the person that everybody worshipped—he decided to bring back some of these comp folks to give lectures at Rutgers. So I saw Don and Dave at a conference, and we were having a drink, and they said, "Are you going to Rutgers this spring?" And I said, "Yeah, they invited me to go,

> isn't that great?" And they said, "Oh my god, we're terrified. We're so nervous about what we're going to say." Now if you print this they'll probably be mad at me for putting them in this light. This is a story; it's taking some liberties with reality, no doubt, but my recollection of the conversation is that they said, "Well, we're really so nervous about going back to Rutgers." I said, "Gee, I'm not." And they said, "What? Don't you want to know who's going to come and hear your talk? What if nobody comes? What if Dick doesn't come to your talk?" I said, "I don't care whether he comes or not; he didn't give me any attention while I was there." [Laughter from both] I don't think Poirier really gave me much attention, or knew I was alive, basically. He knew I was proceeding through the program successfully, but I never got any special attention from him, so going back I don't care who shows up. I wouldn't necessarily expect any of those graduate professors to come; I'm expecting it will be the people in the comp program who will come. So we compared notes afterwards, and we were able to say that, yes, Dick Poirier did come to all of our talks, but I said, "I bet he didn't kiss you. He kissed me." [laughter from both] And they said, "Well, no, he didn't kiss us, but we were just as glad he didn't kiss us." So I felt I was treated very well by my graduate professors, and I got an excellent education at Rutgers, but I didn't feel like I got a lot of mentoring.

Though she succeeded pretty much by winging it without a mentor, and though Holy Cross does not have graduate students, Bizzell does try to offer advice and other kinds of help to graduate students at other institutions and to her junior colleagues whenever and however she can.

> Since I have no colleagues at my school, my professional life has been lived at conferences, and I've made friends in the profession through seeing them at conferences. People whose work I've admired I then go to their sessions and meet them, and if I can help them in some way professionally, I do. I don't know … men and women, really. I don't know whether they would regard me as having mentored them in any way. I don't know whether they would regard what I've done as that much help. It doesn't seem like that much help to me. Since I'm not in a graduate program, I don't have an easy way of establishing ongoing relationships with folks as a mentor, but I've tried to help people. Not because I wanted to help them necessarily but because I thought their work deserved to be known more widely in the profession, so I promoted it. And then they might ask me for advice about what they should do about this or that, so it might develop that way. I don't know that they would regard what I've done as significant mentoring. I've done what I could do given the fact that I'm not in a graduate program with graduate students.

Having a Life

Though Bizzell told us that she doesn't have a serious hobby, it became clear very quickly in our discussions with her that she has a *life* and that her successful career is only one piece of it. She told us that she enjoys reading almost anything—she calls herself an "omnivorous reader." She reads novels randomly, but she especially loves detective fiction and what she calls "junk books: kind of romance/suspense novels with no redeeming qualities whatsoever as far as I can see, except they're amusing." She also loves classical music and all kinds of dance; she has a subscription to the Boston Ballet. Herzberg prefers modern dance, so they go to modern dance concerts as well, including one in western Massachusetts at a venue called Jacob's Pillow: "we haunt Jacob's Pillow in the summer." Bizzell told us she loves to cook, take long walks with her shepherd-huskie mix, and garden a little. She's currently working on her Hebrew and taking some college classes in Jewish intellectual history. And at the time we talked with her, she and Herzberg were planning a long trip to Israel during their 2005–06 sabbatical. When we asked how she manages to fit so many non-work-related activities into her hectic schedule, she told us that she tries to integrate most of her interests into her daily or weekly routine:

> I walk every day. I cook every day. I listen to music every day. Going to a dance concert or a music concert is something that's pretty easy to fit into a weekly schedule. So the things that I do for pleasure are not things that require me to set aside a large chunk of time, separately from my weekly schedule. And I think that's what makes them work.

One of the most impressive and inspiring things we learned in our discussions with Bizzell is that this highly successful and massively busy scholar never fails to observe the Sabbath. That is, despite the crazy demands of teaching up to three courses a semester, directing various college-wide programs, serving as President of the Rhetoric Society of America and chair of the English department, and producing her own scholarship, Bizzell manages to *rest* for one full day each week—and she strongly encourages others in the field to do the same:

> That's why I said earlier that I was chained to the watch six days a week. I'm not chained to it seven days a week because I observe the Sabbath. It's a very valuable thing to have a Sabbath, and I recommend it. From sundown on Friday to sundown on Saturday, we don't answer the phone, we don't turn on the computer, we don't turn on the TV or the radio, we don't drive anywhere. We have a lovely meal Friday night, and we sit at the table for a long time. And then we sit around on Saturday morning, go to synagogue, take a nap—Saturday afternoon, we go for a walk. When the kids were small we would play games with them. This was and is precious family time, and rest time, and you have

to learn how to do it. It's a real discipline. But for someone like me, given everything else that you've learned about me in this interview, you know that I would have to have a religious discipline to get me to stop working for one day a week. And it's been great. It's been a life saver in many, many ways for me and for our family to have that day of rest every week. So I recommend that to people. Have a day of rest. If you can't manage a full day, have a half a day. And the ideal thing is that it's really a day of rest, not the day when you take the kids to the zoo, or you go skiing, or whatever. But you turn off the world. Turn off the world.

Postscript on Changes

By the time the book in which this profile appears is published, Bruce Herzberg and I will be divorced. Quite unexpectedly, for me, he initiated the separation in October 2004. The divorce has been rather "public" in the world of composition and rhetoric, since we were so well known for our work together. The fact that we have divorced may make some readers wonder whether I wish to qualify any of the statements I make here about relationships and careers.

The answer is no. I affirm that Bruce and I had for many years the wonderful partnership that is described here. I affirm my belief that we made good choices together over the years for ourselves and our family. I cannot see how any different choices we might have made would have prevented our marriage from ending. I still feel that the views I express here represent the best advice I can give others about making choices that affect relationships and careers.

If there is perhaps too self-congratulatory a tone about that advice, readers annoyed by it should know that life has now chastened me. But I stand by those views nevertheless.

—Pat Bizzell, 21 February 2005

9

SHARON CROWLEY

Sharon Crowley is professor of English at Arizona State University, where she teaches courses in the history and theory of rhetoric and composition. A prolific and respected scholar as well as a celebrated teacher and mentor, Crowley has published six books devoted to the history, theory, and/or teaching of rhetoric and writing: *Toward a Civil Discourse: Rhetoric and Fundamentalism*; *Ancient Rhetorics for Contemporary Students*, co-authored with Debra Hawhee and now in its third edition; *Rhetorical Bodies*, co-edited with Jack Selzer; *Composition in the University*, which won MLA's Mina Shaughnessy prize for the year's best book on teaching; *The Methodical Memory: Invention in Current Traditional Rhetoric*, which won the Ross Winterowd award for the year's best book in rhetoric and composition; and *The Teacher's Introduction to Deconstruction*, which was commissioned by NCTE. Crowley earned both her BA and MA in English at the University of Nebraska and then her PhD in English at the University of Northern Colorado in 1973. She took her first tenure-track position at Northern Arizona University in 1974 and remained there for 17 years, easily earning tenure and then becoming full professor. She joined the faculty in the Rhetoric Department at the University of Iowa in 1991 and then the Penn State English Department in 1995, where she spent the next three years writing *Composition in the University*. In 1998, she accepted the position at Arizona State, returning to her beloved desert home.

Background

Crowley was born and raised in Nebraska. Both her parents were teachers, and she told us that there was never any discussion about whether she and her sisters would go to college: they were expected to go. There was never any discussion about *where* she would go to college, either—her family lived in Nebraska, so Crowley went to the University of Nebraska, even though the school was considered "a den of evil" by some people in her home town. Her father's friends warned him that his daughter would "lose her religion" if she went to Lincoln, Crowley told us, "and they were right." After earning both her BA and MA in English with a teaching certificate, she taught high school in Columbus,

Nebraska, for a year before marrying a high school counselor and moving to Davenport, Iowa, in 1967. She taught at Central High, a large urban high school, and her husband worked at the junior high school down the street. Central High had "lots of problems, lots of issues," Crowley told us, but she loved to teach, and "it was a really exciting time" to be doing it:

> I discovered that the literature-with-grammar curriculum that was standard was not what my students wanted or needed. Many of my students were only marginally literate because their parents were transient workers. This was on the Mississippi River. Families moved up and down the River, following the crops, so the students never got a chance to stay in school very long. I was charged to teach American literature to a class of 15-year-old kids who couldn't read, for example. So I took the big old American lit book, a big thing, it started with "Sinners in the Hands of an Angry God"—half my class was African American. As one of them said about that, "Shiii-it!" [laughter] And so we started with Thoreau and we read "Civil Disobedience" together. This is the 60s. We read it out loud. It took us a long time because they were just learning to read tougher texts. They picked up reading really fast, and by the end of "Civil Disobedience," we had a revolution on our hands. It was exciting. … [T]hese kids were more receptive to instruction than almost anybody I've ever taught. … I enjoyed teaching high school, but I just couldn't stand the institution.

Crowley and her husband taught in Davenport for five years and then both applied to PhD programs. When he got a scholarship to the University of Northern Colorado in Greeley, she went with him. "I applied elsewhere," she told us. "I got into the University of Iowa, for example. But I didn't know the difference. I didn't know the pecking order. I was still very isolated. So I followed him to Northern Colorado." Later, she questioned this decision, noting that Ross Winterowd had once told her she was "the only person in the profession that had a worse degree than he," meaning that neither had graduated from an ivy or an older state university. But at the time she never considered not going with her husband, who incidentally didn't get into Iowa: "It never occurred to me not to go with him. … For women, up to the second wave, we sort of went with the flow," she told us. "We did what we were told, and it did seem like serendipity if things happened for us. Or we were taught to rationalize it as serendipity. If we made it happen, we told ourselves it was luck."

So Crowley enrolled in the doctorate program in English at UNC, but she told us she knew right away that this very traditional department wasn't going to give her what she was looking for. She couldn't name what it was that she wanted to study—she didn't yet know that it *had* a name—until one day a fellow graduate student told her, "We need to study rhetoric. There's an art here." Crowley agreed. At the time, there were no rhetoric courses in the English department at UNC, so these two English PhD students went over to the speech department and signed up for "lots of hours in the history of rhetoric"—and the rest, as they say, is history.

> So I took these wonderful courses in the history of rhetoric from this very good speech department. I took a course in medieval rhetoric. I took courses in classical rhetoric … . And as Ed Corbett used to say when he told his story about discovering rhetoric, I just fell in love with it. Where has this been all my life? Not only for pedagogical purposes, but for intellectual purposes. But in the meantime I'm slogging through all this English lit and American lit. And it's awful stuff. The more I understand about rhetoric the less I'm interested in literature. And I understand the kids today in graduate school who study rhetoric and then go to their lit classes and say, "Why are we doing this?" So I got some bad grades on papers.

But a few bad grades didn't dissuade her. At thirty, Crowley was older than most of her colleagues in her grad student cohort, and she had as much teaching experience as some of the faculty at UNC, so she had the confidence (she said the "arrogance") necessary to go against the flow in the English department. Her confidence was also considerably bolstered by the amazing cultural, political, and intellectual energy of this particular time period, the *Zeitgeist* of the 70s, during which she found not only rhetoric but feminism, too:

> This was also women's liberation in the '70s and the second wave. Oh, I bit on that second wave. Joined a CR group and of course we smoked dope at our CR group. And I left my husband. That's the story … . We were all stoned all the time, but *everybody* was stoned all the time. It's hard for people who didn't live through that time period to realize how wonderful it was. Politics was in the air. We were articulating systemic analyses for the first time—for me anyhow. I came into contact with leftist discourse for the first time. I'm a good little white girl from Nebraska but liberal. My parents were liberal, and so their politics were different from those of most of the people in the place where we lived, but that was the extent of my political understanding. And then I got involved in women's lib. Reading Robin Morgan and people like that blew my mind. So that was the start of where I was, or where I am. … And it was just wonderful. To be in graduate school, and to be a woman—it was incredible. And I found an appreciation for women that I'd never had because we'd been raised to compete with one another. I made some incredible women friends and learned the strength of female friendship. Wonderful stuff.

Crowley completed her PhD at UNC in 1973 and immediately landed a tenure-track position at Northern Arizona University, which was one of only two jobs "available for something like 400 newly minted PhDs" that year, 18 of whom were her colleagues at UNC. Northern Arizona was looking for someone to write a series of undergraduate courses for English majors and so had advertised for a specialist in technical writing—which Crowley, of course, was not. But she presented herself as a technical writer in the interview, and she must have pulled it off very nicely since she did indeed get the job. She suspects that the search committee "didn't know enough about composition to know that I wasn't what I was advertising." In those days, remember, there was no field called "rhetoric and composition." Her creative self-marketing got her foot in the door, got her the chance to compete on campus with other candidates for the position—candidates who, presumably, actually did have expertise in technical writing. From there the story of her hire, as she put it, turns into "an interesting … story." When she got the on-campus interview, she had to figure out what to wear:

> I was so poor that I didn't own a suit. So I had to borrow a suit from a friend. And I'm a fairly tall woman, and the suit was way short. But that was OK. … The suit was navy blue, and I bought a yellow polka-dotted shirt to wear with it. I could afford to buy a shirt, or blouse, but not the whole thing. So I get down there and, unbeknownst to me, navy blue and yellow are NAU's colors. So I'm wearing their colors, which turned out to be important. And I interview with the president. He ran things. It was a very patriarchal institution. This is before conditions of faculty service, before well-thought-out tenure rules. Later on, I participated in composing the descriptions for tenure and such for the state of Arizona—during the late '70s and early '80s. At that earlier time, appointment to associate was a mystery. Nobody quite knew how it happened. But anyway, I'm getting ahead of myself. So I go in to interview with the president, and I sit down and cross my legs, because I forget for the moment that I'm wearing a skirt. And he looked … energized. The interview with him lasted about twenty minutes. The rest of the on-campus visit went just fine. But I was told in the English department that I was not their first choice, that their first choice was an older person, and that they wanted to hire someone a little bit more senior. I thought it was kind of cool that they were being honest, and I went home thinking, "Well, I'm going to have to go back to work and get a real job." But the next week I got a call that they wanted to hire me. Years later I found out from a friend that the president had called the chair of the department and told them: "I want you to hire that younger woman. I think she will attract our students." But you know what happened. … Isn't that something? But, you know, it could also have been the suit, the blue and yellow suit.

In any case, NAU was clearly pleased with their decision to hire Crowley: she earned tenure right on time and eventually got promoted to full professor there, where she remained for the first 17 years of her career.

Strategies for Success

Graduate School

Crowley told us that if she had it to do over again, she would go to a school that had a better position in the traditional pecking order: "I would have gone somewhere else. I would have had the requisite knowledge to know that I should have gone to Iowa." If she had gone to Iowa, she said, she "would have been in a whole different place now. Because Sam Becker was there in those days, and Don Bryant. It would have been a whole different ballgame. Iowa has always been, since the '40s, a hotbed of innovation in English studies." Indeed, when we asked Crowley what advice she wishes someone had given her in college, grad school, or as a junior faculty member, she could think of only one thing: she wishes someone had told her that there are better schools and that she should go to the best institution she could.

> You know, my friend Bryan Short did his undergraduate work at Yale. And when I was an assistant professor and we were pals, I realized how much better educated he was than I am, or was. The University of Nebraska is a good school, and luckily I took a lot of philosophy, right? I just gravitated—well, I know why: the requirement was either math or philosophy. ... But Bryan had read Nietzsche, and he'd read all this stuff that I hadn't read. So I wish I had known when I was 16 that there were better schools, and that I could maybe go to one. But there's no way my family or anybody that I knew could have understood that.

She wishes she had gone to a better institution not only because of the pecking order, Crowley told us, but also because she feels she could have used a "fuller undergraduate education."

> Bryan could cite stuff—stuff would just fall off his lips. He'd say, "Well, you have to read this or that." And I would say, "When did you read that?" And he'd say, "Oh god, I was 21, maybe." Of course, he lived near New York and so he had cultural advantages too; he heard Pavarotti's debut, for example. It's clear to me that growing up in the Midwest, or probably Texas as well, there's a certain handicap there, a cultural handicap. But there's nothing you can do about that. ... So when I read bell hooks, for example, on her experience going to Stanford—I mean, I can't understand it fully because I am white—but I sure empathize with how she feels such an outsider. And then when she goes back home she's a little bit alienated from home because she's been at Stanford. So I wish someone had told me all about that stuff.

Pre-Tenure Promotion Strategies

When Crowley joined the faculty at NAU, the teaching load was 4/4, which for her meant four sections of freshman English each semester. The publication requirements were minimal, however, and Crowley told us that after having taught what amounted (conservatively) to a 5/5 load at the high-school level, NAU's 4/4 seemed like a snap:

> When I was a junior professor, I was single again, and so delighted to be a professor. I loved the life. I loved the academy. And NAU was perfect for me. The publication expectations were not high in those days. When I started I had a 4/4 teaching load. I taught freshman English. But I was used to that. I was a high school teacher; a 4/4 load was great because in high school you have five classes every day and 150 students. Plus potty duty and all those things. Four sections of freshman English was like falling off a log.

Because she was accustomed to the teaching pace and because a position at NAU didn't put her under the "publish or perish" gun, Crowley told us she spent the first few years as an assistant professor "reading all the books that had been mentioned in my history of rhetoric classes." She read voraciously, read everything—effectively giving herself the education she had wanted in graduate school—and she took the time to talk with her colleagues about what she was learning, to put it into practice in the teaching of composition:

> And so I learned a lot about contemporary currents in composition; in addition to reading *CCC*, of course, Ed Corbett was the editor of that. I learned a lot about administering composition programs and about the politics of composition. But the exciting thing in those days of course was the composing process. And I began to teach that to my colleagues. Everybody in the department taught comp—part of your load was comp. This is the way things were done in the old days. Until you got to be senior you taught comp. And so I began to teach my colleagues about the composing process, and they loved it because it was a lot less work in many ways because the students participated in class in a way that they had never been allowed to when you simply lectured. And grading papers was a lot easier because the students could help you. Students became invested in their work in a way that they weren't under current-traditional instruction. Now this didn't happen over night. But my colleagues thought, "Wow!" So their estimation of me went right up because I helped them have more fun teaching freshman English. I was astonished at how much more fun it was; I just couldn't believe it.

Crowley also spent quite a lot of time getting to know the contemporary movers and shakers in the field, which among other things landed her the editorship of the *Arizona English Bulletin*, high-powered speaking invitations, and the chance to start publishing her talks in some of the field's top journals, such as *College Composition and Communication*.

> Deane Hargrave, who was my colleague there in English education, took me down to ASU and to U of A and made sure that I met Frank D'Angelo and Charles Davis, who ran the writing program at U of A, and the people in English at those two institutions. Ken Donaldson who was Mr. English Education in those days. Bob Schaffer. And her doing that got me an appointment as editor of the *Arizona English Bulletin*, which was one of the premiere regional English journals in those days, and I had that editorship from '75 through '77 or '78 and through that I got to meet an awful lot of people in Arizona, plus nationally people would publish there because they knew Ken or Deane, Frank, somebody who was active.
>
> Somehow I got an invitation to go up to Puget Sound, with Gary Tate, he was the other speaker, and I talked about the composing process. And Gary urged me to send a paper off to Ed, and I did, on the composing process, and Ed published it. I don't even remember how I got in the national scene, but I must have because in '79 I went up to the Wyoming conference as a featured speaker. So I must have. Probably the editorship and just publishing little pieces here and there. I didn't even know that you had to publish. Let's face it, in those days it was very different. You were expected to teach.

During her pre-tenure years, Crowley was actively involved in NAU's faculty senate, as well, joining with the faculty senates of all three Arizona institutions to help write the procedures for promotion to associate and full professor:

> I think this was something that happened across the country. And I attribute this move to formalize these procedures to the increasing number of women and minorities in the academy who knew they needed this kind of protection. This is what's often called the professionalization of the discipline, and at the time, the late 70s and early 80s, it was important and it was politically sound. It's been abused since, or maybe I should say that the old abuses have found a way to use these rules, but at the time it was a good thing.

Obviously, Crowley went on to become one of the most rigorous and prolific scholars in the field, and/but, interestingly, her path was paved in part by NAU's lower publication requirements, which gave her time to read and network, to immerse herself in the field and to serve on some very visible, university-wide committees that earned her name-recognition around campus. Her initial publications grew quite organically out of her various speaking engagements, and she apparently managed in the early days to remain somewhat oblivious to the pressure-cooking anguish often inspired by institutional credentialing machines. Indeed, Crowley stressed to us several times that her pre-tenure time-management strategies were successful precisely because she was not pressured to publish: "Again, I was in a non-research oriented institution, so it might have been different for someone who was at Penn State."

On the other hand, it may also be important to emphasize that Crowley never became the technical writer that NAU thought they were hiring. That is, she did not allow her initial job description much creative power over her long-term professional identity. Whereas a handful of our profilees, all of whom are now extremely successful, went into their first tenure-track jobs with no real career goals and rose to success by doing very well whatever their institution needed them to do at the time—and then developing a scholarly interest in it—Crowley was motivated in the other direction:

> Intellectual hunger is what motivated me. I can remember just consuming Ong's book on Ramus. These are books that had never been checked out of the library. I just consumed them. I was just so hungry for that. I remember reading *Eighteenth-Century British Logic and Rhetoric* cover to cover. Just consumed it. I have no idea where that came from. In '77 Bryan went back to Yale for a sabbatical, and Derrida was there teaching. In '76, of course, *Of Grammatology* came out, and when Bryan came back he made us read it. It's 1978 and we're reading *Of Grammatology* together. We called ourselves the Poststructuralist Luncheon Club. … We met every Friday. There were four of us, and all of us published out of that experience. Our group, which lasted for about eight years, went on from Derrida and read other stuff. I saw right away the connection between deconstruction and sophistry. It isn't exact, and of course you have to consider the historical distinctions. But it was like, Boom! … And I just couldn't stop after that. Just couldn't stop.

There was no book requirement at NAU when Crowley came up for tenure, and she was promoted on the strength of a collection of well-placed articles, which she completed by writing "all the time," whenever she wasn't teaching. "I just wrote whenever I could," she told us. "A vacation. Early morning. Late at night. Just whenever I could." And she put together what she called "a decent portfolio," more than enough to support her promotion. However, the promotion procedures that she helped to establish for NAU had not yet come into effect, so her case was actually decided under the "old system":

> My first promotion didn't come under that system; it came under the old system: that president must have remembered my knees. [Laughter]

> Because one day I got a letter and it said I'd been promoted to associate and here's a raise. … There was no examination of salaries relative to one another. It was completely at the president's discretion. At NAU there was this thing called the Committee of 100. The president would select 100 faculty members, and they would all get in a meeting, and the president would say, "Well, who should we promote?" … And apparently those meetings were grisly. Bad things were said about people. Things have changed a lot since then, and it's my generation you have to thank for that.

The "new system" for promotion to associate not only instituted clearly defined procedures for T&P (tenure and promotion) but also more rigorous publication requirements. To get tenure in rhetoric and composition today, one generally needs to have a book out (or at the very least accepted) with a university press—though some colleges and universities continue to grant tenure in the field on the basis of a collection of well-placed articles, particularly when the candidate does certain kinds of empirical research. In any case, "in today's university you won't survive unless you publish," Crowley observes. The tenure bar continues to rise almost everywhere, and she doesn't see any relief in the foreseeable future:

> I can't see any institutional reason why the tenure bar will ever be lowered; rather there are lots of good reasons (from a provost's or president's point of view) to keep raising that bar. Assistant profs now understand that their tenure book must at least be in press at tenure time, which means that the thing has to be finished and under contract four or five years out of grad school. In addition, humanities and other departments are asking for an edited collection and/or a substantial portfolio of articles at tenure as well. I suppose the upper limit for the tenure bar is human endurance, willingness to remain single and childless and to forgo relationships with parents, friends, etc.

Post-Tenure Promotion Strategies

By the time Crowley went up for promotion to full, her "decent portfolio" had grown into a seriously impressive mass of top-notch scholarly work. She told us that immediately after tenure she got her first sabbatical (1981) and engaged in what she called some "really serious pushes" to complete various articles and manuscripts that she had begun but had never had the time to complete—she had been working on some of them for seven years. During this incredibly productive "leave," she finished four articles in four months. And they were all published.[10] Crowley used part of her sabbatical time to go to Ohio State and attend Ed Corbett's seminar, which is where she wrote the first pages of *Methodical Memory.*

> That was the first time that I'd had continuous access to a library that was old enough to have the nineteenth-century textbooks. If libraries keep old textbooks, it's sort of an accident of personnel, or shelf space. And in Arizona none of the libraries are old enough. Because all those universities were founded in the 1870s, and I needed earlier stuff. So I thought I had died and gone to heaven when I went to Ohio State. "My god, here's Bain on the shelf!" So I wrote the book. And Ed was so inspiring. I wanted to be Ed Corbett. And I don't mean Ed the scholar only. I wanted to be the teacher he was and the person he was. That was really a turning point for me, that seminar.

When Crowley looks back over her professional life, she sees herself always "scrabbling for time to write." She told us she needs at least three days to get into a writing project because it takes her two days just to gear up to where she was when she left off. "So a weekend won't do it." Until her promotion to full, Saturdays and Sundays were always designated "writing days," and she was always trying to get a Friday or a Monday off to provide the stretch she needed for a project. Writing is clearly a passion for Crowley, and the descriptions she offered of the very intense writing "pushes" she engaged in as an associate professor demonstrate a curious mix of pain and pleasure. When she wrote the first edition of her textbook, *Ancient Rhetorics for Contemporary Students*, for example, she was under "very serious pressure" from her publisher to complete the first draft. This project required a different kind of writing than she was used to doing, she had no real models to go by, and she had only the summer to get it done. Yet, her description of that anxiety-pumping situation gives it a somewhat seductive feel:

> But this was in Flagstaff, and the summers in Flagstaff are just glorious. I lived in a pine forest. I would get up early in the morning, write for four hours, and then go for a walk through the woods and run errands, buy groceries and stuff. Then I would write for another four hours, and then I would sleep for a few hours. And then I would write for another four hours. So I started literally working round the clock, 24 hours. There were times when my cat would come up and nudge me, and I'd say, "What do you want?" Lady was old then and she was very dignified but no doubt upset that our schedule was off. "What do you want?" I'd ask her, and then I'd realize I hadn't fed her for twelve hours. I'd look up and the clock would say ten, and I would think, Oh, it's ten at night. But I'd look out and the sun was shining—it was ten in the morning. I've had this happen with other writing projects, too. You get sort of transported to another place and you can't really be with anyone. Even your beloved cat is a distraction. I think you go a little bit crazy. And it's scary to me. It's like an acid trip in some ways. I don't know whether it's chemical, whether you put yourself in that place through sleep deprivation or what.

Administration

When we asked Crowley what she would tell a new graduate thinking about applying for an administration-heavy job, she told us unequivocally that she would advise "new grads to avoid administration like the plague."

> I was a WPA, but I waited till I was an associate professor with tenure, partly so I would have the authority to convince my colleagues to stop teaching current-traditional rhetoric. I had good relationships with my colleagues, but that wasn't enough. You have to have intellectual authority too. I waited till I was an associate also so that I couldn't be fired. I don't know how I knew to do that, but I knew. And then I only kept the job for five years. And I remember taking it because I knew that someday I would leave NAU, and I needed to have that on my resume. But I hated every minute of it. Not every minute of it. But I didn't like it. I got so anxious and controlling that—this was like the third year into my directorship—on the first day of classes I was prowling the halls with a schedule to make sure that everyone had shown up to teach. While I was doing this I ran into Bryan, and he said, "What in hell are you doing?" I told him, and he said, "Oh, go have coffee." And I realized, you just can't do that, you can't give it that much of your energy.

If a new graduate has to take WPAship in order to get a job, Crowley advises that she should, at the very least, surround herself with "excellent staff" and save her emotional commitment for her own work:

> If there's an associate directorship, make sure that's filled by somebody really competent and willing to work hard. And get yourself a good office staff that you can trust. Then don't commit yourself fully to the writing program. In other words, let it run itself. You may be hired to work miracles, but don't. Because any miracle that can be worked in a writing program, given the problems with that institution and with its universal requirement, will fade. As soon as you leave, somebody else will come in and do something different. And the mass of teachers and the terrible hiring practices mitigate against bringing about lasting qualitative change in a writing program. I know that's a controversial thing to say, but that's my experience. I would say to a young person, save your miracle-working for something else and just administer the program. Then go home at night—work 8 to 5 on the program, or whatever it is they make you do—and then go home at night and on weekends and do your research. But the crucial thing is not just the time, it's the intellectual and emotional commitment. You reserve that. You don't give that to the writing program. You give it to your research. The

> writing program will survive no matter what you do. In today's university you won't survive unless you publish. … You have to cultivate a kind of skepticism and cynicism about the writing program. If you don't it will just eat you alive. Unless there are senior compositionists around, nobody in the department will know whether you've done a good job or not. They won't care. What they'll care about is that you've kept down the controversy, kept a lid on kids rebelling and all that. That's what they care about.

Crowley also suggested that if you plan to accept a position that has a heavy administrative load right out of graduate school, you should try to "get in writing exactly what the tenure expectations are." This is somewhat "hollow advice," she admits, since by the time you actually come up for tenure "the dean and the chair probably will have changed," but if you get it in writing "at least you can wave it. I'm not sure that's adequate protection, but it's something."

It's not only new grads that Crowley warns off administration, however; she recommends that women in rhetoric and composition "stay away, stay away, stay away from administration" throughout their career if they possibly can because, among other things, "it turns you into a bureaucrat, and turns you away from—I hope I don't sound sexist in this—but it turns you away from your humanity and your femininity. It turns you away from your graciousness and your kindness and your love for others." While in administrative positions, Crowley told us, she found herself beginning to identify with the institution's goals, "and, oh, god, I become somebody I don't like." So she urges people not to do it if they can avoid it, though she acknowledges that it's not easy to avoid. Her advice to those who find themselves in an administrative position is to "pray every night, or whatever it is you do. [Laughter] Write in your journal. I found a journal to be of enormous help, by the way. Through difficult times, difficult administrative times, keeping a journal is very helpful, and having women confidantes is also crucial. And they should be women who are not in the department. Your neighbors, or friends, somebody who lives far away."

Institutional Survival Strategies

Crowley experienced some resentment from her colleagues at NAU both for her publishing record, which helped to raise the bar of expectation for everyone else, and for the professional "goodies" she got in return for her scholarly and diplomatic efforts.

> In my first job I was one of the few people who did research, because it wasn't expected then. I just did it. And I was resented for that because I was perceived to be changing the way things were done, raising the bar, however you want to put it. And good things happened to me because I learned from my father, who was a politician, I learned how

> to grease wheels and do spin. I greased every wheel, I greased the dean, I greased everybody I could, and so good things started to happen to me. My colleagues began to say that I was getting these goodies because I am a woman. "Sharon gets this because she's female. She got that promotion because she's female, she got that raise because she ... etc." And they would say this to my face.

When we asked how she had handled this situation, she answered ironically: "brilliantly of course. My great rhetorical triumph was to tell one of my colleagues, who was going on about that, to go fuck himself. ... So there went the grease right out the window." But in general, these occasional bursts of unpleasantness at the department level were tempered, Crowley said, by the fact that she had made some very good friends, both in and out of the department. One of her closest friends at NAU, for example, was the department chair:

> Despite all the flak I had great friends at NAU. Bryan Short was the chair of the department, a great friend.[11] He was an Americanist. He sat in on my history of rhetoric classes, and that helped him with his book on Melville. He wrote about Melville's reading of Samuel Newman. Samuel Newman wrote a textbook, and Melville read that while he was in school. So did Dickinson. Bryan later went off to Amherst and read Dickinson's papers, and he found a copy of Newman there. Isn't that cool stuff? ... I sort of turned him on to rhetoric, and he turned me on to administration and showed me how it could be done. He was a brilliant administrator. And if it hadn't been for people like that, it would have been much harder.

Indeed, Crowley encourages our readers to make friends with people all over campus who understand how the university works:

> Make good friends. It's really important to find somebody at any institution, who's maybe not the national star, but somebody who's been at that institution for a long time, who knows how that institution runs, and who has been on a lot of committees and can tell you what committee to get on, and who to cultivate, and how the institution works. One of the things I've noticed doing this migration that I've done over the last ten years is that it pays to know the institution. Right now, I don't know the institution, and it makes a difference. I'm pretty savvy about how universities work, but I don't yet know who the key people are at ASU. I don't yet know the right dean to call, and equally important, she doesn't know me, doesn't know whether she should take my call or not. So that's an important kind of knowledge for a young person to have. Don't just look up to the flashy scholar in your discipline—that person's going to know less about your university because she's gone all the time, off writing, researching.

The important thing is to determine who makes things happen at your institution and get to know them. And according to Crowley, "often they're staff people. The secretaries. That's another good piece of advice: get to know the secretaries. They run things."

> When I was chair of the faculty senate at NAU, I got to know the president's secretary, who was a stalwart woman, and I learned more shit from her; it was one of the most valuable relationships I had. And when I'd go to see him, it'd be: "Hi! I'll get you right in" even if he wasn't particularly happy to see me.

Mentoring

Crowley mentors colleagues and graduate students both inside and outside her home institution, and she told us that she tries to be as honest as possible with people: "though it sometimes hurts, it sometimes backfires, I try to be honest. I wish people had been honest with me when I was coming up." She warns, however, that being an honest and caring mentor is extremely difficult when the task comes shrink-wrapped with an administrative agenda. Recently, for example, Crowley served as the Director of Graduate Studies, and she was charged with whittling "down the number of our graduate students" by urging those who had been dissertating for several years to finally finish. She was ultimately successful, but she found that many who worked with her came in expecting "the typical bureaucratese," the standard institutional line, rather than honesty. And she admits that she went into the situation "thinking like an administrator—'we need to reduce the number of graduate students so we can give more time to each, our time-to-degree is the talk of the graduate school,' and so on." However, she told us that when she began to talk to these students, she changed hats because she discovered that they had "all sorts of personal difficulties that were keeping them from finishing." They had a clear memory of "all the institutional moments where people weren't generous, weren't open, weren't honest," so they tended to "suspect anybody in authority of the same sort of motives. With justice." Still, Crowley tried to be as honest as possible, to be more a mentor than an administrator:

> People had hundreds and hundreds of reasons for not writing their dissertations, and I would finally say something like, "You know, a lot of people have sat in that chair and said these things. But a lot of them have also managed to write their dissertations, so there must be something else going on. Is it that you really don't want to finish?" And that usually brings on a flood of tears. Mentoring is not easy. What I mean by that is, you can't be easy on people. There are times when you just need to put your arm around somebody, but there are other times when you just need to tell them the truth. And I always try to tell them that

> institutions are awful places—bitter, nasty, they bring out the worst in people. Don't expect institutions to behave honorably. Don't expect them to have a memory. Don't expect them to appreciate you. I try to tell all those things.

She is equally direct with her colleagues: we asked Crowley what she would do if some young woman she was mentoring were being discriminated against or persecuted in some way for her scholarship, and Crowley told us without hesitation that she would "console her, make sure she's okay, and then I would go beat the shit out of whoever was doing the discriminating or persecuting." She wasn't joking: "I'd just go put a stop to it. Because I have the kind of stature now where I can do that. I just say, 'I understand that you've been saying such and such. Stop it.'" Then, to the person getting harassed, Crowley would say:

> "your work is valuable." I'd try to indicate how her work connects up with work that other people are doing, and then to discern whether the criticism might be coming to her for unrelated reasons. I'd tell her that when the problem is sexism, or something else you can't do anything about, you just keep doing your work and go on. If you feel up to it, you might try to argue with people, but that's asking an awful lot. That's like my African American colleague who always seems to have to teach white people how to behave. That's not his job. And that's really not the job of a young person who's untenured and doing original and interesting research; it's not really her job to defend that against people who are ignorant. You can't really insist that she do that. I haven't seen that happen so much lately because people are hired now with an eye towards keeping them.

Having a Life

Once she was promoted to full professor, Crowley told us, she was determined to get some texture in her life, to work less and enjoy more. She started taking Saturdays off, but interestingly, it was an effort for her—she had to force herself not to work:

> After I got to be full professor, I said, no more of this 24/7 stuff. I forced myself—this is when I was at Iowa—to take Saturdays off. And it was a forced thing. I was so ingrained in the habit of working all the time, every day. Jan Norton, who's now my colleague, was there as a graduate student. She was trying to write her dissertation, and she thought this would be good therapy for her, too. So we would get in my car—I had a convertible—we would get in my car and drive through cornfields all over middle Iowa on Saturday afternoons, fleeing from

> this discipline we had imposed on ourselves. We had a lot of fun, but we had to work at it to not write on Saturday afternoon, or to not grade papers or whatever.

Crowley was on a year's leave when we spoke with her, and she confessed that she was back to writing and reading every day, though she insisted that she no longer works *all* day: "and if someone says, Let's go up in the mountains, I go." Indeed, it's worth noting that Crowley's description of her writing experience now offers a definite contrast to the high-intensity "writing pushes" she described above:

> I generally write in the morning; I'm trying to write in the morning. I'm on leave this year, and I'm doing small pieces now. Just to keep my hand in, I try to write every day. And then I read all afternoon for the luxury of it. It's just so wonderful. I even read at night. I'm finding that I can continue reading late into the night. Although lately, I don't have enough light. I'm getting old. It's very frustrating. I remember Kenneth Burke talking about this, how your physicality begins to fail you and how frustrating that is because you have this *desire* to read and you can't do it anymore.

Besides writing and reading late into the night, Crowley told us that she is now socializing with friends she has made all over the country through rhetoric and composition, and she's enjoying the many social, cultural, and sporting events that Phoenix offers: "I love the Phoenix urban area because there's more stuff than you can shake a stick at. Museums, galleries, professional sports teams, great Mexican food." She particularly loves to watch sports and to hike. "Anything outdoors is great," she told us. "When I lived in Flagstaff, I ran rivers. That's one of the reasons I moved back to Arizona, it's an outdoorsy state." Crowley also likes to go to shows and just to hang out with her friends and colleagues. The point is that after her promotion to full, she no longer felt she needed to work 24/7, and she has very much enjoyed the added texture in her life:

> I have backed off considerably, and you'll be able to do that later on in your career if you want to. You get to a point where you just say, This is no way to live. My blood pressure's through the ceiling, I'm drinking too much, or whatever it is you do, and I'm fragile. You, for example, will have published sufficiently in a couple of years that any promotion that's available you can have. At that point I think you'll look around and say—I hope you will—that I can back off just a little bit. You can have a garden or whatever your hobby is.

10

CHERYL GLENN

Cheryl Glenn is currently Chair of the Conference on College Composition and Communication (CCCC) and professor of English and Women's Studies at Pennsylvania State University, where she teaches courses in the history and theory of rhetoric and composition. Equally committed to pedagogical and to theoretical scholarship, Glenn has produced three major textbooks—*The Writer's Harbrace Handbook* (third edition, with Loretta Gray, 2005), *Making Sense: A Real-World Rhetorical Reader* (second edition, 2004), and *The St. Martin's Guide to Teaching Writing* (fifth edition, 2003); and three scholarly books—*Rhetoric Retold: Regendering the Tradition from Antiquity Through the Renaissance, Unspoken: A Rhetoric of Silence,* and *Rhetorical Education in America* (with Margaret Lyday and Wendy B. Sharer). She is also co-editor, with Shirley Wilson Logan, of Southern Illinois University Press's "Studies in Rhetorics and Feminisms," which has published several influential works in rhetoric and writing studies. Glenn earned all three of her degrees at Ohio State University, finishing up the PhD in 1989 and immediately beginning a tenure-track position at Oregon State University. She was awarded early tenure in her fifth year and won numerous awards for her teaching and scholarship before accepting the position at Penn State in 1997. In 2004, she put out three books, was promoted to full professor, and won the College of Liberal Arts Outstanding Teaching Award. That same year, she served as an Administrative Fellow with Penn State's Executive Vice President and Provost, and as a Fellow with the Committee on Institutional Cooperation Academic Leadership program.

Background

Glenn was born in Ohio but moved with her family to Wyoming and then to Laredo, Texas, when she was very young. She learned to talk in Laredo, a culturally diverse border town located on the banks of the Rio Grande and situated within walking distance to Nuevo Laredo, Mexico. However, when Glenn began almost exclusively to speak what she describes as "border Spanish," refusing her mother's anxious pleas to "speak English!" her family promptly moved her back to Ohio and signed her up for first grade a year early:

> While living in Laredo, I started speaking too much what my mom thought was "Mexican" but I would call "border Spanish." And she was horrified. I can remember her saying, "Sherry, speak English. Speak English!" But I would play all day in border Spanish; then we left Laredo, Texas. But before we left town, the woman whose husband ran the gas station filled a little tin lunch bucket with cookies for me. Have you ever seen one of those old-fashioned lunch buckets? Mine was a little green and white bucket with a little lid and flower decals on the front. She gave me the bucket of cookies, then we left town and drove to Ohio.
>
> I was five years old, and my mom put me in first grade and said to the teacher, "Sherry won't speak English. She has to start school." And the teacher said, "Well, she's too young." And my mother, young mother that she was, said, "You have to do something." So I started first grade at five years old. And the teacher was supposed to make me speak English. And it's funny: as soon as I got to first grade, I spoke English. No problem. I could do it all along; I just didn't want to. But I think that was a sensitivity lesson to me to find out that some people and their language weren't valued, and some people were.

So Glenn grew up in Ohio after all. Her parents never explicitly encouraged her to go to college, but they did assure her frequently that she was smart, as did her teachers, and by the time she reached high school, she was certain that she wanted a college education. She decided to become a teacher and to pursue a degree in English Education. And because she would be paying for it herself, she decided to go to Ohio State, which was very close to home and a "financial bargain." She found and won a scholarship to cover the cost of her undergraduate tuition, and she worked 20 hours a week to pay for everything else.

> Ohio State was the cheapest place for me to go, and as a 17 year old who wanted to go to college but needed to pay for it, it made sense to go there. I remember going down to some sort of scholarship office, sitting down, and reading through, page by page, a big three-ring notebook that was filled with descriptions of various scholarships and grants. I decided to major in English Education because my teachers had always been good to me and I needed to get a job as soon as possible. Fortunately, I found a specific scholarship for women—girls, we were called—in English education, and I got that scholarship every year, which paid all my tuition. But I had to pay everything else, so I always worked.

Throughout her undergraduate career, Glenn worked as a teacher's aide in elementary and middle schools, as a Home Economics teacher, and then at a local bookstore, each time scheduling her classes around her particular job responsibilities.

She got married when she was 20 years old, graduated the next year, and immediately started teaching at a central Ohio high school. At 24, she had her daughter Anna, and at 28, after some extremely difficult negotiations with her husband, who wasn't thrilled about the idea, Glenn went back to school for an MA in English. The decision was prompted—or, at the very least crystallized—she told us, by the devastating trauma of her younger brother's suicide:

> He was 19, so I was in my mid-twenties, I guess. I took care of him (and my toddler) after he was released from the rehab center. He'd been in an automobile accident and was paralyzed. When he died (he had decided to commit suicide), I thought about life and death, of course—a lot. I realized how very short life is, and I told myself that I had to figure out what I was going to do with my life because it's so short. And that's when I started taking my first graduate course, one night a week. I remember saying to my then-husband, "I have to take a class. I have to." And I found this class (it might have been "Traditional English Grammar"?), and I hoped they'd let me in to the master's program at Ohio State, which they did.
>
> My brother's dying really changed my life. And he also left me a little bit of money because I had taken care of him, which allowed me to consider doing things differently, so I'd drive to Columbus one night a week for my class.

So Glenn began her graduate school career at Ohio State, taking one course at a time, one night a week, and driving an hour each way to Columbia to do it—all while raising a toddler, teaching ESL and technical writing part time for Nestle International and Honda of America, and grieving for her brother. Literature and linguistics were the focus of her studies, but she took her first rhetoric course in the summer of 1981 and told us that she was instantly hooked. When she graduated with her MA, she got a position teaching courses in basic writing and ESL at Ohio State, where her colleagues encouraged her to continue on for a PhD Within the year, and much to her husband's chagrin, she applied and was accepted to OSU's doctoral program in English.

> Other teachers in those programs and some other faculty kept saying, "You know, you ought to go for a PhD." But I couldn't imagine getting a PhD—I think I'm of a generation that I couldn't imagine that I could do it for all sorts of reasons. Besides not feeling "smart enough," I didn't have the support of my husband. But the head of graduate studies kept saying, "I really think you ought to give it a go." So I applied, was accepted, and began my PhD at Ohio State. I was happy to be accepted, still married, with a fourth-grade daughter. I couldn't have attended anywhere else; I was geographically bound. So for those reasons, I did all three degrees in the same place. But, you know, I

> really lucked out by doing a PhD in English at Ohio State. It was a wonderful place to concentrate in rhetoric and composition. I didn't know that when I started, but I surely knew it when I graduated. My luck was dumb luck.

During the course of her PhD, Glenn took a career-defining class with Edward P.J. Corbett, "loved it," and then began to take as many rhetoric courses as she could. She went on the job market with only a half-finished dissertation because she was pouring most of her energy into writing *The St. Martin's Guide to Teaching Writing* with Bob Connors—an opportunity, she said, that was simply too good to pass up. The demands of graduate school in general took a toll on her already strained marriage, however, and two days before she left for her MLA job interviews in 1988, her husband asked her for a divorce. She described the timing as "both devastating and liberating. In some ways it was a gift because I thought, 'Well, I can go anywhere I want now.' I was no longer geographically bound by anything, and I had been wanting to head West, if I possibly could." So she did: she interviewed for and was offered the position at Oregon State. Glenn took the job, finished her dissertation, and then moved herself and Anna (by then in ninth grade) across the country to begin her life as an Assistant Professor of English in Corvallis, Oregon. She earned tenure early, a year ahead of the standard six-year schedule, and she remained at Oregon State for eight years.

Strategies for Success

Graduate School

Due to her financial and domestic situation, Glenn ended up earning all three degrees from Ohio State, and though she wouldn't advise students to do that now if they can possibly avoid it, she herself doesn't regret that decision. "I wouldn't have gone to a different school even if I could," she told us. "My Ohio State professors were very influential on my intellectual and emotional development. Mr. Corbett was really important to me, in some ways especially important because of his teaching style: he was so organized, regimented, and he always had very high expectations of us all. I love that kind of teaching." Still, she does recommend that students not take their graduate degree at the same institution they get their undergraduate degree. "I did everything wrong," she confided. "Because most people on hiring committees still hold it against candidates if they go to the same school for all three degrees." If a beginning graduate student has the ability to move, Glenn suggests that s/he should. On the other hand, Glenn also told us that it may not be a good idea to get your MA at one institution and your PhD at another:

> I did hear, though, that there are search committees—I heard this when I was visiting another university—who feel that if you switch between

> your master's and your PhD it means you didn't get into your PhD program at the school where you got your master's. I hadn't heard that inference before. I don't think our search committee read dossiers that way. It's always interesting to hear about how other schools, other committees read dossiers. I think if students could at least do their undergraduate one place and their graduate another place, that's what I'd advise them to do, but if you've done it the "wrong way" already, as I did, you just have to punt and stay in the game.

If she were given the chance to do graduate school over again, one thing Glenn told us she would do differently is be "kinder to everyone," including herself. She would develop a more "generous all-round outlook" and be more "generous in spirit," which is something she tries to cultivate in the graduate students she works with now. ("If we faculty members worked actively to cultivate mutually supportive graduate school friendships among our students, then we'd automatically be preparing a cohort of mutually supportive new untenured professors.") She couldn't have been more generous with her time back then because she literally didn't have any, but she wishes she had taken the time to demonstrate more often the kindly feelings she had for her grad student colleagues. "If I could do it all over again," she told us, "I would have been less anxious, kinder, and more relaxed emotionally with everyone in my life."

> This feeling comes to me, I think, because I continue to hear too many stressed-out graduate students discuss their own anxieties about productivity, accomplishment, rankings, and work (their own as well as that of their friends). I want to say (and often do): "Try not to worry so much. It'll all work out. There's enough work for all of you so make steadfast friends now because you'll need them the rest of your career. *These* are your best friends ever."
>
> I don't think a graduate school environment naturally cultivates or supports a feeling of generosity and kindliness among graduate students themselves, and it should. After all, graduate school friendships are often some of the most important ones we forge in life; sometimes, those are the friendships, forged when we were all young, nervous, striving, that sustain us throughout our entire professional careers and personal lives. I know those friendships continue to sustain me.

The high anxiety that ran some interference with Glenn's collegial spirit all those years ago was due in large part to the fact that she felt she had so much at stake. The exacting demands of graduate school will put a strain on most any marriage, but Glenn was also holding a part-time job, a graduate teaching assistantship, and raising a young daughter, so she was hyper-aware of the magnitude of her decision to return to school: "I over-determined every syllable I said in class and I wrote in my seminar papers. At the time, I felt that I had everything on the line. I suppose I thought I had more on the line than anybody else. I felt like I had my whole family on the line, like they were making a huge sacrifice for me to do this."

> There were many times in graduate school where I felt like I was hanging on by my thumbs, maybe even my thumbnails. I couldn't meet my friends for drinks very often or even for lunch; I couldn't have long conversations on the phone—I mean, I drove two hours, at least two hours, every day, I had a little girl, I had a husband who lived abroad quite a bit. I couldn't socialize much, and I felt like I really strained those friendships, but I made it through graduate school with those friendships intact. I thought I was a pretty good mother, but I think I was only pretty good. But my daughter and I made it through those tough years, too. I'm really grateful that my daughter and I are very close.

Nonetheless, Glenn now recognizes that her peers and their loved ones were also making their own sorts of sacrifices for graduate school. "Nobody goes to graduate school without sacrificing," she told us. "Everybody pays."

Glenn's marriage ended with her PhD work, and she spent a lot of time in her first years as an assistant professor reflecting on what her graduate degree had cost her. Soon after she got to Oregon, she found a therapist and confided her unshakable concern that her divorce may have been the direct result of her decision to go to graduate school: "maybe I ruined my marriage by getting a PhD." It's not news that many relationships do not survive the strains and growing pains of graduate school, but Glenn's therapist suggested that it doesn't quite cut it simply to *blame* graduate school for a breakup. Instead she asked Glenn to embrace and affirm the fact that there is something about her that's unstoppable, that her level of personal motivation is so powerful that no one—not even a frustrated husband—would be capable of shutting it down.

Glenn told us that she can't account for this personal motivation in any direct way. It's not simply autobiographical, she told us, and "it doesn't seem to be contagious or hereditary. Maybe it can be instilled—I don't know. But I do know that no one has a recipe for *giving* motivation to someone else. I don't think you can automatically give it to your kids." She remembers that it meant a lot to her when the head of graduate studies at Ohio State told her that she should consider applying to the doctoral program, that she could do it, and she feels certain that that level of encouragement made a difference; however, she had wanted to go back to school *before* he encouraged her to consider it.

> I think of people like my good friend Jan Swearingen, whose parents seem like intellectuals to me. They both went to graduate school at Yale (in the 1940s); Jan's the eldest child (of five), so it was expected that *she* would go to college, and of course she would go to graduate school. That kind of upbringing surely accounts for some of her drive

> and direction. Yet, she has four siblings, and although they're all educated, she's the only one who's an academic. My parents, on the other hand, didn't have that same motivation to go to college (I'm not sure they felt any possibility for that). But they did say that I was smart. My teachers encouraged me to think of college, and I did, always, it seems. I mean, even though there wasn't family money put aside for college, I've always been resourceful, and I was able to put myself through college.

Glenn suspects that some of her personal motivation is due to generational and socio-cultural factors. Though she had not participated publicly in the women's movement at all in the 1970s, she was intuitively conscious of salary discrepancies in the public schools and made sure, for example, that she earned the same salary as the male teachers hired the same year she was. But when she started actually reading feminist works, she became conscious of her "female self as a part of an overall pattern," which helped her understand her own struggles with self-esteem and confidence in terms of a larger context. "Feminism for me answered a lot of questions—and offered solutions. It was liberating in so many ways. … It helped me to feel part of a general malaise rather than just experiencing my own shortcomings. So feminism in the early 80s—I kind of missed the earlier part—helped me to focus on my goals and forge ahead." Indeed, Glenn told us that besides her grad school friends, she had some wonderful women friends in Marysville, Ohio, where she lived; these were older women who wanted Glenn to go on because most of them hadn't been able to. "Most of these women were from the *Feminine Mystique*, Betty Friedan sort of generation. And they wanted me to go to graduate school—and 'make it,' however they defined the phrase."

> I had a couple of women friends who were professionals there in Marysville, but whether they were wives of professionals, public school teachers, physicians, psychiatrists, or attorneys, they all seemed to support my decision to go for a PhD. One woman had run the Anna Freud Clinic in Vienna, before escaping in 1938. Another was a physician who had left her practice after twenty-five years to take care of her daughter who had cerebral palsy. Another good friend had been my high school student (when I was 21 and she was 18) and became my attorney. Most of them, though, were women I'd met when I was teaching high school English: they were well-educated, -traveled, -read public school teachers, the kind of influential teachers so many of us benefited from. They were supportive women friends—even when they wanted me to be able to socialize and couldn't understand why, exactly, I had to say no. Mostly, they respected my "no." I had no spare time whatsoever.

But Glenn's motivation runs deeper still. When her brother Skott died (a loss from which she thought she'd never recover), she tapped into the transformative power of her grief and used it to *do* something; as we noted above, it was epiphanic and became a kind of exigence. "My brother's death motivated me in terms of crystallizing some concrete educational and professional goals. … Life is really short. So you better do what you're going to do, because you never know when it's going to be over. Make the best of it." She had always had the drive and the personal motivation, but when her brother died, it was a defining moment in her life. "And then I told myself, 'If you're serious about getting a master's, you'd better get started.' It seems so silly to say this on tape, but I can't think that there aren't other young women who are thinking, 'Dare I try to make a space for myself? Will I make it?'"

Besides her personal motivation and hard work, Glenn told us that part of her success in graduate school was due to her ability to compartmentalize, to concentrate, and—perhaps especially—to say "no."

> I worked really hard. I have a very good ability to compartmentalize. I have a very good ability to say "no" to social things, to say, "Sorry, can't." And to withstand the peer pressure to do X, Y, or Z. … I think it's hard for women to know that they can—generally for women to know—they can say, "I'm sorry I can't do that." And just say no. And I can do it, even though I'm an over-committer and over-worker. Like tonight, when you are here, I'm not answering the phone. I'll check the caller ID to see who it is. If it's Jon [Olson], whom we want to come home to make us margaritas, I'll answer. Otherwise I'll call people tomorrow. I'm very, very good at that, compartmentalizing. I think that's a strategy that I have.

Glenn developed this set of strategies very early, and she considers them crucial to her success both in graduate school and throughout her professional career.

Her ability to compartmentalize, concentrate, and say "no," however, didn't keep her from taking on a lot of extra projects while she was trying to finish her dissertation, which was only half-finished when she went on the market. And though she managed to land several good interviews, campus visits, and job offers anyway, she wouldn't advise graduate students today to follow her lead on this one; she'd advise them instead to focus their undivided energy on their dissertations. "Taking on extra projects has always been my fault," she told us, "even with my ability to say 'no.' I'm part of OCOWA: Over-Committer, Over-Workers Anonymous. Not a very exclusive club, especially for people in our field."

Time Management

Glenn told us that life as a junior faculty member at Oregon State was "mostly a lot of work, especially in terms of teaching." She taught six new courses her first year and five new courses her second year—all of her courses were writing intensive, including the British lit survey she taught every quarter, which enrolled about 50 students. At that time, Glenn was also recovering from her divorce and dealing with the fallout that one would expect to accompany any decision to move a ninth-grade daughter two thousand miles from home. Anna "was doing what she should have been doing: acting out," Glenn told us, which prompted a number of trips to the principal's office and ad hoc parent–teacher conferences. So how did she manage her time?

> I got up about four every day and reviewed my day's work and other obligations, and I would be at the gym at 7:30 for my 7:30 to 8:30 circuit-training class. Then I would come home, get Anna ready for school—or maybe I'd get her ready before I left for the gym—get her ready for school, and then go teach class at ten o'clock.

She'd teach again at 1:00 pm, have office hours, and then get back to evaluating a seemingly endless stream of student papers. "I had so many writing assignments—I wanted to be the very best of teachers, to implement everything I'd learned about teaching. But it was all too much—too much writing, too much responding to student papers. Students lined up in the hallway to see me during office hours, so we could talk about their writing (whether it was for my course or for another course)." She was often in the office until 6:30 or 7:00 pm; then she'd go home, cook dinner for Anna and herself, and work until about 10:30 pm. The next morning at 4am, she'd start all over again.

As an assistant professor, Glenn told us that she was so busy planning courses, teaching, and grading, so busy learning the job itself, that she didn't (really couldn't) write on a daily basis—though she knew that writing was also part of the job. Instead, she wrote mainly during the Christmas and Thanksgiving breaks, which meant that she basically had no breaks to speak of. "So I'd have to say 'no' to things: 'No, I can't come home for Christmas'; 'No, I can't do this; no, I can't do that.'"

> Summers were hard. I moved to Oregon a few days after I received my PhD in June, so that first summer was a moving and settling in summer. Then school started, and I was buried in planning and teaching. So by the end of the first year, I hadn't yet published anything more than what I came in with. I was getting really nervous, afraid I wouldn't publish. I remember after my first year, the chair took me for a walk and said, "You know, you've got to publish something, even if you just get into conference proceedings."
>
> So I began to concentrate on a piece on Margery Kempe. Andrea [Lunsford] had marked one particular section of my then-finished dissertation as being interesting, the part on Margery Kempe's various uses of ethos. It took a while for me to get my foothold on that piece,

> but I did. My first publication as an assistant professor, then, was a piece on Kempe that appeared not in conference proceedings but in *College English*. [Laughter]

During those first few years, Glenn taught a wide variety of writing and literature courses, and she scheduled them during the hours that Anna was at school so she could be home with her in the evenings. After Anna got older and Glenn got tenure, however, things changed: "Now, things are different. I teach only rhetoric courses, so the preps are different and somewhat easier. Plus, I usually teach bistro hours, so I don't teach before 3:30. Rarely do I teach before 3:30, so I can write every day till noon." She rarely works in the evening anymore, and she likes to write at home in the mornings. On days when she doesn't teach, she writes from about 6:30 or 7:00 am until about 3:30 pm, when she takes a shower, gets ready for the day, cooks, and enjoys the evening. "Nothing makes you feel better," she told us, "than to get back to your document about 7 o'clock in the morning, write all day, get off at 3:30, take a shower. You think, 'I have had a good day.'"

> I guess the more established you are in your career, the better your professional life can be, which is really not the way it should be. It's like when you're older and your kids no longer live with you, *then* you finally have money. It's the same thing. The more established you are in your career, the more you can control things that would have made your early career easier. But learning to endure is an important life lesson for us all, just as learning to work hard is. New assistant professors get those opportunities in spades! Those are important life skills.

Tenure and Promotion Strategies

We had heard through the grapevine—an exquisite rumor—that Andrea A. Lunsford had long ago given Glenn the "keys to the queendom," so to speak, and we secretly hoped that she'd pass them along to us in our interview. Unfortunately, however, when we broke our silence and flat out asked her about them, she told us there weren't any: "Oh, what a delicious concept. How I wish it were true. It's a fabulous urban legend, but like such legends, only that." When it comes to securing tenure and promotion in this field, there are no simple answers, no easily replicable keys to pass on to you here; however, Glenn was happy to share with us some of her own strategies for navigating the T&P course. She told us, for example, that developing an optimistic outlook has been crucial to her professional success; the more optimistic she is, the harder she can work and the longer she can concentrate. Embracing this "positive psychology" has allowed her to focus on her own work without feeling threatened by her colleagues' accomplishments. "I believe in abundance, especially professional abundance," Glenn told us. "I think there's plenty of work for us all to do. We don't need to be jealous of anybody else's work, accomplishments, or recognition. There's plenty to do, and there's a never-ending stream of research, teaching, and speaking to keep us all busy in the years to come." It's important, especially if you're in a difficult or troubled department, to be able to assume enough of a distance from departmental politicking to focus on your own work.

> I always think of it in terms of swimming laps: Stay in your own swim lane. I'll swim in my lane; you swim in your lane; she'll swim in her lane. We'll all go down to the other end of the pool; we'll do our flip turns and go as fast as we can. But we're not competing against each other. We're just trying to get our laps done. If you can't do your laps in your own swim lane, don't swim. And quit looking over into another swim lane; that'll just slow you down, maybe even get you hurt.

This may be the most important, and the most difficult, lesson an assistant professor will ever learn. And the key, again, is to develop enough confidence and optimism to not *care* how fast someone else is swimming or what swim lane they're in. "I tell myself to get those goggles on, dive in, get down there, and flip turn," Glenn told us. "That's all we can concentrate on, really, our own work. If we're busy watching someone else's swim lane, then we better get out of the pool and into the stands."

Glenn told us that she learned how to be demonstrably kinder when she learned both to stop watching what's going on in everyone else's lanes and to distinguish between "being kind and being the kind of person that people could walk all over (they are not the same)."

> I learned from Jackie Royster that you can speak up and say your piece. You're not mad; you're just saying your piece. Jackie told me once about giving a half-day workshop, and some man kept acting out. Finally she said to him, "If you're not required by someone to attend this session, feel free to leave. I will not be bothered at all if you choose not to subject yourself to this workshop. I'll be gone by noon. Maybe you would prefer to come back after I'm gone." I said, "Jackie, how did you know to say that? I don't know that I would have." She replied, "I have too much respect for myself to put up with that." "Jackie, I do too." And that's one thing I've really tried to work on, to remember to have respect for myself at the same time that I want to learn from and respect others.

As an assistant professor, Glenn learned a lot by watching other people she respected and by asking them "point blank how they deal with this and that." She told us that she has spent a lot of time "studying other people" and kind of "trying on" their coping strategies: "If they've got a way that works, I often think, 'Hmm, I could wear that, I could slip into that behavior.'" Glenn noted that "there are a lot of really good women in our field that we can all learn from," and she encourages everyone, assistant professors in particular, to do just that. Even today, as a full professor, Glenn continues to learn all she can from others in the field. And when others whom she respects give her advice, she just takes it. "I say to myself, 'OK, I can do that.' We waste a lot of time trying to decide what to do, and if somebody we respect simply sets an example of what we can do, like Jackie, or Cindy [Selfe], or Andrea [Lunsford], then you think, 'You know, I don't have to worry about that anymore. I can do *that.* OK, that's taken care of. Next?'"

Another key to Glenn's success is a keen "political sense" (she actually called it a "survival instinct"): she understands how to approach people, how to ask for things, and basically how to make things happen without upsetting too many people. Friends have told her that she has "very good political sense," and though she's not sure she recognizes it in herself, she does notice when she's around colleagues who *don't* have it.

> I think, "Whoa, what are you doing?" I don't think I am particularly gifted at it, but Roxanne [Mountford] told me I was once, and I thought, "Hmmm, that's interesting." Lisa Ede has also said I have a very good political sense. It's never backfired, which is not the same as saying that I've always been successful in getting what I want. I have not. I have taken calculated risks and lost; I've asked for things and been denied; I've been disappointed. But I've also had a good many rich and satisfying academic experiences as well. So, I would not call it a political sense; I would call it a survival instinct, and given my background, maybe I've always needed one.

It's worth noting that it was very likely this same survival instinct that kept Glenn, in the early years, from opening up about her own emotional struggles to the junior women who came in after her. Some of these women, who are now her good friends, confided to her later that at first they weren't sure if they could like her because she seemed so calm and collected, as if she had everything under control, while they themselves were having a very difficult time adjusting and settling into academic life. They had no idea that Glenn, too, was struggling. "Little did they know that I was going through therapy and crying on the days I wasn't at school! This might be the biggest reason we should be a mutually supportive cohort—the untenured life can be particularly hard." Glenn told us that if she had those early years to do over again, she might have opened up more: "I might have forced myself on some of these women who came in after me, and maybe trusted in myself—and them—enough to tell them that my life was not perfect. We might have been an even better group to one another."

Still, Glenn recognizes that making oneself vulnerable enough for this sort of sharing is not always easy, and, at the time, it may have been impossible for her: "Given that I was seeing a therapist for the first time in my life, telling her seemed to be all I could manage. I didn't feel I could tell anyone, especially in a small department. I didn't want to become a topic of conversation, let alone pity. I imagine I worried if colleagues knew I was seeing a therapist, it might affect my tenure. It might have, too." Indeed, Glenn ultimately concluded that "seeing a therapist and being quiet about it was probably the right thing to do." In any case, and either way, Glenn's most adamant advice to all junior faculty is to *go to therapy*:

> I imagine lots of new faculty feel the same way: worried, nervous, not knowing whom to trust. They should all go see a therapist! Now that's the gift that keeps on giving. Whether you tell your colleagues or not, you've got to see a therapist your first year. … Therapy is the best thing ever invented.

And along with therapy, Glenn recommends another coping strategy: keeping a journal. "If you think you're going to be driven crazy or stressed by something," she told us, one of the best things you can do is think of the whole situation as research material: "keep track of it and think about how you can give a talk on it or publish it. But don't talk about it, let alone publish it if you're angry," she warns. By the time you get ready to publish your thoughts, you should be calm and in genuine problem-solving mode.

Mentoring

Glenn told us that she had several significant mentors when she was in graduate school and that she "loved them all."

> I had my medieval professor, Stanley Kahrl, who's passed on. He was great for several reasons, one of which was that he told me never to write on Margery Kempe, who, of course, I wrote on the most. He told me that she was "crazy." … I also feel indebted to Rolf Soellner, who was my Renaissance professor and is now gone. He, too, was generous and supportive of me. And, of course, Ed Corbett, whom I didn't like so much in graduate school as I admired him. I took every class he offered. I loved him after I graduated and felt very close to him. … Murray Beja was our department chair, and he remains the very best chair I've ever seen in action. I have often called Murray over the years for professional and political advice, and his advice is first-rate. And of course Andrea [Lunsford], too. Notice that she's the only woman on my list—but then there weren't many established female professors back then. Although I didn't officially take any courses from her, I was her research assistant and learned a great deal from her. I learned more about how to be in this profession from her in the two years I worked as her research assistant than from anyone else in all my years in the profession so far. She is a wonderful model for us all—still.

Thanks in part, perhaps, to the fine mentoring she got in graduate school, Glenn is now herself a committed mentor of graduate students and junior faculty both inside and outside her home institution. She is frequently asked for advice on everything from publishing journal articles, writing textbooks, and applying for grants to addressing disciplinary problems, dealing with rejection, interviewing for jobs, and "handling a fellow graduate student who's really acting like a butthead"—and she tries to respond attentively and responsively. When we asked what she would tell an assistant professor who confided that she felt discriminated against or persecuted for her work, Glenn told us she'd first of all try to help her find ways to defend herself.

> I'd listen, and I'd try to repeat what she was telling me to make sure I understood. I would try to help her think of a strategy to take care of herself. I would also work behind the scenes. At a meeting, I might bring up the different kinds of work going on in the field and talk about how exciting it is and how I want to read more about that. I would do that kind of subtle work, to open up the possibilities for receiving this person's work.

Glenn also said if she were to see "the perp in the hallway," she'd be sly but honest, invitational rather than confrontational. She said she's not sure whether her preferred approach is motivated by political savvy or survival instinct and the desire to see everyone get along, but she believes the worst thing to do is make the perp feel defensive, "or as though I know what he's done wrong." So she'd intervene, but not directly; she'd say something like "You know, I don't understand some of the theoretical moves so-and-so is making, but it seems like really exciting work. And, you know, she's been invited to do X, Y, and Z. Did you know that?"

When we asked Glenn if there were anything, any piece of advice she didn't get in graduate school or as a junior faculty member but wishes she had, Glenn told us she wishes one of her mentors would have told her: "You're smart." But she immediately retracted this statement, admitting that her mentors did in fact tell her frequently that she was smart; the problem was that she couldn't hear it. "So I wish they had said it and knocked me upside the head." She wishes someone had given her Carolyn Heilbrun's essay about exceptional women, "about the icky, male-identified women who think they're special, and about how women don't have to be mean to other women because they themselves are plenty smart." She also wishes someone would have given her Adrianne Rich's *On Lies, Secrets, and Silences* and told her to read it every day. Glenn now teaches that book nearly every year to graduates and undergraduates alike. "They all love it," she told us, and it's important to get it out there because "despite all the inroads feminism has made, we remain a male-identified, male-dominated society," which makes success all the more difficult for women.

> Some women do, indeed, make their way—and that's wonderful. But I've found that men, in general, still exercise a greater feeling of entitlement than any woman I've ever known, whether those women are going up for full professor or coming in as an assistant professor. ... And I think that the best thing that a bunch of women could do would be to be kinder to each other and more helpful to each other, and we would really be a frightening group. Because a lot of men are helping each other out, and yet we're still not helping one another enough, not enough.

Having a Life

Glenn married Jon Olson about two years after her first marriage officially ended, and it was a grounding move, particularly for Anna, who was a little older by then and no longer acting out: "The day Jon and I got married, Anna seemed to be very happy. And I never had to go to the principal's office again." Dual academic relationships tend to be a challenge, but Glenn and Olson make it work by carving out at least a little bit of relaxation time together every day. They both work a lot and enjoy working, but no matter what else is going on, they make time to have a glass of wine together nearly every night; they put work aside, tell each other about their day, and wind down together. "Even if we have barely anything for supper," Glenn told us, "we have a glass of wine together. And it might only be half an hour. But it's enough."

Glenn's exceptional ability to compartmentalize work and play gives her somewhat of an advantage over many academics in the "having a life" department: when she's working, she's working very hard, but when she's not working, she's *really* not working. She can let go of it and enjoy herself. Aside from nightly wine-breaks with Jon and daily phone chats with Anna, with whom she remains very close, Glenn told us that when she's at home and in town she's mostly working. At this point in her career, however, she travels almost twice a month to lecture at other schools, and when she does, she leaves her work at home. "When I go to another school, I have fun," she said. "I don't take my laptop; my talk or workshop is already written when I get on the plane." She flies in, gives her talk or workshop, and then takes the opportunity to relax and enjoy some time with the faculty and students who invited her to come in. Glenn and Olson also try to plan a couple of vacations together every year, which are really vacations rather than the "writing retreats," "research trips," or other sorts of "working-vacations" to which so many academics constrain themselves:

> Jon and I compartmentalize trips out west, and we have a wonderful time there. We have a lot of connections out on the pueblos, and my cousin is a Laguna Indian—he's 80—and we see him every time we go, several times a year. So that's really fun to be away from email, telephones. We get a house-sitter. We travel around, rent a car, stay in

> some cheap place, eat lots of green chile, and we package up our fun like that.

Glenn and Olson also like to cook with friends, often with their next-door neighbors: "They do a lot more cooking than I do," Glenn told us, "but we're very good eaters." Glenn says she enjoys reading the newspaper every morning, as well, and catching about five or ten minutes of *The Today Show*:

> My mom and I often talk about what Katie Couric's wearing. I sometimes think, "Well, that's an inspiration for what I could wear to school today." But my daughter's adamant that Katie should not be my fashion facilitator. "Oh god, Mom, she's so old."

Glenn also loves to read novels, especially mystery novels. In fact, she told us that she's never not reading a mystery novel and that she never falls asleep at night without reading part of whatever novel she's currently into. Glenn is what you might call a serious pleasure reader: "I even buy hardbacks," she told us. "Hardback pleasure reading!" Once again, this is a compartmentalized experience for Glenn—pleasure reading is *pleasure* reading and not a covert way of allowing work to spill over into non-work time. Interestingly, however, she did suggest that the joy she takes from reading her novels does manage to spill over into her work-life, pleasurizing her writing experience:

> You probably fall asleep reading Levinas. [Laughter] I fall asleep reading David Morrell. … I read those [novels] all the time. I don't think enough of my colleagues read that kind of stuff. Doesn't writing drain it out of you? I feel like the more words I put on the page during the day the more I need to fill it up with pleasure reading. Pleasure reading enhances my writing pleasure.

11

SUSAN C. JARRATT

Susan C. Jarratt is Professor of Comparative Literature and Campus Writing Coordinator at the University of California at Irvine, where she teaches courses in the histories and theories of rhetoric, feminist theory, and composition pedagogy. Jarratt is perhaps best known for her first book, *Rereading the Sophists: Classical Rhetoric Refigured*, and for her edited collection *Feminism and Composition Studies: In Other Words* (with Lynn Worsham). Jarratt earned her BA in English with a teaching certificate at the University of Texas in Austin 1971 and taught high school in San Antonio for six years. She earned her MA in English at the University of Texas at San Antonio in 1978 and then her PhD in English with a concentration in Rhetoric at UT Austin 1985. She took her first tenure-track job right out of graduate school at Miami University, where she earned tenure (1990) and promotion to full (1997), and served as the Director both of women's studies and of composition. In 1994, she left Miami to accept the Lillian Radford Chair of Rhetoric and Composition at Texas Christian University, returned to Miami the next year, and then in 2001 she joined the faculty at UCI.

Background

Jarratt was born in Topeka, Kansas, in 1948 but moved with her parents and two brothers (one older, one younger) to Austin, Texas, when she was five years old. Jarratt's parents both grew up in "impoverished rural environments," she told us, but they were not from farming families, "so they have rural backgrounds but not really very positive rural identities." Jarratt's mother was the eighth child in her family; her father, a schoolteacher with a certificate (1895) from Central Normal College in Great Bend, Kansas, died in the 1919 flu epidemic a few months before her mother's birth. She was told stories (passed down from her siblings and mother) of his ability to use Latin and play the violin. Jarratt's maternal grandmother "moved their family east because one of the eight children, one of the two boys, was able to go to college. He went to Kansas State in Manhattan, Kansas, and they brought the whole family there to support him." Despite her mother's good experiences in high school, she had to leave home and get a job after graduation because of Depression-era strains on the family finances. Jarratt's father grew up in Comanche County in northwest Texas, "about an hour and a half west of the Dallas/Fort Worth Metroplex. There were six kids in that family," and Jarratt's father had to drop out of high school "during the Depression to help support the family. But he did get a high school degree, was a talented athlete, and earned a football scholarship from SMU. But he wasn't very big and got injured early on; those were the days when if you were injured, the scholarship was withdrawn. Though he never got a degree, he did get a college experience."

Jarratt's mother and father married in 1939, and when World War II broke out in 1941 Jarratt's father joined the navy. The war was a strain on them, but Jarratt noted that it also gave them the opportunity to travel and begin to see themselves as part of larger national and global contexts. She gained perspective on these years through a set of audio-taped memories her mother made in the early 1990s (her father passed away in 1983). When her father got out of the service, they moved to Austin and he took a job with the federal government in what we now call human resources. This was a white-collar, middle-management position and a definite step upward in terms of social class. "Our lives were very shaped by post-war class mobility," Jarratt recalls. "We lived in houses financed by the FHA, and my brothers and I went to excellent public schools." But there were often tensions about money and resentment arising from comparisons with families who were more established in the middle class: "people with college degrees, new cars, and more comfortable family finances." Her family narratives suggest the unevenness of class experiences over the course of a century; these aren't clear patterns of rise or fall.

Though Jarratt's parents struggled financially, it was always understood that she and her brothers would go to college.

> That was completely in the script—part of their understanding of where their kids were going to fit in the social, educational picture. My parents' plan was to locate in Austin because of the University of Texas, a virtually free public university, and we would live at home and go to this university. That would be the way we could afford it.

This plan worked out very well for both of her brothers, Jarratt told us, but not so well for her: "For me it was a little bumpier. I needed out of the house, and I couldn't figure out appropriate ways to leave." She did apply to other schools, some of which not only accepted her but offered her scholarships to attend, but it wasn't in the picture. "My father, for example, could not understand why I would want even to apply to any other school because it cost ten or fifteen dollars for an application." Her mother tried to find other resources to help her accept one of the more attractive scholarships, but in the end, it didn't work out.

Jarratt spent her first year of college as an English major at UT. When her boyfriend, and later husband, was sent to Vietnam in the summer of 1967, she left Austin for the jazz program at Sam Houston State University in Huntsville. After a semester there, she dropped out and headed to San Francisco's Haight-Ashbury. It was the 60s—an exciting, painful, and confusing time. There seemed to be infinite possibilities—many possible life paths. She married in 1968, spent a year as a piano major at Kansas State (where her uncle had studied several decades earlier), and then returned to Austin with her husband to re-enroll at UT for her junior year. She applied to the music department and intended to double major in music and English. She was admitted to the piano program, but when she explained her double major plan to her music professors, "they just laughed, literally. They said, 'We don't have double majors. Essentially, you're ours.'" She needed to make a decision, and with the encouragement of her father, who thought teaching would be a more secure profession than music, she decided to major in English. She graduated with a BA in English and a secondary teaching certificate in 1971.

Her decision to major in English was also influenced, indirectly, by her previous English teachers, one high school teacher in particular:

> His name was John Shelton and he was a very interesting figure who embodied a kind of intellectualism I hadn't encountered anywhere else. He really nourished me and encouraged me and praised me. One time he took a little thing that I wrote and used it as an example for the class, and that stuck in my head. It was a paragraph on John Ruskin's iron words. It's funny isn't it, I can still visualize that paragraph in my high school handwriting. And I have a memory of that when I took freshman composition, too, of a teacher using a composition that I wrote—this one was about Kafka's "Hunger Artist"—as an example for the rest of the class. So I got messages from my teachers that I was good at this. I saved handouts and writing from my high school and undergraduate English classes so that I could use them when I became a teacher. I still have some of them.

Jarratt confided that her decision to become a teacher and to study language and rhetoric may also have been a way to *not* become her mother. Her father frequently wrote letters of protest on a little portable typewriter (which she still has) and engaged her and her brothers in intense discussions about public affairs and politics around the dining-room table, discussions in which her mother wouldn't or couldn't join: "We would have these intellectual discussions, and my mother was constantly trying to break in with offers of more food. This is definitely an arena where she didn't belong or participate, and which she resented. I became identified with my father and with masculinity as the site of intellectual activity and rhetorical performance."

> My mother stayed at home and was the good mother. She made a couple of efforts to work outside the home and to go to college, but it

> was a struggle: fighting with my father just to get out of the house. He begrudged her every inch.

And yet, Jarratt told us that her mother did manage to find productive ways to negotiate the domestic conflict: "She wouldn't stay *inside* the house; obviously, she was a very good housekeeper, but the yard and garden became her sphere." She took correspondence courses in horticulture from Texas A & M and studied plants, ultimately specializing in roses. She became an officer in the American Rose Society, a certified rosarian and judge of roses. "They have contests where people bring roses to be judged," and these contests gave Jarratt's mother the chance to travel "and develop a network of friends outside the family and neighborhood." Her rosarian credentials also opened another door for her, which is for our purposes significant:

> She wrote for a newsletter of the Austin Rose Society, and she would select poems to reprint. Her tastes ran to the Edgar Guest and Hallmark card style. Nonetheless, it was beauty in language she was attracted to. Beauty in the outdoor world and beauty in language, and I think I really benefited from both those inheritances. And then at a certain stage she wrote a column called Girty Gopher's Gardening Guesses. [Laughter] I have these documents she passed along to me: an archive of her advice column about gardening.

So it's not exactly the case that deciding to become an English teacher was a way for Jarratt to construct herself *against* her mother, who turns out to be something of an archivist, a writer, and a lover of language.

Immediately after completing her undergraduate degree, Jarratt applied to UT's graduate program in English, but what she called her "checkered undergraduate career" installed a temporary roadblock. She didn't get a teaching job in Austin that year, either: "I was a pretty alternative person at that point—short skirts and left politics. I'm not sure that that made a good impression in my student teaching. Or maybe I just wasn't the strongest candidate." So Jarratt got a job as a secretary for a bank, used the academic hiatus as a time to have a baby—her daughter Jessica born in 1972—and by the next year was divorced.

Freed from the need to stay in Austin, Jarratt applied for other high school teaching jobs and got offers in Houston and San Antonio "in very beleaguered, inner-city districts." She took a job teaching English and directing the choir at Thomas Edison in San Antonio and taught there for six years. She told us she loved high school teaching, that she had a vocation for it, but that "it was terribly hard." The harsh reality was that students were socially promoted through the eighth grade and then were suddenly expected to earn credits when they hit the ninth grade. It was therefore no surprise that over 50 percent of Thomas Edison's ninth graders were failing—on average, they were reading at the sixth grade level, Jarratt told us, though some "were on about a fourth grade level."

Because 65 percent of the students were Mexican Americans, there were second language issues, as well. "It was *such* a shock," Jarratt recalled. But it was precisely because the situation was so challenging that she had the opportunity to develop a considered pedagogical approach early on:

> I realized there that I couldn't teach literature or writing; I had to teach students. The subject matter only became relevant in the context of who they were. I guess it's a recognition of what pedagogy is, as opposed to "I am an English major and here's this body of stuff." I think it was really valuable to me on many levels. We had the Warner's little blue grammar text. I don't know if you've seen those. Ninth grade was a year of reviewing and consolidating traditional grammar, and so it was an opportunity for me to go back and re-learn it. Very much in the current-traditional model. I remember so vividly starting out with, "OK, we're going to review grammar, so let's start out with parts of speech. You've studied the parts of speech, right?" "No, Miss, we never studied the parts of speech." I'd say, "Yeah, sure, you remember, what about a noun?" "No, we never studied nouns." [Laughter]

The first summer after she started teaching high school Jarratt moved in with her parents in Austin and started taking graduate classes at UT; at that point, her daughter was three. She signed up for Chuck Rossman's British Modernism course, but her "dual identities were still in play," she told us, because the other course she wanted to take was in the history of jazz. Rossman, who was also her advisor, patiently explained that graduate study is more specialized and that she probably needed to take another English course. For the first two years, she taught high school during the fall and spring and then took two courses in the summer. At that time, they were just launching UT San Antonio, and they offered seminars in the evening in order to appeal to schoolteachers wanting an advanced degree. So Jarratt switched to UTSA, where she could take courses all year round. There was a downside to the full-time job plus graduate school: "Who was raising my kid at that point? My parents helped out tremendously with the childcare during my whole graduate school experience, but parenting was a source of guilt for me."

During the course of her MA work, Jarratt considered switching from English to Education and going for a middle-management supervisor certificate. "I thought I wanted to be a curriculum consultant, to teach other teachers. I really enjoyed constructing curriculum." But she told us that taking a few education classes one summer "completely got me over that notion." Some of the courses were "unspeakably bad." Jarratt stayed in English and soon had a composition conversion experience: she met Eileen Lundy, who was the composition faculty member at UTSA at that time and who was instrumental in hiring Jarratt. Lundy made a strong impression on her and helped her imagine what a professional field of composition and rhetoric would look like. When Jarratt finished the MA at UTSA in 1978, she was still teaching high school, but she soon landed a full-time position at UTSA teaching four composition courses per semester. "We were contingent faculty, but full-time," she told us. And this position was "a real breakthrough. High school *so* wears you down. It's so hard." When Jarratt "broke out" of high school teaching and got into college teaching, she took a pay cut, but didn't care: "It was so exciting."

Charles Kneupper taught at UTSA at the time—he and Jarratt became bridge partners—but she never took a rhetoric course from him: "he was a wild man in bridge. It was so fun. But I never took a rhetoric course from him, which is odd. What a missed opportunity." She loved the teaching experience at UTSA, but it wasn't easy and the pay was abysmal. She taught four courses a semester, and there were seven required papers in each course. "We added up the number of pages and divided them into our salary and came up with twenty-five cents a page. But I loved it." She was also in a rock 'n' roll band during that time, and in 1980 she started the PhD program at UT Austin (UTSA didn't have a PhD program). While Jarratt took courses in Austin the afternoon and evening, her daughter would be 75 miles away in San Antonio with a babysitter. "One night I came home and she had been sick—this was before cell phones. That scared me." The crazy schedule finally became too much to handle, and Jarratt was forced to make some difficult decisions: "I was a single parent trying to teach all those courses, work on a PhD, and play in a band. And I couldn't handle it. It was too much. My daughter was protesting. And I could see that it was just too crazy."

Jarratt initially thought that the best decision might be to drop out of the PhD program. However, Lundy took her out to lunch and persuaded her to rethink that choice, "a choice, again, between music and the academy." Thanks mostly to Lundy's efforts, Jarratt decided to devote herself and her life to the academy. She reapplied for a TA-ship at UT, and this time she got one. She and her daughter, now in the 5th grade, moved to Austin in 1982. "And so then from '82 to '85, I was on campus finishing the PhD." She graduated in 1985 and immediately accepted the tenure-track position at Miami University, where she remained for 16 years.

Strategies for Success

Graduate School

Jarratt's decision to get her PhD at Texas was in some ways an effect of circumstances. Traveling far from the support system of her parents would have made graduate school impossible. But she says she feels as if she "ended up in exactly the right place at the right time" in James Kinneavy's rhetoric program. When she was doing the PhD she had no idea whether she'd be able to get a tenure-track position. "I loved this new field I had discovered, rhetoric, and liked going to school," she told us. "I thought, Well, I'll finish this [degree] and then, if nothing happens, I'll go back to high school teaching." But David Jolliffe and Tom Miller went out the year before her, and they both had lots of interviews. The cohort of students at that time era was very friendly and supportive: Beth Daniell, Roger Cherry, and many more rhetoric friends who have remained a solid professional network through the years. Initially not as aware as her classmates of the broader world of the academy, Jarratt began to imagine that it could work out for her, too. When she went on the market, she had only one chapter of her dissertation drafted ("obviously, this isn't advisable now"), and since she had not been required to do a prospectus, she didn't have a very clear view of what she was going to be doing in it. She had no publications and had never been to a professional conference. Still, that was a "very different time," as she said; most programs place much more emphasis on professionalization during graduate school now. And she ended up doing very well on the market, perhaps in part because she was female:

> Let's see, I went on the market with several classmates, all guys, which was interesting on the level of gender. One of them said, Well, of course you're going to get a lot of interviews and land a job because you're a woman. That was probably true, but it was kind of weird to hear that.

All three UT candidates were on the short list for the Miami University job, but Jarratt landed the position. "And I have no problems saying that I got the job in part because of affirmative action."

Tenure and Promotion Strategies

According to Jarratt, to get tenure at Miami University in 1991, one needed "a book or its equivalent," but that requirement "was read pretty openly." Jarratt told us there was a lot of collegiality and support in her department and institution, and that "it just rarely happened that someone didn't get put up for tenure." The English department had recently changed policies concerning leave so that junior faculty could have time off for research before the tenure decision. During that semester of leave, she was able to make some important decisions about moving from dissertation to book, not always a smooth process. Typically, one was expected to have at least five substantial articles to have a solid case, but Jarratt said she knew some people who got tenure with only a few articles. She herself had two or three substantial articles, a book review, and a book manuscript under contract at Southern Illinois University Press. Kenney Withers at SIUP was very helpful and, according to Jarratt, hurried the process along for her when she confided that her tenure decision could be affected by the status of her manuscript. The upside to the press's willingness to fast-forward the process is that Jarratt had the book contract in hand before she went up for tenure; the downside, however, was that she did not get much substantial feedback from her manuscript reviewers. So the rush-order was "kind of a mixed blessing," as Jarratt put it. "The reviewers weren't very critical, and [I] would have liked some critical feedback. Yet, if I had had a critical reader who had said, 'I don't think this is going to fly,' I might not have gotten tenure."

Another very positive aspect of the early years at Miami was a strong network of support among the younger women faculty and opportunities to collaborate. Working with Dale Bauer on the Feminist Sophistics conference was a real high point of that era. Sitting in on a first course in feminist theory co-taught by Dale and Kristina Straub (now at Carnegie Mellon) was another. Her graduate students have also helped her a great deal; she described them as interlocutors and supporters who have given her "much pleasure and balance over the years." Working for a whole year with a group of graduate students on feminist pedagogy was an incredible experience. Later we had a group working on public sphere studies. These "extracurricular" formations have been very sustaining. Another important experience at Miami was a writing group including Vicki Smith, Lori Merish, Alice Adams, and Cheryl Johnson: "We had very different approaches to writing and areas of scholarship, and sometimes one or the other of us would strike the wrong note in our responses. But overall it was a great experience." Jarratt continues to collaborate with Smith on projects in feminist theory, rhetoric, and pedagogy.

Jarratt told us that one of her most serious struggles as a junior faculty member was maintaining confidence in herself as a writer; indeed, she still struggles with it today.

> My coping strategy has been to try to see what is really at stake for me in a project, to think about what I would like to do for others, to think about how my work may contribute a little—perhaps not make a grand, definitive statement but give another "turn to the screw," as my dissertation director Jack Farrell used to say. And of course not to forget to bring other readers in at every stage possible.

Time Management

As professor of comparative literature and UCI's campus writing coordinator, Jarratt is currently trying to balance the demands of teaching, administration, and research. This is no mean feat, and she told us that it has forced her to become more focused on the now: "I'm very driven by what's right in front of me and due tomorrow (or last week, or last September, in the case of the piece I'm working on now)." The administrative load is heavy, and she often finds herself "staying in the office in the late afternoon and early evening to write administrative documents. It's peaceful, but I'm still in the office." Jarratt distinguished between writing she does for the institution and her *own* writing: as she notes above, she writes institutional reports and such mostly in the office in the late evening; her own writing, on the other hand, she does at home in the early morning, but typically only during the summer months or over the winter break.

> I have trouble doing much independent research and writing during a regular school term. The crush of university and professional service is just massive—totally out of control at this point. It's only been in the summer and over breaks that I can clear away other tasks. Then I get up early to write, use the mid-day for running errands, read and revise in the afternoon. It's Walter Pater's formula. He says the evening is for the "labor of the file" (i.e. editing).

Mentoring

Jarratt, who is a tireless mentor, told us that when young women colleagues and graduate students come to her for advice, they generally have issues with "confidence, getting the writing/research agenda up and running, and sometimes coping with students." Yet, she noted that her junior colleagues seem to have much more confidence and to feel more enfranchised than she did at their stage. Indeed, Jarratt told us that her junior colleagues "often take the lead and have little need for mentoring." Still, we asked her what she would do if one of her junior colleagues came to her feeling persecuted or discriminated against by other colleagues in the department. Jarratt told us that she would first listen—a sympathetic and confidential listener is an important first stage—and recount any similar experiences if they seem relevant. Then she would seek out all the university regulations and precedents for their use in similar situations. And because the "official grievance route"—with its "ineffective procedures, the possibility of retribution," and so on—is often not the best route to take, Jarratt told us she would then try to "locate anyone who has had a similar experience and find out what she did about it." She would strategize about whether there is any collective response possible or advisable, take the initiative to change procedures where possible, and find out if there are "national precedents or initiatives that might be of use (even in the language being used)." After researching all the options, Jarratt told us that she'd talk through these options with the junior faculty member being persecuted in order to determine together which one "best fits her personality."

We also asked Jarratt what advice she'd offer to a PhD candidate or recent graduate about to take a WPA position somewhere. She told us she'd rather advise the person before he or she took the job. "Actually, I don't think hiring a WPA at an entry-level is a good idea, so I would discourage that. The authority issues are too difficult." Either way, however, she told us she'd ask a series of important questions:

> If it's any entry-level job, what are the demands for scholarship? Are they reasonable? Will WPA-type writing (training materials, curriculum) count towards tenure? … What does the person really want to do? If this is a time-filler until you get a "real" job, then don't do it. What is the time-frame for the position? If the institution expects you

to be WPA forever, are you ready for that? What are the financial supports in place? What scope of creativity will you have in making changes in curriculum and policy? How is the writing program considered within the unit (department)? Is the department/unit aware of any of the professional institutions and standards related to WPAs? Will you have the support of the dean for your initiatives?

Having a Life

Jarratt told us that balancing work and fun has been and remains a struggle for her. A few years ago, she stopped working in the evenings for the most part because she came to resent the demand to work 12–16-hour days. However, she told us that cutting back her working hours is probably why she's behind on deadlines, and getting behind is also a stress-inducer. Still, in her down time in the evening, she says that she enjoys gardening, watching TV (like Toni Morrison, she's a *Law and Order* aficionado), cooking, reading mysteries, and talking on the phone. "I like exercise, too—going to the gym and taking long walks. Here in California, I've started kayaking, sailing, and hiking in the mountains. Anything that moves my body through space is a good counterbalance to the fixity of academic work."

Jarratt is also a frequent traveler: her "family and friend network" is national rather than local, so she spends quite a lot of time on airplanes, and she actually enjoys that. "It gives me focus, moving through space in that contained little tube." Her new granddaughter, Neely, who lives in Portland, Oregon, is the most common destination lately, and a recent family reunion in Texas brought the now four generations of women in her family together. Her daughter, Jessica, who also saw herself as taking a different path from her mother by going into non-profit development instead of to graduate school, has recently started a consulting business for non-profit groups. But just as in the previous generation, mother and daughter have discovered links: her daughter's profession requires a high level of rhetorical expertise, both oral and written, as she leads meetings, writes promotional materials, prepares funding-raising plans, and drafts speeches for organizational leaders. Their conversations explore the next generation of women's struggle to balance work and family.

Music continues to be an expressive outlet for Jarratt, who was in a woodwind quintet (she's also a flute player) and a choral group for years in Oxford. She has sung in a couple of groups in Irvine as well: "I play the piano for myself now, working up something or other, and still play keyboard and flute with active musician friends in Texas It's only a few times a year, but it's still great fun."

Chapter 12

SHIRLEY WILSON LOGAN

Shirley Wilson Logan is Associate Professor of English at the University of Maryland, where she teaches courses in composition, rhetoric, and African American literature. Her books *"We are Coming": The Persuasive Discourse of Nineteenth-Century Black Women* and *With Pen and Voice: A Critical Anthology of Nineteenth-Century African-American Women* are foundational texts in feminist/womanist rhetoric and provide important insights into African American contributions to the rhetorical tradition. Her numerous journal and book chapters address the intersections of race, gender, and rhetoric and composition studies. She plays a strong leadership role in the profession, having served as Chair of the Conference on College Composition and Communication (2003); Member of the MLA Division on the History of Rhetoric and Composition Executive Committee (2000–05); and President of the Coalition of Women Scholars in the History of Rhetoric and Composition (1998–2000). She earned her PhD in 1988 from the University of Maryland, where she served in various capacities, including Director of the Professional Writing Program for seven years, after being awarded a tenure-track position at that institution. She was tenured and promoted to Associate Professor in 1998. She is the recipient of a number of fellowships and awards, including the American Association of University Women (2003–04) and National Endowment for the Humanities (2006–07) postdoctoral fellowships.

Background

Logan was born in Due West, South Carolina, to a Sunday school missionary and a schoolteacher. Logan's parents both graduated from historically black colleges in North Carolina. Her father went to Johnson C. Smith University, "which is one of the first historically black schools established after the Civil War" (by the Presbyterian Church). Logan explained that her mother attended the "sister school"—Barber-Scotia College, in Concord, North Carolina. Logan still has the Johnson C. Smith yearbook, with pictures "of the sweethearts of the graduates. And my father and my mother are in it. It is a wonderful treasure to have."

Her family moved to Spartanburg, South Carolina, when Logan was about nine years old. She attended elementary, junior high, and high school there in segregated schools. The close-knit community members, including her teachers, knew one another well. Laughing, she said,

> My most embarrassing high school memory unfolded during my junior year—you actually had to tell your teacher who was taking you to the prom. There was sort of an unrecorded but widely known list and at some point, if you hadn't been asked, the teacher (Miss B) would let it be known that there was someone who hadn't been asked. It was downright embarrassing. As the prom drew closer, she would have us push the desks back, and practice formal dancing for the prom. So they [the teachers] were all very much involved in your lives and what you were doing. And I guess that was a good thing. I don't know. People always talk about it now as if it's too bad we don't have those good old days. I don't know that it was all that perfect, but it did mean that you didn't have the anonymity that now allows people to do things that they wouldn't do if they knew somebody was watching. We were probably not any better than kids today, but we just had so many people watching that we had to kind of behave ourselves!

Logan added that she was one of the ones who had *not* been asked to the prom, so her teacher was watching out for her.

The youngest of five children, Logan was born six years after the fourth child and referred to herself as "an afterthought." Her elder siblings were busy or were already out of the house when she grew up, so she had to entertain herself. There were many books in her home, "so," she said, "I sort of took to reading." While a childhood of reading portends a future in English studies, Logan had other ambitions: she wanted to be a hairdresser. "I adored my hairdresser, and I wanted to go to school to learn cosmetology," she said, laughing. However, her destiny—as a daughter of two first-generation college graduates—awaited her in college, not cosmetology school. "As second generation college students, we were atypical. The whole idea is that you don't achieve less than your parents. It was never a question. Even *where to go* wasn't much of a question!" She went to the same Presbyterian school, Johnson C. Smith University, following in her father's footsteps.

While Logan's siblings were older, they watched out for her. By the time Logan was old enough to go to college, both her parents were deceased but she was fortunate to have an amazing stepmother, who, marrying her father when Logan was five years old, showered love over all of them. Logan's sisters became teachers and her brother served in the Marine Corps. Annually, they pooled their resources to support Logan through college. Although she received a small scholarship and worked in the summers, her brother and four sisters supplemented her tuition for the entire four years of her undergraduate education. “They never made me feel like this was a tremendous burden,” she noted, “although I’m sure it must have been, because they were all just starting out with their own families.”

Once in college, Logan declared math and French as her majors, until she took her first math class, which ended up being an advanced course *and* a “disaster,” she recollected. Although she could not recall why she finally selected English, she graduated *summa cum laude* with departmental honors with majors in English and French. She did remember one English professor who “turned [her] on to James Baldwin” and, she admitted, “I think I actually had a crush on him.”

> He handed me *Go Tell It On the Mountain*, and he was just an excellent teacher—and at that time a rather unusual teacher. He would come and eat with us in the dining hall. He was just wonderful. He was so excited about the material. He was personable. Most of our teachers were stand-offish and proper. And here was this man who was a sitting-on-the-desk kind of a teacher. He was talking about all of these issues, which at that time [the early 1960s] we weren’t necessarily talking about very much. I think that’s what really turned me on to literature, so to speak. His introduction. And Faulkner. We read Faulkner, too.

Mr. Blue not only ignited Logan’s love of literature, but he also planted the seed of further study of English at graduate school. “He said in pretty much these words, ‘You should go on and put your application in for graduate school.’”

Graduate school was out of the question, however, because Logan could not afford it. She said, “it was out of the question to ask my family to support me for more than the four years that they already had. So I wasn’t going to ask for any more assistance … . Mr. Blue encouraged me to apply for a Woodrow Wilson Fellowship. And I was a finalist, but I didn’t receive it.” So, instead of going to graduate school, Logan began teaching high school in Charlotte, North Carolina, after she graduated in 1964. While teaching, she attended the University of North Carolina, Chapel Hill, during summer sessions, earning her master’s degree in English in 1966. Her thesis was on Richard Wright’s short stories. “We didn’t know much about writing by women then,” she added.

She told us that soon after this time she knew she was “ready to leave Charlotte,” which was embroiled in racial tensions exacerbated by integration. She was “one of the first teachers to teach in the newly integrated Charlotte-Mecklenburg schools.” Although she didn’t “have any stories of violence or rocks being thrown or anything like that,” she recalled the constant, underlying tension, exhibited in scenes such as the memory of “one student who took great pleasure one day in raising his hand and asking a question totally unrelated to the discussion: ‘Miss Wilson, I was wondering if you are familiar with the novel by Joseph Conrad, *The Nigger of the Narcissus*?’ Just to get my reaction … . It was not a particularly good time. [But] I had a job.”

She found her exit one summer, when she was teaching at Mount Holyoke at the "head-start," "leg-up" program, "A Better Chance," aimed at encouraging young African American students to attend private preparatory schools. During this summer, she met someone who told her, "'You should come teach at Howard.' And I said, 'Oh, I have relatives in Washington, DC.' So I wrote a letter and used his name and got a job [as an instructor of Freshman English] at Howard University. So that got me out of Charlotte." It also got her out of public high schools and into higher education. She noted that this was an important move for her, because it "helped [her] to see that world and recognize its advantages." She explained, "I just kind of knew that I wanted the freedom to express myself and to do the kind of work that I wanted to do that I couldn't do in high school. There wasn't that same kind of structured environment, requiring me to have individual lesson plans for up to five classes a day."

She soon found herself back in that "day-to-day" routine, however. When she met and married her husband, she took a job teaching in Prince George's County public schools, in a suburb of Washington, to earn more money. But then she "started having kids, and so the brief cycle of childbirth, maternity leave, and return to work began." She realized she needed more flexibility in her work, so returned to teaching at Howard. This time, however, she enrolled in wonderful courses with "people like Arthur P. Davis, who edited the *Negro Caravan*" and who knew people like Langston Hughes and Richard Wright personally. She said, "Arthur Davis would say [*sotto voce*], 'Well, *Langston* and I … . And *Richard Wright* … .' So it was very exciting to be at Howard during that time—I also heard Sterling Brown read "Strong Men" and Margaret Walker (during a campus visit) read "For My People." Although she enjoyed her time at Howard, when her youngest child was four years old and she had completed another childbirth cycle, she grew restless. She was living near Walter Reed Medical Center, where her husband was serving as an Army physician. She said to herself; "'Okay, I'm ready to get out of here and do something.' And then I said, 'the University of Maryland is over there! I wonder if they need a writing teacher?' It was totally serendipitous. It wasn't as if I applied and waited. I wrote a letter and it turns out it was the year that they were starting their professional writing program … . So, they needed all of these writing teachers … . And that got me to the University of Maryland," where—in between lots of carpooling—she earned her PhD in 1988.

Balancing doctoral work and motherhood proved to be a challenge. She would deposit her children at their piano lessons or soccer practices and then go to class. Or, when her kids returned from school, she would "lock them in [the house] because they were old enough to be left at home (somehow I had rationalized that I was just a few minutes away)," while she attended her courses. Her dissertation, "An Ethnographic Study of Computer Writers," has "Cindy Selfe … all over [it]," as a pioneer in the area. Logan noted that it is "strange" to look at her dissertation now, given the rapid change of technology. "My research question," she revealed through laughter, "was: '*Should* we use computers to teach writing?'" At that point, the field of rhetoric and composition was still in the process of professionalizing itself as a discipline; Logan noted, "at that point, you couldn't get a PhD in rhetoric and composition," so her "emphasis was in education. It was curriculum and instruction." Logan's first introduction to rhetoric "in a systematic way" was through courses taught by then recent hire Jeanne Fahnestock.

After earning her degree in 1988, she thought to herself, "Okay, I have a PhD, and I'm still teaching professional writing as a part-time instructor." She began applying for both African American literature and rhetoric and composition positions. She ended up landing a tenure-track position at her alma mater. When the University of Maryland advertised for a rhetoric and composition specialist, "the chair of the department, who at that time was a rhetoric and composition person, said, 'You know, Shirley, we would really like to hire you'" for the position. This was a huge relief for her, four years after earning her degree. "I was beginning to worry, after awhile, that people would think 'What's taking this person so long?' I knew that search committees consider how long it's been since the degree was awarded. So in 1992, I was appointed to a tenure-track position at the University of Maryland, directing the professional writing program. I was then *directing* the same professional writing program that hired me way back when to teach my first writing course at Maryland."

Strategies for Success

Finding a Passion

When asked what advice she would give to someone at the beginning of her career, Logan did not hesitate. She said, "Try to find your passion, because that's going to have to sustain you in times when it's not all roses." She explained that one's research has to be motivated by a genuine interest. "[I]t can't just be about the profession, or about advancing, or about promotion," she said. "You have to *want* to know or find out whatever it is that you're" researching. She offered an example:

> I remember that what got me going with my research on nineteenth-century black women was the Ida Wells stamp that was issued in the 1980s. I was just curious about it; I had heard just a bit about her. It got me looking into her and some of the work she had done. I really enjoy my work … . Whatever I'm working on, I would do it anyway. And that's why I decided to go ahead and apply for a tenure-track position because I was working on *With Pen and Voice* before I was on tenure track. And I thought, 'Well, I'm going to do this anyway. I might as well get credit.' I would have done it anyway. That's what's so rewarding. So that would be one piece of advice I would offer young

> scholars—figure out what it is that's going to sustain them and what brings them that kind of pleasure.

Logan's research gives her pleasure, and it sustains her when other aspects of her life are difficult. She said, "I feel motivated to get up in the morning and get started again. For example, I'm currently researching black sites of rhetorical education in the nineteenth century and find new material daily .... And, of course, one discovery leads to another and then there are all the connections. I'm eager to share my work" with others.

When asked if she had ever felt like quitting or just walking away from her career, Logan responded, "No, I can't really think of a time when I just wanted to quit." But,

> Every now and then I get some student evaluations … I don't read student evaluations anymore. I mean it's almost like, you know, you think you're doing such a great job, and you're having this wonderful engagement with the students, and then you read the evaluations. And you realize that they were just *there* for the grade! It was a one-night stand! [Laughs.] Sometimes that's a little bit discouraging.

Indeed, Logan admits that her work is often what gets her through other difficulties in life. She confessed, "I often use work as my way of absorbing personal issues. I just kind of bury myself in my work. That's not necessarily very good. Work has enabled me to sustain other activities I have been tempted to abandon." So for Logan, her passion for her research is especially evident—it is her sustaining and motivating force.

Administration and Tenure

Although Logan was deeply gratified to become the director of the program for which she had served as an adjunct professor for so many years, she had an understandable concern: how to serve as a writing program director and still make successful progress toward tenure and promotion. Although some, such as Cynthia L. Selfe, do not see a conflict between program administration and scholarship, others, including the majority of our online survey respondents, believe with Logan that it is a difficult negotiation, especially pre-tenure. Indeed, Logan said, "So then I was directing the program and on tenure track, which is, of course, not a good combination." However, Logan was fortunate to be at a supportive institution. She said the department "was very accommodating. I was granted a year off to write and assigned a mentor-colleague to shepherd me through the tenure and promotion process and to foster productivity."

Mentoring

Logan identified several mentors who aided her during her beginning years as a tenure-track assistant professor. She mentioned Sue Oswald, to whom she dedicated her book. She also singled out Jane Donawerth, as "one of the most helpful":

> *With Pen and Voice* was published in time for my third-year review. But I knew that an anthology wouldn't do it at Maryland. It was actually Jane who said, when I was working on *With Pen and Voice*, "You're spending too much time with this in terms of writing the introductions and going into analysis of the speeches. Save this for the book! A little blurb, a little head note will do, because it's still going to be an anthology, and even though you may have some good stuff in there, you want to try to save that for a separate single-authored volume."

Donawerth helped refocus Logan's scholarship toward a single-authored book, which was required by her institution for tenure and promotion. *With Pen and Voice* is "an anthology. You know they [the college] would say, 'All you did was just assemble these texts.'" Thanks in part to Donawerth's intervention, Logan regrouped and "by the time my clock was up, I had the manuscript and the contract for *'We Are Coming,'* so that pretty much got me through that." Donawerth's exceptional mentoring was also characterized by Logan as

> paying attention to opportunities for me, for things to which I could apply—grants, fellowships—and putting me on panels with her. She was selected a distinguished scholar/teacher at Maryland one year, and the winner could ask two people to give mini-papers with her, and she asked me [in order to] give me an opportunity to showcase my work.

Throughout the process, Donawerth helped Logan work the system so that she would get tenure. "[S]he wants to be sure that you get it, that you understand how the system works. And she's quite vocal about her opinions about doing the right thing. She's one of these people who will do the right thing—a very honorable person." Logan characterized her as a feminist teacher and mentor.

Another mentor Logan identified was Jeanne Fahnestock. "What Jeanne did for me was make me feel that I had something to offer. She's the kind of person who, whenever you talk to her, makes you think, 'Well, I must be brilliant!'" Although Logan revered Fahnestock and deeply appreciated her mentoring, they did not always see eye to eye.

> I had tremendous respect for her as a scholar. She's just brilliant as far as I'm concerned. Jeanne and I, as far as politics, we are like this

> [gestures with hands far apart]. We just sort of came to terms with that; we won't talk about that. [Logan laughed.] This is one case where I do just want to be polite, because this is a person I treasure so much, and I know that this is something that we don't agree on, so I don't even want to talk about that because I don't want to be in a place where I'm disagreeing with this person that I greatly respect. We sort of joke about it now. But only *mildly.*

Regardless of the differences in political points of view, Logan stressed, "what Jeanne did for me was, with her body language, with her comments on drafts of things, just say, 'You know, you can do this, you have something to say, you have a mind.' And to have that coming from her was just very, very reaffirming." At her first conference talk, Jeanne "was sitting in the audience ... and she was just locked in to my every word, as if she thought, 'This woman is saying such amazing things.' She was just nodding, 'Yes, yes, yes.' She was writing stuff down. I thought, 'Okay, this must be going pretty well.'" Logan summed up the method and value of a true mentor: "It doesn't take many people, just one person, really, one person to kind of validate you."

Committee and Professional Service

In her early years as an assistant professor at the University of Maryland, Logan found herself on a lot of committees, because, she explained: "You know, not that many black people on the campus, and I'm a black woman—so you got your two-for here." Logan values committee service and recognized its importance, but this "two-for" service ended when mentors advised her, "You've done enough of this. You got that box—we can check service off." Obviously, she continues post-tenure to serve the greater profession of rhetoric and composition, most notably by her past service as Chair of the Conference on College Composition and Communication. What leads her to such time-consuming and service-oriented posts is a personal characteristic that motivates her research and scholarship as well: curiosity. She recalled:

> I've always been curious about what happens, you know, under the table. Not that it's all under the table, but behind the door. A curiosity about that. Always wanting to know, "When was that decided? I wonder how that unfolds?" It's gotten me into a lot of trouble, but I think that's what motivated me. I remember when Chris Farris from Indiana was chairing the nominating committee. She called me and said that my name had come up and are you interested? I hadn't thought about it at all. There are people for whom being chair of 4Cs is their lifetime goal, a dream come true. I'm not being dismissive of it, but it wasn't something that I ever thought much about one way or another until about a month before I was doing it. And so I'm trying to

> think, "Why did I accept?" You know, it's exciting to be the head of your professional organization! All these people that you have admired for so long—suddenly to have the opportunity to work with them in another way was quite an honor. And I was just kind of curious. You know, even though you go to 4Cs conventions for years and years, you are just sort of there. You don't stop to think about how it all happens. And it was in a time in my life when the kids were gone, and I was looking for stuff to do to keep busy. Actually, they told me, "Mom, go ahead. You can do it!" They'd say, "You know, you told me to do so-and-so." They'll bring up a time from their past when I encouraged them to pursue something.

One of Logan's key strategies as chair of CCCC was the effort to conduct successful and *smooth* meetings of the Executive Committee. Her method was to keep an index card propped up in front of her, "a verse from James in the New Testament, which is, 'Quick to listen, slow to speak, and slow to anger.' I've put that on a card because of those meetings," she laughed. "[I]n any kind of professional organizations, you've got differences of opinion. So I write it on an index card and prop it up in front of me, so I can look at it every now and then."

Politics of Academe

Along with other women in this volume, Logan noted her discomfort with conflict caused by differences of opinion or of racial tension. She explained,

> One thing I don't like about myself … is that I don't think I'm assertive enough. I don't handle confrontation well. I can almost feel something inside of me when there's a conflict arising. I wish I were more willing to engage in controversial encounters. I think I would have more of an impact if I could do that … . I'm the kind of person who will walk away from a situation and then a day later think, "I could have said … ." Or, "Why didn't I do this?" Whereas somebody like my good friend Joyce [Middleton] would just be right on point. I'll think about it and then go off and mope and then think of what I could have said or done.

Recognizing this tendency as a weakness, she encouraged young scholars to surround themselves with professionals who are better at handling controversy. She said, "surround yourself with good people. Find them. Just find them. I think I was fortunate that I was around people who were supportive. It just takes one or two people to keep you going." She also advises that one or more of those good people be savvy about "working the system and negotiating" and so forth, and that person wouldn't be her, she laughed: "I've never been good at working the system. It [requires] that same kind of confrontational assertiveness that I don't have. But it doesn't hurt to … surround yourself with people who have it so that maybe some of it will rub off. You do need some of that. You can't go into this work with such naïveté. You will get exploited."

Having a Life

Because Logan is no longer an administrator, she has no typical daily routine. Her activities vary from day to day, from role to role. When she was Director of the Professional Writing program, she would spend most all her days in the office, with the door open. "And it's [people] in and out[, saying] 'You got a minute?' 'You got a minute?' 'You got a minute?' Everybody wants a minute. But it was a wonderful experience because you're interacting with people all day. But you can still kind of control it—if you want some down time, you could kind of go off." No longer in this role, Logan finds her days more isolating,

> Because you can actually enter the building from the back stairs, and not even see anybody. Go to the fourth floor; go to your office. If it's not a teaching day, you can close your door, and nobody will even know you're there, which I do a lot. It's nice, but it is really kind of isolating. I'll teach and then have office hours. A few students will come by with some issues or help with a paper. I'll go down to the main office and hang out a little bit, because I still miss that interaction.

Rising at 6:30 or 7:00 a.m., Logan will do "some kind of [spiritual] devotional before I head out. Or, I'll get up and walk … around the neighborhood and try to read a little bit. If it's a regular academic year, I usually get a late morning class. I'll go in and teach." Many days, she'll attend committees ("diversity this or something or other that"), and if there is time, and "I feel like it," she'll go to the gym at the end of the work day, return home to work or go to the library to search the archives. Her husband is away often, as his job requires travel, and because her children are grown and out of the house, when she arrives home, she has the space and time to work late into the evening, if she desires. "Because that's the thing about an academic life," she said. "You're always working." That doesn't mean that her role as a mother is over. "They still manage to need me a lot. And that's okay," she said, although she admitted that she thought at this point in her life that they'd be beyond it. "But then," she said, "every now and then, they'll call and remind me that they're not quite out of the woods … . I just sort of thought that I would draw a line, and it doesn't quite happen that way. It is more of a zig zag kind of thing."

Logan draws a great deal of strength from her spiritual practices. When asked if there were certain principles that guide her, she responded:

> I'm a Christian. I'm Presbyterian. I'm an elder in my church. I'm very active in my church, because it's my way of maintaining a link to a world outside of the academy. In times when I want to scream because

> I'm torn, I've always maintained an active participation in my church. Because it's a kind of a source of strength for me to believe that there is some ultimate power out there, somebody who is concerned (I don't know if it's a person), but a force controlling and helping guide us.

In turn, her religious beliefs form a foundation for her personal ethics. Logan said, "I believe in fairness, in being honest, trying to be considerate of other people, so that I can look at myself in the mirror at night. To try to be a good person. To try to do something for other people *because* of my own experience."

Although her life is full, she often wishes that she had some hobbies outside of work, motherhood, and church activities. She advises others to "try to have something that you can do that's just for pleasure outside of the work." However, she admitted that, in fact, her work is truly a pleasure. She gave an example: "People will say, 'Oh, you *have* to go to a conference.' And I moan and say, 'Yeah, I *do*.' Meanwhile, I'm packing and just grinning. I know I'm going to see Joyce [Middleton] and Jackie [Royster]!" Thinking further about developing a hobby, she admitted, "Sometimes … [it] scares me that *this* [academic work] is my pleasure. I think, 'Well, maybe I should have something else!' … I keep thinking, 'Shouldn't there be something else?' You know, knitting or *something*. Cross-stitching or something." She laughed.

Chapter 13

ANDREA A. LUNSFORD

Andrea A. Lunsford is currently Louise Hewlett Nixon Professor of English and Director of the Program in Writing and Rhetoric at Stanford University. Perhaps best known for her advancement of collaborative writing, Lunsford has also contributed to scholarship in the teaching of writing, feminist rhetoric, literacy studies, and intellectual property rights. She is co-author or co-editor of 14 books, including several popular composition textbooks and readers. Her scholarly work includes *Singular Texts/Plural Authors* (with Lisa Ede); the edited books *Reclaiming Rhetorica: Women in the Rhetorical Tradition* and *Crossing Borderlands: Composition and Postcolonial Studies*; and innumerable journal articles and chapters in books. Lunsford is a tireless spokesperson for the field, having presented more than 500 speeches, lectures, workshops, and papers since 1997. Her professional leadership includes Co-chair of the Alliance of Rhetoric Societies International Conference (2002–03), and Chair of the Conference on College Composition and Communication (1989–90). She has received many awards and honors, including the Exemplar Award from the Conference on College Composition and Communication, the MLA Mina P. Shaughnessy Award for best book on the teaching of writing, and the YWCA Women of Achievement Award, City of Columbus. Lunsford earned her BA and MA in English from the University of Florida, and her PhD in English from the Ohio State University. After her PhD, she accepted a position at the University of British Columbia; she continued there as Associate Professor and Director of Writing until 1986, when she was appointed Distinguished Professor of English at the Ohio State University. She served there until 2000, performing several administrative roles, including Director of the Center for the Study and Teaching of Writing and Vice-Chair for Rhetoric and Composition.

Background

Lunsford was born in Ardmore, Oklahoma. Her parents moved to the foothills of the Smoky Mountains in eastern Tennessee when Lunsford was quite young so that her father could find work. Lunsford's mother, Myrtle Lee Cunningham, had grown up in these foothills and was one of nine children, seven of whom survived. Because of the kindness of an uncle, Lunsford's mother was the only child in her family to go to college; Lunsford explained, "[f]or some reason he took a shine to my mom." She graduated with a degree in French, and thereafter "taught for awhile in a one-room schoolhouse" until Lunsford was born. Lunsford's father, Gordon Grady Abernethy, was unable to "finish college because he and his brother were both in college, and his parents could only afford for one to go." Lunsford has very few memories of these early years, but she does remember her love of reading: "From the minute I could read, that's what I was doing. I really think I kind of was 'lost in a book' for a lot of my childhood." She also remembers being "punished for reading things I wasn't supposed to be reading. I would have to stay after school to get a talking to by the teacher because I had been reading my *Nancy Drew* or *Cherry Ames, Senior Nurse*, or all those *Hardy Boys* books."

When Lunsford was in seventh grade, her father's work in aviation took them to Hagerstown, Maryland, and then later to St. Augustine, Florida, where she finished high school. Of these Florida years, she has very fond memories of going to the beach for hotdog roasts with her family. She was a high school cheerleader and a good student (receiving mostly As), but her studies didn't "captivate" her. Her decision to go to college was born partly of "peer influence," since two of her closest friends were college-bound, although she noted, "not that many people from my high school at St. Augustine went on to college." However, convincing her father that she should go to college was not easy. She said, "I started asking at the end of the eleventh grade if I could go to college. My father wasn't too enthusiastic about it," in part because she hadn't shown much interest in school. Her father thought that she should become a secretary, since his daughter had proved her keyboarding skills by winning the typing medal in the ninth grade. But, Lunsford reported, "then I got really lucky." After the launch of Sputnik in 1958, the nation was increasingly concerned about the paucity of college graduates and its need for more teachers. The State of Florida sponsored scholarships to college-bound students who agreed to teach for a specified number of years upon the completion of their degrees. When Lunsford was awarded one of these scholarships, her father finally agreed to let her go. She worked year-round to supplement the scholarship, and her parents sent her an additional $50 a month to support her ("it was a sacrifice for them," she said), along with boxes of chocolate chip cookies and roasted peanuts.

Lunsford majored in English and minored in political science; she graduated (*magna cum laude*) and married a law-school student. She admitted,

> We had no more business being married than the *man in the moon*. We were good friends. I really liked him; I still like him. We thought we were in love, and my mother was really, really sick at the time. And I kept going back and forth from Gainesville to St. Augustine on the weekends to help take care of the kids who were still [at home] … . I think I thought, 'I have to get out of this somehow.'

An alcoholic until the last eight years of her life, her mother was the most important person in Lunsford's youth, the person Lunsford credits with "[m]y love of words and my linguistic abilities." (Her mother died of breast cancer in 1980.) Lunsford believes she married her first husband in part to absolve her from the responsibility of taking care of siblings when her mother could not.

After Lunsford's marriage, she and her new husband moved to Oklahoma so that he could serve in the Army, and nine months later they moved to Florida so that he could finish his law degree. After his graduation, they moved to Orlando so that he could join his father's law firm. Although she adored her family-in-law, she bristled at parts of their social world and the expectation that she would join it: "his family wanted me to be in a women's club that puts on a debutante ball every year. [My mother-in-law] was in the League of Women Voters. She belonged to a bridge club. And that's the sort of thing I was expected, silently, to do. And I just said, 'I can't do it. I've got to get a job.'" In order to fulfill her obligation to the State of Florida for her scholarship, she began teaching high school in Florida. After four years of teaching and five years of marriage, she was divorced.

While her former husband (later to become chief justice of the Supreme Court of Florida) was studying law, Lunsford pursued her MA in English at the University of Florida; her thesis was on William Faulkner. She recalled, "I had no idea what I was doing. I had exempted all the writing courses. Like so many people, I had no idea how to sustain a big project like that. And of course nobody helped me." Going on for a PhD seemed out of the question then, not only because of her marriage, but also because of the sexism of the times. Lunsford said, "My adviser discouraged me from going for further education. He said, 'You don't want to get a PhD; you want to go home and have babies." After her divorce, she moved to St. Petersburg, Florida, near where her parents were living and took a high school teaching position there. Later she became a faculty member at a new community college, Hillsborough Community College; she taught there until 1972.

By 1970, Lunsford reported, "I was really *mad*" at "that old man" who had "advised" her to "go home and have babies." At Hillsborough she had been asked to write booklets on the major modes of writing, which she undertook without any knowledge of scholarship on rhetoric and composition.

> These little booklets were on how to write a descriptive paper; how to write a narration paper; how to write an exposition paper; how to write a persuasion paper. I made up one all on my own called "How to Write the Combination Paper," because even then I intuited that these modes were not out there in the real world. That was the very beginning of television in schools. I recorded all of these lessons as television shows. Then, Ed [Corbett]'s book [*Classical Rhetoric for the Modern Student*] came and I started reading it. I had been knocking myself out trying to figure out how to write a persuasion paper. I started reading this stuff and I thought, "Oh my gosh. Look what I don't know!"

Lunsford had a desire to know more about the teaching of writing, so she applied for the graduate program in English at Ohio State. She moved to Columbus, Ohio, in 1972 with the man who would become her second husband. He, too, attended Ohio State—as a doctoral student in Philosophy. He was younger than Lunsford, and—she remembers—"I completely, utterly fell in love with him—the first and only time for me."

Although she had moved to Ohio State to study rhetoric and composition with Ed Corbett, she found that Corbett was only teaching literature; indeed, she told us, "During my graduate career, I studied almost nothing but literature in my formal requirements. Outside, however, I audited courses on rhetoric and writing in the Communication Department and the School of Education." When she realized that Corbett was not teaching rhetoric, she went to see him and said, "I came here because of this book, *Classical Rhetoric and the Modern Student.*" He responded by asking her to serve as the assistant editor of *College Composition and Communication*, a position she held all through her doctoral studies. "That's how I taught myself composition studies," she explained. "You couldn't have a better course than that. Ed let me read all the submissions that came in along with him. Then we would talk about what ones he was going to select and why." Eventually, she undertook directed readings with Corbett, examining key, primary rhetorical texts. She chose rhetoric and composition as one of her four doctoral exams, becoming the first student at Ohio State to be allowed to do so. In her dissertation, she focused on basic writers.

She earned her degree in 1977 and because there were so few scholars who marketed themselves in writing and rhetoric, she had many interviews at MLA and several offers. "I was lucky, really lucky, to be right at the time and place, when there was some interest in writing. In 1976 was that big 'Johnny Can't Write' furor (a so-called literacy crisis … happens every 15–20 years) and Mina Shaughnessy and Geneva Smitherman's books, both published in 1977, had created quite a discourse around student writing." She and her husband decided what job to take by looking at the map to locate where each offer would take them: "And I said, 'You know, I have hardly ever been west of the Mississippi River. There's this offer from *British Columbia*. Let's go there!'" So they did. One of the job offers she rejected was from the University of Michigan.

Hired as a rhetoric and writing specialist, Lunsford not only developed three undergraduate courses in the area, but she also directed the University of British Columbia's first-year writing program. "It was a very hard first job," she said. Although she loved Vancouver, enjoying its beauty and outdoor activities, she said, "the department was very, very contentious." The early 1980s were turbulent ones in Lunsford's private life as well (she lost both parents and her brother, and her husband left their relationship unexpectedly). However, she published prolifically and joined Ohio State in 1986 as Professor of English, where she helped build the graduate program in rhetoric and composition.

Strategies for Success

Graduate School

For many years, Lunsford has suggested that students—but particularly women—delay the start of their PhD until they have gained outside experience. Lunsford herself did not begin her PhD until she was 30 years old. The working conditions she experienced before beginning her PhD gave her a better perspective. She reflected, "I had been teaching in high school and community college six and seven classes a day. I taught big writing classes at the community college. When I got … into the graduate program [at Ohio State], I thought, 'What a piece of cake!' I was taking these really interesting courses … . And I was teaching *one class* instead of seven!" But in addition, Lunsford felt completely focused: "I knew myself better by then. I was much more mature; I understood what I wanted to learn."

Lunsford also believed that delaying the start of her PhD allowed her to put local university politics in perspective. She said, "I was in the business of getting this degree. I didn't get caught up in the graduate organization, which was always petitioning about this and writing letters about that, and complaining about xyz, having elections. I just was more focused on keeping 'my eyes on the prize.'" Instead, Lunsford found real pleasure in the process of her education. She recalled, "I really enjoyed graduate school … . By the time I got to read for exams, I just couldn't believe that I was getting paid to sit around and read and think and try to connect the dots. I really enjoyed that time and was very, very grateful for it. Graduate school was a financial struggle … . But intellectually, it just seemed like I was at this big banquet having a wonderful time." Of course, Lunsford's success in graduate school depended in part on her work with Corbett, since there was no coursework available in rhetoric and composition at that time. So another key factor in Lunsford's success was finding a mentor early in her career.

The Value of Work

Lunsford grew up a driven first child in a family marked (in both good and bad ways) by her mother's alcoholism.

> [My mother] was wonderful, a magical presence in my life, and I loved her beyond words. But I had a really conflicted relationship with her, too, because I hated it when she was drunk. In fact, now, if I'm around people who get drunk, I hate it. You know, drunk people are not really there, not present. And that is what I associate with my mother, whom I wanted to be there desperately … . Anyway, a lot of the care of my brother and sisters fell to me, especially when my mother was most ill.

In comparing herself with her younger sister (a writer), she said, "I never was the brightest person in my family, not by a long shot. My younger sister is just made of intelligence." But in her own estimation, whatever she may have lacked in intelligence was compensated for by her work ethic. "I've worked hard!" Lunsford said. "There's no doubt about that … . I'm that typical first child. I fit that profile to a T."

Lunsford started publishing and writing grants as a graduate student. Her first essay, "Those Freshman Composition Blues," was published in the *Freshman English Newsletter*. She also wrote a grant that helped co-found the Basic Writing Program at Ohio State. Since then, work (both writing and teaching) has sustained her through difficult times, including the dark years of 1980–87, when she lost many people dear to her. She elaborated on those years: "[M]y mother died a really gruesome death from cancer in 1980. My brother, the youngest in our family and 10 years younger than I, died another extraordinary pain-ridden death in 1984 … . And then my father killed himself practically the minute I got to Ohio State [in 1987]. So, the losses in the 1980s in my life just accumulated." (Lunsford's other younger sister died of the same disease as her brother, in 1996.)

Lunsford's husband was a significant part of her life, and she had every reason to believe that he would be there to comfort her. Indeed, given the situation at British Columbia, Lunsford felt she needed his support. The department was legendary for its contentiousness—"whole series of books have been written about this English department," she said. When she arrived, Lunsford recalls,

> There were … *wars* going on. As a new person, I didn't really know what they were. In my first year, the director of graduate studies was just *excoriated* on the floor of our faculty meeting, subjected to ad hominem attacks like I had never seen before. It seemed to me utterly vicious! And it was over some petty thing about the graduate exam … . So I saw this kind of behavior, and that department was very British in that F.R. Leavis acerbic, let-me-cut-you-down-to-size way … . That was a kind of badge of courage and a good thing—you wanted to be able to do that. I didn't want to be able to do it. So, I didn't fit in all that well.

When asked how she survived the department, Lunsford responded, "I just put my head down and tried to do my work." Her teaching "was really well received" and she "was publishing, so it was kind of hard for them to just go back on their decision to hire" her, even though she stood up for the part-time faculty and "rubbed people the wrong way" because of it.

Well before she expected it, Lunsford was promoted—but not tenured. "I was promoted to associate professor I think in my fourth year," she said. "I still don't know why. They just called up and said, 'We're not tenuring you, but we're promoting you early.' It had something to do with my publishing. So I thought, 'That must be good.'" But the department's enthusiasm for the volume of her work could not get them over the fact that she was publishing in an area they did not fully value. So, in 1982 when Lunsford came up for tenure, "it was so contentious that they met for two days." In the end, the department voted to tenure Lunsford, but the controversial nature of the decision left her feeling "shocked and hurt" and "very undercut." As she put it, "It wasn't that they disliked me, or my work, I don't think, but they didn't know if they wanted to tenure somebody in our field. That was what the argument was about." She survived because she had published so much, but it was "really unpleasant."

Lunsford's work ethic continued to sustain her through the worst thing that ever happened to her, so far (she said, laughing): her divorce from her second husband.

> [I]n the summer of 1985, there was this cataclysm with my husband—he just kind of imploded. I've never seen anything quite like it. He just turned into someone else. This is a very common story, but it didn't seem common at the time. He just turned into somebody that I didn't know. He was my very, very best friend. The best friend I've ever had—or at least that is how I perceived it. The loss of that relationship rocked the foundations for me.

She fondly recalled their early days together when she was teaching at the community college and he was finishing college; they took trips together to the White Mountains in New Hampshire, the Green Mountains in Vermont, and even to Ireland. "It was so exciting!," she said. "It was also kind of illicit, too, because we weren't married."

She believes that the seeds for the dissolution of the marriage were sown, as such seeds often are, much earlier. And while she has thought about it and puzzled over her own responsibility for the breakup of this most important relationship over the years, she says she eventually had to accept the fact of moving on and making a life on her own. But that acceptance was a long way off:

> [T]hat summer, while my marriage was dissolving, I went to Penn State to teach a summer course. Of course, my husband had been planning to go with me, but he didn't. I taught a course on the history of invention that summer. Linda Ferreira-Buckley, that wonderful scholar/researcher who is at Texas now, was in that class. And I wrote two articles that summer, and I go back and look at those articles and think, 'Where did that come from? Who on earth wrote these?' Because I was really working by remote control; I remember very, very little of that summer. But, work got me through. My work—and my sisters and my invaluable women friends—are what have always sustained me.

Lunsford acknowledged that her belief in the value of work to sustain and even heal a person "may be awfully old-fashioned," but she has good reason to believe in it. Given her history, her own survival is remarkable and a testament to the power of this strategy.

Luck vs. Self Worth

When asked what advice she would give to someone just beginning her career, Lunsford said: "Believe in yourself." She explained:

> It's so easy to think of yourself through others' eyes. It's a kind of internalized, not racism or sexism, but internalized "not-good-enough-ism." I certainly experienced that a lot. Not so much in graduate school, but certainly in the profession. My work on textbooks has never been valued in the academy, for instance. But I really believe that if we want to change things, we have to work on things like textbooks that are going to be out there, making a big impact, touching a lot of students' lives. And the way to believe in yourself is to attach yourself to the integrity of your work.

The work that Lunsford particularly values is teaching. She returned to this theme several times in the interview. "I am the luckiest," she said. "When I think about falling into teaching like I did … ! I'm so happy when it comes September and the new students come back. I don't think I'll ever feel old as long as I'm teaching. I get a lot from it, and I love making up new classes, and I've loved building programs." She founded Stanford's Writing Center "from scratch," and has enjoyed working with others to build it. She believes that the kind of work scholars in rhetoric and composition do "touches people," and the integrity of this kind of work is particularly sustaining.

Near the end of the interview, Lunsford circled back to the issue of luck. She had credited luck for discovering teaching as well as for auspicious timing at key moments in her career (particularly Sputnik in 1958 and the "Johnny Can't Read" controversy of 1976). However, pausing to reflect on her language, Lunsford said, "I think how lucky I feel is characteristic of women. I don't think men necessarily think they are 'lucky.' I think they think they earned it. I may be wrong about that." When we confirmed that we had heard that theme repeatedly in the interviews, she smiled wryly and said, "Keep your eye on that." Then she went on to say, "I do think that is characteristic [to feel lucky], but certainly I've worked hard!" Feeling lucky can go hand in hand with feeling unworthy to sit at the table.

Building a Support Network

Lunsford strongly advises younger women scholars to build a support network. She said, "I think early in my career, I didn't understand how important that network was to who *I* was. I've learned that hard. It's been a hard lesson." Like many women, she thought of her partner as the main source of her support network. She said,

> I think I thought of my husband and myself as this little unit that was sort of inviolable. When I didn't have that anymore, I had to really re-evaluate: where does my support and strength come from, if it's not this thing that I thought was the heart and soul of who I am? So I really had to claim a new identity. I think all people have to do that. We are not the same at 60 as we were at 40 or 20 or whatever. We keep reinventing ourselves. I think that's a good thing. But I've tried not to ever forget that I get to be who I am by virtue of the people I am connected to. And I better not forget it!

Lunsford has many life-long friends whom she spends time with regularly, including colleagues from her community college teaching days; they still travel together regularly. Other dear friends include former Ohio State colleagues, former graduate students, friends, students, and colleagues associated with the Bread Loaf School of English (as Lunsford says, "the very best MA and professional development program for teachers on the planet"), and her sister and sister-in-law (wife of her deceased brother), with whom she is very close. She is also aunt and godmother to some very special young people and, most recently, she is "Aunt A" to Audrey, her nephew's daughter and much loved great-niece. That her social circle includes so many former students is a testament to Lunsford's mentoring, which is legendary. She received strong mentoring from Corbett for her academic work, but she had to invent the style of feminist mentoring for which she is known. Lunsford treats her graduate student advisees as colleagues, passing on her wisdom with great compassion. But she considers the relationship a two-way street. She has written that teaching is a gift exchange. "When I think of my own experiences as a receiver of such gifts, I think most often of students who have been my teachers … . [So many of my students] have been and continue to be exemplars for me" ("Metaphors" 7–8). Lunsford builds the self-esteem of her students by considering them teachers of *her*, thus emphasizing mentoring as a dialogical, not hierarchical relationship. Lunsford's practice suggests that sometimes the act of mentoring can sustain the mentor, because good mentoring is a gift that is returned.

Collaboration

For many years, Lunsford has preached the value and importance of collaboration—particularly of women collaborating together on scholarship. Her experience with collaboration was born of her storied friendship with Lisa Ede, her close friend and former classmate at Ohio State.

> Lisa and I became friends in graduate school … . My husband and I and Lisa and her husband did tons of stuff together. When they moved away from Columbus, we spent the whole day at their apartment, cleaning it up so they could get their deposit back. Every once in a

> while I say, "You really owe me, for making me clean out that disgusting refrigerator!" But anyway, they got their Uhaul packed up, and Greg was driving, Lisa was looking down, and I was crying. And I said [in a tearful voice], "Oh, bye Lisa!" It was a really wrenching experience. But then I was still at Ohio State for a year. We visited them in Brockport, but then after I moved to BC, Lisa got an offer from Oregon State. She then moved to the West coast … [and] we were able to start up a more formal kind of working together. Our collaboration grew out of our friendship.

When Lisa Ede and Lunsford began collaborating on scholarly work, collaboration in the humanities was unusual. Lunsford recalled,

> [T]he first thing we wrote together was an essay in Ed Corbett's honor [for their edited volume *Essays on Classical Rhetoric and Modern Discourse*]. When we told him we were going to do it, he just looked at us and said, "*How* can you do it?" He could not understand how we could do this *physically*. He never could get over it. He was talking about it until the day he died—that strange thing we did. And our colleagues thought it was very peculiar. So, it was not at all a common practice … . And then once people reacted so strangely to us, we kind of got our chins set. So we said, "We're just going to do this."

Ede and Lunsford worked in what they would later call the "dialogic" mode in *Singular Texts/Plural Authors*, their study of the nature of authorship in the workplace and the academy. They share the work of preliminary research, but when it comes time to write, they like to meet in a hotel or one of their homes and write each line together, one person at the keyboard, both working through each sentence, one by one. In order to emphasize that they truly share the responsibility and credit for the work, they have alternated the order of their names on their many publications (about half list Ede as first author, the other half Lunsford).

Nevertheless, the romantic notion of the solitary author is deeply entrenched in English studies. Once Lunsford and Ede experienced resistance to their work together, they refocused their research and publications on collaboration, publishing their first essay on collaboration in 1983, in *Rhetoric Review.* Their colleagues continued to worry about their prospects. Ede and Lunsford write, "Some in our field cautioned us … that we would never receive favorable tenure decisions or promotions if we insisted on publishing coauthored articles. Even those who did not caution us about the dangerous consequences of our habit professed amazement at our ability to write together …" (*Singular* 6). As it turned out, there *were* some consequences for their work together. Lunsford recalls, "I got tenure before we really started in on this collaboration. But when Lisa came up for tenure, I had to write an 'unsolicited' letter that detailed line counts—how many lines she wrote; how many lines I wrote. I had to make up something, because when we write together, we really write *together.*" Despite prevailing prejudices against collaboration, Ede did get tenure at Oregon State, and when Ohio State called Lunsford for a position in 1986, they promoted her to full professor in the process, even with her growing list of collaboratively written publications. Lunsford believes that collaborative writing is subversive of modern concepts of authorship. She encourages women to write and work collaboratively in part to undercut lingering attachments to the single-authored articles and books as the penultimate evidence of scholarly worth. Collaborative work in rhetoric and composition studies is common now and far more respected, thanks in part to the work of Lunsford and Ede.

Having a Life

Lunsford works long hours at Stanford University. A typical day for her begins when the alarm rings each morning around 6:30 am; having developed an allergy to caffeine some 15 years ago, she is, as she reported, "on her own" in her attempt to wake up, so she performs a "series of yoga-like back exercises" to get herself moving. She arrives at her office at 8:00 am if she has a meeting, or 9:00 am if not. She spends the day with a "couple of office hours, three or four meetings, a class or two, and one or two evening events, especially in the Stanford Writing Center, where we host many readings and performances." She tries to arrive at home by 8:30 pm. The time she spends writing are "in between meetings and then in the down time between about 5:00 and 7:30 pm, when evening events start." She said, "Those two and a half hours are gold for me. I also work part of Saturdays and Sundays, when I can really concentrate." She works out at the gym on Saturday and Sunday mornings, and, if possible, one evening during the week. And every few days she has a date with Audrey, now two-and-a-half years old: "It's hard to express how much sheer fun I have playing with Audrey; that little girl is sunshine itself." "My days since I got to Stanford are just packed," she said, including many events that are requested by students themselves and put on by the Writing Center. "Lately, I've been in the dorms constantly. Kids want to hear about writing—and increasingly about speaking and performing. It's all been very interesting to me."

Lunsford's schedule is busy but sustaining. As she reflected on the things she does for and with others, she said, "I think that [work] can sustain us through enormous turmoil." But, she added with a grin, "It also helps to have lots of girlfriends. Can't have too many girlfriends. Or, too many sisters, in my experience."

14

JACQUELINE JONES ROYSTER

Jacqueline Jones Royster is currently Senior Vice Provost and Executive Dean of the Colleges of the Arts and Sciences, and Professor of English at the Ohio State University. Prior to her move to Ohio State in 1992, Royster taught English and served as an administrator at Spelman College, an historically African American college that is her alma mater. From 1976 to 1992, she held several positions there, including Director of the Comprehensive Writing Program and Associate Dean for Advising. While she has written on literacy and the teaching of writing, Royster is best known for her work on African American women writers and Afra-feminist research methods. From 1983 to 1996, she was part of the editorial collective of *SAGE: A Scholarly Journal on Black Women* (serving as editor of their final issue, published in 1996). With the editorial collective, she published the anthology *Double Stitch: Black Women Write About Mothers and Daughters* in 1991. Perhaps her best-known work in this area is *Traces of a Stream: Literacy and Social Change among African American Women*, which won the MLA's Mina P. Shaughnessy Award for best book in the teaching of English. Royster was Chair of the Conference on College Composition and Communication (in 1995); her chair's address, "When the First Voice You Hear Is Not Your Own" is frequently cited and was anthologized in *Cross Talk in Composition Theory: A Reader* (second edition, 2003). Her scholarship, leadership, and service to others has led to many awards, including Ohio Pioneer in Education by the State of Ohio Department of Education (2000); the Ohio State University Distinguished Diversity Award (2002); the Ohio State University Distinguished Lecturer (2003); YWCA Woman of Achievement Award (2004) for the City of Columbus; and the Exemplar Award (2004) from the Conference on College Composition and Communication.

Background

Royster was born in Greensboro, Georgia, a small town in the Piedmont region. An only child, Royster was strongly influenced by her mother, a public school teacher. According to Royster, she was "something of a revolutionary," and she became "an outcast in her own hometown [because] she was very outspoken." When Royster was just a toddler, her mother, several other teachers, and an administrator were fired for protesting the inequitable funding of a new school that had recently been constructed for the black students in the town. Those who protested were also barred from teaching in other schools in the county. Everyone moved to seek employment elsewhere—everyone except Royster's mother. She stayed in the same town, despite the controversy that surrounded her, and traveled to surrounding counties to teach. Royster recalled,

> Because it was the segregated South and the power dynamics were what they were, people were afraid to be friends with her. There were real consequences for being friends. If my father hadn't been from a family that was also well-respected and had a kind of power matrix of his own, he might have gotten caught up in it. But they always felt sorry for him for being married to such a wild woman.

Long after Royster's mother was fired, her mother's reputation influenced the size of her social circle; "there was always that 'she is so-and-so's daughter' syndrome that carried on," Royster explained.

One of the pivotal events of Royster's childhood was the death of her maternal grandmother, who took care of Royster while her mother worked. Unable to find childcare, Royster's mother—by then the principal of a two-teacher school, not unusual in the rural South before *Brown vs. Board of Education*—decided to take Royster to school with her at the age of three. She was easily included with the other children (despite her age) and advanced through the elementary and middle school curricula, entering Floyd T. Corry High School in her home town at age 13. She never attended an integrated school. As she put it, "I could have because the schools were actually integrated by the time I got to high school, but who wanted to go to the white high school?" Because she attended the lower grades in another county, Royster didn't have many friends from her hometown until she entered high school. She graduated high school at age 15. Remarkably, she was invited to go to college as early as age 14 through early admissions programs. But her mother encouraged her to slow down, saying, "It's not socially healthy for you to go to college at 14." Royster was always one of the youngest members of her class. However, she kept her age to herself. "I was much more sensitive then to being younger than everyone else—all through college, even in graduate school. I never talked about my age."

In choosing her classes and eventually her major, Royster followed her passions. A prodigious reader, she majored in English at Spelman College, but she pursued other interests as well. "All I ever liked to do was to read and write and, actually, draw. When I first went to Spelman, I was an English and art major." She also always loved languages. She placed in the second level of

Spanish when she entered Spelman and kept taking Spanish courses. After she took an art course that was really a home economics course, she dropped the art double major and chose Spanish instead. A scheduling conflict dashed her plan to graduate with a double major in English and Spanish, and she switched to a Spanish minor, which meant that she had a double minor in Spanish and secondary education. Her mother had always urged her to choose a minor in secondary education no matter what because her mother felt that a college-educated black woman might need to teach someday and certification was important. In the end, her mother's advice proved to be influential on her career.

Royster never doubted that she would pursue a master's degree. "I never thought too much about it … . In my family, the line was, 'once you get your master's, you can think about other things.' So, I really never thought about anything beyond the master's while I was in college." Because of her exposure to Indo-European languages, she looked for a master's degree in English that would allow her to pursue her growing interest in the history of languages. "I came from a small liberal arts college[,] [so] I didn't know about [graduate programs in] linguistics … [and] anthropology. I knew about English." She applied to and was accepted by her top three choices: Michigan, Brown, and Indiana. She chose Michigan because the head of the English department at Spelman, a man whom Royster deeply admired, was an alumnus of Michigan. She entered the MA program in English at Michigan, where she focused on the history of the English language and was trained by "historical linguists and very much by socio-linguists." She completed the degree in one academic year, at the age of 20.

Many women scholars in rhetoric and composition have experience in teaching primary or secondary education, and Royster is no exception. After finishing her MA, she taught third grade for one year in her hometown. As she explained, anyone from her community in Greensboro who earned a college degree was offered a teaching position when they graduated.

> I taught third grade reading and writing and second grade reading … . I did feel prepared to do that because the linguistics training had helped a lot in terms of language acquisition, but [the students] just didn't know enough to make it interesting to me. My mother was an elementary school teacher, although by the time I was in high school she had switched to special education, and her best friend was the best elementary school teacher that there was. I would look at this woman and look at myself and say, "Why are you doing this [teaching elementary school]? If you can't be like this woman, then you are wasting your time." I believed that, that only the best teachers should be elementary school teachers, and she was the best.

At the end of that year, she said to herself, "that's enough of that" and began to turn her sights toward journalism. She applied to and was accepted into the school of journalism at Michigan for the fall of 1972. But on the way to studying journalism, Royster got a chance to teach at the college level for the summer. A friend and fellow Spelman/Michigan classmate was teaching at Northern Illinois University and told her about an opening in their summer bridge program. She encouraged Royster to apply. Still intending to enter Michigan's journalism program, Royster accepted the summer position at Northern Illinois. At the end of the summer, however, she was offered an appointment as an instructor in the English Department. She accepted and decided to delay graduate school.

This teaching experience revealed to her the usefulness of her training. "I realized that my training in linguistics and the English language did really help me help the students who were in the program." While teaching the students first-year composition, she began thinking about the process of writing and observed that "given what [the students in the summer program] were saying and doing, that they [didn't understand] what they wanted to do." She took a "problems-based" approach to the issues they presented her, asking them, "What is the task? What kinds of things do you already have at your fingertips? What kinds of questions do you need to ask yourself?" Her approach worked well and propelled her to reconsider her career plans.

Royster's interest in teaching writing was developing just as her friend and former classmate began to explore the doctor of arts program at the University of Michigan. Royster went along with her friend for an informational meeting about the DA program; in the end, both applied and were accepted. She crafted a course of study that would continue her master's work and fill gaps in her knowledge, which included contemporary language theories and methodologies for language study. "I really did love that program," Royster said. "I felt that I was just learning everything, and of course, we were at the University of Michigan, which is a very intellectually stimulating environment. I was surrounded by people who were doing all of these incredibly interesting things. So I was excited about every course I took," including in the emerging fields of cultural studies, women's studies, and "rhetorical studies, [which] was emerging in a different way from composition studies." For her dissertation, "Communicating in Writing: A Rhetorical Model for Developing Composition Skills," Royster returned to the site where her interest in the teaching of writing began: the problems her students experienced in first-year composition. Her observations "ended up being translated into my dissertation project, in which I developed a rhetorical model for the development of communication skills."

At the age of 24, Royster earned her doctor of arts degree and accepted a teaching position at Clayton Junior College in Morrow, Georgia. The following year she accepted a position at her alma mater, Spelman College, beginning a 16-year career as a tenure-track professor of English and administrator (she was made assistant dean at the age of 28). In 1992, Royster and her husband took positions at Ohio State, where they are both academic administrators.

Strategies for Success

Graduate School

Royster emphasized that her career decisions have always been guided by her ability to pursue work that was interesting to her. In college she learned that she was "pretty good at everything," so when given a choice, she pursued work she enjoyed. In her first year in college, she sailed through her biology course, so her professor tried to persuade her to consider majoring in science. She responded, "'Don't you have to do math with that? … Then no!,'" and laughed. She explained,

> [A]lmost all my decisions have been triggered by whether I like doing something or not. It's not that I had grand goals to do anything. I haven't done anything that I can think of that was really a specific goal other than school. I had a goal to finish college. I had the goal to go to graduate school. Once I got into graduate school and realized that I didn't want to teach at the public school level, I had a goal to have a doctorate degree. At first it was a PhD, but I liked thinking about writing and thinking about rhetoric, and there was no way in 1971 [to study that], so I had to make one [a program] up. The place that I was able to make that up was the University of Michigan's doctor of arts program. So even that wasn't a goal. That was because that structure allowed me to do something that I wanted to think about.

While Royster said that she wouldn't recommend this way of making decisions "for most people," her strategy clearly worked for her. By ensuring that she had interesting work to do rather than pursuing the most recommended paths, she moved into each phase of her career with energy and passion. However, she acknowledged that such an approach carries liabilities. Royster chose a DA degree over a PhD, which carried less prestige in the 1970s, and, as she explained, "If you care about those things, then you don't choose a doctor of arts."

To discover a graduate program that would meet her needs, she "poured through university catalogs to actually look at descriptions of courses." When searching for a master's program, she closely reviewed the catalogs of graduate-level English courses at the University of Michigan, Massachusetts Institute of Technology, the University of California at Berkeley, Brown University, and Indiana University, among others. "I don't know if students actually do that these days, but I did," she said. She chose Michigan for the MA and when she wanted further training, she again chose Michigan for their doctor of arts program because it permitted her to study what she wanted to study at a high-quality institution.

> [T]he reason the program was attractive to me was that there were only two core courses: one was popular culture and the other was (I forgot what it was called), but it was … about how language worked, what we know from across disciplines that would have bearing on what it means to construct pedagogies for teaching writing … . They used this wonderful range of readings that helped me to rethink everything I knew about the history of English—which was already a strong suit for me—about people's perceptions of communication and how it works, how it breaks down.

The program allowed her to study rhetoric and writing (primarily through linguistics) before graduate programs in rhetoric and composition existed. So an important strategy for Royster was knowing what she wanted to study and carefully researching programs to find the right one.

Social Responsibility

Royster grew up in a small, segregated Southern town, and she clearly shares the social ethic she learned there. Taking a third-grade teaching position was not so much about Royster's natural interests, but rather about fulfilling a responsibility to her community. "I was raised to be socially responsible," she said, so when the principal of the African American elementary school in Greensboro offered Royster and her friends jobs following their graduation, "all three accepted." Later, when she encountered a troubling, arbitrary administrative decision at Spelman that delayed her tenure case (discussed below), she chose not to sue the individual involved because she would, in effect, be suing her own community (Spelman was her alma mater as well as her employer). Of this decision she said, "My ethical position was Spelman was my school. I don't sue my school. That was an ethical choice. I feel that ethical choices happen in people's lives more than you think, and I try to be very conscious of that."

Her willingness to challenge the pervasive racism of mostly white institutions and organizations is based on this ethic, and one needs only to consider her mother's courageous witness—before *Brown v. Board of Education*—to see where Royster's inclination to speak out comes from. We witnessed it during a meeting of the Coalition of Women in the History of Rhetoric, which included in its title "Lifting As We Climb," the motto of the National Association of Colored Women. During the Q&A following the panel presentation, Royster asked the chair (who was a white feminist, as was most of the audience), if she knew where this motto came from, and made the point that, too often, white academics borrow the intellectual work of African Americans without crediting them. In her interview, Royster brought up this case as an example of the importance of being "true to my own cultural, social, and political identity, and to be steadfast, when it seems worth it, about letting people know when they are violating things, even when they are friends." She continued,

> On the surface it seems very innocent, because the theme was "Lifting As We Climb," but there was no acknowledgement of how clearly that phrase or that clause is tied to black women's experience. There was no acknowledgement of that. Well, you know, among friends I could have let that go, but my ethical backbone would not allow that. So I had to speak up and in public. Because of the nature of the program, speaking up in public was the only way to do it. If I hadn't spoken up, there would have been a whole room of people who would not have been pointed to the fact that we owe a debt. We could talk about it as plagiarism. That's the kind of thing, and there are little things like that, that kind of make life difficult.

Royster affectionately called her mother and herself "knuckle-brains" for speaking out when doing so was bound to "make life difficult." But for Royster, ethical commitments and family come before all else.

Tenure and Promotion

Royster has been an administrator for most of her career, beginning only two years into her appointment at Spelman as an untenured assistant professor. "If I had been advising me," Royster retrospectively noted, "I would have said to me, 'don't do that,' but nobody was advising me." Her list of responsibilities was long. She was assistant dean for freshman studies for three years, developing in the general education curriculum a strong focus on writing, reading, and critical thinking as co-director of the College-wide Writing Program, with Pauline Drake, Dean for Faculty Development. The program included a writing center and a writing-across-the-curriculum (which she established and directed) and a faculty development program, which her colleague coordinated. She was then promoted to associate dean for advising, revamping the college's advisory systems. When Spelman's newly founded Women's Research and Resource Center (for which she had been a member of the organizing team) established a research associate position, she stepped away from the academic dean's office to fill it. After this appointment, she had intended to rejoin the ranks of full-time faculty in order to spend more time on her research and teaching. However, while Royster was associate dean, Spelman had submitted a proposal for Title VI funding which included support for the writing program, changing the title to the "Comprehensive Writing Program." When the funding was granted, the president and the dean for institutional development approached Royster and pleaded with her to head the program, since she had helped write the grant. Royster responded, "Why don't you hire somebody? But they didn't do it." She agreed and held the position from 1983 until she left Spelman nine years later.

Her administrative appointments directly interfered with her achievement of tenure. Unbeknownst to her, with her appointment to assistant dean in 1978 she had, in effect, given up her tenure-track appointment. The president had indeed assured Royster that the administrative post would permit her to retain a tenure-track status, but their agreement was not in writing. Royster recalled, "trusting my home institution, I didn't pay attention to how that line kind of dropped out of my contract after two years." In her sixth year at Spelman, she prepared her dossier for tenure and promotion, and the president informed her that she was "not eligible" for tenure and promotion. Blindsided, Royster responded,

> "What are you talking about, I'm not eligible?" You know, I was still teaching. I was still developing curricula. I was still running academic programs. It wasn't your run-of-the-mill administrative stuff. I was coordinating all of the support programs, all of the tutoring programs. I was running one for the writing program. I was teaching one course a term, and I was active in 4Cs. I was really hurt. I was so taken aback and really disappointed that a person at an institution that I was loyal to would stab me in the back. So his compromise was that he was willing for me to complete my portfolio for promotion—I actually had more in mine than most people who were teaching full-time had in theirs—but that I would be promoted without tenure. Which was unheard of. I had never heard of that. So, I was the only person, I felt, in the United States of America who was promoted before being tenured.

The bottom line for Royster was that during those years she was very busy serving the institution, and she had trusted the Spelman administration not to abuse her loyalty and trust. Thereafter, when Royster accepted new administrative positions, she "had them put everything in writing, and … paid attention" to each contract renewal she signed.

Royster went back on the tenure clock once she left the dean's office (which she did immediately upon learning she was not eligible for tenure as a dean). But her tenure case, which was, as readers can imagine, a slam-dunk, was held up yet again when she became involved in a political controversy involving the president. She was "elected faculty representative to the Board of Trustees as an untenured faculty member," which is, she said, "another thing that I would not advise my students to do." Service in this position required Royster to compose reports.

> I wrote a report that the President didn't like and during the year that I was being reviewed! You know, nothing like being knuckle-brained. Now, even if I had been aware that there were consequences, I wouldn't have taken one word out of it. So, I'm not saying that even if I had known I never would have said it. *But*, if I were to advise others about a similar situation, I would point out the necessity of such a decision being a deliberate choice, so that the person is aware that there is something risky about doing such things.

And indeed, there were consequences. Her file breezed through the review process, but when it reached the president, he refused to act on it. "He didn't say no. He just refused to put it forward to the Board of Trustees. What he told me was that he was just afraid that the Board would say no. So I said, 'You should've let them make that decision.'"

In the end, the president sat on Royster's tenure file until the next year, a move she considered to be politically motivated. Royster recalled, "I knew that there were only about three people at the whole college who had a better record than I had, even though I had spent four years as an administrator. And what I did was to annotate for him my vitae and to say, based on an external evaluation that I solicited and received in support of my case, that I had all the evidence I needed to sue him and the institution." She chose not to say another word about the case, however, and did not reapply for tenure as instructed. The next year the president took her then year-old file to the Board, "and it was unanimously passed." Royster, already an associate professor, was then, finally, granted tenure.

Royster regrets two key decisions in her pre-tenure years: 1) taking an administrative appointment so early in her career, and 2) failing to keep track of changes made to her contract. Having accepted an elected position to the Board of Trustees before tenure, she would not have rewritten any of the reports she presented, even given the consequences for her tenure, but she would not advise others to accept such a high-profile position without tenure.

Promotion to Full Professor

In 1992, Royster moved to the Ohio State University. She had fully expected to "die at [her] desk [at] Spelman," but Ohio State offered positions to both her and her husband. He had been serving as assistant dean for freshman studies at Morehouse College. Of the move, Royster commented,

> One of the things that made [OSU] attractive to me was that it was the first time I got a rhet/comp community. But what I left was a black women's community, so you lose and you win … . [But the gain] was having that community and being [at] a Research One university, where I was supposed to be able to do my own work. That's what I struggled so hard to do at Spelman, because it was a small liberal arts college, and there wasn't that much support for research. There wasn't that much time for it. Here it was supposed to be different. Well, how many hours was I here before [I was asked] to be director of the writing center?" [She laughed.]

Directing the writing center was difficult but enjoyable work that inevitably delayed progress on *Traces of a Stream.*

> I came with all but two chapters done, with work done on those two, but the first two years I was concentrating on that program [the Writing Center]. Because I was the first official faculty director, I was concentrating on setting that up well, and I really didn't mind doing it because as I recall, I was the only one in the department who had really run a writing center before. I hadn't been in a research context, but you know, I'd been a national consultant for writing centers, so I had some sense that I could really do it well. So, I took two years trying to get structures in place that would allow it to function as a unit with a faculty liaison who could garner a little bit more visibility and authority for it as a substantive program and one that could actually be a research site for graduate students. I thought I was well on my way, but then the budget went bad. They cut me [the Writing Center] in half, and I quit. I was really furious, because I felt that I had taken away two years of time from my own work for something that the university was committed to that it clearly *wasn't* committed to. I was *furious* … . I was ready to leave by then.

Royster didn't leave, however, because "Well, I just hate moving so much, so I cooled down and I didn't go. I said to myself fine, I'll just concentrate on my own work. So, that was the more important battle for me." She completed her book, was promoted to full in 2000 (for the second time, since her promotion to full at Spelman in 1992 was confirmed at the very same time that she accepted the offer to move to Ohio State).

Administration

Because Royster has spent so much of her career as an administrator, her advice in this area is particularly relevant. She acknowledged that the reason so many rhetoric and composition scholars are tapped for administrative roles is that they are so willing to take on the job. And indeed, they are trained well for work. "[W]e actually have some skills across the board that make us easy to tap [for administration]. The other thing is that we are people-centered and that's one of the skills [that enables successful academic administration]." But Royster's experiences at Spelman changed her approach to administrative work. "[T]here wasn't anything that they could have asked me to do that I would not have tried to do, and that's what got me into trouble in the first place. I didn't have anybody to say to me, there are some things that they shouldn't be asking you to do." In advising others, Royster said scholars in rhetoric and composition should ask some key questions before accepting administrative work. "[W]hat do you get out of it based on what you put into it? How do you balance administration with your own work?" She argued that women should not say yes to something just because they can do it or just because they feel socially responsible for their institution. "Unfortunately for us, not only are we talented people, we are trained very usefully to do lots and lots of things. My advice is to be careful what you say yes to. Stop acting like an amoeba that can absorb everything. My self-reflection is to think twice about whether I *should* do something just because I know I *can* do it well."

Mentoring

Royster strongly believes in the importance of mentoring others. "I do explain to students that the notion of mentorship is a relatively new thing, and you could not in the past count on anyone to really give you advice or try to help you make decisions that were positive, or negative, really. So, I didn't have mentors as such, but I did have people who cared about me and supported me." Throughout our interview with her, Royster repeatedly stressed that she would not advise *most* people to follow in her footsteps. The qualification is important. From Royster's point of view, students and untenured faculty need help in considering the *consequences* of their choices. The purpose of mentoring is not to advise others on what choices they should make, but rather to make known the possible consequences of their actions. A good decision accords with one's life principles, which only an individual can know. Therefore, what Royster wishes she had had early in her career was someone who could have explained to her what her institution was supposed to do for her (and, more importantly, not do *to* her) and to warn her about the potential risks of the choices she made.

One of the consequences of choosing rhetoric and composition as a career is its status within institutions, particularly English departments. For Royster, choosing our field was a deliberate choice, but not an easy one. She advises students accordingly.

> Why would anybody choose rhet/comp in light of the power structures in English studies? Right? … So, I always encourage graduate students to be very deliberate about the choices that they make … . I don't say, you know, this [the field of rhetoric and composition] is great. I do acknowledge that there are jobs, but I don't make the politics of those jobs seem simple. The politics of those jobs is not simple.

She offered two examples. When she was fighting the battle for tenure at Spelman, she had to write a professor at Michigan and ask him to explain her area of specialization within English studies to Spelman's president. Her second example was about how her colleagues at Spelman viewed rhetoric and composition. She laughed and said, "I remember the conversation quite well. Everyone [in the English Department] at Spelman taught writing, and they were committed to teaching writing. I had to explain that still their commitment to composition was a little 'c,' and mine was a big 'C.'"

Mentoring is particularly important for students from underrepresented groups. At Ohio State, Royster grew concerned that so few African American students were going on for further graduate work in English. The problem seemed to be a lack of attention to the students on the part of the faculty. She gave an example of a student she had in one of her classes.

> He was one of the best writers that I had ever had in my class, and he had a good solid GPA as a major and generally. He was quite well-spoken. He was an active participant in class, and he had never had a conversation with a faculty member in the department before I talked with him. He was a senior. Nobody had asked if he ever thought about going to graduate school. I was the first person. His dad is a lawyer, and so he was headed to law school. That's an example of where our problem is.

Students from underrepresented groups were simply invisible to the mostly white faculty in her department. While her example is of undergraduate English majors, her point can be extrapolated to graduate students, part-time and untenured faculty as well as to who may be less likely to score informal mentoring from professors in the majority culture.

Race and Academe

In *Traces of a Stream*, Royster reveals her frustration with the frequent resistance her project on the literate practices of black women received while she was writing it. White audiences simply couldn't believe that black women were literate (on any level) before Emancipation. No one thought that Royster had any material for her book. In her Chair's address to the CCCC, she tells another story of a white student who wanted to hear Royster speak in her "real" voice (which the student assumed to be Black English Vernacular). For Royster, racism in academe is most pernicious (and persistent) in its undervaluing and misinterpretations of African Americans.

These struggles are consistent facets of her everyday life that "come along with being African American and female in the United States of America." Racist behavior is so consistent that she simply ignores much of it. When she does choose to pay attention, her responses are "quite automated." She offered an example. "After I had become vice chair, I was in a meeting in which people who should have known better were talking about students at risk in the English major." It soon became clear to me in the conversation "that they were thinking of these students as black students." But she knew that the English department had no idea who the at-risk students really were. So she asked, "'Do you have a way of finding out who all of these African American English majors are and what their record is?'" The Director of Undergraduate Studies said yes, and so they reviewed the African American students' records.

> Well, all of them were strong students. They were not all straight As.

> Almost to a one they were good B students—you know, that proverbial black B. So, I said, "What makes you think that these students are any more at risk than any other students?" I would say the problem with our students of color generally, and with African American students in particular, is that they get absolutely no attention from anyone in the English department.

Royster's point in telling this story was that discrimination is pervasive and people like herself often have to ignore much of it in order to sustain a positive attitude. However, she noted that what she and other African American women put up with on a regular basis would be considered real battles if encountered by others. Because there are so many such incidents, they are often called upon to downgrade them as background noise in order to do their work. Women of color must learn, then, to choose when to speak up and when to let the race and gender politics go on by. But, most importantly, they still have to "consider" what they say in response to the behaviors of colleagues and be cognizant of not allowing the persistence of this behavior to affect the foundations on which they stand. As Royster said of herself, "I'm too self-defined" to allow that to happen.

Having a Life

Given the race and gender politics of higher education that Royster conceded she faced on a regular basis, we wondered what she did when the politics *did* get to her. She responded that her real problem was not in "feeling down" from others' behavior, but rather in handling her anger towards them.

> [W]hen I get so mad that I know I run the risk of saying things to people that I will regret, I take myself home because I do—on an individual basis—like most of the people that I know. I haven't met too many people that I really dislike. There are lots of people that I'm impatient with, but there are not too many people that I dislike. So, I don't want to have my frustrations push me to say things that are unconsidered. When I get really, really angry, what is likely to come up might just come out without me thinking about it. When I can't find patience, I know that there are people whom I can call that I can say to, "I know that I'm not the one who's crazy," and they will say, "You're right,"—or not as the case may be.

Royster was quite clear that life is elsewhere, that her job is not her life, not her foundation or source of stability: "This job doesn't get me there. It's not capable of getting me there." What does provide her security is family and friendships. A clear source of support is her family (Royster married Patrick Royster in 1980; her daughter Rebecca was born in 1982, her son Giles in 1984). "Now when I really need love and warmth," Royster stated, "I go home to my mom." Another source of support is being in contact with long-term friends who make her feel "joyful." "Fortunately," she noted, "I do make the kind of salary where I can put myself on a plane" to visit friends when she needs to be rejuvenated. Or, "I can pick up the telephone."

Royster has three key values that guide her in her career. First, she only chooses things to do that interest her. Second, she tries to keep her priorities straight, "and none of them are job-related." Third, people in her life count. As she put it, "There is nothing in any job that I can imagine that would cause me to subvert my commitment to my family or what makes me feel like I'm living a good and ethical life."

15

CYNTHIA L. SELFE

Cynthia L. Selfe is currently Humanities Distinguished Professor at the Ohio State University, where she teaches courses in computers and composition, a relatively recent specialty that her scholarship has helped to define. She is the author of several books examining digital literacy and computer-assisted instruction, including her most recent *Technology and Literacy in the Twenty-First Century: The Perils of Not Paying Attention*. In addition, she has co-authored and co-edited 16 books, including her most recent (with Gail Hawisher) *Literate Lives in the Information Age* and *Writing New Media: Theory and Applications for Expanding the Teaching of Composition* (with Anne Wysocki, Johndan Johnson-Eilola, and Geoffrey Sirc). She is also a founding editor of the journal *Computers and Composition*, and she continues to serve, along with Hawisher, as the print editor of that journal today. She has served as Chair of the Conference on College Composition and Communication (1997–98) and on several key NCTE and MLA committees that deal with computers and composition interests. She earned her Master's of Education from the University of Texas at Austin 1977 and then her doctoral degree, again from UT, in 1981, focusing on curriculum and instruction as well as English and composing processes. Following her graduation from Texas, Selfe was hired by Art Young, then the Head of the Humanities Department at Michigan Technological University. She earned tenure at Michigan Tech in 1987. She was promoted to full in 1991 and served as Chair of the Humanities Department until 1999. While on the faculty of Michigan Tech, Selfe served as a Visiting Professor of Composition and Communication at Clemson University and as the Watson Professor at the University of Louisville. In 2005, she left to join the faculty at the Ohio State University.

Background

Selfe was born in Rochester, New York, and lived there until the age of six, when she moved to Richmond, Virginia. When she was twelve, her family moved to Philadelphia, and when she was sixteen they moved to Houston, Texas, where she attended Memorial High School and where she met her future husband, Richard J. Selfe, Jr. ("Dickie"), a student at that very same high school.

She graduated in the bottom eighth of her class—and she was grateful to do so. "I was not college material," she laughed, but given the fact that her parents were "professional people and had gone to college," she was sent to Stevens College, "which was in those days a finishing school, or thought of as a finishing school, and it was an if-you-have-enough-money-you're-in kind of thing." Selfe majored in equestrian sciences, but she fell off a lot of horses, and after waking up in a hospital "with all kinds of injuries," she decided she'd choose another major: English. One might say, then, that Selfe is an "accidental academic" in the field of rhetoric and composition.

Selfe acknowledged that there was no great motivation behind her decision to major in English: "I don't know. I just have always liked to read and my parents were great readers, and I always thought reading was pleasant." Not painful, like falling off horses, nor "grotesque" like working as a journalist, which Selfe experienced while attending college. During the summers, Selfe returned to Texas, where she would work as a "stringer" for the local papers. A "stringer," Selfe explained, is a journalist hired on "a part-time or temporary basis," assigned to do the stories that no one else wants to do, like "feature stories on giant zucchinis and wild bees, and obituaries, [and] city council meetings." As she chased down stories, she realized there were problems with the profession.

> The awful part of it was that you had to go bother people when they were going through horrible times, like if someone got killed, you had to go pester their relatives for the story. I came to the conclusion that newspaper people, or the reporters I worked with, I should say, acted badly, and dressed badly, and were badly paid. And they were mostly guys. In fact there were no women. And I thought that that was grotesque. I thought, "Why do I want to hang around these folks?" So, I decided not to do that for a living.

She decided instead to teach.

In "the arrogance of youth," she found Stevens College "too parochial … because we had to dress for dinner, and it was known as a finishing school even though it wasn't—it was an all-women's school, and a good one, but I was a poor student." She and her roommate decided they wanted to finish their degrees elsewhere. Their favorite textbooks helped them decide where to go: her roommate "took out the psychology book. I took out the English textbook. And we looked in the back to see where the people who had contributed to the book had gone to school, and we picked our schools based on that. She chose Auburn and some other place. And, I chose Stanford and Wisconsin. Stanford turned me down flat, and Wisconsin took me. I was lucky." She hadn't yet experienced a major in English, so her decision was like a spin of the "wheel of fortune." Fortunately, she found the right degree. "I got a degree in teaching secondary school in English. So, that was very pleasant. I always liked to teach, too—I like kids, and I liked the satisfaction of teaching … . And I liked to read."

After receiving her degree from Wisconsin, she applied for the Peace Corps but was denied, because she "had been protesting a little bit too much and was on somebody's black list." So, she responded to a notice she saw on a bulletin board, which led her to teach for a while in Auckinloch, a small coal-mining town in Scotland. When she returned to the States, she moved back to Houston, Texas, where her parents lived, and found a teaching position at "a very small school in an all-black school district outside of Houston." She credited the students at this institution with teaching her "what it meant to teach." To explain, she said, "Let me just describe the first day, before lunch."

> I went into the classroom. I taught the Combined Vocational Academic Education class—18 males and no females in the class. I went in there having taught at the University of Wisconsin high school. I thought I knew what to do. Right? So I went in there the first day and thought I'd give a diagnostic test and find out what they know. I had it all typed and paper-clipped and stapled. It was good-looking. I had them sitting in rows, I handed it out, and I said, "I want you to take a lot of time, to be very careful. I really want to know what you know so I can do a better job of teaching you." I told them to "take your time, check your work, and raise your hand when you are finished," and by the time I got to the 18th kid, the first kid in the first row had his hand up. I said, "Can I help you? Do you have a question?" He said, "No, I'm finished." And I said, "No, I really want you to take your time. I really want to know what you know. I want you to check your answers … ." He said, "No, I'm finished." So, I picked up his paper and on the front page, in big, bold, carefully printed block letters, was his message "FUCK YOU!" So, that was the first teaching experience I had. Later when I told that story to Marilyn Cooper, she said, "Boy, that student was smart!" And she was right; that student knew exactly what kind of help I was prepared to give him—not much.

She learned that she had a long way to go as a teacher, and buckled down to the job for the next three years

Meanwhile, Dickie Selfe wrote her letters, knowing that they "were going to be together. He just knew that—he said he knew that from the beginning." However, she "didn't even consider him a possibility." Although she was now in Houston where Dickie and his family lived, he was away working on his undergraduate degree at Texas Tech University and then his master's degree at the University of Texas. As she said, he "kept writing and kept writing and kept writing." "Eventually," she told us, after eight years of letters, "he just wore me down," and the "idea of marrying Dickie just sort of grew on me." So, Selfe moved to Austin to be with him, and thanks to an unknown University of Texas graduate student "who got pregnant the day before the term was about to begin and turned down a teaching assistantship," she was funded for study and began her graduate work. "I was an unpromising undergraduate, and I was lucky to get into college, and the only reason I got into graduate school was because … they were desperate! So, I … started the next day in English Education, because I wanted to learn more about teaching … because [as my previous experience demonstrated] it was very clear that I knew very little about what I was doing." She went on to earn her master's and PhD degrees from the University of Texas in Curriculum and Instruction.

When she graduated with her doctorate, Selfe didn't apply for jobs because she hadn't been advised to do so.

> I didn't know you *had* to search for a job. I didn't even think about it. Good grief, I didn't even think I'd graduate! MLA happened to be in Dallas, and the 4Cs was in Houston. So, another graduate student told me I should go … . So I went to Dallas and the MLA, and I walked into this hotel. I checked in and got on the elevator, and saw this woman, Carol Berkenkotter, whom I had met at Linda Flower's protocol workshop at Carnegie Mellon while I was doing my dissertation. Linda Flower was very kind and let me come for free as a graduate student. And I got into the elevator and Carol said, "What are you doing here?" And I said, "I think I'm supposed to be looking for a job." She said, "Well, we have a job at Michigan Tech. Do you want to meet Art Young?" And I said, "Yeah!" She introduced me to Art Young, and he walked me across a set of railroad tracks to have a barbeque sandwich with Bill Powers, who was then Dean of Humanities at Michigan Tech, and that was the job I got. [T]hat was how I searched for a job. It was very good. It was very swell. That was it. So, that was 1980, and folks they didn't exactly search for jobs like they do now. Now, they're all very smart about the process!

As a result of that serendipitous elevator encounter, Selfe landed a position—or, in her words, "stumbled into a job"—as a tenure-track assistant professor at Michigan Technological University.

It was at MTU that she developed an interest in computers and writing. Like the position at MTU, she says the specialization came to her. She recalled, "So I got to Michigan Tech, and I didn't know much about computers or anything. But I had used one to type my dissertation and in 1980 that made me an expert. And that's how I got into computers." Her arrival coincided with the release of the first fully assembled microcomputers in the United States. Because she had some computing experience, the Department of Humanities let her run with it. "The University said, 'Look, this is a microcomputer.' And I said, 'That's cool.' So, we decided to use those, and that was it. I did not plan to go into technology studies or anything." It wasn't long before Selfe turned her nascent expertise into a subfield: computers and composition.

Strategies for Success

Mentoring

Selfe's tale of having "stumbled into a job" indicates that she did not receive a lot of mentoring about the process of applying, interviewing, and finding a job. Selfe concurred. "Mostly I would say my peers mentored me. Although I wouldn't say that the faculty didn't *try* to help me. They *really* tried to help me—but I was such a slow learner!" She did identify faculty who mentored her in various ways—Jim Kinneavy, Lester Faigley, Steve Witte, Maxine Hairston, and Ed Farrell, who, she claimed, "taught [her] how to write, which was something you should try to figure out how to do by the time you are graduating with a PhD." But mainly, during her graduate school days, she pointed to her peers—Hugh Burns, Tom Miller, Tom Newkirk, Sue Rodi—as her main mentors. She wrote an article with Sue Rodi, and she learned how to use a computer from Hugh Burns. Once at Michigan Tech, she found Art Young, then the Head of the department, to be a generous mentor, and during our interview with her, she referred to him multiple times as providing various forms of support—funding for *Computers and Composition* and help through the tenure process, as well as serving as an ideal model for administrative style and research productivity.

When asked if she, herself, now mentors, she responded emphatically:

> I hope I do. I would like to think I do. I never consider it that formal of a thing. But I would hope that I mentor in the editorial work that I do, both the book series and the journal. I hope that I mentor in the graduate program and the undergraduate program. But any of those relationships that I have seem to be so two-way, you know, there's a duality that's going on there. If it's a mentoring relationship, I can never tell which way it is going. So, it's a lot of give and take with people I like to be around, whether they are graduate students or undergraduates, or authors that we are dealing with or whatever. But I would like to think that in that there are times when I'm doing things that help other people—and especially women. I'm very conscious of that. I would say that if there is something I have a bias about in my life, which I do, I certainly have lots of them, but I have a bias towards working with women. I notice that I hire women, or ask women to help out on the journal or do a book.

Indeed, she makes a conscious effort to support other women by providing them opportunities to publish in both *Computers and Composition* and in her book series. She said, "We try to have feminist values and gender neutral language in the journal; we try to get women graduate students to serve as the associate editor of the journal, as well as men." In the early days of the journal, she remembers that she and Gail had to fight with their publishers to change the style so that women's work would be recognized. She said, "[W]e changed our bibliographic style so that we don't use only the first initials only of authors. We include an author's full name because people—reading first initials only—might think, by default, that the author is a male .... We think about this kind of small potent gesture every time we do projects."

Although Selfe has never been professionally hurt by a female colleague, she does observe that there are women who exhibit symptoms of "Queen Bee Syndrome," where a woman "makes it" and "then doesn't seem to want to help other women." She said, "I have been conscious of that. And I try *not* to do that." Her advice to junior faculty trying to deal with a Queen Bee?

> I think all I can tell that person is what I would do .... I would try to tell that young faculty member what her strengths were, try to provide her plenty of options to do work away from that person or without that person, and tell her that she is going to encounter people like that all along her life. That's a scant comfort, but that's the truth. You're always going to have people in your life who aren't always interested in your success. If you pay attention to those people, or ... if you let their *problems* flavor your life, then you've lost the battle; you've *become* them. My advice is, "Hey, look, you've got to look after yourself. Here's the cool work you can do here. Here are the opportunities. If opportunity knocks, open the door. Do your work. Do what you want to do. Have some fun. And ignore the behavior that is unproductive, because if you let it influence you, you *become* that problem or that kind of person. You can do better than that."

Tenure

When Selfe went up for tenure, the requirements for tenure and promotion did not include the now-current tenure touchstone of the "single-authored book." Rather, she told us, her scholarship at Michigan Tech requirement was "an article a year or something like that." MTU was beginning to focus on scholarship as a requirement for tenure. She said,

> [W]hen I first came to Michigan Tech, tenure was granted after four years .... [H]alfway through my run at tenure, they changed the decision to the sixth year, and also the requirements became more oriented toward scholarly publication. Teaching was still considered very important, and service, of course, was just stuff you did for the department. I think over the years that I spent within the profession, publication and scholarship have been an increasingly important part.

Her progress toward promotion and tenure was smooth, because the Head of the department (Art Young) was "a great feminist, even in those days," supportive of women, hiring them, giving them prominent roles in the department. She did not feel as if there were any gender-related obstacles to her work, because "Michigan Tech was just so pleased to have women. And we were very important to its diversity." The only potential obstacle, in retrospect, was the fact that her degree was in English Education and not in English, but by the time she figured out that it might be an issue, she told us, it was no longer an issue.

Administration

Although many junior faculty are warned against accepting administrative roles prior to tenure, Selfe assumed several such positions, including director of the writing center and a member of the writing across the curriculum research group before she received tenure, and then the director of the Scientific and Technical Communication program and director of graduate teaching assistant education after receiving tenure. No stranger to administration—and grateful for the opportunities, Selfe claimed that it is not always unwise "to assume a job as a WPA, or director of the writing center as a junior faculty member." On the contrary, she argued, accepting such roles can be a "healthy" choice because it provides the opportunity for a multi-dimensional career:

> It's a one-dimensional kind of life when all your attention is focused on scholarly production. You must feel like a cog, like you crank out the articles. You're not cranking them out for a reason, like to be a better teacher, or be better at mentoring graduate assistants, or to talk to your colleagues. Scholarship is an exchange, a dialogue, and an examination, a reflection on your own teaching, for your work in an institution and a profession. It shouldn't be scholarship for its own sake. There's no inherent value in pieces of paper .... So, it seems to me that limiting those opportunities is not always the right answer. I can understand when people are overburdened by work and attention to bureaucratic issues. But, I also think if you integrate scholarship into your administrative work, your service work, your teaching work, that you can make opportunities within the duties of that job.

When asked about junior faculty who serve as a WPA pre-tenure but whose scholarship is not in the teaching of writing, Selfe said that she would advise such a person to *find* something to publish on that grows out of her administrative experience.

After she received tenure and promotion, Selfe served as Assistant Chair of the Humanities Department at Michigan Tech, and finally Chair of that same department, a position she found very challenging. Indeed, when asked if there were one thing she could do over in her academic career, she responded, "I would have liked to have done a better job as a chair. Because I think that it is such an important job to make an environment in which faculty and students can succeed." Again, she pointed to Art Young as the model: "He was very smart about making a good working environment for faculty, … one within which people could succeed and within which they feel valued and know that their contributions were important to the department. He was very good at that." When asked the most difficult part of the job, she responded:

> I think trying to live your theory. We're very quick to spout democratic sorts of theory and liberatory pedagogy, … but how do you fashion a curriculum that reflects your theory, how do you shape a faculty meeting? How do you foster an environment in which staff and faculty and students can work together? How do you substantiate theory in the daily fabric of people's lives?

In addition, Selfe admitted that she is "a bit of a control freak," so she found it difficult when problems arose that she couldn't "control or help or fix." Inevitably, such problems lead to conflict, and, as Selfe put it, "I'd prefer not to see conflict or problems or anything like that because I want to get in there and fix it. It's a very limited way of thinking, isn't it? Because conflict is a part of growth."

Productivity/Integrating Research

One of the most astonishing and inspiring characteristics of Selfe's working style is her ability to integrate her scholarship, academic and administrative service, teaching, and life outside academe. Whereas most academics live a "fragmented" life, roughly represented by a series of conflicting demands—40 percent research, 40 percent teaching, 20 percent service, and life, which is elsewhere—Selfe reported that she leads a "pretty seamless" life, in that her various professional activities are integrated. Again, she attributed Art Young with providing her with the blueprint for such an achievement.

> Art was very good in helping us [turn … teaching and administrative work] into scholarly work. So Art and Toby [Fulwiler] would get a book contract, and say, "Let's write about this!" and ask us to write, so we would write chapters for that book. It was more that they led us through the process of making our teaching and administrative work into the subject of our study, so that the scholarship and the teaching were never separate for me. And the scholarship and the administration were never separate, either, They were all the same thing. And I think that's one of the reasons I've been able to be so productive, because I don't have to separate those parts of my life. So, when I'm doing something, I'm thinking, do other colleagues have to do this? How can I write about it? What am I doing that other people might want to know about? Are other people experiencing these same challenges? And it

> becomes a very integrated way of thinking of your academic life, where service and teaching and academic scholarship are one thing.

Her publications, then, represent her responses to questions or problems that arose as she attended to teaching and administrative tasks. It is for this reason that she believes junior faculty can be productive scholars while serving in administrative positions.

Selfe's writing style is a further manifestation of her belief in integration. Whereas most scholars set aside a block of time to write, often at home where they will be uninterrupted, Selfe works on her writing between appointments and teaching. She reported, "I always write in my office. I very seldom take work home … . I always write in the interstices of my day … . I write in little bitty chunks and all the time … in between students, in between meetings with colleagues." She admitted that "[i]t's a very unusual writing style." Again, she credited Art Young for this practice. "Art always taught me to have two or three writing projects going at all times. He compared it to a stovetop. You know, you have one or two big pots on the back burner, but you always have a little pot on the front burner. You do some second-tier journals and some first-tier journals." As her day permitted, she said, she "attended to writing when [she] could."

Another characteristic of her writing style—and productivity—is collaborating with other authors. We asked her, given the emphasis on and value of single-authored manuscripts, whether untenured faculty who wish to collaborate should worry about doing so. She responded:

> I think you should be concerned about it, and I think you should know what the terrain is like at your home institution … . You should find out how collaboration is viewed at your institution. You should help educate people about the nature of collaboration, and you should meet the requirements at your institution … . But with that given, I think collaboration is a much better way of going about the process because you bring multiple perspectives to bear on some of these really strong problems or difficult issues, so you can do a better job with them … . [And] I do think you can be more productive if you collaborate than you can be when you're not.

Finding a good collaborator is the key. Like Andrea A. Lunsford, Selfe works primarily with one colleague—Gail Hawisher—with whom she has collaborated for many years. Selfe could not praise Hawisher enough: "She brings 120 percent to any collaborative project. So, she never is late on a deadline; she is always professional; she is smart as a whip; she knows exactly what to do; *and* she has a memory like an elephant! Every success of my career I really do owe to Gail—she makes me do better work than I think I can."

Having a Life

Selfe's collaborative and integrated writing and research styles, not surprisingly, manifest themselves in her approach to her entire life. The traditional separation between work and home life simply do not apply to her. "My work and my life are the same thing," she admitted. "I really do have a life and Dickie is a marvelous part of that. Dickie … is right there [working at the same institution], so we carry our work home and carry our home to work." Selfe and Dickie never had children. When asked if the decision not to have kids had anything to do with her professional life, she responded:

> I suppose it did. I just had never thought I'd make a particularly good parent. And I know some really good parents … . So, it just didn't seem like something I could do well, and I thought parenting was so important of a thing that I had better leave it up to someone who was really good at it. We know some excellent parental role models—and they do great work.

She and Dickie have two dogs: an Australian shepherd named Gracie and a mutt, Bosco.

On the weekends, she socializes with her colleagues—and their dogs. When in Houghton, during the winters, for example, "every weekend Dickie and I [had] a doggie potluck scrum, where people like Nancy Grimm and Diana George and Marilyn Cooper and Randy Freisinger and Jill Burkland and Erin Smith and graduate students and friends all bring their dogs over, and there were about 20 people and 20 dogs, and we'd all go out in snowshoes or ski and then we'd all come back and have a potluck on Sunday afternoons and then we'd all go home." It is clear that they did not lack for company in Houghton, a small town dominated by the university. It took a little getting used to at first. Selfe gave an example.

> Early in my time there, I remember going through the line in the grocery store. I bought a box of Grape Nuts. I had it in the cart along with some other stuff. The woman who did the check out picked up my Grape Nuts and said, "You don't need that. Dickie was just through here, and he got a box."

Because of the size of Houghton, she said that people made their own fun: "So you didn't have a professional symphony, but you had a symphony in which the dean played the cello, and that included electrical engineering students in the horn section. If you wanted to have Habitat for Humanity, Diana George's husband, Chuck Harris, ran it. If you wanted to have a book group, Jill Burkland started it and Marilyn Cooper did the calling. So everybody had to help." And at Ohio State, she notes, she gravitates toward colleagues like Scott DeWitt, Jackie

Jones Royster, Louie Ulman, Beverly Moss, and Brenda Jo Brueggemann, who "have a strong work ethic … and an understanding of how scholarly work can make a difference in people's lives."

She advises others in the profession, especially those just finishing up graduate school, to make professional decisions with this integrated perspective:

> Really do something you enjoy because you want to get up in the morning and believe that you are doing something good. And, unless you're doing something you believe in and think is a good thing to do, that's not going to happen. So, you have to do something that makes a positive difference in your life, in the lives of others that you care about. You should choose your work based on those criteria, I think, that make you proud to do what you do … . You should make a positive difference in the world. I think you can. I'm very old-fashioned about that. I really think we can make changes in the world that are productive. I think we *should*. I think it's a job we have to do, an obligation. And we have to do it for ourselves and for others … . I would also say collaborate, because you are more than the sum of your parts when you collaborate. It adds up to a third thing that is greater than the two of you, or the three of you or whatever.

Of course, Selfe's example suggests that serendipity can become opportunity when one applies these principles. She said, "It always does astound me that [my] luck has been so terrific. I'm grateful for that—and I recognize that many people don't have it that easy, that they don't have the chance to be lucky in that way." Nevertheless, she took advantage of every opportunity, including those that came with the performance of administrative tasks. "I was grateful for the circumstances," she said. "I thought the circumstances were opportunities."

16

LYNN WORSHAM

Lynn Worsham, currently professor of English at Illinois State University, is both a leading theorist in the field of rhetoric and writing studies and the editor of one of its top theoretical journals, *JAC*. Worsham is well known for her sophisticated approach to the rhetorics of gender, race, trauma, and emotion, so it was not much of a surprise to learn that she earned her BA in psychology and English at the University of Colorado at Boulder in 1976. She earned her MA in English and then her PhD in Humanities at the University of Texas at Arlington in 1988, and she immediately accepted a position in the English Department at the University of Wisconsin at Milwaukee. She earned tenure at UWM right on time (1994), and four years later she joined the faculty at the University of South Florida, becoming a full professor well ahead of schedule (1998). Shortly after arriving at UFS (1998), Worsham also became the editor of *JAC*, accepting the reins from co-editors Sidney Dobrin and Thomas Kent. In 2004, she—along with Olson and *JAC*—left USF for ISU, where she currently teaches in the English department's Rhetorical Studies Program.

Background

Though she claims Texas as home, Worsham moved around a lot as a child; her father was an engineer and an oil field specialist, so they followed the oil. Nonetheless, she and her siblings were expected to earn straight As in every school they attended: "It was our first job," Worsham recalls, "and we received no rewards for having done so." Given her parents' strict academic standards, she presumed at a very young age that she was headed for college. It wasn't until she got to high school, where students were tracked into either "vocational" or "college prep" courses, that she discovered that her father had very different ideas about how she, as a woman, should spend her life:

> Something of a battle royale ensued in which my father insisted that I enroll in vocational courses, while my mother insisted that I enroll in college prep courses. (I clearly had the ability and the grades.) My father held the strong (though not winning) opinion that men and boys

> should prepare themselves for professional lives by going to college and professional schools; women, he believed, were to spend their lives taking care of men and boys and therefore needed no college education.

The battle went on for several years: "first when I made it clear that I expected to go to college, again each year when I wanted to return to college, and finally when I announced that I wanted to attend graduate school." Against her father's wishes but with some financial support from her mother, Worsham paid her way through college at the University of Colorado at Boulder.

She chose to go to CU because of its excellent program in clinical psychology, planning at the time to continue on for a PhD before practicing in a clinical setting. While completing her BA and applying for graduate programs, however, she was selected for an internship program in clinical psych at a state-of-the-art mental hospital, and while there, she told us, she decided against pursuing an advanced degree in psychology:

> I saw first-hand what it meant to "warehouse" patients and chemically "lobotomize" them. I witnessed many instances of patient abuse and neglect, and too many instances of unethical if not criminal behavior on the part of staff. Now, this experience occurred after the mental health system had been completely overhauled in an effort to provide more humane treatment. It was a sad and sobering experience, one that was quite disillusioning to me. During this time, I also realized that the discipline of psychology was much too focused on the individual, on the adjustment of the individual to social norms, rather than on a diagnosis of what has been called social pathology—the ways society makes the individual "ill."

During this same time period, Worsham's mother was diagnosed with cancer, so Worsham returned to Texas to be with her. Her decision to go to the University of Texas at Arlington to pursue an MA in English was a direct effect of this familial crisis: "There was only one reason for my initial choice of UTA: to be near my mother." Worsham's mother passed away shortly after she began graduate school.

She completed her MA in English, but by that time she no longer wanted to pursue a PhD in literature: "For me, it was too narrow. I wanted to find an interdisciplinary program that would accommodate my interests in philosophy, psychology, sociology, history, anthropology, and critical theory." And as luck would have it, she told us, Victor J. Vitanza had just arrived at UTA with a mandate to create an interdisciplinary graduate program in rhetoric as part of a humanities PhD. "I looked at the program he was developing," Worsham recalled, "and it seemed to be a perfect fit for me because it defined rhetoric in the broadest, most intellectually rigorous terms." Worsham became the very first graduate from that program in 1988, and she maintains that "it was the best education available." She completed her PhD without support of any kind from her father, who believed until the end that she should find her future in marriage and children:

> The most clarifying moment in my struggle to obtain the education I wanted occurred one hot August afternoon when I went to see my father to ask for a loan to pay tuition so that I could finish my dissertation. I was literally in my last semester, and I needed about 600 dollars. Knowing how he felt, I wouldn't have gone to him if I weren't really desperate. He refused to loan me the money; instead, he offered to pay my full tuition (no loan involved) if I wanted to become a legal secretary, since it was clear, he said, that I would never marry and would need some means of self-support. He was surprised when I finished my degree and was appointed to a university position. He died believing I was a failed woman because I had not married and had children.

Worsham described this experience with her father as "a terrible, heartbreaking education: the discovery and gradual understanding that my father had such a limited—indeed, ignorant and sexist—view of women and that he would make no exception for his own daughter." But she acknowledges that this "education" has also been useful to her: "Over the years, whenever I have met sexism's smiling face, I have recognized it almost immediately."

Strategies for Success

Graduate School

Worsham told us that the only way to succeed in graduate school "is to work constantly, which is what I did. Everything else went to the back burner." Given all that one must accomplish in graduate school, Worsham observed, graduate programs are typically very short; in the few years dedicated to graduate study, one must build a broad and deep knowledge of a field and its history, enter an intellectual conversation through conference participation and publications, and establish some minimal professional credentials. Therefore, as Worsham put it, "there is and was simply no time to waste."

When we asked her for a few of her specific graduate school success strategies—beyond working constantly—she told us that she spent every Friday afternoon in the current periodicals section of the library: "There I browsed around and discovered journals I didn't know about and read articles I might not have discovered otherwise. I learned a tremendous amount about my chosen field and various debates in other fields. This activity was one way I turned 'work' into productive play." Though internet databases have made research much easier in many ways, Worsham noted that it has also made "the sort of diffuse, non-goal-directed research that I found so productive appear to be unproductive. To use the internet databases, you have to have some idea of what you are looking for. What I learned on my Friday afternoons was the result of pure serendipity, and it made all the difference in my intellectual formation and development."

Worsham told us that she also tried to "work smart," to organize her work economically but "without sacrificing intellectual curiosity." For example, she said, "if you are writing a seminar paper on, say, body politics, then it would be smart to find a recently published book in this area and try to get a book review commissioned. Reading the book supports your preparation for writing the seminar paper, and your publication of the review helps to build your professional credentials. This is something I did in graduate school."

Nonetheless, when we asked Worsham what advice she wishes someone had given her while she was in grad school, she told us that she wishes someone had told her "not to take it all so seriously." When her grad students come to her now in various stages of panic, she reminds them that "academic work is not brain surgery: no one's life is hanging in the balance." The key is to work constantly but without stressing excessively:

> Once [my students] have calmed down, I also tell them that those graduate students who take graduate school seriously (just not *too* seriously) from the beginning and place all other activities second to it are precisely the ones who are most likely to be successful. I tell them about the graduate student who called me right before a seminar meeting to say he was not going to attend class that day because he had "some errands to run." Then I tell them that this student never got his degree. No one should pursue a PhD unless he or she has a driving passion for intellectual work. It requires real dedication—and, frankly, not everyone is cut out for this work.

Time Management

It became immediately apparent in our discussions with Worsham that she is extremely organized; unlike many academics, she schedules her time carefully and effectively. "The only trick there is to juggling the demands of academic work," she told us, "is to set firm and clear boundaries with yourself and with others. So, for example, if you have a manuscript to review for a press, you must set aside a block of time—a reasonable amount of time—and you complete the task in that amount of time. Academics tend to train themselves over time not to be very good at time management. Success demands that we retrain ourselves, and that retraining often occurs when one discovers one has much more to do than time allows." The often overwhelming demands of teaching and service can easily give one's own scholarship the squeeze, but Worsham found a way to protect it: Before she got tenure, she tried to teach only classes that met once or twice a week, preferably in the evening so that she could use the daytime to prepare for those classes, and she devoted Fridays, Saturdays, Sundays, Mondays, and Wednesdays to her own scholarship. When she was appointed Coordinator of the graduate program in rhetoric in the early 1990s (pre-tenure), she had to modify that schedule to accommodate the new administrative duties; nonetheless, she still made every effort to schedule appointments and committee meetings on the days she taught in order to keep her writing days and nights free. This wasn't always possible, of course, especially during "crunch" times, when admissions decisions had to be made or when grades were due. And it became even more difficult when, in 1994, she was appointed Coordinator for the modern studies graduate program at UWM.

There is no way around it: when one assumes administrative work, something—frequently scholarship—necessarily gets squeezed. However, Worsham told us that by staying organized she managed to keep that "squeeze" fairly evenly distributed—that is, until she began editing *JAC*:

> For example, when I took on administrative work, I stopped over-preparing for class, which is my tendency, or maybe I would do fewer manuscript reviews. Certainly, my writing days and my scholarship got squeezed, too. As I recall, I devoted one of my scholarship afternoons to administrative duties. Since I became editor of *JAC*, there has been no such thing as free time or "unsqueezed" time. I live, eat, breathe journal. That doesn't mean I work on it constantly, but I am constantly thinking about it: what needs to be done, what I'd like to do for the next issue, what must be done today, etc. I still try to compartmentalize the labor by designating "*JAC* days," which is usually three days a week. We publish four book-length issues a year, which means that we're always in production with an issue. Editing the journal is certainly equivalent to being the CEO of a small business but without sufficient support staff to make the workload reasonable. When I am pressing to get an issue out, everything—and I mean everything—goes by the wayside to get the issue off for final printing.

Administration

We asked Worsham what she would say to a new graduate who is offered an administration-heavy job, and she told us that she'd caution those interested in research positions to avoid administrative work before tenure. "However," she added, "there is a growing number of students who are more interested in WPA work than in research positions. I tell these students to consider any job offer they might get in the context of the institution and its history of awarding tenure to composition faculty. You need to know what the institution's track record is for granting tenure to composition faculty, especially WPAs." If an untenured person does find herself in the position of being a WPA, by choice or necessity,

Worsham advises that she develop very clear boundaries and organize her schedule so that a certain amount of time is slated each week for doing her own scholarship. "I would tell her that under no circumstances should she allow *anything* to take that time away from developing her research agenda," Worsham added. "I would tell her to keep her eyes on the goal: the date in five years when the case for tenure will or will not be made." Worsham says that very often untenured female professors become "their own worst enemies" when they do not establish and maintain a weekly schedule for doing their own scholarship:

> Now, this may sound as if I'm blaming the victim, but I've seen numerous junior professors try to take on too much, both personally and professionally, refusing to accept how tenure decisions are actually made. In any given tenure decision, departmental faculty are basically dealing with three different scenarios: they know the junior professor and are looking for reasons to award tenure; they know her and are looking for reasons to deny tenure; they don't know her well enough to render an informed and just decision. The untenured WPA will inevitably make her presence felt in her department through her administrative work; hopefully, if she's good at what she does and no one is gunning for the WPA, her colleagues will know why she is an asset to the department and to the university. However, she still must publish enough and in the appropriate venues so that any question about publications is moot.

Professional Identity

Worsham told us that one of the most important things she has learned over the years is that it is a mistake to invest too much of one's professional identity in one's department. "It makes you vulnerable to departmental politics, which, in English departments, can be deadly." Of course, "you have to be a good 'citizen' and do the work of your department," she adds, "but you also need to keep in mind that some small or large part of the scope of your professional activities and identity should involve the university and the field at large. That's what I mean by not investing too much of your professional identity in your department."

As it happens, both UWM and USF were involved in massive English department scandals not too long before Worsham left each institution. She was not involved in either one, but we asked if the nastiness of the situation had influenced her decision to leave either place. Her response, because it offers a peek into the slimier side of departmental politics, is worth quoting at length:

> My reasons for leaving both institutions really had nothing to do with these so-called scandals; my reasons were both personal and professional. However, the work environment in each place made it much

easier to leave with no sense of remorse or misgiving. Let me explain. Faculty misconduct (ethical and/or financial) was at the heart of the scandals, which was what was reported in the *Chronicle*. In each case, what occurred during the investigation of allegations of misconduct was even more scandalous and went unreported by any news agency. Both departments were already deeply polarized when the investigations occurred. Each was mired in a deep ideological split between those who wanted to reform the department and those who wanted to maintain the status quo. The investigations had the effect of further polarizing the faculty into overtly warring camps. For the first and then second time in my life, I gained firsthand knowledge of what the term "blood feud" means, how it begins, and what is at stake in such a feud. In each case, members of the department (faculty and graduate students alike) were expected, in effect, to sign what amounts to a loyalty oath, swearing unwavering loyalty to one camp or the other. The camps were formed during the investigation into wrongdoing and according to a single, simple, unstated question: regardless of any facts or evidence of misconduct, do you hold harmless the person (or persons) under investigation? If your answer didn't clearly emerge from your comportment in the department, rumor and innuendo answered for you. If the eyes of the university and community were on the department as a result of newspaper reports, faculty and students were expected to lose all capability of independent thought and sing some version of "be true to your school/department."

In each case, graduate students were instrumentalized and became pawns in the bitter feud between faculty members, a feud that was not so much about the facts of the given case but about who supported whom. And there were real and lasting consequences, not only for the persons under investigation. Many suffered significant psychological and material harm. Reputations were destroyed; careers ended; tenure cases were threatened. Those who suffered the most (and, from my point of view, they were not the persons under investigation) were expected to do so in abject silence, and they were punished even further if they had the temerity to voice any form of complaint. Needless to say, in both cases, the workplace was not conducive to productive activity of any kind (not to mention sanity). The only thing these two situations taught this postmodernist is an appreciation for (indeed, a longing for) the fictions of reason and principled conduct; I've come to regard both as necessary fictions.

When the opportunity arose to move on down the road, I packed my books. I left UWM to join a nationally known graduate program that had a sharp focus on theoretical scholarship, which, of course, is my primary research interest; I had also begun a personal relationship with a faculty member at USF. I left USF, whose graduate program in rhetoric had begun to disintegrate (thanks to the feud), to join a graduate program that is truly unique and innovative in its attempt to integrate all aspects of "English studies."

Discrimination

Worsham told us that she had faced many sorts of discrimination over the years around which she has had to find ways to negotiate and navigate. She has met with gender discrimination very frequently over the course of her career, she told us; sometimes it is subtle, in the form of everyday interactions with colleagues and administrators, and sometimes it's explicit, as when she has occasionally been denied certain professional opportunities due to her gender. She has tried various ways of responding to the more subtle versions, "from simply tolerating the isolated sexist remark to filing a formal complaint." But Worsham suggests that the best strategy for handling discrimination is, first, to create a paper trail: "At the very least, keep a contemporaneous log of the details of the discriminatory behavior: when it occurred, who was present, what was said or done." Second, she says, "tell someone you trust, a friend or a mentor." And last, "tell an accountable officer—if not your own supervisor than your supervisor's supervisor." So, for example, if a junior colleague suspected that that her annual review might be negative because her scholarship wasn't valued by the committee charged with doing the review, Worsham says she'd tell her to "obtain from the chair a written statement that her work would be valued equally to that of her counterparts in other subfields within the department. She might need to see the dean or associate dean of her college and obtain a similar statement. I think it's important to always create a paper trail about any sort of professional matter, especially if it has the potential of becoming a contentious or actionable one."

When we asked Worsham if she had faced any particular professional struggles, pre- or post-tenure, that it might benefit other women in the field to know about, she told us about three situations. When she was an assistant professor, more than one senior male professor expected her "to follow him around like a groupie and admire his every word." She managed that situation by "showing due respect while conducting myself as an individual and as his equal who expected his respect." Later, her tenure case was threatened by another senior professor who was charged with academic misconduct. "This person believed I had given damaging testimony during the investigation, which I had not." Worsham told us she "simply endur[ed] the dreadful situation" and held on to the belief that "my academic record would prevail the day the tenure vote was taken in the department, which it did." She has weathered post-tenure professional struggles, as well. She felt comfortable sharing one in which she was marginalized by a professor who believed she didn't vote for him for department chair. He was elected chair, and she was subsequently passed over for certain administrative positions she had been in line for. He treated another female professor in "a very hostile manner, and her strategy for dealing with this situation was to meet with the chair face-to-face and tell him that although she did not vote for him, she felt she could work productively with him and would support his tenure as chair." Worsham, however, "could not and would not say this to him," so she accepted her marginalized state "and got busy with other things. In other words, I redirected my energies to other intellectual and professional opportunities." Incidentally, her female colleague's more direct strategy "was ultimately unsuccessful; she resigned her administrative position in the department within six months because of the overtly hostile manner in which she was treated."

When we asked Worsham what advice she wishes she had gotten in college, graduate school, or as a junior faculty member, she told us she wishes someone would have warned her not to be surprised about certain things. For example, she wishes someone would have clued her in to the sheer amount of invisible labor (labor that goes unrecognized and unrewarded) that is typically required of faculty. And she wishes someone would have prepared her for those graduate students who are "quite comfortable engaging with a female professor on the level of the 'personal' (hairstyles and fashion trends) but who resist engaging seriously with that same professor about an intellectual project; or the 'old-boy system' of top-down departmental governance and the fact that the 'old-boy system' might just include some carefully selected 'girls' who claim to be feminists but whose behavior suggests otherwise."

We told Worsham that several of our survey respondents had guardedly admitted that while they were junior faculty members they were discriminated against, persecuted, or otherwise blocked not by sexist male colleagues but by senior women in the department—one of the field's dirty little secrets—and asked if she had witnessed this phenomenon. She told us that she has, but she noted that "the hostility that fuels it occurs throughout the ranks of women professors and among women students. Differences in rank and accomplishment allow the hostility to take particular forms and give it an especially destructive edge, but the hostility is not restricted to senior women versus junior women." Worsham's "best guess" at explaining this nasty behavior among women is that "while sisterhood is powerful, not all women are sisters, as it were." That is, some women are "thoroughly identified with and invested in patriarchal values and beliefs." Obviously, this identification can express itself in many ways, "all of which are likely to be unconscious," but the bottom line is that these women "loathe other women, which in turn may be a displaced self-loathing"—something they've learned from patriarchal culture, which defines women as inadequate and defective.

> What gets expressed as some sort of hostility may be the kind of *ressentiment*, or soul-withering rage, that Nietzsche describes as the pathos of subordination. At its core, *ressentiment* is created by profound, existential shame—that is, a deep sense of inadequacy at the

> core of one's being. Patriarchal culture is, among other things, a highly efficient shame-producing machine because it defines one-half of the population as inadequate. It works on men (threatening to expose their "inadequacies," which are coded as "feminine" traits), but it is designed for girls and women, for reproducing a certain kind of girl and woman who does not identify as a member of the class or group of women (who would want to be a member of that club of lesser beings?) and instead casts her lot with men. Second-wave feminists called them "male-identified women" to indicate the kind of woman who derives her sense of meaning and being from patriarchy.

Worsham noted that while the American academy today has many more women faculty and students than it has ever had, "it is still a male world and a patriarchal one." Senior women professors, by virtue of their rank, have achieved recognition in this world and, "as Pierre Bourdieu observes, recognition is the most valuable (and coveted) symbolic capital in academic culture because there is precious little of it (especially in the humanities where we don't make huge salaries or bring in multi-million-dollar research grants and therefore are not valued by an institution that more and more values us according to how much external funding we bring in)." Women who have managed to acquire the "tokens of recognition in this patriarchal subculture (tenure, promotion, reputation)" have achieved "more being, as it were," than those who haven't. And Worsham suggests that these senior women may behave badly toward junior women because they don't want to share: "it's an economy of scarcity, after all." So they block junior professors or hold them to increasingly higher and impossible standards. "It's a sorry situation that pits one woman against another, but that's what a patriarchal system does." And given that "much of this psychodrama is played out at a deeply unconscious level," it's not easy to talk about or rectify; that is, "it's hardly a subject for two women to discuss rationally."

Worsham told us that she has also witnessed another twist of this sexist power play: "female graduate students and female professors (of every rank) use what I would call sexist practices to curry the favor of male professors and administrators." They behave in a blatantly flirtatious manner and "play some version of the starry-eyed bimbo or the seductive southern belle in an effort to gain the recognition that they need or the advantage that they desire but don't know how to achieve in another, less sexualized and more professional way." Sometimes these same students and professors are openly hostile to female professors, and they typically don't take female professors of any rank seriously; they don't treat them with the same kind of respect with which they treat male professors of every rank.

> The students usually prefer to work with male professors, and the professors seek male mentors because they feel more comfortable acting out a familiar heteronormative and patriarchal subtext or script. I have also seen male professors, who claim to be feminists, hold

> female students to a different, less rigorous standard than their male students and thereby ensure that the female students are less competitive academically than their male counterparts. Ah, what inglorious things are done in the name of feminism! Again, I think much of this transpires at an entirely unconscious level, but it certainly does make academic work more complex (and also more boring and predictable) than I think it should be.

Having a Life

We asked Worsham what sorts of issues her junior colleagues and graduate students come to her with most frequently, and she told us that "they want to know how to have it all: the plum job, publications, tenure, children, a dual-career family, European vacations, a star-studded career." But Worsham gives it to them straight:

> I tell them that academic life typically does not come without some hard choices and even some sacrifices. I tell them, for example, that they should wait to have children until after tenure or until tenure is assured because they've done enough to get tenure. I don't think anyone has ever followed this advice, but I give it anyway. I think there's a generational difference at work in the formulation of this advice and in the way it is received. In other words, I come from a generation in which women's place in the academy was not assured and was often resented. I haven't had the luxury of taking anything for granted. My students are part of a different generation, a third or fourth or fifth generation of academic women who seem to believe much of the struggle for women is over. Yet, there are still faculty in positions of power and influence who discriminate against women professors, especially those who start a family while on the tenure track. At one of my previous institutions, a woman in my department was denied tenure. The official reason was that she had not published enough, but I believe the department was not motivated to produce a strong case for her because they hardly knew her. I think there was resentment that she spent a good part of her time starting a family and was not considered much of a presence in the department. Years later she was part of a federal gender discrimination suit brought against the university, and she won a monetary settlement and tenure at a branch campus where she had worked as an adjunct after being denied tenure at the main campus. But imagine her heartbreak at being denied tenure originally, imagine what the loss of salary meant to her young family, imagine the years of emotional labor (not to mention actual labor) that she spent in trying to rectify this situation. Hers was a career derailed, one that never recovered.

When we asked Worsham if she feels she has a "life," if it's even possible to be successful in this field and also to "have a life," she, being a good deconstructionist, turned the question around on us:

> I don't mean to sound glib when I say that "life has us" whether or not we make time for it. Bills have to be paid, groceries have to be bought, children have to be taken care of, loved ones die and have to be mourned. (Both my mother and my brother died while I was in graduate school.) What you are asking about is balance, how to achieve balance in your life. To be honest, balance has been elusive in my life—there has been more of what others would recognize as "work." But that doesn't mean I don't have a life. I have choices; I make choices. These choices constitute my life. I no longer think of balance as a state you achieve and never lose. Balance is an ongoing process; sometimes you have more and sometimes you have less. It's important to know what is necessary to your well-being and to your sense of yourself, what your limits are, and how to say no. "Having a life" or finding balance requires that you know at least these three things.

Worsham tries very hard to say "no" when she's offered excessive academic work, particularly the "invisible" variety:

> Just the other day at a meeting of the graduate committee, the director of the graduate program asked for three volunteers to read five dissertations that had been nominated for an award. She looked around the table, looked each one of us in the eye, and reminded us of our duty as graduate faculty and members of the graduate committee. She described the projects and why a given project should interest a given committee member. She implored and she pleaded. It took an agonizingly long period of time to get those three volunteers. I am happy to say I was not among them, although I knew everyone in the room expected me to volunteer because I'm a senior professor with loads of experience reading dissertations, and because I'm new to ISU's English Department and should want to pitch in and impress my new colleagues. In spite of the pressure, I remained silent and felt guilty for about three seconds because I knew at the time that in the near future I would have ample opportunity to say "yes" or "no" to more invisible labor.
>
> Saying "no" may not always be easy, but we should cultivate the skill as if our very lives depended on it—which it often does. In this context, I think it's important to remember that typically there is a core group of people, typically a relatively small group of faculty, who do the bulk of the department's work. It didn't take me long to realize that I was always in that core group of people who always served on the important committees in the department, always attended departmental

> meetings, and so on. I also realized that this core group did not include a number of highly competent people, who, I imagine, must know how to say "no." So now I think of saying "no" at appropriate times as one step in an effort to distribute labor more evenly. Again, you have to be a good citizen of your department and do your fair share of the labor, but you can pick and choose what is most appropriate for you to devote your energy to in any given context.

It's not easy to make a dual career relationship work in this business, so we asked Worsham how she and Gary Olson have managed it, if she has any strategies she'd like to share. She told us that she has only been in a dual academic career situation for about ten years, and that she was single through the early and hardest part of her career—"that is, before tenure and promotion." On the positive side, that meant that she didn't have any constraints on her decisions about job offers and that she was free to establish her scholarly credentials and pursue her research "without the encumbrances of family obligations." On the downside, though, she recalls being very lonely. "Academia is a thoroughly coupled environment, and I experienced significant social discrimination because I wasn't married or coupled. I wasn't invited to parties and other social events because I was single." As an untenured professor, Worsham was also concerned that her single status might negatively affect a tenure decision. "In a society that insists on defining marriage as a union between a woman and a man and any other arrangement as abnormal or at least 'different,' it is not paranoid to suggest that people tend to discriminate against those of us who do not fit neatly into the proper mold, and that includes single people over the age of, say, forty."

Still, dual academic relationships are very challenging, Worsham noted. Very often one partner finds a tenure-track position while the other ends up following along, taking a non-tenure-track position at the same institution or at another one in the same area. Worsham calls this "the trailing spouse" syndrome, in which "one person is forced to view his or her career as secondary, less real and important." In part because she and Olson came together after both their careers were going strong, and because they each admired the other's work before the relationship began, they have been determined to avoid this "syndrome" and have so far succeeded:

> We were both content as faculty members pursuing our joint and independent research agendas, but when the opportunity presented itself about five or six years ago for Gary to move from the faculty to central administration, we made a joint decision that this would be good for us both. He went on to serve as the chief academic officer—provost, in effect—at USF in St. Petersburg for a couple of years. Later, we made another joint decision: that another move would be good for us both. We moved to ISU where he serves as Dean of the College of Arts and

> Sciences and where I joined the faculty of the English Department. We both benefited: he is pursuing a line of work that he is quite good at, and I have joined a wonderful faculty in a department that has created genuinely innovative programs on the graduate and undergraduate levels. Before deciding to move to ISU, we considered a number of other opportunities, including some provostships, but it was important to both of us that I did not feel like a "trailing spouse," and that is certainly the case at ISU. We both came as professionals in our own right, and we have been accepted as such by the ISU community.

Finding time to relax together has become more of a challenge since Olson moved into central administration. He works fifteen or more hours a day, Worsham told us, and most weekends. Still, they manage to spend some time every evening together to talk about the day, and they try to attend each other's professional meetings and "to make a little vacation of it." "We take a few extra days and spend them together taking in the sights and enjoying the local restaurants. Since we've been in Illinois, we've gone to Florida regularly to see our friends there, and we've gone to Chicago often."

We asked Worsham what she does for fun on a regular basis, to add texture to her life, and she told us that physical activity is vitally important to her, that she makes time for it every day. That, she says, is non-negotiable. "For many years, I've done long-distance walking; I've done core strength training, yoga, pilates, and spinning. I'm also an avid observer of popular culture. I watch some television late at night. I catch all the reruns I can of the programs that are doing interesting cultural work, and I watch films at night after I can't (or don't want to) work anymore. I'm not the sort of person who needs to travel the world to feel that I have lived. I need friends and companion-animals and books." We asked who her current companion animals are, and Worsham's response indicates their significance in her life:

> Thank you for asking. I recently adopted an Abysinnian kitten named Pickle, who is so named because he is always in a pickle, so to speak. He came to live with us just after the love of my life passed away. He was a big tabby named Max, who adopted me when I was in graduate school. He and I lived together for seventeen and a half years. When I was at home, he was, quite literally, always at my side, usually with one paw on me as if to say "you're mine." We were soul-mates, and I'm afraid I'll never know another being as blessed as he. I also live with a sixteen-and-a-half year old cat named Bear who, at the time of her naming, looked like a black bear cub and who had no fur on her nose. Then there is the tabby named Riley; he was named after a 1950s sitcom entitled "The Life of Riley." The TV character "had the life" because he didn't work (I don't remember why) and puttered around all day; my Riley was the offspring of a barn cat, and he would have

had to work for his supper if I had not adopted him. Now he has the life—and major medical.

We asked if Worsham would do anything differently in her professional career if she could go back and do it over again, and she told us that, of the things she could change, she has no regrets, no sense that she would do something differently. “I have been fortunate in my career,” she told us, “and I know that others have had more difficult choices to make than I have.”

APPENDIX I

Questionnaire for Survey of Women in Rhetoric and Composition

1 According to your definition of success, please name one woman you think has "made it" in the field of rhetoric and composition and/or from whom you would most like to learn about succeeding in our field:

2 What is your age?
___ 25–30
___ 31–35
___ 36–40
___ 41–45
___ 46–50
___ 51–55
___ 56–60
___ 60 or above

3 What category best describes your racial identity?
___ African American
___ Caucasian, Hispanic
___ Caucasian, non-Hispanic
___ Asian
___ Pacific Islander
___ Native American
___ Bi/Multi Racial
___ Other ____________________

4 What category best describes your family constellation?
___ single, no children
___ single with children
___ partnered, no children
___ partnered with children
___ married, no children
___ married with children

5 Are you responsible for the care of dependents other than children? If so, please explain.

___ no
___ yes: ___________________

6 What category best describes your sexual identity?

___ lesbian
___ straight/heterosexual
___ bisexual
___ other ___________________

7 If you currently hold an academic appointment, is it a

___ non-tenure-track appointment
___ tenure-track appointment, assistant professor
___ tenured assistant professor
___ tenure-track appointment, associate professor
___ tenured associate professor
___ tenured full professor
___ emeritus/retired
___ other ___________________

8 If you currently hold or have held an academic position, what is the highest degree awarded by the institution?

___ doctorate
___ master's degree
___ baccalaureate degree
___ associate's degree
___ other ___________________

9 If you hold a current appointment, where is the institution located?

___ Northeastern United States
___ Southeastern United States
___ Midwestern United States
___ Southwestern United States
___ Northwestern United States
___ Alaska/Hawaii
___ Puerto Rico
___ other ___________________

10 If you are in a tenure-track position, how many years did you spend at the rank of assistant professor?

11 If you have been promoted to full professor, how many years did you spend at the rank of associate professor?

12 When you look back on your career thus far, what has been the most difficult challenge you faced? (Please explain.)

13 If you were able to begin your career all over again, what would you do differently? (Please explain.)

14 If you were to give one piece of advice to a woman about to begin a career in rhetoric and composition, what would it be? (Please explain.)

15 In our preliminary research, we discovered that women professionals often experience problems that shake their confidence but are very difficult to talk about. For example, some untenured assistant professors are sexually harassed by male undergraduates or subjected to emotional abuse by senior colleagues who should know better (e.g., other women or other rhetoric and composition faculty). In the interests of helping other women in our field, please tell us about a problem that was especially surprising and/or difficult for you to handle. What did you do to respond to it (if at all)? If you did respond, what happened? Please remember that your answers will be kept strictly confidential.

APPENDIX II

Quantitative Data Collected from Survey

2 What is your age?

4	25–30
20	31–35
23	36–40
12	41–45
18	46–50
37	51–55
19	56–60
9	60 or above
1	did not respond

3 What category best describes your racial identity?

0	African American
4	Caucasian, Hispanic
131	Caucasian, non-Hispanic
0	Asian
0	Pacific Islander
3	Native American
1	Bi/Multi Racial
3	Other ____________________

4 What category best describes your family constellation?

31	single, no children
11	single with children
14	partnered, no children
14	partnered with children
20	married, no children
52	married with children

5 Are you responsible for the care of dependents other than children? If so, please explain.
   122 no
   17 yes
   3 did not respond

6 What category best describes your sexual identity?
   17 lesbian
   117 straight/heterosexual
   4 bisexual
   2 other
   2 did not respond

7 If you currently hold an academic appointment, is it a
   14 non-tenure-track appointment
   31 tenure-track appointment, assistant professor
   1 tenured assistant professor
   9 tenure-track appointment, associate professor
   37 tenured associate professor
   31 tenured full professor
   0 emeritus/retired
   15 other
   4 did not respond

8 If you currently hold or have held an academic position, what is the highest degree awarded by the institution?
   110 doctorate
   15 master's degree
   5 baccalaureate degree
   9 associate's degree
   3 other ____________________

9 If you hold a current appointment, where is the institution located?
   26 Northeastern United States
   27 Southeastern United States
   54 Midwestern United States
   23 Southwestern United States
   6 Northwestern United States
   1 Alaska/Hawaii
   0 Puerto Rico
   2 other
   3 did not respond

10 If you are in a tenure-track position, how many years did you spend at the rank of assistant professor?
Responses ranged from 5 to 13 years.
Average was 5.59 years
(The authors acknowledge, in retrospect, that the question, intended to document years in the rank of assistant professor before being promoted to associate, could be, and most probably was, read as asking years currently in rank as assistant professor.)

11 If you have been promoted to full professor, how many years did you spend at the rank of associate professor?
Responses ranged from 3 to 12 years.
Average was 6.59 years.
(The authors acknowledge, in retrospect, that the question, intended to document years in the rank of associate professor before being promoted to full, could be, and most probably was, read as asking years currently in rank as associate professor.)

NOTES

1 The body of literature concerning the argument that rhetoric and composition is a "feminized" field is extensive and spans multiple claims, such as: the teaching of writing is (or should be) a maternal pedagogy, based on an ethics of care and a desire to foster a learning environment as well as a discourse style that aims for collaboration rather than conflict and agonistic argumentation (see Caywood and Overing; Flynn; see also Jarratt's critique); additionally, some claim that the field is "feminized" precisely because it is seen as "women's" work and is performed mostly by women, and hence devalued (see Enos, *Gender Roles and Faculty Lives*). For a sampling of additional claims and conversations, see Susan Miller, "The Feminization of Composition"; Lauer, "The Feminization of Rhetoric and Composition Studies?"; Ashton-Jones, "Collaboration, Conversation, and the Politics of Gender"; Phelps, "Becoming a Warrior: Lessons of the Feminist Workplace"; and Kirsch et al's edited collection *Feminism and Composition*, which contains as reprints many of the articles mentioned here.
2 See also *The Chronicle of Higher Education* 3 (December 2004): A11.
3 A few good ones include Hume's *Surviving Your Academic Job Hunt: Advice for Humanities PhDs*; Goldsmith, Komlos, and Gold's *Chicago Guide to Your Academic Career*; and Formo and Reed's *Job Search in Academe*.
4 Although beyond the scope of this volume, you may also be asked—or aspire—to hold non-writing-program administrative roles, including department head or dean or university president. If so, we recommend the following sources: Susan H. McLeod's "Moving Up the Administrative Ladder" and David E. Schwalm's "Writing Program Administration as Preparation for an Administrative Career." Other sources include: Walter H. Gmelch and Val D. Miskin's *Chairing an Academic Department*; Allan Bolton's *Managing the Academic Unit*, and Robert M. Diamond's edited *Field Guide to Academic Leadership*.
5 Here are a handful: "Writing Administration as Scholarship and Teaching" by Duane H. Roen; "Scholarship Reconsidered: A View from the Dean's Office" by Susan H. McLeod; *The Writing Program Administrator as Theorist: Making Knowledge Work* edited by Shirley K. Rose and Irwin Weiser; "Reconsidering and Assessing the Work of Writing Program Administrators" by Duane Roen, Barry M. Maid, Gregory R. Glau, John Ramage, and David Schwalm; *The Writing Program Administrator as Researcher: Inquiry in Action & Reflection* edited by Shirley K. Rose and Irwin Weiser.
6 A publication that is a "must-read" for administrators who oversee tenure

and promotion cases and is helpful, as well, for faculty who make tenure and promotion decisions is *Good Practice in Tenure Evaluation: Advice for Tenured Faculty, Department Chairs, and Academic Administrators*, a publication of the American Council on Education, American Association of University Professors, and United Educators, available online at http:www.acenet.edu/bookstore.

7 See Chapter 3 for some advice about how to research citations of your work (see page 110).

8 In Chapter 3, we discuss Boice's advice to write in brief sessions every day. The successful writers he studied were *happier* than their bingeing counterparts because of their habits. In his research, he found that the most successful academic writers "devote only moderate amounts of time to writing each day" (no more than 90 minutes each day), "write in brief sessions that require little warm-up time"; "include acts of pausing and slowing that keep the writing on track"; stop "in time to permit other daily activities such as socializing and exercising"; have "prewritten, planned, and approximated enough so that prose writing goes quickly"; "routinely practice ways of treating inevitable interruptions with calm and tolerance, either by returning to the present moment and its process orientation of working, or, when … taking breaks and gaining perspective on what they were writing"; "welcome criticism, learn and grow with it, and moderate reactions to it"; "let other people, including critics, do some of the work of writing"; "work, mindfully, toward mastery but … tolerate failures and mediocrities along the way with patience and humor"; and "produce more writing in less time because they work with an economy of action" (187–8).

9 See also *This Fine Place So Far from Home: Voices of Academics from the Working Class* by Barney C. L. Dews and Carolyn Leste Law, and *Coming to Class: Pedagogy and the Social Class of Teachers* by Alan Shepherd, John McMillan, and Gary Tate. We also recommend the dissertation "Making of a Modern Scholar: Class and the Academy as Configured Through the Words of Working Class Scholars" by Lori Church.

10 Crowley did note that "in those days it was a lot easier to get published in comp because few people were doing it. Victor [Vitanza] was just starting up *Pre/Text* then and was very supportive of everybody's work."

11 Sadly, Professor Short died unexpectedly in December 2003, after this interview was completed.

WORKS CITED

Allison, Maria T., and Margaret Carlisle Duncan. "Women, Work, and Flow." *Optimal Experience: Psychological Studies of Flow in Consciousness*. Ed. Mihaly Csikszentmihalyi and Isabella Selega Csikszentmihalyi. New York: Cambridge UP, 1988. 118–37.

American Council on Education. "An Agenda for Excellence: Creating Flexibility in Tenure-Track Faculty Careers." 19 Oct. 2005. *American Council on Education*. 13 Nov. 2006 <http://www.acenet.edu>.

——. *Good Practice in Tenure Evaluation: Advice for Tenured Faculty, Department Chairs, and Academic Administrators*. Washington, DC: ACE, 2000.

——. "Quick Facts: Traditional Path to Academic Success Unfriendly to Women, According to New Report." 10 Mar. 2005. *American Council on Education*. 13 Nov. 2006 <http://www.acenet.edu>.

Armstrong, Robert. "The Dissertation's Deadly Sins." *Scholarly Publishing* 3 (1972): 241–7.

Ashton-Jones, Evelyn. "Collaboration, Conversation, and the Politics of Gender." Phelps and Emig 5–26.

Astin, Helen S., and Jeffrey F. Milem. "The Status of Academic Couples in U.S. Institutions." Ferber and Loeb 128–55.

Barr-Ebest, Sally. "Gender Differences in Writing Program Administration." *WPA: Writing Program Administration* 18.3 (Spring 1995): 53–73.

Basow, Susan A. "Student Evaluations: The Role of Gender Bias and Teaching Styles." Collins, Chrisler, and Quina 135–56.

Bateson, Mary Catherine. *Composing a Life*. New York: Atlantic Monthly P, 1989.

Battle, Conchita Y., and Chontrese M. Doswell, eds. *Building Bridges for Women of Color in Higher Education: A Practical Guide for Success*. Dallas, TX: UP of America, 2004.

Benjamin, Lois, ed. *Black Women in the Academy: Promises and Perils*. Gainesville: U of Florida P, 1997.

Bennett, Graham, and Jason Lindsey. "The Perfect Offer." 3 Aug. 2005. *Chronicle of Higher Education*. 2 Sept. 2005 <http://chronicle.com.ezproxyl.library.arizona.edu/jobs/news/2005/08/2005080301c/careers.html>.

Bennett, John B., *Collegial Professionalism*. Phoenix, AZ: American Council on Education/Oryx P, 1998.

Benokraitis, Nijole V. "Working in the Ivory Basement: Subtle Sex Discrimination in Higher Education." Collins, Chrisler, and Quina 3–36.

Berlin, James A. *Rhetoric and Reality: Writing Instruction in American Colleges, 1900–1985*. Carbondale: Southern Illinois UP, 1987.

Biaggio, Maryka. "What I've Learned About Addressing Sexual Harassment, Protecting Students, *and* Keeping a Job." Collins, Chrisler, and Quina 271–3.

Blair-Loy, Mary. *Competing Devotions: Career and Family among Women Executives*. Cambridge: Harvard UP, 2003.

Boice, Robert. *Advice for New Faculty Members*. Boston: Allyn and Bacon, 2000.

Bolker, Joan. *Writing Your Dissertation in Fifteen Minutes a Day: A Guide to Starting, Revising, and Finishing Your Doctoral Thesis*. New York: Henry Holt, 1998.

Bolton, Allan. *Managing the Academic Unit*. Philadelphia, PA: Open UP, 2000.

Boyer, Ernest L. *Scholarship Reconsidered*. San Francisco, CA: Jossey-Bass, 1997.

Bradshaw, Sara M. "The Bachelorette in Academe." *Chronicle of Higher Education* 51.18 (2005): C3.

Brereton, John C. *The Origins of Composition Studies in the American College, 1875–1924: A Documentary History*. Pittsburgh: U of Pittsburgh P, 1995.

Britt, Elizabeth C. *Conceiving Normalcy: Rhetoric, Law, and the Double Binds of Infertility*. Tuscaloosa: U of Alabama P, 2001.

Brown, Stuart C., and Theresa Enos, eds. *The Writing Program Administrator's Resource*. Mahwah, NJ: Lawrence Erlbaum, 2002.

Brown, Stuart, Rebecca Jackson, and Theresa Enos. "Doctoral Programs in Rhetoric and Composition." *Rhetoric Review* 18.2 (Spring 2000): 244–373.

Cantor, Paul. "The Graduate Curriculum and the Job Market: Toward a Unified Field Theory." *The Future of Doctoral Studies in English*. Ed. Andrea Lunsford, Helene Moglen, and James E. Slevin. New York: MLA, 1989. 9–14.

Caplan, Paula J. *Lifting a Ton of Feathers: A Woman's Guide for Surviving in the Academic World*. Toronto: U of Toronto P, 1993.

——. "The Maleness of the Environment." Caplan 186–219.

Carli, Linda L. "Coping With Adversity." Collins, Chrisler, and Quina 275–97.

Carr-Ruffino, Norma. *The Promotable Woman: Advancing through Leadership Skills*. 2nd ed. Belmont, CA: Wadsworth, 1993.

Caywood, Cynthia, and Gillian Overing, eds. *Teaching Writing: Pedagogy, Gender, and Equity*. Albany: State U of New York P, 1987.

Chrisler, Joan C. "Teacher vs. Scholar: Role Conflict for Women." Collins, Chrisler, and Quina 107–27.

Chrisler, Joan C., Linda Herr, and Nelly K. Murstein. "Women as Faculty Leaders." Collins, Chrisler, and Quina 189–209.

Church, Lori Ann. "Making of a Modern Scholar: Class and the Academy as Configured Through the Words of Working Class Scholars." Diss. U of Arizona, 2003.

Coiner, Constance. "Silent Parenting in the Academy." Coiner and George 237–49.

Coiner, Constance, and Diana Hume George, eds. *The Family Track: Keeping Your Faculties While You Mentor, Nurture, Teach, and Serve*. Urbana: U of Illinois P, 1998.

Collins, Lynn H., Joan C. Chrisler, and Kathryn Quina, eds. *Career Strategies for Women in Academe: Arming Athena*. London: Sage, 1998.

Comfort, Juanita Rodgers. "Making a Space in the Profession for One's Scholarship." CCCC. Chicago, 2002.

Connors, Robert J. *Composition-Rhetoric: Backgrounds, Theory, and Pedagogy*. Pittsburgh: U of Pittsburgh P, 1997.

——. "Overwork/Underpay: Labor and Status of Composition Teachers Since 1880." *Rhetoric Review* 9.1 (Fall 1990): 108–26.

Cooper, Joanne E., and Dannelle D. Stevens. *Tenure in the Sacred Grove: Issues and Strategies for Women and Minority Faculty.* Albany: State U of New York P, 2002.

Crowley, Sharon. *Composition in the University.* Pittsburgh, PA: U of Pittsburgh P, 1998.

Csikszentmihalyi, Mihaly. "Towards a Psychology of Optimal Experience." *Review of Personality and Social Psychology.* Ed. Ladd Wheeler. Vol. 2. Beverly Hills: Sage, 1982.

DeNeef, A. Leigh, and Craufurd D. Goodwin, eds. *The Academic's Handbook*, 2nd ed. Durham, NC: Duke UP, 1995.

Dews, Barney C. L., and Carolyn Leste Law, eds. *This Fine Place So Far from Home: Voices of Academics from the Working Class*. Philadelphia, PA: Temple UP, 1995.

Diamond, Robert M., ed. *Field Guide to Academic Leadership*. San Francisco, CA: John Wiley 2002.

Dillman, Don. *Mail and Internet Surveys: The Tailored Design Method*. 2nd ed. New York: John Wiley & Sons, 2000.

Drago, Robert, Ann C. Crouter, Mark Wardell, and Billie S. Willits. "Faculty and Families Project: Work-Family Paper #01–02." 14 Mar. 2001. Pennsylvania State University. 18 July 2006. <http://lsir.la.psu.edu/workfam/FFFinalReport.pdf>.

Elgin, Suzette Haden. *The Gentle Art of Verbal Self-Defense*. Englewood Cliffs, NJ: Prentice-Hall, 1980. [New edition: *The Gentle Art of Verbal Self-Defense at Work.* Paramus, NJ: Prentice Hall, 2000.]

Ellig, Janice. *What Every Successful Woman Knows*. New York: McGraw-Hill, 2000.

Enos, Theresa. "Gender and Publishing Scholarship in Rhetoric and Composition." Rpt. in Kirsch et al 558–72.

——. *Gender Roles and Faculty Lives in Rhetoric and Composition*. Carbondale: Southern Illinois UP, 1996.

——. "Mentoring—and (Wo)mentoring—in Composition Studies." Gebhardt and Gebhardt 137–46.

Erwin, Robin W. "Reviewing Books for Scholarly Journals." Moxley and Taylor 83–90.

Evans, Gail. *Play Like a Man, Win Like a Woman: What Men Know about Success that Women Need to Learn*. New York: Broadway, 2000.

Farris, Christine. "30 Things I Can Say I Know for Sure about Dealing with the Dysfunctional Department." CCCC. Chicago, 2002.

Ferber, Marianne A. and Jane W. Loeb, eds. *Academic Couples: Problems and Promises*. Urbana: U of Illinois P, 1997.

Fitzpatrick, Jacqueline, Jan Secrist, and Debra J. Wright. *Secrets for a Successful Dissertation.* Thousand Oaks, CA: Sage, 1998.

Flynn, Elizabeth. "Composing as a Woman." *College Composition and Communication* 39 (1988): 423–35.

Fogg, Piper. "Paper Trail." *The Chronicle of Higher Education* 51.45 (15 Jul. 2005), A20–22.

Formo, Dawn M. and Cheryl Reed. *Job Search in Academe: Strategic Rhetorics for Faculty Job Candidates*. Sterling, VA: Stylus, 1999.

Gabor, Catherine, Carrie Shively Leverenz, and Stacia Dunn Neeley. "Mentor, May I Mother?" Unpublished essay, 2006.

Gallagher, Carol A. *Going to the Top: A Road Map for Success from America's Leading Women Executives*. New York: Penguin, 2000.

Garcia, Mildred, ed. *Succeeding in an Academic Career: A Guide for Faculty of Color.* Westport, CT: Greenwood, 2000.

Gardner, Howard, Mihaly Csikszentmihalyi, and William Damon. *Good Work: When Excellence and Ethics Meet*. New York: Basic Books, 2001.

Gebhardt, Richard C. "Evolving Approaches to Scholarship, Promotion, and Tenure in Composition Studies." Gebhardt and Gebhardt 1–20.

——. "Mentor and Evaluator: The Chair's Role in Promotion and Tenure Review." Gebhardt and Gebhardt 147–66.

——. "Preparing Yourself for Successful Personnel Review." Gebhardt and Gebhardt 117–28.

——. "Scholarship and Teaching: Motives and Strategies for Writing Articles in Composition Studies." Olson and Taylor 35–46.

Gebhardt, Richard C., and Barbara Genelle Smith Gebhardt, eds. *Academic Advancement in Composition Studies*. Mahwah, NJ: Lawrence Erlbaum, 1997.

George, Diana, ed. *Kitchen Cooks, Plate Twirlers, & Troubadours: Writing Program Administrators Tell Their Stories*. Portsmouth, NH: Boynton/Cook, 1991.

Germano, William. *Getting It Published: A Guide for Scholars and Anyone Else Serious about Serious Books*. Chicago: U of Chicago P, 2001.

Gmelch, Walter H., and Val D. Miskin. *Chairing an Academic Department*, 2nd ed. Madison, WI: Atwood P, 2004.

Goldsmith, John, John Komlos, and Penny Schine Gold. *The Chicago Guide to Your Academic Career: A Portable Mentor for Scholars from Graduate School through Tenure*. Chicago: U of Chicago P, 2001.

Goodburn, Amy, and Carrie Shively Leverenz. "Feminist Writing Program Administration: Resisting the Bureaucrat Within." Jarratt and Worsham 276–90.

Greenblatt, Stephen. "A Special Letter from Stephen Greenblatt." 28 May 2002. The Modern Language Association. 15 Nov. 2006. <http://www.mla.org/resources/documents/rep_scholarly_pub/scholarly_pub>.

Gross, Kim Johnson, and Jeff Stone. *Dress Smart Women: Wardrobes That Win the New Workplace*. New York: Warner, 2002.

Gross, Robert A. "The Adviser-Advisee Relationship." 28 Feb. 2002. *The Chronicle of Higher Education: Chronicle Careers*. 13 Nov. 2006. <http://chronicle.com/jobs/2002/02/2002022802c.htm>.

——. "From 'Old Boys' to Mentors." 28 Feb. 2002. *The Chronicle of Higher Education: Chronicle Careers*. 17 May 2007. <http://chronicle.com/jobs/news/2002/02/2002022801c/careers.html>.

Gunner, Jeanne. "Professional Advancement of the WPA: Rhetoric and Politics in Tenure and Promotion." Ward and Carpenter 315–30.

Hairston, Maxine. "When Writing Teachers Don't Write: Speculations about Probable Causes and Probable Cures." *Rhetoric Review* 5.1 (Fall 1986): 62–70.

Halpenny, Frances G. "The Thesis and the Book." *Scholarly Publishing* 3 (1972): 111–16.

Haworth, John T. *Work, Leisure and Well-being*. New York: Routledge, 1997.

Heiberger, Mary Morris, and Julia Miller Vick. *The Academic Job Search Handbook*. 3rd ed. Pittsburgh: U of Pennsylvania P, 2001.

Henley, Nancy. *Body Politics: Power, Sex, and Nonverbal Communication*. Englewood Cliffs, NJ: Prentice-Hall, 1977.

Hofmeister, Heather. "Commuting Clocks: Work and Leisure." Moen 60–79.

Holbrook, Sue Ellen. "Women's Work: The Feminizing of Composition." *Rhetoric Review* 9 (1991): 201–29.

Holmes, Olive. "Thesis to Book: What to Do with What is Left." *Scholarly Publishing* 6 (1975): 165–76.

Hornig, Lilli S. "Academic Couples: The View from the Administration." Ferber and Loeb 248–69.

——, ed. *Equal Rites, Unequal Outcomes: Women in American Research Universities*. New York: Kluwer, 2003.

Hourigan, Maureen. "From Dissertation to Scholarly Monograph." Olson and Taylor 75–88.

Hume, Kathryn. *Surviving Your Academic Job Hunt: Advice for Humanities PhDs*. New York: Palgrave Macmillan, 2005.

Hunter, Gordon. "What We Talk about When We Talk about Hiring." *Profession* 94. New York: MLA, 1994. 75–8.

Jarratt, Susan C., "Feminism and Composition Studies: The Case for Conflict." Rpt. in Kirsch et al 263–80.

Jarratt, Susan C., and Lynn Worsham, eds. *Feminism and Composition Studies*. New York: MLA, 1998.

Kerber, Linda K. "We Must Make the Academic Workplace More Humane and Equitable." *The Chronicle of Higher Education* (18 Mar. 2005): B6–B9.

King, Julie Adair. *The Smart Woman's Guide to Interviewing and Salary Negotiation*. Franklin Lakes, NJ: Career, 1995.

Kirsch, Gesa E. , Faye Spencer Maor, Lance Massey, Lee Nickoson-Massey, and Mary P. Sheridan-Rabideau, eds. *Feminism and Composition: A Critical Sourcebook*. Boston: Bedford/St. Martin's, 2003.

Kolodny, Annette. "Creating the Family-Friendly Campus." Coiner and George 284–310.

Kouzes, James M., and Barry Z. Posner. *The Jossey-Bass Academic Administrator's Guide to Exemplary Leadership*. San Francisco, CA: John Wiley, 2003.

Lauer, Janice M. "The Feminization of Rhetoric and Composition Studies?" Rpt. in Kirsch et al 542–51.

——. "Graduate Students as Active Members of the Profession: Some Questions for Mentoring." Olson and Taylor 229–35.

Layard, Richard. *Happiness: Lessons from a New Science*. New York: Penguin, 2005.

Leverenz, Carrie. "Tenure and Promotion in Rhetoric and Composition." *CCC* 52.1 (September 2000): 143–7.

Logan, Shirley W., ed. *With Pen and Voice: A Critical Anthology of Nineteenth-Century American Women*. Carbondale: Southern Illinois UP, 1995.

Lott, Bernice, and Lisa M. Rocchio. "Standing Up, Talking Back, and Taking Charge: Strategies and Outcomes in Collective Action Against Sexual Harassment." Collins, Chrisler, and Quina 249–71.

Madsen, Mary K. "Women Administrators in Higher Education." Collins, Chrisler, and Quina 209–12.

Mason, Mary Ann, and Marc Goulden. "Do Babies Matter?: The Effect of Family Formation on the Lifelong Careers of Academic Men and Women." 2 Feb. 2002. *Academe*. 2 Dec. 2006. <http://www.aaup.org/AAUP/pubsres/academe/2002/ND/Feat/Maso.htm>.

McKay, Nellie Y. “Minority Faculty in [Mainstream White] Academia.” DeNeef and Goodwin 48–61.

McKeachie, Wilbert J. *Teaching Tips*. Lexington, MA: Heath, 1994. 251–61.

McLeod, Susan H. “Moving Up the Administrative Ladder.” Brown and Enos 113–24.

——. “Scholarship Reconsidered: A View from the Dean’s Office.” Gebhardt and Gebhardt 177–90.

McNaron, Toni A.H. *Poisoned Ivy: Lesbian and Gay Academics Confronting Homophobia*. Philadelphia, PA: Temple UP, 1997.

Meeks, Lynn, and Christine Hult. “A Co-Mentoring Model of Administration.” *WPA: Writing Program Administration* 21.2–3 (Spring 1998): 9–22.

Micciche, Laura R. “More than a Feeling: Disappointment and WPA Work.” *College English* 64.4 (March 2002): 432–58.

Miller, Hildy. “Postmasculinist Directions in Writing Program Administration.” Ward and Carpenter 78–90.

Miller, Naomi J. “Following Your Scholarly Passions.” 25 Mar. 2002. *The Chronicle of Higher Education: Chronicle Careers*. 13 Nov. 2006. <http://chronicle.com/jobs/2002/03/2002032501c.htm>.

——. “Of Parents Born: Changing the Family Care System in Academe.” Coiner and George 255–60.

Miller, Susan. “The Feminization of Composition.” Rpt. in Kirsch et al 520–33.

——. *Textual Carnivals: The Politics of Composition*. Carbondale: Southern Illinois UP, 1991.

Mintz, Beth, and Esther Rothblum. *Lesbians in Academia: Degrees of Freedom*. New York: Routledge, 1997.

Modern Language Association Ad Hoc Committee on the Professionalization of PhDs. “Professionalization in Perspective.” n.d. Modern Language Association. 15 Nov. 2006. <http://www.mla.org/professionalization>.

Modern Language Association Committee on the Status of Women in the Profession. “Women in the Profession 2000.” *Profession* 2000: 191–217.

Modern Language Association Taskforce on Evaluating Scholarship for Tenure and Promotion. “Executive Summary.” Modern Language Association. 2 Apr. 2007. <http://www.mla.org/tenure_promotion>.

Moen, Phyllis, ed. *It’s About Time: Couples and Careers*. Ithaca, NY: Cornell UP, 2003.

Montgomery, Mark. “All in the (Small College) Family.” *The Chronicle of Higher Education* 52.49 (11 Aug. 2006): B5.

Moore, Cindy, and Hildy Miller. *A Guide to Professional Development for Graduate Students in English*. Urbana, IL: NCTE, 2006.

Mountford, Roxanne. “From Labor to Middle Management: Graduate Students in Writing Program Administration.” *Rhetoric Review* 21.1 (2002): 41–52.

Moxley, Joseph M. “If Not Now, When?” Moxley and Taylor 3–18.

——. *Publish, Don’t Perish: The Scholar’s Guide to Academic Writing and Publishing*. Westport, CT: Praeger, 1992.

Moxley, Joseph M., and Todd Taylor, eds. *Writing and Publishing for Academic Authors*. 2nd ed. Lanham, MD: Rowman & Littlefield, 1997.

Murphy, Christina. “Breaking the Print Barrier: Entering the Professional Conversation.” Olson and Taylor 5–18.

Murray, Donald M. “One Writer’s Secrets.” *College Composition and Communication* 37.2 (May 1986): 146–53.

Neuleib, Janice. "Special Challenges Facing Women in Personnel Reviews." Gebhardt and Gebhardt 129–36.

Okawa, Gail Y. "Diving for Pearls: Mentoring as Cultural and Activist Practice among Academics of Color." *College Composition and Communication* 53.3 (Feb. 2002): 507–32.

Olson, Gary A. "Publishing Scholarship in Rhetoric and Composition: Joining the Conversation." Olson and Taylor 19–34.

Olson, Gary A., and Todd W. Taylor, eds. *Publishing in Rhetoric and Composition*. Albany: State U of New York P, 1997.

Ostrow, Ellen. "An Academic Life Out of Sync." *The Chronicle of Higher Education* 49.48 (8 Aug. 2003): C5.

Phelps, Louise Wetherbee. "Becoming a Warrior: Lessons of the Feminist Workplace." Phelps and Emig 289–339.

Phelps, Louise Wetherbee, and Janet Emig, eds. *Feminine Principles and Women's Experience in American Composition and Rhetoric*. Pittsburgh, PA: U of Pittsburgh P, 1995.

Phillips, Gerald M., Dennis S. Gouran, Scott A. Kuehn, and Julia T. Wood. *Survival in the Academy: A Guide for Beginning Academics*. Cresskill, NJ: Hampton Press, 1994.

Ratcliffe, Krista. "What I Didn't Learn in Graduate School." CCCC. Chicago, 2002.

Richardson, Steven M., ed. *Promoting Civility: A Teaching Challenge*. San Francisco, CA: Jossey-Bass, 1999.

Roehling, Patricia V., Phyllis Moen, and Rosemary Batt. "Spillover." Moen 101–21.

Roen, Duane H. "Writing Administration as Scholarship and Teaching." Gebhardt and Gebhardt 43–56.

——, Barry M. Maid, Gregory R. Glau, John Ramage, and David Schwalm. "Reconsidering and Assessing the Work of Writing Program Administrators." *The Writing Program Administrator as Theorist: Making Knowledge Work*. Eds Shirley K. Rose and Irwin Weiser. Portsmouth, NH: Boynton/Cook, 2002. 157–70.

Rose, Shirley K., and Irwin Weiser. *The Writing Program Administrator as Researcher: Inquiry in Action & Reflection*. Portsmouth, NH: Boynton/Cook, 1999.

——. *The Writing Program Administrator as Researcher: Making Knowledge Work*. Portsmouth, NH: Boynton/Cook/Heinemann, 2002.

Ruark, Jennifer K., and Gabriela Montell, "A Wake-Up Call for Junior Professors." 2 July 2002. *The Chronicle of Higher Education: Chronicle Careers*. 15 Nov. 2006. <http://chronicle.com/jobs/2002/07/2002070201c.htm>.

Schell, Eileen E. *Gypsy Academics and Mother-Teachers: Gender, Contingent Labor, and Writing Instruction*. Portsmouth, NH: Boynton/Cook, 1998.

Schilb, John. "Scholarship in Composition and Literature: Some Comparisons." Gebhardt and Gebhardt 21–30.

Schwalm, David E. "Writing Program Administration as Preparation for an Administrative Career." Brown and Enos 125–35.

Shepherd, Alan, John McMillan and Gary Tate, eds. *Coming to Class: Pedagogy and the Social Class of Teachers*. Portsmouth, NH: Boynton/Cook, 1998.

Sherman, Stephanie S. *Make Yourself Memorable*. New York: AMACOM, 1996.

Smelser, Neil J. *Effective Committee Service*. Newbury Park, CA: Sage, 1993.

Sorcinelli, Mary Deane. "Dealing with Troublesome Behaviors in the Classroom." *Handbook of College Teaching*. Ed. K.W. Prichard and R. Sawyer. Westport, CT: Greenwood P, 1994. 365–73.

Stanton, Domna. "On Multiple Submissions." *PMLA* 109 (1994): 7–13.

St. John-Parsons, Donald. "Continuous Dual-Career Families: A Case Study." *Psychology of Women Quarterly* 3.1 (Fall 1978): 30–42.

Talburt, Susan, ed. *Subject to Identity: Knowledge, Sexuality, and Academic Practices in Higher Education*. Albany: State U of New York P, 2000.

Taylor, Shelley E., and Joanne Martin, "The Present-Minded Professor: Controlling One's Career." *Research Papers Series*. Research Report No. R717. February 1985. Graduate School of Business—Stanford University, 1985.

Tebeaux, Elizabeth. "Re-Envisioning Tenure in an Age of Change." Gebhardt and Gebhardt 191–200.

Toth, Emily. "Fear of Committee-ment." 16 Nov. 2001. *The Chronicle of Higher Education: Chronicle Careers*. 29 Jan. 2003 <http://chronicle.com/jobs/2001/11/2001111602c.htm>.

——. *Ms. Mentor's Impeccable Advice for Women in Academia*. Philadelphia: U of Pennsylvania P, 1977.

Trower, Cathy A. and Richard P. Chait. "Faculty Diversity: Too Little for Too Long." *Harvard Magazine* (March/April 2002). 2 Dec. 2006. <http://www.harvardmagazine.com/on-line/030218.html>.

Varner, Amy. "The Consequences and Costs for Delaying Attempted Childbirth for Women Faculty." The Family Faculty and Families Project. Pennsylvania State U. Sept. 2000: http://lsir.la.psu.edu/workfam/delaykids.pdf (accessed on 18 July 2006).

Ward, Irene. "Developing Healthy Management and Leadership Styles: Surviving the WPA's 'Inside Game.'" Ward and Carpenter 49–67.

Ward, Irene, and William J. Carpenter, eds. *The Allyn & Bacon Sourcebook for Writing Program Administrators*. New York: Longman, 2002.

Warr, Peter. *Work, Unemployment, and Mental Health*. Oxford: Clarendon, 1987.

Welsch, Kathleen A., ed. *Those Winter Sundays: Female Academics and Their Working-Class Parents*. Lanham, MD: UP of America, 2005.

West, Martha S., and John W. Curtis. *AAUP Faculty Gender Equity Indicators 2006*. Washington, DC: AAUP, 2006.

Whicker, Marcia Lynn, Jennie Jacobs Kronenfeld, and Ruth Ann Strickland. *Getting Tenure*. Newbury Park, CA: Sage, 1993.

White, Edward M. "Use It or Lose It: Power and the WPA." *WPA: Writing Program Administration* 15.1–2 (1991): 3–12.

Williams, Joan. *Unbending Gender: Why Family and Work Conflict and What to Do About It*. New York: Oxford UP, 2000.

Wilson, Robin. "A Higher Bar for Earning Tenure." *The Chronicle of Higher Education* 47.17 (5 Jan. 2001): A12–14.

——. "Off the Clock." *The Chronicle of Higher Education* 52.46 (21 July 2006): A6–10.

INDEX